Roman Republic
at War

To Marilyn Taylor
and
the memory of Professor Ira Taylor – a giant
from whose shoulders a boy could see forever.

Roman Republic at War

A Compendium of Battles from 498 to 31 BC

Donathan Taylor

Pen & Sword
MILITARY

First published in Great Britain in 2017 by
PEN & SWORD MILITARY
An imprint of
Pen & Sword Books Ltd
47 Church Street
Barnsley
South Yorkshire
S70 2AS

ISBN 978-1-47389-442-6

Typeset by Concept, Huddersfield, West Yorkshire.
Printed and bound in Great Britain by TJ International Ltd, Padstow, Cornwall.

Pen & Sword Books Ltd incorporates the imprints of Pen & Sword Archaeology, Atlas, Aviation, Battleground, Discovery, Family History, History, Maritime, Military, Naval, Politics, Railways, Select, Social History, Transport, True Crime, and Claymore Press, Frontline Books, Leo Cooper, Praetorian Press, Remember When, Seaforth Publishing and Wharncliffe.

For a complete list of Pen & Sword titles please contact
PEN & SWORD BOOKS LIMITED
47 Church Street, Barnsley, South Yorkshire, S70 2AS, England
E-mail: enquiries@pen-and-sword.co.uk
Website: www.pen-and-sword.co.uk

Contents

Acknowledgements

I wish to express my appreciation to the staff of the Rupert and Pauline Richardson Library whose aid was invaluable in bringing this work to fruition. The director, Mrs Alice Specht, was very gracious in permitting me the opportunity to retain ample portions of the library's collection of Loeb Classics for months at a time, and the acquisitions department is second-to-none in its ability to garner rare published materials from various special collections. A note of thanks must also be extended to the staff of the British Library for their kind and patient assistance, as well as to Mr Ian Taylor for drafting the maps. Thanks also to David Jones of David Jones Photography for the photograph of the cover painting.

The author also wishes to thank William Heinemann Ltd, Harvard University Press and the Loeb Classical Library. A very grateful word of thanks must go to Philip Sidnell, Matt Jones and the firm of Pen & Sword Books for their generous guidance throughout this project. Also, a special note of appreciation to Tony Walton for his editorial wizardry; any errors are mine.

Also, a heartfelt word of gratitude to my mentors Donald W. Engels and Thomas Kennedy. Thanks also to Colin Wells for much needed and appreciated words of encouragement years ago.

Finally, I want to offer a very special thank you to my family – Joy, especially, but also Autumn, Ian and Corrender – for providing me with constant encouragement. They are four points of light which forever steady my course and draw me onward.

Preface

The primary purpose of this compendium is to provide readers a basic reference of the most significant battles in Roman Republican history. The information in each entry is drawn exclusively from ancient, late antique and early medieval texts, in order to offer a brief illustration of each battle based solely on the information provided by the earliest surviving sources which chronicle the event. Such an approach will provide the reader with a concise foundation of information to which they can then confidently apply later scholarly interpretation presented in secondary sources in order to achieve a more accurate understanding of the most likely battlefield scenario.

In writing the battlefield descriptions I have not sought to subject the evidence contained in the original sources to intense analysis, nor have I attempted to embellish upon the surviving accounts beyond that which was necessary to provide clarity to the modern reader. In essence, I've allowed the original writers to speak for themselves. My task was simply to harmonize the disparate information in order to provide a better appreciation of what the ancients describe as occurring on the field of battle.

A task of this nature cannot be truly and properly addressed unless one is willing to undertake an exhaustive reading of the ancient authors. Otherwise, one runs the risk of overlooking any number of battles to which the classical writers will in many cases devote only a few lines in their texts.

The names of battles included in this work are typically derived from one or more of the ancient sources consulted, and so in many cases may not bear the name perhaps more commonly used to identify a specific engagement in general or popular studies of Roman history. When an exact name is not given by primary sources, the battle is identified by the nearest community or recognizable geographical feature. Likewise, the dates used in this study are largely those provided in various editions of the Loeb Classical Library.

I cannot claim emphatically that this work includes every Roman battlefield contest mentioned in the original sources that might be deemed by some modern historian to be a major encounter. Engagements which, in this author's judgment, appear to have been nothing more than skirmishes – relatively small, brief, unintended clashes of no significant strategic value for either hostile party involved – have not, with rare exceptions, been selected for inclusion.

Also not included are those battles discussed or alluded to by one or more ancient writers for which there is simply no identifiable name, location or landmark. Likewise, I have generally avoided sieges, a particular form of hostile encounter that occurred throughout the history of Rome. Some of these more celebrated events are included nonetheless, so readers will find descriptions of sieges ranging from Alesia to Veii.

For the convenience of the reader, an effort has also been made to disentangle the confusing knot of names that often denote Roman individuals associated with a particular battle or military campaign. While perusing Livy, Polybius or any number of ancient sources, young researchers are oftentimes perplexed by the unexpectedly redundant nature of Roman names and so commonly mistake, for instance, the general Publius Cornelius Scipio – whom Hannibal defeated at the Ticinus River – with the general Publius Cornelius Scipio, responsible for defeating Hannibal at Zama, or with the general Publius Cornelius Scipio Aemilianus, who destroyed Carthage. Then, to make matters worse, in the course of their reading students may also encounter the generals' cousins Publius Cornelius Scipio Nasica, Publius Cornelius Scipio Nasica Corculum or Publius Cornelius Scipio Nasica Serapio, as well as any number of Lucius Cornelii, Gnaeus Cornelii, etc. All of this would be made a bit easier to sort out if it were not for the fact that ancient authors rarely offer the reader an individual's entire name. So Livy may very likely refer to a particular character in his text as only 'Publius Cornelius', and thereby leave the budding scholar with the uneasy feeling that another Publius Cornelius might have crept into the text when they momentarily turned away from their readings. I have therefore elected to include, when possible, the *prenomen*, *nomen*, *cognomen*, and *agnomen* if available, of each Roman to which the text alludes.

Part One

Introduction to Warfare during the Roman Republic

The Army of the Roman Republic

From Republic to Empire

As the Roman Republic gradually evolved from a small city-state to a large empire by the first century BC, its army necessarily adopted practices that addressed the changing nature of the state's security needs. The altered circumstances arising from some five centuries of expansion dictated a shift from robust regional defensive strategy to one that incorporated a projection of power beyond the natural geographical limits of the Italian peninsula. In so doing, the composition of the army grew more complex and sophisticated in order to capably and consistently address the diverse challenges faced by troops wherever they might be deployed, whether in the arid reaches of Syria and Palestine or snowy forests of northern Europe.

During Rome's early history, the army demonstrated a tactical composition akin to those of other armies in central Italy, possessing organizational characteristics clearly influenced by the Etruscans, a powerful people living north of the Tiber River in the region of Etruria. By comparison to its later manipular and cohortal offspring, the early Roman legion was somewhat primitive in construction. The composition of the early Roman army was based on the communal division of Rome into three ethnic tribes – the Luceres, Tities and Ramnes. Each *tribus* was in turn subdivided into ten *curiae*, each of which consisted of a number of *gentes* (families). An individual tribe typically mustered 1,000 men for service in the army, each *curia* committing 100 men, for a total manpower 'levy' of 3,000 – hence the *legio*, or legion.[1] Some 300 horsemen, also provided by the tribes, likely supplemented this formation. The tactical deployment of the legion during this period is not definitively known, but within a century a new battlefield system compelled the complete alteration of Rome's social structure and moved the army away from a configuration based on the tribe.[2]

By the early sixth century BC, Greek-inspired hoplite tactics began to alter the nature of warfare practiced by the Etruscan peoples, and these changes were in turn destined to reshape the construction of the Roman legion.[3] As the leading power block in the region, the confederation of twelve cities which formed the Etruscan League greatly influenced the smaller Latin towns to the south of Etruria.[4] These new tactical innovations eventually spread from the Etruscans to the Romans and other Latin peoples of central Italy. Tradition ascribes the adoption of the new hoplite tactics to the Roman king, Servius

Tullius (reigned *c.*580–530 BC). Simultaneous with the introduction of these martial reforms was a reordering of Roman society. Such changes were born out of military necessity, resulting from Rome's ongoing struggle for supremacy in Latium. The continual cycle of exhausting conflicts with her Latin neighbours depleted Rome's available manpower, and compelled the state to expand its body of citizens to include many immigrants now settled in the city and countryside. To achieve these expectations, Roman authorities introduced a property census that joined military service with wealth.[5] From this new census arrangement were levied soldiers for inclusion in the legion: the wealthiest segment of the population, the *equites*, formed the cavalry, and the remaining census pool provided infantry.[6]

By the mid-sixth century BC, the Roman army was composed of militia, infantry and cavalry, organized around a Greek-style phalanx, the *classis clipeata*.[7] The new legion included a total manpower complement of approximately 4,000 heavy infantrymen, a sizeable force of some 600 cavalry, and light infantry drawn from the *infra classem*.[8] Most significant of these were the heavily armed *milites* – each equipped with a *panoplia* comparable to the Greek hoplite of the same period: bronze helmet, cuirass, greaves, spear, sword and round shield. At some later date, perhaps in the following century, the concentration of infantry was increased to 6,000 men.

This phalangial tactical formation served the Romans well enough in their wars against neighbouring Italian peoples, but in the second decade of the fourth century BC a sizeable force of invading Gauls inflicted a crushing defeat on a Roman army at the Allia River northeast of Rome. Here, the Roman hoplite phalanx disintegrated in the face of the Gallic onslaught. Following this disaster, the enemy occupied the city of Rome for seven months before their chieftain Brennus elected to withdraw his forces from the peninsula. Roman tradition ascribes the departure of the Gauls to the actions of the celebrated dictator Marcus Furius Camillus, whose sudden arrival at Rome with a fresh army resulted in a complete victory over the interlopers. Despite the credit Roman literary sources assign to Camillus for recovery of the city, the reality of the matter was that the defeat of the Roman army at the Allia, followed by the Gallic occupation of the capital, was a disastrous and humiliating episode in the history of the Roman people.[9]

The fateful events of 387/386 BC inspired a new generation of modifications to the legion during the following decades. By the time the Samnite Wars began in the latter fourth century BC, the Romans had incorporated tactical changes built around the inclusion of a 120-man unit called the *manipulus*.[10] While this reorganized legion traditionally employed only 4,200 *milites*, both light and heavy infantry, plus cavalry, the application of the maniple offered greater tactical flexibility on the battlefield than was provided by the larger, more compact phalangial arrangement.[11] Some early dramatic expressions of its capability can be seen in the third-century engagements fought against the Epirot phalanx of King Pyrrhus at Heraclea (280 BC), Asculum (279 BC) and Maleventum (275 BC). In the first two battles, the opposing infantry formations appear relatively evenly matched, but the Roman victory at Maleventum clearly demonstrated the greater tactical elasticity of the legion. The success of this new arrangement meant that the basic structure of the Roman legion did not again experience significant change until the co-hortal reforms of the first century BC. Until then, the manipular legion would carry the Roman state through some of its most difficult centuries of warfare.

The Roman Legion, Early Third Century BC to Late First Century BC

'The Roman army, clashing their shields and spears together, as was their custom and uttering their battlecry, advanced against the foe.'

Polybius 1.34.2–3

A decade after Rome's victory over the Epirot army at Maleventum, a far more lethal contest erupted which challenged the capacity of the Roman army to overcome an opponent. If the struggle against Pyrrhus proved a potent test of the manipular formation's capability on the battlefield, this demonstration was completely dwarfed by the later conflict with the North African state of Carthage. The First Punic War, which began in 264 BC over disputed affairs in Sicily, plunged the Roman state into more than a century of war with the Carthaginians, and ultimately grew to include hostilities with the Macedonians as well. Rome's eventual triumph after three Punic and four Macedonian wars (264–146 BC) came at a savage cost to its people. Battlefield disasters like that in 216 BC near the village of Cannae in southeastern Italy pushed the Roman army to the brink of collapse. Collectively, the manpower losses in these wars were appalling, but the duration and severity of the long contests, and Rome's ability to emerge victorious, served to permanently secure its pre-eminent place in the Mediterranean world once hostilities ended. With the conclusion of the wars against Carthage, Macedon and the Seleucid Empire of Antiochus III by mid-century, Rome quickly exerted major commercial and military influence throughout the entire region.

The end of these great wars also saw a reduction in the overall number of legions. The demands placed on the Roman army in the latter stages of the Second Punic War (218–202 BC) inspired a temporary increase in the number of standing legions from the normal four. This figure jumped to as high as twenty-three during the difficult years after Cannae, but fell to six with the restoration of peace.[12]

Like the number of legions traditionally maintained by the Roman state during its long history, the complement of troops in each legionary formation – *hastati*, *principes* and *triarii* – remained unchanged throughout most of this age. The only notable alteration to the legion came in 211 BC, when a contingent of skirmishing troops called *velites* was added to the existing maniples of heavy infantry.[13] Thereafter, the army went without significant modification until the consulship of Caius Marius at the end of the second century BC. In the meantime, the manipular legion continued to be the most potent instrument for the projection of Roman power in the Mediterranean.

Manipular Legion, *c.*299–105 BC

A single manipular legion consisted of three ranks of heavy infantry: the *hastati*, *principes* and *triarii*. The first two lines were then further subdivided into ten maniples, each composed of two centuries of sixty men; and the third line also into ten maniples, but each formed of two centuries of thirty soldiers. In raw numbers, this distribution of troops among the legion amounted to 1,200 heavily-armed *hastati*, 1,200 *principes*, and 600 *triarii*. A body of 1,200 lightly armed soldiers called *velites* rounded out the full complement of the legion.[14] These latter troops were distributed evenly among the thirty maniples of infantry. The flexibility which resulted from this complex arrangement of units was the hallmark of the manipular formation.[15]

As it was for all Romans since the time of the Servian reforms, wealth remained a criterion for military service. The manpower of the legions was drawn from the ranks of the *adsidui*, the community of male citizens. Those who possessed property worth at least 400 *denarii* were eligible for military service between the ages of 17 and 46.[16] In an emergency, citizens up to age 50 might be levied into the ranks.[17] Among the heavy infantry, the *hastati* consisted of younger men in their late teens and early twenties; the *principes* included more seasoned veterans, perhaps in their late twenties to midthirties; and the *triarii* was drawn from the oldest and most experienced legionaries. The lightly armed *velites* were derived from those individuals identified by census as the poorest citizens eligible for military service.

Modifications in the type and use of weapons carried by the legionaries accompanied these new tactical innovations. Each soldier in the first two lines of Roman infantry was armed with a sword and two throwing spears (*pila*). The *triarii* were similarly armed, though they bore long thrusting spears (*hastae*). In order to meet their own unique battlefield responsibilities, the *velites* were armed with sword and javelins.[18] Unlike the *hastati*, *principes* and *triarii* who were equipped with the heavy, oval *scutum*, the *velites* carried a smaller round shield for defensive purposes.

Each of the thirty maniples was commanded by a centurion elected by the tribunes of the legion (the first centurion selected was that of *primus pilus*, the

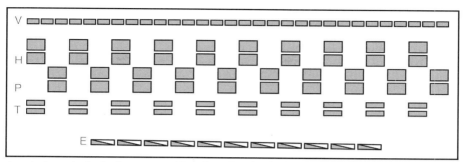

A typical manipular legion arranged in a three-line battle formation (*triplex acies*). Additionally, the individual maniples are staggered in a *quincunx*, or checkerboard arrangement. V=*velites*; H=*hastati*; P=*principes*; T=*triarii*; E=*equites*.

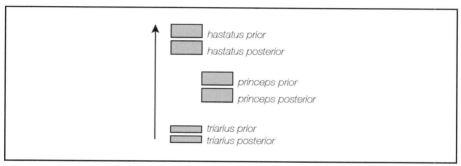

Three maniples of a Manipular Legion.

senior centurion of the legion). These thirty officers then individually selected a second centurion to command the remaining century in each maniple. The senior centurions in the maniple were recognized as *prior centurions* and the junior centurions were identified as *posterior centurions*. Because the distribution of the centurions reflected the three-part division of heavy infantry-men (*hastati*, *principes* and *triarii*), each centurion was identified specifically as: *hastatus prior*, *hastatus posterior*, *princeps prior*, *princeps posterior*, *triarius prior* or *triarius posterior*.

Finally, the manipular legion had an attached force of 300 cavalry (*equites*), which was divided into ten squadrons, or *turmae* (sing. *turma*) of thirty men. Each *turma* was subdivided into three squads of ten men, and each squad was under the command of a *decurion*. The senior decurion of the three commanded the *turma*.[19]

The *Ala*

On campaign, a contingent of allied troops called an *ala* (wing) supported each legion.[20] This force of approximately 5,400 infantry consisted of troops

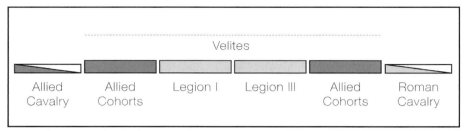

A consular army in battle formation during the time of the Second Punic War (218–201 BC) and First Macedonian War (214–205 BC).

drawn from Rome's Latin allies (*socii Latini*). When deployed for battle, the two *alae* of a consular army assumed positions on the wings, or flanks, – *dextera ala* (right wing) and *sinistra ala* (left wing) – of the two legions.[21]

The tactical organization of an *ala sociorum* differed from its legionary counterpart. A 600-man unit of infantry called a *cohors* (pl. *cohortes*) served as the basic building block. When brigaded with the legions of a consular army, the *alae* were commonly bivouacked separately (ten cohorts apiece), but it is not completely certain that this decuple arrangement reflected a fixed tactical disposition when deployed for combat operations (see camp diagram below). In addition, Polybius reports that three times the number of cavalry was attached to the *alae* as normally accompanied the legions. These were divided into thirty *turmae* of allied cavalry.[22]

From the ranks of these units, the twelve allied commanders, the *praefecti sociorum*, assembled an elite detachment of cavalry and infantry called *extra-ordinarii*. According to Polybius, the number of troops chosen as *equites extraordinarii* amounted to a third of the allied cavalry and those selected as *pedites extraordinarii* totalled a fifth of the allied infantry.[23] The responsibility of the *extraordinarii* was to assume the vanguard when the army was on the march and to undertake other hazardous tasks when called upon by the consul or legate, such as reconnaissance or picket duties or that of rearguard.[24]

The *ala sociorum* remained a potent component of the Roman army until its dissolution in the early first century following the Social War (90–88 BC). Thereafter, the distinctions between the Latin and allied divisions of the army no longer existed.

Cohortal Legion, *c.*105–31 BC

At some point during the late second or early first century BC, the manipular construction of the legion was superseded by a tactical organization based on the *cohors*. The exact evolution of this change is unknown. The historians Livy and Polybius allude to the cohort in their accounts of fighting in Spain during the Second Punic War, but the *manipulus*, or maniple, was still the basic tactical unit around which the 4,200-man legion was constructed, and appears to have remained so until at least the end of the second century BC.[25] The cohort was essentially an amalgamation of three maniples, and early uses of a *cohors*, like that described by Polybius in his account of Scipio's battle against Indibilis, suggest this modification was valuable under certain situations as a more robust tactical response to an enemy threat.

By the first century BC, a new 'cohortal' legion, consisting of approximately 5,200 men arrayed in ten cohorts, replaced the earlier manipular formation. In composition, the cohort consisted of 480 soldiers, divided into six centuries of eighty men.

With the change from *manipulus* to *cohors*, the tactical distinctions between the older unit's heavy infantrymen called *hastati*, *principes* or *triarii* disappeared. In addition, the accompanying light-armed skirmishers known as *velites* were completely eliminated as a distinct fighting force. All troops were now armed alike with a *pilum*. These changes are typically ascribed by many modern scholars to the body of reforms introduced by the *consul* Caius Marius, partly because the last textual references regarding the maniple and *velites* in battle are found in Sallust's account of Caecilius Metellus' campaign against Jugurtha, in 109–108 BC.[26]

Another notable change during this period was the disappearance of Roman and Italian allied cavalry in the wake of the Social War at the latest, a circumstance perhaps more attributable to changing social and political, rather than military, factors in the concluding decades of the Republic.

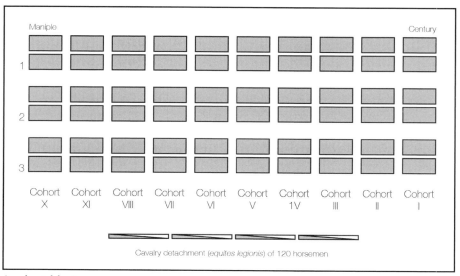

A cohortal legion.

Command structure of the Republican-era Legion

At the time of the Republic, a government magistrate called a *consul* typically commanded a legion in wartime. The people of Rome annually elected two such officers of state, and their duties ran concurrently. As the senior elected civil magistrates in Rome, each *consul* held *imperium* for a period of twelve months, and during that time was entrusted with the most important military responsibilities. During national emergencies, each *consul* possessed authority to assume command of a 'consular army' comprised of two legions. These legions were numbered I–IV.[27] A second annually-elected magistrate, subordinate to the *consul*, called a *praetor*, also possessed authority to command a single legion when necessary. Should a crisis or threat to the state warrant such action, additional legions could be mustered. Under such emergency circumstances, the Senate might also choose to extend the *consuls'* period of service by the granting of proconsular status.

Subordinate to the *consul* and *praetor* were the *tribuni militum*, six military tribunes who served as the most senior staff officers in a legion.[28] These individuals were drawn exclusively from the ranks of the *equites*. If placed in command of the legion, the tribunes normally divided themselves into three pairs, each assuming command for a period of two months.[29]

By the end of the third century BC, demands of the Punic and Macedonian wars compelled some *consuls* to appoint experienced staff officers to command single legions, but conventional practice still dictated that senior magistrates remain in overall command of the army. In the post-war period, provincial governors increasingly relied on legionary and/or auxiliary troops to assist in the maintenance of order in their region of authority. By the early second century BC, the responsibility for command of these military forces increasingly devolved to the governor's deputies or assistants, called *legati* (sing. *legatus*). A governor typically selected such appointees from among family, personal friends or political supporters. Consequently, competent leadership on the battlefield was not guaranteed, meaning that some military actions inevitably ended with dire results. Nonetheless, the divestment of consular authority continued apace, and adjustments were gradually made regarding the selection of field commanders. Over a century later it was common for consuls to remain in Rome during their year in office, and for men of talent and/or battlefield experience to be appointed by the Senate to conduct military operations.

It was during his subjugation of Gaul in the first century BC that Julius Caesar first introduced the practice of routinely placing a *legatus* in command of a single detached legion. Such appointments were intended to be only temporary, but growing reliance on such officers during the final stages of the Republic ensured that by the reign of Caesar Augustus a *legatus legionis* was recognized as holding permanent command of a legion by special appointment of the emperor.

Vital to the ability of these senior officers to execute their responsibilities on the battlefield was the skill and discipline of the legion, whose battle-readiness was in turn directly attributable to a corps of experienced professional officers called centurions. One such officer commanded each of the sixty centuries comprising a manipular legion, and of these, the thirty senior centurions were charged with responsibility for the maniples. The senior centurion of the legion, the *centurio primi pili*, commanded the maniple of *triarii* on the extreme right of the legionary formation. The shift from manipular to cohortal organization did not result in any drastic changes to this existing structure. Because the distribution of the centurions in the cohortal legion continued to reflect the older three-part division of heavy infantrymen (*hastati*, *principes* and *triarii*) found in the manipular model, each centurion continued to be identified by one of six titles derived from the earlier formation: *hastatus prior*, *hastatus posterior*, *princeps prior*, *princeps posterior*, *pilus prior* or *pilus posterior*.

Battlefield Tactics

During the mid- and late Republic, the tactical arrangement of the Roman army was constructed around manipular and later cohortal organization of the legionary unit. Ancient sources attest to a variety of battlefield formations employed by the later Republican army, but the most common was the *triplex acies*, consisting of heavy infantry deployed in three ranks.

In the manipular system, the thirty maniples were drawn up in three lines, with lateral intervals between each maniple equal in width to a single maniple. According to Polybius, each space was then overlapped by a maniple in the next line.[30] The result was a *quincunx*, or checkerboard pattern formation. With the advent of the cohortal legion, Roman commanders continued to employ the *triplex acies*, but like their consular predecessors also freely resorted to a *simplex acies*, *duplex acies* or *quadruplex acies*, depending on the dictates of the battlefield.[31] The extent to which these tactical formations were accepted by Roman generals of the Republic is strikingly revealed at Ilerda during the civil wars of the first century BC. Here, Julius Caesar deployed his cohorts in a *triplex acies*, while the opposing general, Afranius, arrayed his legionary force in a *duplex acies*. According to Caesar, 'The Afranian line was a double of five legions. The third line of reserves was occupied by the auxiliary cohorts. Caesar's line was threefold, but the first line was held by four cohorts from each of the five legions, next to these came three reserve cohorts, and again three more, each from its respective legion.'[32] Evidence suggests that both the *triplex acies* and *duplex acies* remained a standard battlefield system into the imperial era, though in fact no textual

account survives which directly ascribes the use of the double-ranked formation in any specific engagement.[33]

Such tactical arrangements were the result of generations of battlefield
experience. Factors such as topography and the composition of an opposing
army necessarily determined the constitution of a Roman battle formation.
The more sophisticated armies which evolved in Mesopotamia and the
Mediterranean basin incorporated combined-arms tactics, and hostile inter-
action with these powers in the third and second centuries BC had a profound
impact on the Roman army.

The manipular construction addressed deficiencies in articulation that
existed in the Greek-style phalanx adopted during the Regal and early
Republican periods. The greater elasticity of the new formation afforded the
Roman army a basic tactical arrangement whose inherent flexibility allowed
the legion to accommodate itself to any enemy's particular tactical disposition, regardless of size or sophistication.

The great wars of the third and second centuries BC introduced Rome
to the complexities of large combined-arms armies, some units of which
possessed specialized skills. The nature of these contests in turn meant that
the actual duration of a battle could be, and often was, impacted by the particular tactical arrangements adopted by the opposing armies. Battles could
last a matter of minutes or, like Cannae, unfold over the course of a few hours.

As a rule, such clashes, whether of long or short duration, generally unfolded in similar fashion. Following a bout of skirmishing by opposing light-
armed troops, the primary divisions of each army then joined in a general
struggle.

A battle involving a manipular legion typically began with the deployment
of light-armed *velites*, who served to not only harass the enemy but probe
for weaknesses in the opposing formation. Once this initial assault had been
pressed to maximum effect, the *velites* were withdrawn and the *hastati*
formed their line in preparation for the primary attack; each maniple moving
the latter of its two centuries left and forward to close the adjacent interval
and thereby present a solid wall of men along the entire length of the
formation.

Having ordered their line for battle, the *hastati* moved forward at a given
signal. When the advancing maniples were within 15m (50ft) of the enemy,
the legionaries discharged their *pila* in unison in order to disrupt the integrity
of the awaiting line or to check the momentum of an approaching offensive
charge. The measurable impact of this opening salvo by the Roman heavy
infantry was largely predicated on the composition of the enemy. Against
generally unarmored opponents like some Celtic and German foes, this initial
volley of *pila* often proved devastating; whereas the better-protected

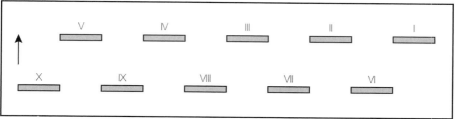

The cohorts were assembled right to left, with Cohort I positioned on the extreme right of the front line.

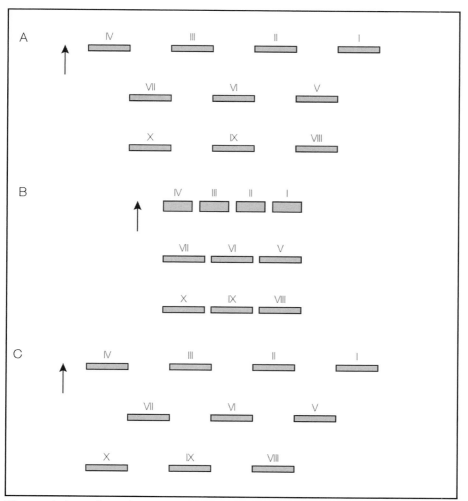

Three variations of a *triplex acies*.

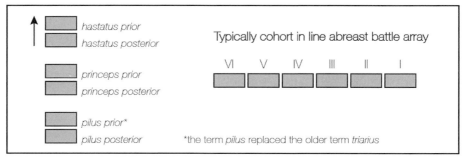

hastatus prior
hastatus posterior

Typically cohort in line abreast battle array

VI   V   IV   III   II   I

princeps prior
princeps posterior

pilus prior*
pilus posterior

*the term *pilus* replaced the older term *triarius*

A cohort and accompanying centurions when arrayed in file; and in line abreast battle array.

Macedonian, Carthaginian and Near Eastern armies tended to absorb such attacks with greater success.

Typically, after the *hastati* loosed their *pila* they advanced behind their *scuta* at a relatively methodical pace with drawn *gladii*. Upon contact with the enemy formation, intense fighting immediately erupted along the entire length of the front line as the legionaries, moving forward in a semi-crouch to permit use of a stabbing thrust, pressed the attack.[34] Polybius notes that according to the Roman manner of fighting, 'each man must move separately, as he has to cover his person with his long shield, turning to meet each expected blow, and as he uses his sword both for cutting and thrusting'.[35]

The physical demands of sword-fighting inevitably depleted the strength of this first assault, necessitating the withdrawal of the *hastati* and replacement by the *principes*, who advanced forward to resume the engagement. This process continued until the integrity of the enemy line collapsed under the sustained pressure of the maniples' attack. As the opposing troops began to flee the field in disorder, the cavalry and *velites* – whose primary offensive role until this moment was to attack the flanks and rear of the enemy – now undertook a pursuit to inflict significant casualties on the retiring forces and bring an end to the contest.[36]

The *Castra*: The Legionary Camp (Polybius, *Histories*, 6.27–32)

An integral component of Roman tactics throughout Republican history was the fortified marching camp, the *castra*. A daily ritual for any Roman army deployed in the field was the construction of a temporary camp sizeable enough to safely quarter the entire force. The building of the *castra* was very labour intensive and required several hours of strenuous work by the soldiers, but resulted in a secure base from which the army could safely conduct operations in hostile territory. A hallmark feature of such camps was the uniformity of design. All Roman legions, whether deployed in the forests of Gaul or the deserts of Palestine, erected marching camps in a similar fashion using a preconceived plan. Each encampment incorporated common features, such as a fortified wall and trench system, and a standardized street layout.

Polybius offers a detailed description of a camp during the Republican era. Ideally, the shape of the Roman marching camp was square, but variations were common, depending upon the size of the force encamped and the dictates of local topography. The remains of these temporary fortifications demonstrate a wide array of rectangular shapes, though the interior plans almost always generally conform to the illustrations provided by the Greek historian.

The camp arrangement followed a predetermined formula. In the sixth book of his *Histories*, Polybius describes a *castra* intended to quarter a force of two legions, or approximately 10,000 men.[37] The streets were arranged to facilitate ease of movement and access in conformance to an established plan, and every legion, maniple, cohort and century possessed an assigned location in the camp. Each unit could thus anticipate where they would be quartered in relation to the other elements of the army.

An earthen wall (*vallum/agger*) and trench (*fossa*) encompassed the camp and provided the first and most substantial line of defence. The size and extent of the trench varied, but was typically 7ft deep and 9ft across. The excavated earth was then used to construct a rampart immediately inside the *fossa*. The wall was raised to a height of about 5ft, and was reinforced by turf from the

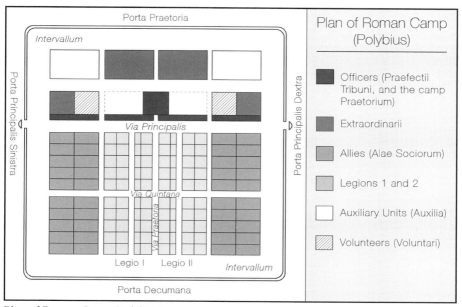

Plan of Roman Camp (Polybius).

trench, *fasces* or both. When completed, each side of the *castra* was enclosed by a 750yd expanse of linear earthworks for a total defensive perimeter of approximately 3,000yds. Finally, thousands of stakes (*sudes/pila muralia*) were planted atop the wall to form a palisade (*vallum/vallus*). Four gates, approximately 40ft in width, provided access into the enclosure. Each entrance was essentially nothing more than a break in the trench and rampart, with additional earthen constructions around the exposed openings to restore the defensive integrity of the compound.

Organization was quite orderly inside the *vallum*. An open expanse of ground called the *intervallum* separated the actual encampment from the walls. This space was used for the marshalling of troops, as well as the insulation of structures and personnel in the camp from spears and other projectiles thrown from outside. A perimeter road, called the *via sagularis*, aided traffic inside this area. According to Polybius, a series of main and side streets facilitated movement throughout the camp itself. The primary thoroughfare, called the *via principalis*, passed in front of the senior officers' tents, and was anchored on each end by a camp gate, appropriately identified as the *porta principalis dextra* and *porta principalis sinistra*. A secondary street known as the *via quintana* ran parallel to the *via principalis* through that area of the camp occupied by the legions and contingents of the *alae sociorum*. Situated perpendicular to the *via principalis* was the *via praetoria*, which intersected the *via principalis* opposite the senior commander's tent, the *praetorium*. The other end of the street terminated at the *porta decumana*. A fourth gate located behind the *praetorium*, and called the *porta praetoria*, provided entry into the camp near the tents of the *extraordinarii* and *auxilia*. Each of these main avenues of traffic was in turn joined to a number of lesser streets, providing easy access to every part of the encampment.[38]

The Navy of the Roman Republic

Crucial to the expansion of Roman power in the Mediterranean basin was the navy, an instrument central in strategic value to the Republic only after the outbreak of hostilities with Carthage in 264 BC. While Rome's strategic designs remained confined to the Italian peninsula, there was very little attention given to the construction of war fleets to project the will of its Senate and people. Consequently, Roman maritime activity in the early Republic was largely confined to protection of coastal communities and colonies against piracy, or to periodic naval operations involving specially assembled fleets under the command of two popularly elected magistrates called *duoviri navales*.[39] Livy and Polybius relate very little in their narratives about early Roman naval activity, likely a reflection of the state's modest participation in such pursuits.

The extension of Roman authority into southern Italy, especially in the third century BC, was accompanied by the acquisition of greater seaborne capability following the addition of several coastal cities that possessed fleets. These naval allies (*socii navales*) thereafter offered Rome a more robust medium through which it could address its growing military and diplomatic challenges in the central Mediterranean.

The first great test of Roman naval ability came in 264 BC, when a series of provocations resulted in a twenty-three-year war with the North African city of Carthage, master of the greatest fleet in the western Mediterranean Sea. It quickly became apparent to the Senate that the potentially negative strategic implications of the war for Rome in southern Italy and Sicily demanded at the very least naval parity with the Punic state, and if the conflict was to be won the Romans must overcome Carthaginian supremacy on the high seas. In 261 BC, the certainty of this situation resulted in the construction of a war fleet that included a hundred quinqueremes and twenty triremes.[40]

Because Rome's true military strength emanated from its army, an effort to redress the imbalance created by Carthage's indisputable maritime mastery was further achieved through the introduction of a novel invention called the *corvus* (κόραξ); this wooden boarding bridge enabled a Roman vessel to affix itself to an enemy ship by means of a heavy iron spike, allowing legionaries to board the opposing craft – thus, for all practical purposes turning each ship-to-ship contest into a miniature land battle.[41] The tenacity of the Romans to overcome Punic naval superiority, even in the face of horrendous losses at sea, ultimately resulted in the defeat of Carthage in 241 BC.

At the centre of Rome's achievement was a willingness to commit to the construction of state-of-the-art warfleets, and this meant the adoption of oared war galleys: the quinquereme (πεντήρης), quadrireme (πεπρήρης) and trireme (πριήρης).[42] The mainstay of Roman warfleets were the quinqueremes or 'fives'. According to Polybius, each quinquereme was manned by a crew of 300 and a detachment of 120 marines.[43] The size of the ship's complement suggests the vessel was somewhat larger than the dimensions of the Classical trireme, which was approximately 120ft in length with an 18ft beam, and manned by 170 rowers.[44] Though the design and dimensions of the quinquereme remain points of debate among modern scholars, the vessel appears to have possessed three banks of oars and a comparable length to that of the trireme, but with a broader beam to accommodate the larger number of rowers.[45] The adoption of the quinquereme placed the Roman navy in a position to challenge Carthage, the Greek states and various Hellenistic kingdoms for supremacy on the high seas.

Rome's emphasis on fleet-building lasted only so long as it faced a major maritime threat. The conclusions of the Second Punic War (218–202 BC) and the Second Macedonian War (200–197 BC) denoted major milestones in the Republic's progress toward complete naval supremacy of the Mediterranean. This dominance was further solidified with the defeat of Seleucid fleets in 190 BC near Myonessus and at the hands of Rome's Rhodian allies at the Eurymedon River. Following the addition of Rhodes as a permanent ally of Rome in 164 BC, Republican fleets faced no other maritime threats from states or kingdoms in the Mediterranean basin.[46]

This turn of circumstance led to the gradual diminution of the Roman fleet, accompanied by a commensurate growth in the Republic's reliance on the eastern Greek states for the supply of both ships and personnel when needed. In time, the security afforded for so long by the robust presence of Roman warships plying the waters of *Mare Nostrum* declined, leading to a more ominous problem by the early first century BC – a resurgence in piracy. To resolve this situation, the Senate appointed Cnaeus Pompeius Magnus in 67 BC. Within three months, Pompey's fleets largely eliminated piracy throughout the Mediterranean, though it remained a persistent if isolated problem in eastern waters until mid-century.[47]

By 50 BC, Rome was on the cusp of the Civil Wars. These struggles, particularly the later naval contests between Sextus Pompeius, Octavian and his lieutenant Marcus Agrippa, and finally Marcus Antonius, resulted in the last great sea battles of the Republican era. The final climactic clash came in 31 BC between the 400-ship fleet of Octavian and the less nimble warships of Antony and Cleopatra off the promontory of Actium in Greece.

For approximately the next two-and-a-half centuries, major imperial fleets continued to reside at Misenum (*classis Misenatium*) and Ravenna (*classis Ravennatium*), with lesser fleets stationed in such locales as Britain, Egypt, Syria and on the waters of the Danube River. These ships continued to support the needs of the army as it expanded and defended the borders of the growing empire, but the great age of Roman sea battles, which began at Mylae in 260 BC against a Carthaginian war fleet, came to an end with Octavian's victory at Actium.

The Ancient Sources

The Reliability of Ancient Sources

The corpus of ancient sources available to modern historians seeking to reconstruct an accurate understanding of a battle from the era of the Roman Republic is not abundant, and those sources that may be obtained are almost invariably prejudiced to some extent in interpretation of facts. Roman works are many times burdened by the bias of their creators, whether subconscious or deliberate, making the information available to a modern researcher problematic at best for an accurate analysis of events.

Works of Roman history belong to either the annalistic or monographic traditions, and biographies are counted as a part of the latter. As the name implies, works categorized in the annalistic tradition – for instance Livy's *History of Rome from its Founding* (*Ab Urbe Condita Libri*) – record Roman history year-by-year, and most begin from the city's foundation; whereas monographs, such as Sallust's *Catiline's War* (*Bellum Catilinae*) and *Jugurthine War* (*Bellum Iugurthinum*), usually address a single topic of relatively limited time and scope.

The earlier of these two traditions, the annalistic, finds its origin in the *Annales maximi*, the public record maintained by the *Pontifex Maximus* of each year's magistrates and major events in Rome.[48] Rome's earliest historians drew upon this chronicle for both information and stylistic inspiration, and their influence is indelibly stamped on the works of some of the most well-known historians of Roman history, among them Livy and the Greek historians Polybius and Dionysius of Halicarnassus.[49]

One common characteristic found in Roman-produced histories of the Republican era is the moralistic overtones which colour the narratives. Livy, Sallust and other Roman historians documenting the state's early history, whether of the annalistic or monographic traditions, spoke to their audiences as moralists. Such writers recounted history in ethical terms in an effort to present their audience moral lessons derived from the past, and these works are typically imbued with the authors' sense of allegiance to the Roman state and its moral ideals. This tendency serves to prejudice the value of the accounts as unbiased records of events.[50] Though Livy, for example, derived information from Polybius' *Histories* for use in his own narrative, his work nonetheless demonstrates characteristics that reveal the author's inclination to glorify Rome and Italy and their traditional values in a way not expressed by the Greek writer, who was himself an admirer of the Romans.

Such sentiments commonly influenced the Romans' interpretation of history, including their accounts of wars and conflict with other peoples. A commonly held belief among Roman writers, for example, was that Rome's many conflicts of the early and central Republic were defensive in nature, fought to preserve the state or in defence of Rome's allies. Livy was such a proponent, and did not deviate markedly from this perspective even when his accounts moved from the confines of the Italian Peninsula to the greater Mediterranean world.

Consequently, the modern historian must be cognizant of the fact that Roman works of history are neither unbiased nor were they written for the exclusive purpose of providing an exhaustively scrupulous compilation of facts pertaining to an event. Roman histories, like all works of ancient history in general, are coloured by the character and intent of the author. This does not negate the fact, however, that Roman sources offer a viable historical record, and there is no reason to reject the historicity of the evidence *in toto*. Despite the patriotic and moralistic forces at play in Livy's work, for instance, his fundamental concern – like that of Polybius – was historical truth.

As such, and in varying degrees, these and other works offer valuable insight into periods of Roman history for which the role of the army was central to the events described. Other notable sources include the writings of Velleius Paterculus, Sextus Julius Frontinus and Julius Caesar.

Julius Caesar is exceptional among all Roman historians chronicling the Republican era in that he offers a first-hand account from so unique a perspective as that of an experienced soldier, politician, commanding general and *triumvir*. His *Gallic War* and *Alexandrine War* are invaluable windows into the Roman army of the late Republic, despite the fact that these works are compromised as an unbiased historical record because of the intended political aims for which they were designed to serve. To a far lesser degree in value are the contributions of the former soldiers Velleius Paterculus and Sextus Julius Frontinus. Paterculus, the author of *Roman Histories*, was himself a prefect of cavalry and *legatus* under Tiberius before the latter subsequently became emperor in AD 14, and as a consequence acquired a practical understanding of military matters through service in a number of campaigns. His work, though a relatively brief historical account, does record aspects of Roman history not found in Livy's surviving books. Such military experience likewise influenced the thoughts of Frontinus in his *Stratagems*, a compilation of military stratagems from Greek and Roman history. His experiences as an army commander and governor of Britannia lend authority to his elucidations for the benefit Roman officers.

Lastly, there are the surviving biographies. Much discussion has circulated among modern historians as to whether biographers such as Plutarch or Cornelius Nepos should be included within the list of ancient historians, but the information they offer provides a unique perspective that is in itself of certain intrinsic historical value. Plutarch's biographies of men like Marc Antony or Scipio Africanus, or Nepos' accounts of Hamilcar and Hannibal Barca, cannot be overlooked as potential sources of illumination for the discriminating scholar. These works provide an additional dimension to modern scholarship's overall understanding of some of the key figures who shaped Roman warfare through their actions on the battlefield.

Note Regarding Battlefield Numbers

One of the most unrelenting problems facing the student of ancient warfare is the validity of numbers related to an army's size and to the casualties suffered as a result of a battlefield encounter. In truth, all numbers cited in ancient sources should be viewed with scepticism by a modern historian. There was very rarely any means by which ancient writers, often far removed in time and place from the actual event, might acquire an accurate count of the casualties suffered in a major engagement, let alone deliver a figure with the level of accuracy expected of today's military authorities. For these same reasons, information pertaining to the size of a field army at the moment of battle is also problematic, and so must likewise be approached with due caution.

Some ancient writers offer figures which are very evident exaggerations, while others provide numbers that are seen to be more plausible by modern researchers. The acceptance of the latter is typically based on a variety of factors, including the type and volume of evidence present, the availability of supporting or corroborating information and the overall reliability of the particular writer or source from which the numbers are drawn.

It should also be understood that ancient writers were susceptible to the expectations of their audience, and the temptation to skew the numbers in order to satisfy the bias of their readers, or to reflect the author's own political or social prejudice, was certainly great. In like fashion, the transmission of numbers through subsequent editions and translations of a work only enhanced the likelihood of human error, and it is reasonable to conclude that over time such changes might occur either by accident or design while in the hands of a scribe.

Ancient Authors and Their Works Relevant to this Study

It is important to have a general understanding of the original sources from which the accounts are drawn when studying an ancient battle. Though no historian should slavishly adhere to the descriptions provided by ancient and medieval writers, their works do serve as the fundamental starting point for any further critical investigation. To this end, basic insight into the background of an early author provides the modern researcher with an appreciation of the inherent value of the extant source.

APPIAN. Born around AD 95 in Alexandria, Egypt, to an upper-class family of equestrian rank, Appian served in high offices in his native province before moving to Rome, where he worked first as *advocatus fisci* before being appointed *procurator* during the reign of Antoninus Pius. Appian died about 165 AD. He composed his *Roman History* in twenty-four books, though only eleven are extant. Most significant are books 13–17 of the *Roman History*, which focus on the civil wars of the later Republic. In his writings, Appian shows a genuine interest in warfare, though the text often reveals the author's lack of understanding regarding the topic. (Loeb)

CAESAR. A member of one of the most distinguished families in Rome, Caius Julius Caesar was born in 100 BC in an area of the city known as the Subura. At age 31 he was elected *quaestor*, the first significant political office of his career, and six years later won election as *pontifex maximus*. The following year he served as *praetor*, and then *proprietor* in Spain before attaining the consulship in 59 BC. Following the establishment of an informal political alliance between himself and fellow senators Cnaeus Pompeius Magnus and Marcus Licinius Crassus, Caesar prosecuted an aggressive decade-long war of conquest in Transalpine Gaul. His growing political power eventually culminated in civil war against Pompey and Senatorial forces. Caesar's victory in the conflict left him in supreme authority of the Roman state until his murder by senatorial conspirators in the March of 44 BC. Of the numerous works he wrote during the evolution of his career, only two are extant: *The Gallic War* (*De Bello Gallico*) and *The Civil War* (*De Bello Civili*). Tradition ascribes three other works to Caesar: *The Alexandrine War* (*De Bello Alexandrino*), *The African War* (*De Bello Africo*) and *The Spanish War* (*De Bello Hispaniensi*), but each is likely the work of another author. (Meier, Loeb)

CASSIUS DIO (DIO CASSIUS). Born sometime around AD 160 in Bithynia in Asia Minor, Cassius Dio Cocceianus (though commonly rendered in Greek, Δίων ὁ Κάσσιος) came from a prominent Roman family. Already a member of the Senate by the time of Commodus' emperorship (AD 180–192), Dio subsequently had a distinguished career as *praetor*, *suffect* consul, *proconsul* of Africa and governor of Dalmatia and Upper Pannonia. During these years he wrote his seminal work, *Roman History*, which recounts in eighty books some 1,400 years of Roman history from the age of Aeneas to the year 229. Books 36–54 and 56–60 are almost complete. All other volumes of the history survive only in part or in fragments. (Loeb)

DIODORUS SICULUS. The Greek historian Diodorus Siculus was by his own admission born in the city of Agyrium (mod. Agira) in Sicily. Though his birth year is unknown, his death occurred around 20 BC. His most notable achievement was the writing of the *Library of History* (Βιβλιοθήκη ἱστορική), a universal history in forty books. Of the complete collection, only books 1–5 and 11–20 are fully extant: the remainder is fragmentary. In its original form, the first six books presented a geographical survey of North Africa, Egypt, Ethiopia, Arabia, Mesopotamia, Scythia, Greece and portions of southern and western Europe. The remaining books thereafter addressed a history of the world from the Trojan War to the eve of Julius Caesar's Gallic conflict. Of this voluminous account, only that portion covering the years 362–302 BC survives. (Loeb)

DIONYSIUS OF HALICARNASSUS. A native of the Greek city of Halicarnassus (Bodrum) in Caria, southwestern Anatolia, Dionysius moved to Rome around 30 BC and remained there until his death sometime during the latter part of Caesar Augustus' reign. He taught rhetoric while studying Latin. It was during this time that he also wrote his twenty-volume *Roman Antiquities* (Ῥωμαϊκὴ Ἀρχαιολογία), which recounted the history of Rome from its mythological origins to the First Punic War. Of the original work, only ten volumes are extant, with the remainder surviving only through fragments and excerpts. (Hill, 1961; Schutt, 1935)

EUTROPIUS. Supporting evidence indicates that Flavius Eutropius, the latter fourth-century AD Latin author of the *Abridgement of Roman History* (*Breviarum ab urbe condita*), was a *magister memoriae* in the city of Constantinople, and that his public career may have spanned a rising echelon of offices, most notably under the emperors Julian and Valens. Compiled in ten books, the *Breviarum* broadly records Roman history from Romulus through to the emperor Jovian, and the narrative generally focuses on the military events of each age. (Burgess, Jan., 2001; Rohrbacher, 2002).

FESTUS. The late fourth-century AD historian Festus of Tridentum, author of the *Breviarium rerum gestarum populi Romani*, was a career bureaucrat whose service included *magister memoriae* and *Proconsul* of Asia. The *Breviarum* was completed about AD 370, and is a largely superficial compilation of Roman history from its foundation until AD 369. The author dedicated the work to the emperor Valens, and chose to concentrate primarily on the political and military exploits of the Roman state during both the Republican and Imperial eras. Of particular note is the second half of the *Breviarum*, which offers a chronological survey of Rome's wars with Persia. (Kelly, 2010)

FLORUS. Born in North Africa during the emperorship of Vespasian, Lucius Annaeus Florus was the author of *Epitome* (*Epitome de T. Livio Bellorum omnium annorum DCC Libri duo*), a work which broadly describes the history of Rome from Romulus to Caesar Augustus. The information in the *Epitome* is drawn primarily from the work of Livy, though Florus' text suffers from certain deficiencies, such as chronological and geographical inaccuracies. Annaeus Florus died around AD 130, during the final years of Hadrian's reign. (Den Boer, 1972)

FRONTINUS. Sextus Julius Frontinus was a distinguished senator and provincial governor during the first century of the Principate. In AD 75, he assumed the governorship of Britain and retained that office until succeeded by Cnaeus Julius Agricola three years later. In AD 97, the emperor Nerva appointed him to the office of *curator aquarum*, responsible for overseeing Rome's water supply. In this capacity, Frontinus authored *The Aqueducts of Rome* (*De Aqueductibus Urbis Romae* or simply *De Aquis*), a report given to the emperor detailing the condition of the city's aqueducts. During this same time he also wrote *Stratagems* (*Strategemata*), a collection of devices for overcoming an enemy which were taken from Greek and Roman history and compiled for the benefit of Roman officers. His previous military experiences as governor of Britain and legate in Germania under Domitian inspired not only the penning of *Strategems* but a now lost work of military theory entitled *On Military matters* (*De re militari*). Both *De Aquis* and *Strategems* survive, the latter extant in four books, though modern scholars debate the authorship of the final volume. (Loeb)

JOSEPHUS. The first-century AD Jewish historian Yosef Ben Matityahu (Flavius Josephus) was born in Jerusalem to a wealthy family connected to the former Hasmonean rulers of Judea. In the First Jewish War (AD 66–73), he commanded Galilean forces during the Roman army's siege of Jotapata. Following the capture and destruction of the city, Josephus gained the patronage of the Roman general and emperor, Vespasian, as well as the friendship of Vespasian's son, Titus. Through his association with the imperial family, he received Roman citizenship and elected to adopt the name *Flavius*. After the war, Josephus completed *The Jewish War* (*Bellum Judaicum*), which covers Jewish history from the reign of Antiochos IV Epiphanes to the Roman destruction of Jerusalem in AD 70. Less than two decades later, he wrote *Jewish Antiquities* (Ἰουδαϊκὴ ἀρχαιολογία), which together with his earlier work provides modern historians with valuable insight into the social and religious events of first century AD Judea. (Loeb)

LIVY. Born at Patavium (Padua) in Cisalpine Gaul in either 64 or 59 BC, Titus Livius moved to Rome as a young man, where he remained the rest of his life composing his 142-volume *History of Rome* (*Ab Urbe Condita Libri*). Today, only thirty-five books are extant (books 1–10 and 21–45), covering the periods 753–243 BC and 219–167 BC. The remaining 107 books are only partially preserved through fragments, extracts, fourth-century summaries called the *Periochae* and a partially damaged and incomplete papyrus scroll called the *Oxyrhynchus Epitome*. Livy died in AD 17 in his home city of Patavium. (Loeb)

NEPOS. The offspring of a prosperous family from Cisalpine Gaul, Cornelius Nepos was born around 100 BC. As a young man he moved to Rome, where he died sometime around 24 BC. In the course of his life he composed a number of works, most of which are now lost. The most significant of these, and the only one that survives in any notable length today, was *On Famous Men* (*De Viris Illustribus*), a multi-volume collection of biographies of notable men in the ancient world, including the Greeks Miltiades, Themistocles and Epaminondas; the Persian satrap Datames; the Carthaginian leaders Hamilcar and Hannibal; and the Romans Marcus Porcius Cato and Titus Pomponius Atticus. (Loeb; Conte, 1994)

OROSIUS. Born in the latter fourth-century AD, the historian and Christian writer Paulus Orosius began the composition of his most widely-recognized work, *Seven Books of History against the Pagans* (*Historiarum adversus paganos libri septem*), while in the North African city of Hippo Regius. The work is a superficial treatment of world history from the Creation until AD 417, though the author did draw upon earlier historians like Livy, Caesar and Suetonius among others. Modern historians place most value on the record of events from AD 378–417. (Rohrbacher, 2002)

PATERCULUS. Velleius Paterculus was born in Campania, perhaps in the town of Capua, around 19 BC. His family possessed a long history of service to Rome, including his maternal great-grandfather Minatius Magius; paternal grandfather Caius Velleius, who served successively under Pompeius Magnus, Marcus Brutus and Tiberius Claudius Nero; and father Velleius, who occupied the post of *praefectus equitum* (prefect of cavalry) at the time Velleius Paterculus succeeded him. Paterculus, the author of *Roman Histories* (*Historiae Romanae*), was after AD 4 a commander of cavalry and *legatus* under Tiberius before the latter became emperor following the death of Caesar Augustus in AD 14. His work, though a relatively brief historical account, is often labelled by modern historians as amateur, but is nonetheless of value because it records aspects of Roman history not found in Livy's surviving books. In the end, the value of his work is overshadowed by that of Livy, Sallust and Tacitus. (Loeb; Yardley and Barrett, *Introduction*, 2011; Sumner, 1970)

PLUTARCH. Born about the mid-first century AD in the small Greek town of Chaeronea in Boeotia, the philosopher Plutarch died after AD 120. The author of numerous works, among the most significant is his *Parallel Lives*, largely written between 105 and 115; a collection of fifty biographies, most of which are arranged in twenty-three extant pairs that include both a distinguished Greek and Roman political or military figure. In his work, the author reveals an ethical concern, measuring the character of his subjects as exemplars of moral conduct, but his assessments at times suffer from unsound judgements, erroneous conjectures or a colouring of truth. (Loeb)

POLYBIUS. Born at Megalopolis in Greece around 200 BC, Polybius was the son of a wealthy Arcadian landowner, Lykortas. In his early thirties, he served as *hipparchos* (cavalry commander) in the Achaian Confederation, an ally of Rome in its struggle against Perseus during the Third Macedonian War (171–168 BC). Roman distrust of the league's motives in the concluding events of the conflict resulted in Polybius and hundreds of other Achaians being deported to Italy following the Macedonian defeat at Pydna in 168 BC. This turn of circumstance dramatically changed the course of his life, and from his original employment as a tutor in the home of Lucius Aemilius Paullus, he became friends with Paullus' younger son, and future Roman general, Publius Cornelius Scipio Aemilianus. In this capacity he was with Aemilianus during the Third Punic War (149–146 BC), and perhaps again at the end of the Numantine War in 133 BC. A dedicated researcher, Polybius' pursuit of factual accuracy and technical understanding of his subject matter made him a valued historian to both later Roman historians and modern scholars. He died in his eighty-second year after being thrown from a horse. (Loeb; Sihler, 1927; Walbank)

SALLUST. Around 86 BC, Caius Sallustius Crispus was born to a provincial plebeian family in the town of Amiternum, northeast of Rome. Possessed of political aspirations, he served as tribune in 52 BC, and as a member of the Senate supported Julius Caesar during the tumultuous years following the outbreak of civil war in 49 BC. This relationship ultimately proved advantageous for Sallust, and in 46 BC, while serving as *praetor*, he aided Caesar in successfully prosecuting the African campaign against Pompeian forces at Thapsus. Afterward, Caesar appointed Sallust governor of the strategically important province of *Africa Nova* (Africa and Numidia). Sometime during this final decade of his life, Sallust wrote two historical monographs: *The Catilinarian War* (*Bellum Catilinae*) and *The Jugurthine War* (*Bellum Iugurthinum*). A third work entitled the *Histories* (*Historiae*) recorded the history of Rome from 78–67 BC. Of this latter piece, composed in five books, only fragments remain extant. Sallust employs a traditional moralizing tone in his works, using his accounts to portray what he perceives as a moral and political decline within Roman society. Despite the presence of certain detracting features within the texts, such as factual inaccuracies and the author's own proclivity toward prejudice, his works remain particularly valuable sources for acquiring insight into the events of the last century and a half of the Republic. (Loeb)

STRABO. The Greek philosopher and historian Strabo was born to a prominent family in the Pontic city of Amasia in 64 or 63 BC. He completed his most significant work, *Geography* (*Geographica*), sometime in the early first century AD, most likely immediately prior to his own death. For modern scholars, the *Geography* is a valuable source for insight into the different regions of the Near Eastern and Mediterranean world. (Loeb)

SUETONIUS. The life of the Roman writer Caius Suetonius Tranquillus appears to have spanned the latter third of the first century AD and perhaps the first three decades of the one to follow. He came from an equestrian family, his father Suetonius Laetus having served as a *tribunus angusticlavius* in the Thirteenth Legion during the Battle of Betriacum. Among his numerous extant writings, the only complete work is the *Lives of the Caesars* (*De Vita Caesarum*), a biography of Roman leaders from Julius Caesar to the emperor Domitian. The *Lives* is notable for its invaluable insight into the histories of the first emperors, but the text is commonly anecdotal. (Loeb)

SEXTUS AURELIUS VICTOR. Very little is known about the Roman historian and politician Sextus Aurelius Victor. Extant evidence suggests he was born in the early fourth century AD in North Africa near the city of Cirta (Constantine, Algeria), perhaps on a small prosperous farm in the vicinity of the capital. Though apparently of humble birth, Victor achieved an illustrious career as a politician and bureaucrat. The emperor Julian appointed Victor consular governor of Pannonia Secunda in the summer of AD 361, and almost three decades later he attained the prestigious office of urban prefect of Rome, suggesting that he had obtained important posts during the intervening years, perhaps including a proconsulship. It appears Victor completed his most important historical work, *De Caesaribus*, sometime immediately before the assumption of his governorship in Pannonia. The work is a brief survey of the Roman emperors from Caesar Augustus to Constantius II, but unlike contemporaries such as Eutropius and Festus, Victor is a moralist. The text is thus punctuated with passages which express the views of the author, and his style is clearly influenced by the work of the late Republican writer, Caius Sallustius Crispus. (Bird, 1994)

ZONARAS. John Zonaras was a twelfth-century Greek historian and author of the *Epitome of Histories* (*Epitome historiarum*), which chronicled events to the death of the Byzantine emperor Alexios I Komnenos in 1118. Zonaras draws upon both the works of Flavius Josephus and Cassius Dio Cocceianus, though his late Roman sources are much disputed by modern scholars. (Banchich and Lane, 2009)

Part Two

Battles of the Roman Republic

Alphabetical and Chronological List of Battles

The dates used in this compendium for all battles before 300 BC are in large measure those 'traditional' dates derived from the chronology of the ancient Roman writer Marcus Terentius Varro (116–27 BC), which was itself posited by Titus Pomponius Atticus (110–32 BC) in his *Liber annalis* (no longer extant). Because of its subsequent pervasive use in the Roman imperial era, the so-called Varronian Chronology has been long used in Western scholarship pertaining to the early Roman republic, and is still commonly employed as a matter of convenience in many scholarly works to the present day, despite the fact that modern researchers are fully alive to its obvious shortcomings. Thus, such celebrated events in early Roman history as the Battle of Lake Regillus or the more seminal Battle of the Allia River, traditionally assigned to 496 BC and 390 BC respectively, should according to other extant texts be more accurately dated to 493/492 BC and 387/386 BC. Students of ancient Roman battles should therefore make themselves aware of the limitations generally assigned to this traditional chronology and proceed in their research with due caution.

Alphabetical List of Battles

Chronological List of Battles

600–500 BC
502   Pometia

499–400 BC
496   Lake Regillus

496   Aricia
495   Anio River
482   Antium
482   Longula
480   Veii

478   Cremera River
477   Cremera River
477   Temple of Spes
477   Porta Collina
476   Janiculum Hill
475   Veii, 475 BC
468   Antium, 468 BC
468   Antium, 468 BC
465   Algidus Mons
458   Algidus Mons
455   Algidus Mons
449   Algidus Mons
449   Algidus Mons
449   Eretum
437   Anio River
437   Fidenae
435   Fidenae
431   Algidus Mons
426   Fidenae
418   Algidus Mons

399–300 BC
396   Veii
391   Gurasium
390   Allia (18 July)
390   Mount Marcius
390   Veascium
389   Lanuvium
389   Bolae
389   Sutrium
386   Satricum
385   Ager Pomptinae
382   Velitrae
381   Satricum
380   Allia
377   Satricum
362   Signia
361   Ferentinum
361   Anio River
360   Porta Collina
358   Pedum
357   Privernum

346   Satricum
343   Gaurus Mons
343   Saticula
343   Suessula
340   Trifanum
340   Veseris
339   Fenectane Plains
338   Pedum
338   Astura River
325   Imbrinium
321   Caudine Forks
316   Saticula
315   Saticula
315   Lautulae
315   Lautulae
314   Tarracina
314   Caudium
311   Sutrium
310   Sutrium
310   Sutrium
310   Vadimonian Lake
310   Talium
308   Perusia
308   Mevania
307   Allifae
305   Tifernum
305   Bovianum
302   Thuriae

299–200 BC
298   Bovianum
298   Volaterrae
297   Tifernum
297   Maleventum
296   Volturnus River
296   Camerinum
295   Sentinum
295   Tifernus Mons
295   Caiatia
294   Rusellae
294   Volsinii
294   Interamna Sucasina

294	Luceria	217	Iberus River
293	Aquilonia	216	Gereonium
293	Herculaneum	216	Litana
283	Arretium	216	Cannae
283	Vadimonian Lake	216	Nola
282	Tarentum	215	Grumentum
280	Heraclea	215	Nola
279	Asculum	215	Carales
275	Maleventum	215	Iberus River
264	Messana	215	Iliturgi
264	Messana	215	Intibili
262	Heraclea Minoa	214	Nola
262	Agrigentum	214	Acrillae
262	Toros Hill	214	Leontini
260	Lipara	214	Castrum Album
260	Mylae	214	Beneventum
260	Thermae	213	Iliturgi
258	Camarina	213	Munda
258	Sulci	213	Aurinx
257	Cape Tyndaris	212	Syracuse
256	Ecnomus	212	Beneventum
255	Adys	212	Capua
255	Bagradas River	212	Capua
255	Hermaeum Promontorium	212	Herdonia
252	Lipara	211	Himera River
251	Panormus	211	Baetis River
249	Drepana	211	Ilorci
249	Phintias	211	Capua
245	Aegimurus Island	211	Porta Collina
241	Aegusa (10 March)	210	Sapriportis
225	Clusium	210	Herdonia
225	Telamon	210	Carthago Nova
223	Clusius River	210	Numistro
222	Clastidium	209	Canusium
222	Mediolanum	209	Canusium
219	Pharos	208	Petelia
218	Rhodanus River	208	Locri
218	Lilybaeum	208	Clupea
218	Ticinus River (November)	208	Baecula
218	Trebia River (December)	208	Castulo
218	Cissis	208	Bantia
217	Trasimeno Lake	207	Carmone

207	Grumentum
207	Venusia
207	Metaurus River (23 June)
206	Ilipa
206	Astapa
204	Locha
204	Utica
204	Croton
203	Campi Magni
203	Cirta
203	Utica
202	Zama
200	Cremona
200	Athacus
200	Ottolobum

199–100 BC

198	Aous River
197	Cynoscephalae
197	Mincius River
196	Comum
195	Sparta
195	Gytheum
195	Turda
195	Iliturgi
195	Emporiae
195	Litana (summer)
194	Mediolanum
193	Mutina
193	Ilipa
193	Toletum
192	Toletum
192	Pisae
192	Gytheum
191	Thaumaci
191	Thermopylae
191	Cyssus
190	Phoenicus
190	Myonessus
190	Magnesia
190	Lyco
189	Cuballum

189	Olympus Mons
189	Ancyra
189	Magaba Mons
188	Cypsela
188	Tempyra
186	Hasta
186	Calagurris
185	Toletum (spring)
185	Tagus River
181	Aebura
181	Contrebia
180	Manlian Pass
179	Caravis
179	Complega
179	Alce
179	Chaunus Mons
178	Timavus River
177	Scultenna River
176	Letum et Ballista
173	Carystus
171	Callinicus
171	Phalanna
170	Uscana
168	Scodra
168	Elpeus River
168	Pydna
153	Baldano Valley (23 August)
153	Numantia (September)
153	Axinium
153	Ocile
152	Carmone
151	Cauca
151	Intercatia
149	Nepheris
149	Carthage (149–146 BC)
148	Pydna
147	Tribola
147	Nepheris
146	Alpheus River
146	Scarpheia
146	Chaironeia
146	Leucopetra

146	Venus Mons		83	Canusium
144	Baecor		83	Mount Tifatum
143	Venus Mons		82	Fidentia
142	Itucca		82	Aesis River (spring)
141	Termantia		82	Sacriportus
140	Erisana		82	Glanis River
133	Numantia		82	Saturnia
130	Leucae		82	Clusium
130	Stratonicea		82	Spoletium
121	Vindalium		82	Faventia
121	Rhodanus River		82	Placentia
113	Noreia		82	Clusium
109	Suthul (January)		82	Porta Collina
108	Muthul River		80	Mellaria
106	Cirta		80	Baetis River
105	Arausio		79	Anas River
103	Scirthaea		79	Segovia
102	Aquae Sextiae		77	Campus Martius
101	Vercellae		76	Lauron
			75	Italica

100–31 BC

90	Aesernia		75	Turis River
90	Venafrum		75	Sucro River
90	Grumentum		75	Turis River
90	Acerrae		75	Segontia
90	Tolenus River (11 June)		74	Chalcedon
90	Teanum		74	Rhyndacus River
90	Falernus Mons		74	Cyzicus
90	Firmum		74	Granicus River
90	Asculum (90–89 BC)		73	Lemnos Island
89	Fucinus Lake		73	Vesuvius
89	Nola		72	Lycus River (spring)
89	Aeculanum		72	Cabeirus
89	Aufidus River		72	Garganus Mons
89	Canusium		72	Mutina
89	Teanus River		71	Camalatrum
88	Rome		71	Cantenna Mons
88	Protopachium		71	Petelia
86	Chaironeia		71	Silarus River
86	Orchomenos		69	Cydonia
86	Athens-Piraeus		69	Tigranocerta (October)
85	Tenedos		68	Artaxata
			68	Comana Pontica

67	Zela	49	Corfinium (18–24 January)
67	Coracesium	48	Salonae
66	Nicopolis ad Lycum	48	Dyrrhachium
66	Cyrnus River	48	Pharsalus (9 August)
65	Abas River	47	Salonae
63	Jerusalem	47	Salonae
62	Pistoria	47	Tauris
61	Solonium	47	Alexandria (48–47 BC)
61	Valentia	47	Nilus River
59	Arar River	47	Nicopolis ad Lycum
58	Bibracte	47	Zela (2 August)
58	Vosegus	47	Tegea
57	Axona River	46	Hadrumentum
57	Sabis River	46	Ruspina
57	Jerusalem	46	Thapsus (6 April)
57	Octodurus	46	Hippo Regius
56	Morbihan Gulf	46	Carteia
56	Sotium	45	Munda (17 March)
55	Mount Tabor	43	Forum Gallorum
55	Mosa River	43	Forum Gallorum
54	Aduatuca (October)	43	Mutina (14 April)
53	Carrhae (June)	42	Laodicea
53	Avaricum (53–52 BC)	42	Myndos
52	Noviodunum	42	Rhodes
52	Agendicum (spring)	42	Scyllaeum Promontory
52	Gergovia (spring)	42	Philippi (3 October)
52	Alesia (spring–summer)	42	Philippi (23 October)
51	Uxellodunum	39	Syrian Gates
51	Antigoneia	38	Mount Gindarus
51	Amanus	38	Cumae
49	Massilia	36	Mylae
49	Sicoris River	36	Tauromenium
49	Ilerda	36	Naulochus (3 September)
49	Curicta	36	Phraata Atropatene
49	Utica	31	Actium (2 September)
49	Bagradas River		

Battles of the Roman Republic
498–31 BC

Abas River, 65 BC (Third Mithridatic War, Wars against Mithridates the Great) – While in pursuit of Mithridates VI Eupator, king of Pontus, the Roman general Gnaeus Pompeius Magnus learned that the peoples of Caucasian Albania were again in revolt. Turning his army around to deal with the new threat, Pompey retraced his path eastward across the Cyrus River and its two tributaries, the Cambyses and Abas. With his legions safely over the last of these three water courses, word arrived of the approach of a hostile army led by Oroeses, king of Albania. Eager to engage the Albanian monarch before he could accurately measure the size of the Roman force and avoid battle, Pompey arrayed his cavalry before the infantry cohorts and ordered the legionaries to kneel behind their shields and remain motionless, so as to obscure the true size of the army. When the enemy neared the Roman position, the king observed only Pompey's mounted squadrons, and quickly ordered an assault against the foreigners. Overconfident in his belief that his force of 60,000 infantry and 12,000 cavalry could easily defeat the Roman horse, Oroeses failed to recognize the trap. As the Roman horsemen rushed forward, the Albanians responded with an equally enthusiastic countercharge. While both armies were joined in fighting, the Roman cavalry suddenly feigned flight, followed by Oroeses' forces in headlong pursuit. The Roman withdrawal passed directly through the ranks of the concealed legions, which opened gaps in their battle line to permit the cavalry to make good its escape, and then closed around the unsuspecting Albanians, who quickly found themselves surrounded by thousands of Roman infantrymen. As the legions clashed with Oroeses' army, Pompey's cavalry circled around the developing struggle to attack the enemy rear. After an intense engagement, in which each army suffered heavy casualties, the Albanians were finally defeated.

Dio Cassius, *Roman History*, 37.3.6–4; Plutarch, *Pompey*, 35.

Acerrae, 90 BC (Social War, Marsic War) – The Samnite general Caius Papius Mutilus besieged the Campanian town of Acerrae with an army of 10,000 infantry and 1,000 cavalry, the latter being forcefully conscripted from the subjugated territory around the community of Nuceria. In response, the *consul* Lucius Julius Caesar (also called Sextus Caesar) moved against Papius with a force of 10,000 Gallic infantry and a mixed detachment of Numidian and Mauretanian cavalry and infantry. The Samnites attacked the Roman army while it was encamped near Acerrae and successfully breached the camp defences, compelling Caesar to attack with a sally of cavalry. The unexpected counter-assault killed some 6,000 Samnite and allied troops. Afterward, the Roman army withdrew from Acerrae.

Appianus (Appian), *Civil Wars*, 1.42.

Acrillae, 214 BC (Second Punic War, Wars against Carthage) – West of Syracuse, near the Sicilian town of Acrillae, a Roman army under Marcus Claudius Marcellus surprised a Syracusian force of 10,000 infantry and 500 cavalry while in the process of pitching camp. The Romans, already alert to the possible danger of encountering Carthaginians on the highway, were travelling in battle-readiness and upon encountering the Syracusians immediately charged the ill-prepared encampment. The attack proved irresistible. The whole of the Syracusian infantry quickly surrendered, while the cavalry offered only brief resistance before fleeing with the army's commander, Hippocrates.

Titus Livius (Livy), *History of Rome*, 24.35.8–36.1.

Actium, 31 BC, 2 September (Roman Civil Wars, Wars of the Second Triumvirate) – This naval battle marked the end to a series of inconclusive engagements between the forces of Marcus Antonius and Caius Octavianus, and the decisive turning point in the Roman domination of Ptolemaic Egypt. The two fleets engaged one another at dawn, west of the Actium Promontory at the mouth of the *Sinus Ambracius* (Ambracian Gulf) in western Greece. Although Antony's fleet possessed a numerical and size advantage in ships over that of Octavian's squadrons, the latter ultimately benefitted from lighter, faster and more manoeuvrable Liburnian vessels (though the exact figures offered by ancient sources vary widely for both fleets). The centre squadron of Octavian's fleet was commanded by Arruntius; the left wing by Marcus Vipsanius Agrippa; and the right by Octavian himself. Arrayed against this formation on the right was Antony; with Publicola, Marcus Octavius and Marcus Insteius in the centre; and Sosius commanding the left wing of the fleet. The Egyptian squadron of Cleopatra VII remained behind this line, held in reserve. The battle was initiated by the Antonian left. Octavian immediately responded to this attack by ordering the ships of his right to backwater, so as to draw Sosius' squadrons out of the gulf's narrows and into deeper waters of the Ionian Sea, where his lighter Liburnian craft would be at most advantage. Cohesion finally eroded in the Antonian formation when Agrippa sought to extend his left and envelope Antony's right, forcing Publicola to advance against him and thereby separate from the centre. The combination

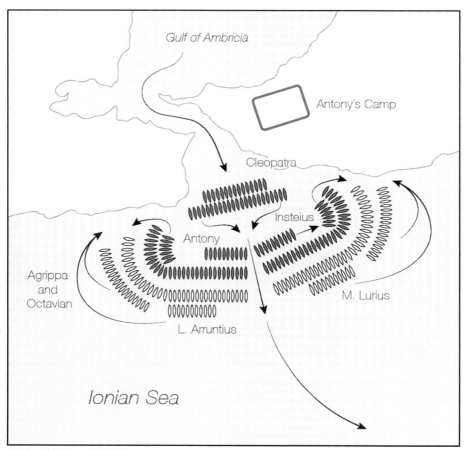

Battle of Actium, 31 BC

of these moves weakened the left and centre of the Antonian formation. It was at this decisive moment that the sixty ships of Cleopatra's squadron took flight through Antony's line, further disrupting the hard-pressed fleet. At sight of the Ptolemaic queen's withdrawal, Marcus Antonius abandoned his forces and followed the retiring Egyptian vessels. The battle continued despite the absence of Antony. After ten hours of combat, the beaten remnant of the now leaderless fleet finally surrendered to Octavian, having suffered 5,000 dead.

> Plutarch, *Antonius*, 60.50–62.4; Appianus (Appian), *Civil* Wars, 1.5, 6; Lucius Annaeus Florus, *Epitomy*, 2.21.4–9; Dio Cassius, *Roman History*, 50.12–35.

Aduatuca, 54 BC, October (Gallic War) – In the territory of the Eburones, near the winter legionary camp at Aduatuca (situated in modern Belgium,

NW of the Meuse River), a Gallic army led by Ambiorix clashed with a Roman force under the command of Quintus Titurius Sabinus and Lucius Aurunculeius Cotta. The camp was unsuccessfully besieged by the Eburones shortly after the legions went into winter quarters. Having failed to take the enemy position by force, Ambiorix offered the Romans safe passage to the distant legionary camps of Quintus Cicero or Titus Labienus, but only if they would agree to abandon the site. This proposal initially divided the Roman command at Aduatuca, with Sabinus favouring its acceptance and Cotta and the senior centurions strongly opposed for fear of treachery. Cotta was, however, finally persuaded to concede, and the Romans evacuated the camp. Once on the march, the column was ambushed approximately 2 miles from Aduatuca. Briefly thrown into confusion by the attack, the cohorts ultimately formed into a defensive square (*consisterent in ordem*), though too late to avert disaster. Trapped on unfavourable ground and in a poor defensive posture, the Roman formation was largely destroyed, Sabinus and Cotta being among the 7,500 slain.

Julius Caesar, *The Gallic War*, 5.24–37.

Adys, 255 BC – While engaged in military operations in North Africa, the Roman *consul* Marcus Atilius Regulus besieged the town of Adys, approximately 15 miles south of Tunis. This action resulted in the deployment of a Carthaginian army under the generals Hamilcar and Hasdrubal, son of Hanno. On reaching the vicinity of Adys, the army occupied a hill overlooking the Roman position, but the elevated location severely limited any tactical advantage offered by the Punic cavalry and elephants. This handicap was readily identified by the senior Roman officers, who quickly moved their legionary forces against the enemy position before the error could be redressed. The Romans advanced on the hill from two sides at daybreak. A strong charge by Carthaginian mercenaries put the first legion to flight, but the momentum of the attack exposed the victors to the Roman forces assaulting the hill from the opposite side. In the ensuing engagement, the mercenaries were routed and the entire Carthaginian army driven onto level ground and scattered.

Polybius, *Histories*, 1.30.4–14; John Zonaras, *Epitome of Histories*, 8.13; Paulus Orosius, *Seven Books of History against the Pagans*, 4.8.

Aebura, 181 BC – In early spring, a Roman army led by Quintus Fulvius Flaccus, *praetor* of *Hispania Citerior* (Eastern Spain), advanced into the region of Carpetania and encamped near the community of Aebura. Several days later, a numerically superior Celtiberian army of 35,000 men established a camp approximately 2 miles distant. For several consecutive days, Flaccus dispatched a force of allied cavalry under command of his brother, Marcus

Fulvius Flaccus, to reconnoitre around the enemy camp, but avoid any confrontation. Finally, the Celtiberi elected to offer battle, and for four days assembled their infantry and cavalry on the open plain between the opposing camps. Each time the Romans declined to take action, and instead remained in their *castrum*. The Celtiberi posted guards and dispatched mounted patrols as a precaution, but ceased the daily deployment of their army. Once Flaccus was convinced that the inaction of his army had lulled the enemy into a sense of complacency, he sent a squadron of cavalry and 6,000 provincial auxiliaries under cover of darkness to occupy ground behind the hills to the rear of the Celtiberian position, and ordered the detachment's commander, Lucius Acilius, to await his signal to attack. The following day, a provocative display by allied horsemen under Caius Scribonius drew the opposing army away from the safety of its encampment. Overconfident, the enemy arrayed within 500 yards of the legions' earthworks, permitting Flaccus to launch a sudden, massive assault against the unsuspecting formation. The commotion served as a signal to those Roman forces hidden in the hills, which then attacked and quickly overran the enemy camp, capturing its entire garrison of 5,000 men. Meanwhile, the battle raged on the nearby plain. Following the loss of their encampment, which was shortly thereafter burned by its captors, the Celtiberi fought with grim determination. In the centre, the Fifth Legion exerted tremendous pressure against the enemy line, but on the Roman left flank the native auxiliaries wavered under the initial clash, and were only saved by the timely deployment of the Seventh Legion. While the fighting continued, additional Roman troops from the small garrison in Aebura, as well as those from the destroyed camp, fell on the Celtiberian rear. Now trapped between these reinforcements and the primary Roman battle formation, the enemy line began to disintegrate. As the defeated troops fled the field in every direction, hoping for safety in the surrounding countryside, Flaccus dispatched two columns of cavalry to overtake the fugitives. The subsequent slaughter was great. Celtiberian losses totalled 23,000 killed and 4,700 captured. Roman deaths, including legionary troops, Latin allies and provincial auxiliaries, amounted to 3,400 men.

Titus Livius (Livy), *History of Rome*, 40.30–32.

Aeculanum, 89 BC (Social War, Marsic War) – The legions of the Roman general Lucius Cornelius Sulla prepared to invest Aeculanum, a town of the Hirpini tribe of Samnium in southern Italy. An initial attempt by the citizens of the community to stall negotiations with the Romans in anticipation of a Lucanian relief expedition failed, and the city soon capitulated. Because the residents of Aeculanum resisted his overtures, Sulla permitted his army to plunder the city.

Appianus (Appian), *Civil Wars*, 1.50.

Aegimurus Island, 245 BC – Near the small Mediterranean island of Aegimurus, located off the North African coast near the Bay of Carthage, a Punic fleet bound for Italy encountered Roman warships, and was subsequently defeated.

Lucius Annaeus Florus, *Epitomy*, 1.18.30.

Aegusa, 241 BC, 10 March (First Punic War, Wars against Carthage) – A fleet of 200 quinqueremes under the command of the Roman *consul* Caius Lutatius Catulus intercepted a Carthaginian flotilla led by Hanno near the *Aegates Insulae* (Egadi Islands) off western Sicily. The Punic fleet, which included 250 warships, was seeking to deliver supplies to the army of Hamilcar Barca at Eryx, north of the Sicilian port of Drepana (Trapani). The engagement occurred near Aegusa, the largest island in the Aegates group, 10 miles southwest of the harbour. As the Carthaginians neared the easternmost islands in the group, a large armada of Roman galleys met the approaching fleet in line-astern battle-formation. Despite being burdened by a strong westerly wind and large swells, the Roman ships capably manoeuvred against the heavily laden enemy vessels. The Punic force was decisively defeated with a loss of fifty ships sunk and another seventy captured. Roman losses amounted to thirty ships destroyed and fifty damaged. With its naval forces now badly crippled, Carthage finally accepted peace terms, ending the First Punic War.

Polybius, *Histories*, 1.60–61; Eutropius, *Abridgement of Roman History*, 2.27; Paulus Orosius, *Seven Books of History against the Pagans*, 4.10; Diodorus Siculus, *Historical Library*, 24.11.1–2; Titus Livius (Livy), *Summaries*, 19; Cornelius Nepos, *Great Generals of Foreign Nations*, 22.1.3; Lucius Annaeus Florus, *Epitomy*, 1.18.33.

Aesepus River, 74 BC – see Granicus River, 74 BC.

Aesernia, 90 BC (Social War, Marsic War) – A Roman force under the *consul* Lucius Julius Caesar (also called Sextus Caesar) attempted to relieve the besieged town of Aesernia, but was defeated by an Italian army led by the Marsic general Vettius Scato. Roman losses amounted to 2,000 killed. Following this victory, the Samnites invested Aesernia and eventually reduced the community by famine.

Appianus (Appian), *Civil Wars*, 1.41; Titus Livius (Livy), *Summaries*, 72, 73; Paulus Orosius, *Seven Books of History against the Pagans*, 5.18.

Aesis River, 82 BC, spring (Roman Civil Wars) – In the spring, the Sullan general Quintus Caecilius Metellus Pius, marching his army through Picenum and Umbria toward Cisalpine Gaul, was met at the Aesis River on the frontier of Picenum by Carrinas, a lieutenant of the *consul* Papirius Carbo. The ensuing battle proved an intense struggle that lasted from early morning until noon, and ended only when Carrinas' army was routed from the field with heavy losses. During the engagement, Gnaeus Pompeius, who had recently joined with Metellus, distinguished himself by routing the cavalry forces recently sent by the *consul* to aid Carrinas, and driving them on to difficult terrain where they were compelled to surrender. Following his victory, Metellus assumed control of the surrounding territory.

Appianus (Appian), *Civil Wars*, 1.87; Plutarch, *Pompey*, 7.3.

Agendicum, 52 BC, spring (Gallic War) – This battle was the result of Julius Caesar's spring campaign to suppress the Gallic uprising of 52 BC. As Caesar advanced toward the town of Gergovia with six legions, Titus Labienus and four legions (including the Seventh and Twelfth) were deployed in the region of Lutetia (Paris) against the Senones and Parisii. As Labienus approached Lutetia from the left (west) bank of the Sequana (Seine) River, a sizeable Gallic army under the leadership of Camulogenus was drawn up ahead of the main Roman body. This route was likewise blocked by the marshes of a lower tributary (the Esonne), forcing the Roman column to affect a crossing of the Sequana at the Senone community of Metiosedum, which was then occupied by legionary elements. The armies were encamped on opposite banks of the river near Lutetia when word arrived of Caesar's reverse at Gergovia. This news compelled Labienus to abandon the present campaign and withdraw back to Agendicum (Sens). Camulogenus, having anticipated this decision, moved to block the Roman army from recrossing the Sequana even as a second Gallic army, that of the Bellovaci, now approached Labienus' position from the north. Faced with this new threat, the Romans sought by means of a ruse to execute a night crossing. Ordering five cohorts to remain in camp and the remaining units of the same legion up river to serve as a decoy, Labienus and the main force of three legions successfully forded the Sequana downstream. This movement was masked by a storm, permitting the Roman formation to cross and reassemble unopposed before daybreak. In the ensuing battle, the three legions were arrayed with the Seventh Legion anchoring the right and the Twelfth deployed on the left wing. Fighting was intense on the Roman left, and the battle remained undecided until resistance on the Gallic left collapsed, permitting the Seventh Legion to wheel and envelope Camulogenus' right wing. Trapped by the legions, the main body of the Gallic force was completely destroyed.

Julius Caesar, *The Gallic War*, 7. 57–62.

Ager Pomptinae, 385 BC – Upon learning of the presence of a sizeable Volscian army in the Pomptine marshlands southeast of Rome, the dictator Aulus Cornelius Cossus mobilized a legionary force to confront the hostile foe. The enemy consisted of a large concentration of Volsci, together with additional elements of Latins, Hernici, Circeii and Roman colonists from Velitrae. The Volsci opened the battle with a charge, but were quickly stopped by the legions, which then assumed the offensive and drove the opposition's front line backward. The pressure of this initial legionary assault disrupted the cohesion of the entire enemy formation, which was further undermined by a timely charge of Roman cavalry against its flanks. The twofold attack broke the enemy ranks at several points, causing the integrity of the entire Volscian formation to disintegrate into a total rout. The Roman cavalry squadrons, under the command of Titus Quinctius Capitolinus, quickly pursued the fleeing remnants of the enemy and held them in check until the legions successfully overtook the Volsci and their allies. In the fighting which followed, the entire enemy army was destroyed and the Volscian camp completely sacked.

Titus Livius (Livy), *History of Rome*, 12.1–13.7.

Agrigentum, 262 BC (First Punic War, Wars against Carthage) – Following the outbreak of war with the North African city of Carthage, Roman legions landed in Sicily under the command of the consuls Lucius Postumius Megellus and Quintus Mamilius Vitulus, and quickly concentrated both consular armies on besieging the town of Agrigentum, which served as the major supply depot and assembly point for the Carthaginian army. The Romans established their camp less than a mile from the town and prepared for extended siege operations by sending out foraging parties throughout the surrounding grain fields. While many of the legionaries were dispersed over the countryside, the Carthaginians suddenly launched a sortie which scattered the foragers. Following this success, a portion of the Punic force advanced against the Roman encampment, while other units moved to assault the supporting force detailed to guard the foragers. These Roman troops maintained their position, and, though badly outnumbered, put up an intense struggle that resulted in heavy casualties on both sides. Finally, after desperate fighting, the cohorts gradually turned the momentum of the battle against the enemy and drove the Carthaginians back into the town with great loss.

Polybius, *Histories*, 1.17.6–13.

Aisne River, 57 BC – see Axona River, 57 BC.

Alce, 179 BC (Iberian War) – Near the Spanish town of Alce, a Roman army under the command of the *propraetor* Tiberius Sempronius Gracchus arrived in anticipation of engaging an encamped force of Celtiberian tribesmen. Following their arrival, the Romans initiated daily attacks against the enemy's outposts using light infantry. The size of this assaulting force increased incrementally each day in order to draw more and more enemy troops out of their fortified camp. Finally, having compelled the deployment of the entire Celtiberian force by means of these daily actions, the *propraetor* ordered his officers of light infantry to feign defeat on the battlefield, allowing the line of Roman auxiliaries to waiver before retreating in headlong disorder toward their own camp, where the main Roman army would be assembled in anticipation. On the day of the final battle, the commanders and *auxilia* executed Sempronius' plan as instructed. By this ruse the enemy enthusiastically pursued the fleeing light infantry back to the Roman *castrum*, where the entire force of legionary heavy infantry was clandestinely assembled behind the ramparts of the camp. As the *auxilia* rushed toward safety through the nearest camp gate, followed closely by the Celtiberians in loose order, the legions suddenly sallied from the remaining gates and fell upon the unsuspecting attackers. The enemy was badly defeated in the battle which followed, suffering some 9,000 killed and 320 captured. Roman losses amounted to only 109 dead.

Titus Livius (Livy), *History of Rome*, 40.48.

Alesia, 52 BC, spring-summer (Gallic War) – This was the decisive engagement in Caesar's campaign to suppress the great Gallic revolt of 52 BC, the success of which assured Rome's mastery of Gaul. In early spring, following his failure at Gergovia, Caesar rendezvoused with one of his subordinate commanders, Titus Labienus, and four legions near Agenticum. His command now consisted of eleven legions, including the Eighth, Tenth and Thirteenth. Once assembled, the army advanced southeastward toward the fortress of Alesia, situated in the territory of the Mandubii (north of Dijon). While in transit, the legions were attacked by a large formation of Gallic cavalry under the command of the Arvernian chieftain Vercingetorix. The assault, though executed by a three-pronged attack on the Roman position, ultimately failed after Caesar's German auxiliary cavalry routed the Gallic left. With this setback, and the failure of the Gallic horse to disrupt the legionary formation, Vercingetorix withdrew toward Alesia, his rear now harassed by elements of Roman cavalry. Once the Roman army arrived at Alesia, Caesar initiated the construction of an extensive and complex system of siege works, consisting of a double line of earthen works extending approximately 11 miles, which completely circumvallated the stronghold. Confined within this static parameter were 50,000–80,000 Gallic warriors. While the Roman works were still in their formative stages, a brief engagement was fought which was capably turned to Caesar's favour by German cavalry. This failure of the Gauls to decisively breach the Roman position now ensured a long siege. Confined in Alesia with the infantry, Vercingetorix was determined to send his entire force of cavalry out through the uncompleted Roman lines, in order to both lighten the logistical burden on the trapped army and to garner outside reinforcements. The need to conserve vital stores also led the Gallic leadership to eject the civilian population from the city. With Alesia fully invested by Caesar, a substantial Gallic army led by

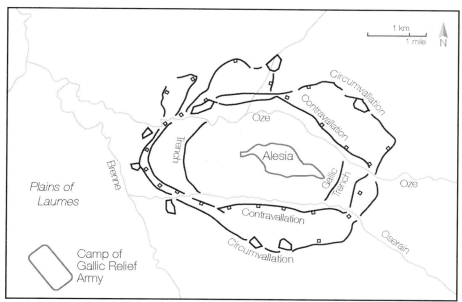

Battle of Alesia, 52 BC

the Atrebatian chieftain Commius sought to relieve the besieged force, but was driven off after several hours' fighting by a counter-attack of the German auxiliary horse. This defeat was followed two days later by a major night assault led by Commius against the outer Roman perimeter, simultaneous with an attack on Caesar's interior defensive works by Vercingetorix. Engaged by these two powerful Gallic formations, the Roman line was hard-pressed until fresh legionary reinforcements, drawn from locations not under attack, were delivered by Marcus Antonius and Caius Trebonius. The battle continued until daylight, when Gallic forces broke off their attack. The third and final assault to relieve Alesia was directed against the exterior Roman lines by a force of 60,000 Gauls led by Vercassivellaunus, a leader of the Arverni and kinsman of Vercingetorix. The main thrust of the attack was concentrated at a weak point in the linear works defended by two legions under the command of Caius Caninius Rebilus and Caius Antistius Reginus. Concurrent with this primary onslaught, a second, diversionary attack was directed against the Roman earthworks by Gallic cavalry in order to further attenuate the legionary force. At the same time, thousands of Gauls under Vercingetorix initiated an assault on Caesar's interior defences. This three-pronged attack was repulsed by the judicious deployment of numerous cohorts under Labienus, Decimus Junius Brutus, Caius Fabius and Caesar himself. Having first stemmed the attack on the interior defences, Caesar redeployed legionary units to reinforce Labienus on the northwest ramparts.

In accordance with this move, elements of Roman cavalry were dispatched around the outer entrenchments in order to attack the enemy in the rear. The effect of this action was to cause the Gauls to waver in their assault. As the cavalry drove in the flank of the main Gallic formation, the Roman foot surged forward from the redoubts, now reinforced by additional cohorts. Their attack broken, thousands of Gauls fell in the ensuing retreat and Vercassivellaunus himself was captured. Now entrapped with no hope of relief, Vercingetorix was compelled to surrender.

Julius Caesar, *The Gallic War*, 7. 63–90.

Alexandria, 48–47 BC (Roman Civil Wars, Alexandrian War) – Having pursued Pompey to Egypt after the Battle of Pharsalus, Caesar became embroiled in the arbitration of a dynastic dispute between the kingdom's co-rulers, Ptolemaeus XII and Cleopatra. The young queen submitted to outside mediation in the matter, but Ptolemy challenged Caesar's intrusion and ordered his general, Achillas, to move against Roman forces in the city of Alexandria. With a royal army of 20,000 men, including a number of ex-Pompeian legionaries from the army of Aulus Gabinius, Achillas advanced from Pelusium and besieged Caesar's force of two legions and 800 horse near the Great Harbour. An initial Egyptian assault against this main Roman position failed, though intense street fighting erupted simultaneously near the port, where royal forces sought to gain possession of the harbour together with

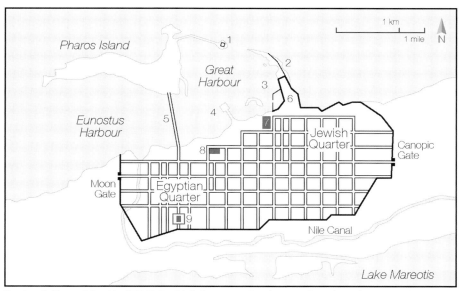

Battle of Alexandria, 48–47 BC (1=Lighthouse; 2=Lochias; 3=Royal Harbour; 4=Timonium; 5=Heptastadium; 6=Palace Area; 7=Mouseion/Library; 8=Theatre; 9=Serapeum)

seventy-two Alexandrian warships, so as to deny Caesar a means to re-supply and reinforce his position. Unable to adequately defend the wharfage with his small force, and unwilling to risk the capture of the anchored galleys, Caesar ordered the entire fleet of quadriremes and quinqueremes to be burned. He soon deployed a contingent of Roman troops to garrison the Pharos Island tower as a means of securing the harbour entrance, even while continuing to strengthen his landward defences. The opportunity was like-wise taken to summon reinforcements from Asia Minor, together with the Caesarian fleet from Rhodes, Cilisia and Syria. The arrival of this flotilla preceded a naval battle in which an Egyptian war fleet unsuccessfully sought to destroy the force of galleys and transports carrying the *Legio XXXVII* in relief of Caesar. This failure was followed by a second battle in the shallows near Pharos Island and the Eunostos Harbour, in which the Romans capably dispersed an assorted formation of ships and shallow-draft vessels attempting to block seaborne access to the city. This latter action compelled Caesar to secure all of Pharos Island, and the Heptastadium linking the island to the mainland. Both were successfully occupied, but a subsequent action to over-run a fort situated at the southern end of the mole resulted in a decisive Roman defeat, with the loss of 400 legionaries and a slightly larger number of allied seamen. Even so, Caesar retained control of that portion of the city already occupied by Roman forces.

Julius Caesar (Aulus Hirtius), *The Alexandrian War*, 1–32; Julius Caesar, *The Civil Wars*, 3.106–112.

Algidus Mons, 465 BC – A sudden raid into Latium by the Aequi, an Italian people occupying the Alban hills south of the Tiber River, broke a year-long truce brokered between the tribe and Rome. In response to this incursion, the Roman *consul* Quintus Fabius sent envoys to the Aequian council demanding a cessation in hostilities, but their overtures were dismissed. An Aequian army was dispatched to Mount Algidus shortly afterwards. These events compelled the Roman senate to deploy two armies under Fabius and his co-*consul* Titus Quinctius to confront the Aequian threat. Both consular forces converged at Algidus and, following an intense battle, inflicted a sharp defeat on the Aequi. Far from serving as a deterrent, the engagement was followed by Aequian raids into Roman territory. Once again, Roman armies were sent into the field. Titus Quinctius failed to make contact with the enemy but Quintus Fabius, having anticipated the route of the Aequian raiders back to their homeland, surprised the unsuspecting enemy and largely destroyed the marauders.

Titus Livius (Livy), *History of Rome*, 3.2–3.3.9.

Algidus Mons, 458 BC – The Aequi broke a treaty concluded with Rome the previous year and invaded the region around Labici and Tusculum, 15 miles southeast of Rome. In response, the Senate dispatched a delegation of envoys to the Aequian camp on Mount Algidus, but the army's general, Cloelius Gracchus, dismissed the representatives without audience. Following this rejection, the Senate directed the *consul* Caius Nautius to invade the territories of the Aequi, and his co-*consul*, Lucius Minucius, to lead a second army against the Aequian force presently encamped on Algidus. Once in the vicinity of Gracchus' position, Minucius hesitated to offer the enemy battle, choosing instead to remain safely behind the ramparts of his marching camp. The Aequian army quickly responded to this cautious posture by surrounding the Roman *castrum* with earthworks and besieging the consular legions within their own fortifications. Alarmed by this developing crisis, and unsure of Nautius' ability to redress the situation, the Senate elected to grant dictatorial power to Lucius Quinctius Cincinnatus. On reaching Mount Algidus with a newly levied army, Cincinnatus deployed his legions around the Aequian position and began construction of circumvallating earthworks, intending to trap the Aequi between his troops and those of Minucius. Recognizing the danger, Gracchus attempted to disrupt the work of Cincinnatus' force but was prevented by Minucius' legions, who initiated a sustained night assault against the Aequian position. With sunrise, the army of Quinctius, having completed the outer rampart and re-armed, suddenly launched a fresh attack against the now battle-weary Aequi. Unable to withstand this new offensive after the previous night's fighting, the enemy quickly sued for peace. Following the surrender of its principal officers, including Cloelius Gracchus, Quinctius permitted the remainder of the Aequian army to return to its homeland on condition that the entire force of men first passed under the yoke.

Titus Livius (Livy), *History of Rome*, 3.25.9–3.28.

Algidus Mons, 455 BC – By the middle of the fifth century BC, the Aequi had established themselves on the col of Mount Algidus, using the elevated heights as a base from which to initiate periodic forays into the Anio and Trerus valleys. Around this time, the Senate received a disturbing report that the Aequians were raiding the territory of Tusculum, a community 12 miles southeast of Rome. In response, Roman armies were deployed under the consuls Caius Veturius Geminus and Titus Romilius. The legions located the enemy and routed them on Mount Algidus. Approximately 7,000 Aequi were killed, and the remainder driven into flight.

Titus Livius (Livy), *History of Rome*, 3.31.3–4.

Algidus Mons, 449 BC – The Aequians badly defeated a Roman army commanded by the general Marcus Cornelius Maluginensis. While survivors managed to flee to the city of Tusculum, the legionary camp was overrun and thoroughly pillaged.

Titus Livius (Livy), *History of Rome*, 3.42.3, 5–6.

Algidus Mons, 449 BC – Regional hostilities again flared between Rome and her neighbours when Aequian and Volscian armies joined together in an effort to threaten territories in the Anio and Trerus valleys. The Senate responded to this invasion by deploying legions under the command of the *consul* Lucius Valerius Potitus. On the slopes of Mount Algidus, some 13 miles southeast of the city, the Romans established their camp approximately a mile from the main enemy position. Confident in their strength, the Aequi and Volsci repeatedly sought to entice the *consul* into open battle, but failed. Finally, convinced by their inaction that the legions possessed no desire to fight, the bulk of the enemy troops began pillaging the lands of the Latins and Hernici, leaving behind a garrison-strength force in the camp. This dispersal of manpower provided Valerius the tactical opportunity he sought. By defeating one element of the opposing army, he could thereby undermine the collective strength of the enemy and destroy the invaders piecemeal. He shortly thereafter offered battle to the occupants of the encampment, but this initial overture was rejected. Alarmed by the Romans' sudden show of force, the garrison dispatched couriers to recall some of the errant divisions then raiding in the immediate vicinity. The Romans again assembled in arms the following day, determined now to carry the assault to the ramparts of the enemy, should a second challenge be refused. Not until late afternoon did the legions finally advance to the attack, a provocative move that inspired the Aequi and Volsci to sally out of their enclosure in force. As the enemy surged through the gates of the camp, Valerius suddenly ordered the legions to charge before the opposition could properly assemble into battle formation. Caught off-guard, the Aequi and Volscians reeled from this first shock but quickly rallied. Fighting continued unabated until the integrity of the enemy formation, already compromised by the initial infantry attack, was irretrievably lost when a strong charge by Roman cavalry broke through its lines. This penetration triggered a general rout, that was further magnified when a second formation of riders swept over an expanse of unoccupied ground and scattered the remnants of the fleeing army. In the midst of the chaos, Valerius and his legions successfully overran the camp's defences and took possession of a large store of booty. The Roman victory was total by nightfall.

Titus Livius (Livy), *History of Rome*, 3.60–61.1–10; Dionysius of Halicarnassus, *Roman Antiquities*, 11.47.

Algidus Mons, 431 BC – The Aequi and Volsci again disrupted the tranquility of the Anio, Trerus and Tiber valleys. Strong armies from both nations rendezvoused on Mount Algidus in preparation for incursions into neighbouring territories. Because of the acute nature of the threat and persistent dissension between the two serving consuls, the Senate recommended the appointment of a dictator to undertake the campaign. Aulus

Postumius Tubertus was selected and immediately set out from Rome in command of a legionary army. Drawing near the enemy's position, the dictator observed two enemy camps, and likewise elected to divide his forces. The Romans almost immediately began skirmishing as a means of testing the strength of their opponents. Such encounters gradually undermined the confidence of the enemy troops and persuaded them that a regular battle possessed little chance of success. Instead, they chose to pursue a night action against the second of the two Roman camps, that of the *consul* Titus Quinctius Cincinnatus Poenus. Postumius, observing the attack from his unassailed position, immediately sent reinforcements to aid his fellow general. At the same time, he deployed a second detachment of troops under Marcus Geganius which successfully overran one of the enemy camps left poorly manned. The dictator himself then led the remainder of his command undetected behind the attackers, and at dawn launched a massive assault against the enemy's rear which trapped the Aequi and Volsci between Quinctius' camp and his own legions. Surrounded, the enemy soldiers put up a vigorous struggle, and despite suffering heavy casualties, managed to successfully battle their way to the relative security of the remaining encampment. The protection offered by the palisade was short-lived, however, as the legions continued to press home their onslaught and, after intense fighting, finally compelled the surviving Aequians and Volscians to surrender.

Titus Livius (Livy), *History of Rome*, 4.26–29.1–4

Algidus Mons, 418 BC – Once again the Aequi began preparations for war, and recruited the Labicani as allies in their campaign. Alerted to the situation, the Senate dispatched a Roman army under the command of two military tribunes, Lucius Sergius Fidenas and Marcus Papirius Mugillanus. From the very beginning, the legions' success was jeopardized by the animosity between the two tribunes. Their mutual hatred left no room for a single leader, and so each agreed to assume supreme command on alternate days. This divided authority proved disastrous. Having fallen victim to a ruse, the tribunes permitted the army to be caught in an unfavourable position too near the enemy encampment, where it was ill-prepared to resist a sudden attack by the Aequi. The unexpected assault routed the Roman formation, and many were slain in flight. The legionaries defended their camp with difficulty throughout the remainder of the day and into the next. Discipline failed the Romans when it appeared that the enemy would soon close off all means of escape. Many abandoned their fortifications and sought safety in the city of Tusculum, while other soldiers simply disappeared into the surrounding fields in flight to Rome. Upon learning of the defeat, a second army marched against the Aequi and Labicani under the command of an experienced general, the dictator Quintus Servilius Priscus. Badly misjudging the abilities of Servilius and his army, the enemy was swiftly routed from the battlefield and their camp over-run by the legions. The remnants of the beaten army fled to the town of Labici, which was captured by Roman siege the following day.

Titus Livius (Livy), *History of Rome*, 4.45.5–47.1–6.

Allia River, 390 BC* (Gallic Invasion of Italy) – Learning of the approach of a sizeable Gallic army toward Latium, the city of Rome deployed a force of 40,000 troops under the command of Quintus Sulpicius Longus to check the invasion. The two armies met approximately 11 miles north of the *urbs*, near the Allia River and its confluence with the Tiber. The speed of the Gallic advance through Etruria denied Sulpicius any opportunity to select a site suitable for engaging a larger army. In order to discourage envelopment by the Gauls, Sulpicius deployed the principle legionary formation along a broad front extending from a low rise of hills on the right to near the Allia on the left. This action dangerously attenuated the Roman centre, making it susceptible to enemy penetration. A secondary force, held back as reinforce-ment by the military tribunes, was deployed on higher ground to the imme-diate right of the primary Roman position. It was this reserve that bore the initial charge of the Gauls. Uncertain of his opponent's strength and fearing a counter-attack on his left once battle was joined, the Gallic commander, Brennus, initiated a sharp attack on the Roman right, shattering the reserves. The cumulative effect of this first assault was to cause the entire Roman line

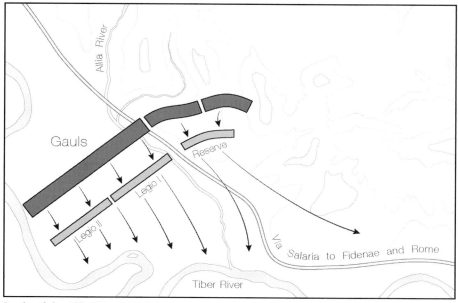

Battle of the Allia River, 390 BC

to waver, permitting the Gauls to strike the main body of the army, collapsing the centre and driving the Roman left into the river, where it was destroyed. Though sources are unclear as to the number of Roman dead, all agree the defeat was total and catastrophic.

> Titus Livius (Livy), *History of Rome*, 5.36.11–39.2; Plutarch, *Camillus* 18.4–7; Diodorus Siculus, *Historical Library*, 14.113.3–115.2. *Despite the chronology of Livy, which gives a date of 390 BC for the Battle of the Allia River, evidence from Diodorus Siculus, Polybius, Heracleides and Theopompus indicate a date of 387/6 BC.

Allia River, 380 BC – The Praenestini marched against Rome upon learning that the Roman people were presently distracted by domestic strife and had failed to enrol an army. The arrival of these Latin troops at the Colline Gate on the northeast side of the city inspired such popular panic that the government was moved to appoint Titus Quinctius Cincinnatus as dictator. This news caused the Praenestini to withdraw to the Allia River, where they believed the psychological dread inspired by the Gallic victory over the Romans ten years earlier would serve to undermine the legions' self-confidence and result in defeat. Contrary to the enemy's hopes, the newly recruited Roman army was certain of its ability to defeat the Latin force, which was at present engaged in a campaign of pillage throughout the surrounding countryside. When the armies finally joined in battle at the Allia, the Romans routed the Praenestini with the opening charge. The enemy line broke and fled in disorder under the simultaneous pressure of cavalry and infantry assaults.

> Titus Livius (Livy), *History of Rome*, 6.28–29.3.

Allifae, 307 BC (Second Samnite War, Samnite Wars) – Approximately 20 miles northeast of Capua, a Roman army under the command of the *proconsul* Quintus Fabius defeated a Samnite army near the city of Allifae in south central Italy. The legions successfully drove the Samnites from the field and then proceeded to invest the enemy in their camp. The determined prosecution of the siege was interrupted by nightfall. The Samnites surrendered the following morning, and were sent under the yoke.

> Titus Livius (Livy), *History of Rome*, 9.42.6–8.

Alpheus River, 146 BC (War of the Achaean League) – The growing political tensions in the Balkans finally spilled over into war between Rome and the member states of the Achaean League. The *strategos* Critolaus, leader of the league, openly expressed his hostility toward the Romans by insulting envoys sent to meet him. In response to this overt expression of hostility, the legions of the *propraetor* Quintus Caecilius Metellus marched southward from Macedonia. The Romans defeated an Achaean army along the banks of the Alpheus (Alpheios) River in Elis.

> Lucius Annaeus Florus, *Epitomy*, 1.32.2–3.

Amanus, 51 BC – A short time after Marcus Tullius Cicero assumed his proconsular duties as governor of Cilicia, he orchestrated a campaign against a band of brigands whose strongholds were situated on Mount Amanus (Nur Daglari), a range near the Mediterranean coast which straddled the border between his appointed province and Syria. In order to seize control of the mountain, Cicero led his army to the location under cover of darkness. Before making the ascent, the *proconsul* divided his *auxilia* and legionary cohorts into four columns, and placed each under the command of a *legatus*. The army was already in the process of climbing the rugged slopes at various locations when dawn broke. The assault caught the enemy completely unaware. The main settlement of Erana, along with Sepyra and Commoris, fell after several hours of intense fighting. A number of fortified citadels were also destroyed, and the majority of the inhabitants on Mount Amanus were either captured or slain. Following the assault, the army encamped on the lower spurs of the mountain, near the Issus River. Over the next four days, the Romans hunted down and slew any remaining fugitives, and thoroughly ruined all of the agricultural land on the mountain which was inside Cilicia.

> Marcus Tullius Cicero, *Letters to Friends*, 'Cicero to M. Porcius Cato, January, 50 BC' (Shuckburgh trans., 1899, ccxxxvii = F xv 4, pp. 100–8); Plutarch, *Cicero*, 36.6.

Anas River, 79 BC (War against Sertorius) – At the Anas (Guadiana) River in southwestern Iberia, Quintus Sertorius' lieutenant, the *quaestor* Lucius Hirtuleius, defeated an army under the command of Marcus Domitius Calvinus*, *proconsul* of *Hispania Citerior* (Eastern Spain). Domitius died in the fighting.

> Plutarch, *Sertorius* 12.4; Eutropius, *Abridgement of Roman History*, 6.1; Lucius Annaeus Florus, *Epitomy*, 2.10; Titus Livius (Livy), *Summaries*, 90; Paulus Orosius, *Seven Books of History against the Pagans*, 5.23. *Eutropius and Livy both identify the Roman officer as Lucius Domitius.

Ancyra, 189 BC – After two aborted attempts to conclude terms of settlement with the Tectosages, the Roman *consul* Cnaeus Manlius Vulso agreed to a third meeting with leaders of the Gallic tribe. Both parties elected to convene at a location situated approximately halfway between the camp of the Gauls and that of the Romans at Ancyra. Five miles from the Roman *castrum*, a superior force of 1,000 Gallic horsemen unexpectedly engaged Manlius and his guard of 500 cavalry. The assault was capably resisted at first, but the pressure of the attack eventually put the Roman column to flight. The Gauls immediately gave chase and killed a number of Manlius' guardsmen, but the pursuit was disrupted by the timely arrival of a 600-man detachment of Roman cavalry deployed in the area to protect a party of foragers. These fresh squadrons of horse charged the Gallic attackers, drove them off and pursued them hotly. Most of the Gauls were slain in the running battle which followed.

Titus Livius (Livy), *History of Rome*, 38.25; Polybius, *Histories*, 21.39.

Anio River, 495 BC – A Sabine army burning and pillaging farms near the Anio (Aniene) River, a tributary of the Tiber, was intercepted by a force of Roman cavalry under the command of Aulus Postumius. Enemy stragglers were quickly captured before the entire Sabine contingent was compelled to capitulate following the arrival of a column of infantry led by the Roman *consul* Publius Servilius.

Titus Livius (Livy), *History of Rome*, 2.26.1–3.

Anio River, 437 BC – The town of Fidenae, 7 miles north of Rome across the Anio (Aniene) River, revolted against Rome and unexpectedly entered into an alliance with the Etruscan city of Veii. When an embassy was sent by the Senate to enquire into the reasons for such a change in policy, the Fidenates murdered the four envoys. Accordingly, an army was dispatched under the *consul* Lucius Sergius Fidenas. The legions defeated a force of Veientes in a bloody but indecisive battle south of the Anio River. Still alarmed by the strategic threat posed by the new affiliation, the Romans appointed a dictator, Mamercus Aemilius Macerinus, to continue the prosecution of the war.

Titus Livius (Livy), *History of Rome*, 4.17.1–8.

Anio River, 361 BC – Almost three decades after a powerful band of Gauls under Brennus destroyed a Roman army at the Allia River, Italy was again subjected to a Gallic invasion. The encroaching army advanced as far south as the further bank of the Anio (Aniene) River, and there camped beside the *Via Salaria*, at the third milestone from Rome. In response, the dictator Titus Quinctius Poenus encamped with his legions on the nearer bank of the water-course, intent on blocking the enemy's approach to the city. Skirmishes inevitably erupted as the two sides sought to gain control of the Salarian Bridge. These clashes proved indecisive, and the violence culminated with a single contest between champions representing each army. In the resulting match, the Roman fighter Titus Manlius defeated his much larger opponent. This unexpected turn of events stunned the Gauls, who abruptly withdrew to Tibur (Tivoli) and formed an alliance with the Tiburtes. They then marched into Campania after acquiring provisions from their new allies.

Titus Livius (Livy), *History of Rome*, 7.9.3–11.1.

Antigoneia, 51 BC (Parthian Wars) – The defeat of Crassus at Carrhae in 53 BC emboldened the Parthians, who systematically recovered all of the lands east of the Euphrates River in the months following the battle. The next year, Crassus' former lieutenant, Caius Cassius Longinus, repelled an invasion of Syria by a small force of Parthians. This penetration was the precursor to a more significant attack a year later by a Parthian army under the leadership of general Osaces and prince Pacorus, the young son of King Orodes II. The invaders first tried to seize Antioch (Antakya), but were repulsed by Roman forces. Osaces then prepared to occupy Antigoneia, a town over 4 miles to the northeast, but this effort also proved unsuccessful when his cavalry could not safely penetrate an overgrown stand of woods outside the community. Frustrated in their attempts to clear away the trees, and continually harassed by Cassius' men, the Parthians eventually chose to abandon the location and withdraw. In the meantime, the Romans prepared an ambuscade along the enemy's path of retreat. Confronting Osaces with a small detachment of troops, Cassius, by means of a feigned withdrawal, induced the Parthians to give chase. The running battle carried both parties directly into the midst of the concealed Roman divisions. The resulting clash ended in the defeat of the Parthians and the death of their general. Pacorus afterward retreated from Syria with the remainder of the army.

Dio Cassius, *Roman History*, 28–29

Antium, 482 BC – The Volscians initiated hostilities during a period of domestic turmoil in Rome. In response, the Senate dispatched an army under the *consul* Lucius Aemilius Mamercus to the community of Antium (Anzio), located 30 miles south of Rome on the Tyrrhenian coast. The legions encamped on a hill adjacent to the enemy and awaited an opportunity for battle. After several days of moderate activity, the two armies finally descended onto the intervening plain and entered into a decisive engagement. The size and martial talents of the Volscian force ensured that both sides were equally matched. Following a lengthy struggle, the Volsci began an orderly withdrawal from the battlefield, which the Romans erroneously concluded was the beginning of a retreat. As the enemy started running toward their encampment, the increased speed of the pursuit disrupted the legionary formation, which now gave a disordered chase. When the fleeing Volscians finally reached the breastworks of their camp, they turned and launched an unexpected counter-attack which was reinforced by additional reserves from inside the camp. The elevated location contributed to the impact of the Volscian charge. The momentum of the downhill assault not only drove the legions back toward their own encampment, but overran those Romans already engaged in plundering the Volscian dead at the original site of the fighting. While the infantry fell back in disorder, the arrival of Roman cavalry in late afternoon, together with the advent of a violent rainstorm, ended the day's action. The following night, Aemilius abandoned his camp and withdrew, conceding the field to the Volscians.

Dionysius of Halicarnassus, *Roman Antiquities*, 8.83.3–85.4.

Antium, 468 BC – Once again faced with war against the Volsci and Aequi, who coveted the more fertile northern territories of Latium, the Romans responded by deploying an army under the command of the *consul* Titus Quintius Capitolinus Barbatus. The legions marched south toward the coastal community of Antium (Anzio) and there encamped not far from the location of the enemy. Soon thereafter, both armies entered battle on a nearby plain and became embroiled in a long and desperate struggle that lasted until midday. As each side was forced to commit its total reserves to action, the numerical superiority of the enemy gradually began to shift the engagement against the Romans. Wishing to extricate the exhausted legions from the fighting, but fearful a withdrawal would be misconstrued by the opposition as the beginning of a rout, Quintius deliberately misled his flagging right wing into believing that the legionaries on the left were at the point of victory. Revitalized by this ruse, and suddenly emboldened as they witnessed their general personally charge into the midst of the enemy line, the entire wing surged forward and put the Volscian formation to flight. Quintius then quickly spurred his horse to the opposite end of the Roman battle-line and exhorted the legionaries there to repulse the enemy in the same manner. The rout proved total, the Volscians and Aequians both being driven from the field in disarray.

Dionysius of Halicarnassus, *Roman Antiquities*, 9.57.3–7; Titus Livius (Livy), *History of Rome*, 2.64.5–6.

Antium, 468 BC – Having days earlier lost a closely contested battle with the Romans near the community of Antium (Anzio), the Volsci, together with reinforcements from other allied tribes, launched a night assault against the legionary encampment located some 3½ miles from the town. As the enemy's foray proved unable to breach the camp's defences, the army's consular commander, Titus Quintius Capitolinus, refrained from any major counter-response until daybreak. Then, at first light, a sudden and unexpected charge by Roman cavalry from the confines of the camp signalled the beginning of an intense struggle between the two armies. The mounted sortie was shortly followed by the arrival of the legions, which quickly assembled into battle formation. In the ensuing clash, the enemy, exhausted from the previous night's action, offered only brief resistance before retreating to a nearby hill. There the Volscians made a final determined stand. The struggle continued unabated for most of the day before the sheer pressure of the Roman attack drove the defenders from their position. Unable to escape the relentless onslaught of the enemy, most of the Volsci, Aequi and their allies died in flight. The following day, Quintius advanced against Antium in preparation for investing the town, but the community resolved to surrender without resistance.

Dionysius of Halicarnassus, *Roman Antiquities*, 9.58.2–8; Titus Livius (Livy), *History of Rome*, 2.65.

Aous River, 198 BC (Second Macedonian War, Wars against Macedon) – Following failed peace negotiations between King Philip V of Macedon and the Roman *consul* Titus Quinctius Flamininus, the forces of both commanders prepared for an armed encounter near the Aous (Aoos or Vijose) River in Epirus. The Macedonian force amounted to 20,000 men, while Flamininus had two legions available. The armies converged in a mountainous region where the Aous is forced through a narrow valley. After an initial episode of skirmishing on the valley plain, Philip's phalanx withdrew to the heights overlooking the river. Flamininus followed, but the rugged mountainous landscape hampered the tactical flexibility of the legions, resulting in further inconclusive fighting which finally subsided with the onset of nightfall. The stalemate was finally broken when local shepherds offered to guide some of the Roman cohorts to a point behind the Macedonian position. The *consul* covertly dispatched 4,000 select infantry and 300 cavalry on a three-day march around the enemy. In order to distract the suspicions of Philip, the main body of Romans continued to draw the Macedonians into skirmishes for two more days. On the third morning, Flamininus divided his force into three columns and marched against the enemy; two advanced along the sides of the valley, and a third moved down the narrowest portion of the ravine, following the river. When the earlier deployed detachment of selected troops finally reached its destination, the tribune in command alerted Flamininus by means of a prearranged smoke signal. The *consul* immediately initiated an intense assault of the Macedonian position. After protracted fighting, the secretly dispatched cohorts suddenly launched an attack on the enemy rear, causing Philip's army to panic. Within a short time the rout was complete, though unfavourable terrain limited pursuit by elements of Roman cavalry. The brevity of the chase offered Philip the opportunity to reconstitute his force and retire from the area in reasonably good order, having lost only about 2,000 men.

Plutarch, *Flamininus* 3–5.1; Titus Livius (Livy), *History of Rome*, 32.5.8–6.4; 10–12.

Aquae Sextiae, 102 BC (Germanic Invasions) – After years of migratory movement, three powerful Germanic tribes, the Cimbri, Teutones and Ambrones, advanced toward Italy. They approached the peninsula along two major fronts, the Cimbri moving northward to cross the eastern Alps through the Brenner Pass, and the Ambrones and Teutones pursuing a more westward Alpine penetration through southern France along the Mediterranean coast. In response to the threatened invasion, the Roman *consul* Caius Marius moved a legionary army into southern Gaul and there established a fortified base near the mouth of the Rhodanus (Rhone) River, ahead of the southern advance of Germans. Upon reaching the plain of the river, the Teutones encamped for several days near the Roman position, seeking to draw the legions

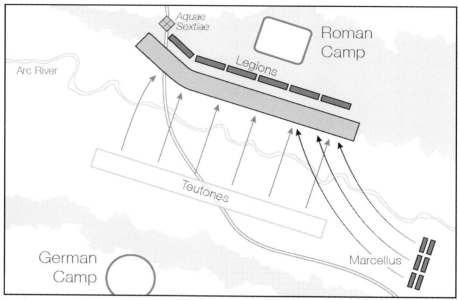

Battle of Aquae Sextiae, 102 BC

to battle. Marius refused all opportunity for open engagement, preferring to hold his forces in reserve behind their fortifications. Unable to breach the Roman position, the Germans determined to bypass the site and continue on to Italy. Once the Teutones and Ambrones resumed their advance toward Cisalpine Gaul, Marius decamped his army and followed at some distance. While both armies were camped near Aquae Sextiae (Aix-en-Provence), a Roman effort to secure access to the Arc River as a means of water supply provoked a preliminary battle with the Ambrones. The main body of the enemy began fording the river as the skirmish intensified, prompting Marius to deploy some of his Italian *socii*, the Ligurians, to attack the Ambrones before they could achieve a successful crossing. This initial assault was quickly followed by a more intense charge by the Romans, who drove the Germans back across the Arc. In the ensuing battle, some 30,000 Ambrones warriors were killed. Roman losses were negligible. Two days later, the Romans engaged the far larger army of the Teutones. Having earlier deployed his lieutenant, Claudius Marcellus, and a force of 3,000 legionaries into a wooded defile behind the main German encampment, Marius prepared to offer battle. He assembled the legions for action, accompanied by elements of Roman cavalry. Observing this buildup, the Teutones responded with a massive attack against the Marian position. The momentum of this effort was disrupted, however, by an expanse of rough and sloping terrain forward of the Roman lines, which permitted the legions to capably turn the assault. As a

Roman counter-attack drove the Germans backward in disorder, Marcellus' force suddenly engaged the Teutones in the rear, shattering the cohesion of the enemy formation. German resistance quickly collapsed. Some 100,000 Teutones were slain or captured in the battle which followed, including their king, Teutobodus.

Plutarch, *Caius Marius* 17–21; Lucius Annaeus Florus, *Epitomy*, 1.38.6–10; Titus Livius (Livy), *Summaries*, 68; Paulus Orosius, *Seven Books of History against the Pagans*, 5.16; Velleius Paterculus, *Roman History*, 2.12.4; Eutropius, *Abridgement of Roman History*, 5.1; Frontinus, *Stratagems*, 2.4.6.

Aquilonia, 293 BC (Third Samnite War, Samnite Wars) – While a Samnite army of 40,000 gathered in the city of Aquilonia in preparation for war, two Roman consular armies prepared to invade Samnium. The veteran legions from the previous year's campaign were given over to the *consul* Spurius Carvilius Maximus, while a newly levied army was led by the second consular magistrate, Lucius Papirius Cursor. The two armies advanced into Samnite territory along separate fronts, the forces of Carvilius capturing the Samnite community of Amiternum and Papirius likewise gaining the city of Duronis by assault. After devastating the Samnite region of Atina, Cavilius moved his army before the town of Cominium while Papirius encamped outside Aquilonia approximately 20 miles away. The following day, the two consuls launched simultaneous assaults, Cavilius mounting a sustained attack on Cominium in order to prevent the town sending relief to Aquilonia, and Papirius engaging the main Samnite army. Command of the Roman right was assigned to Lucius Volumnius, the left wing to Lucius Scipio and the cavalry to Titus Trebonius and Gaius Caedicius. The legate Spurius Nautius, along with three auxiliary cohorts and the army's mules, was ordered to repair to a nearby hill and await a prearranged signal from Papirius. The battle was hotly contested. As the intensity of the engagement approached its apex and the momentum of the struggle began to shift in favour of the Romans, a dust cloud suddenly appeared on the horizon, suggesting the approach of Roman rein-forcements after the capture of Cominium. In reality, the dust cloud was gen-erated by Nautius' detachment of auxiliaries and mules to simulate advancing legions. The implication created by the ruse caused the Samnite line to waiver. At that moment, a well-timed Roman cavalry charge broke the enemy line completely, initiating a complete rout. From the battle and its aftermath, Samnite losses totalled 20,340 killed and 3,870 captured.

Titus Livius (Livy), *History of Rome*, 10.38–42.

Arar River, 58 BC (Gallic War) – During the early summer, Caesar learned that a large formation of Celtic Helvetii was crossing the Arar (Saone) River by boat and rafts, moving toward Roman Provence. Faced with the possibility of a sizeable movement of thousands of Celtic peoples out of lands north of the Rhodanus (Rhone) River and Lake Geneva, Caesar resolved to march his legions forward in an effort to block the migration. Advancing toward a point north of the confluence of the Rhodanus and Arar Rivers, Caesar was informed by Roman scouts that three-quarters of the Celtic force had already crossed the river, with only the last of the four Helvetic cantons, the tribe of the Tigurini, yet to complete the crossing. After several hours, Caesar reached the vicinity of the Arar undetected, and immediately attacked with three legions. The unexpected assault resulted in the almost total destruction of the Tigurini, with thousands dying under Roman arms or fleeing into the surrounding forests. Caesar then took up the pursuit of the remaining Helvetii.

> Plutarch, *Caesar*, 18.1–2; Julius Caesar, *The Gallic War*, 1.12; Dio Cassius, *Roman History*, 38.32.4.

Arausio, 105 BC (Germanic Invasions) – In response to the invasion of Transalpine Gaul by the powerful Cimbri and Teutones nations, the Senate of Rome deployed an army under the command of the *consul* and *novus homo* Gnaeus Mallius Maximus to reinforce the legions of Quintus Servilius Caepio, *proconsul* of Gallia Narbonensis (southern France). Because of his loss of independent command, and a patrician bias for a 'new man', Caepio refused to subordinate himself to Maximus' authority. This disunity of leadership severely undermined the armies' ability to successfully resist Germanic forces. Unable to achieve an accord, the two Roman generals encamped their legions separately, with Caepio establishing a *castrum* between that of the Cimbri and the army of Maximus. Once battle was joined, the two consular armies were engaged separately by the Germans and destroyed piecemeal, with a loss of 8,000 killed. Arausio was the single greatest battlefield disaster to befall Rome since Cannae in 216 BC.

> Paulus Orosius, *Seven Books of History against the Pagans*, 5.16; Titus Livius (Livy), *Summaries*, 67; Eutropius, *Abridgement of Roman History*, 5.1; Dio Cassius, *Roman History*, 27, fragment 91.1–4.

Aricia, 496 BC – A delegation of Aurunci, whose homelands were situated to the south of the Volsci, threatened the Senate with war unless the Volscian territory was evacuated by the Romans. An Auruncian army simultaneously advanced northward as far as the community of Aricia, situated on the slopes of Mount Alban 16 miles southeast of Rome. In response, a Roman force under the command of the *consul* Publius Servilius Priscus moved against the Auruncian danger, and briefly encamped near the town before joining battle the following day. The fighting lasted from early morning until noon. Because the rugged terrain was largely unsuitable for deployment of cavalry, a 600-man detachment of Roman horse led by Aulus Postumius Albus Regillensis dismounted in order to provide additional support for the beleaguered infantry. Finally, after an intense struggle, the Romans successfully drove back the opposing right wing of the Aurunci before routing the entire enemy formation. Both armies suffered heavy casualties.

Titus Livius (Livy), *History of Rome*, 2.26.4–6; Dionysius of Halicarnassus, *Roman Antiquities*, 6.32.3–6.33.

Arretium, 283 BC (Etruscan War) – Learning of the Gauls' siege of Arretium (Arezzo) north of Lake Trasimeno in north-central Italy, the Romans dispatched an army to relieve the city. The legionary force was defeated in the battle which followed with the loss of the *praetor* Lucius Caercilius Metellus Denter. A subsequent delegation of legates sent to negotiate with the Gauls was murdered. This treachery inspired the Romans to deploy a second army into the field under the command of the *praetor* Manius Curius Dentatus. On their march northward, the Romans entered the territories of a Gallic tribe called the Senones, and were intercepted by a significant concentration of warriors. The legions defeated and largely destroyed the attacking army of Gauls in the resulting engagement. The Romans thereafter drove the tribe out of its homeland and established a colony called Sena in the newly acquired region.

Polybius, *Histories*, 2.19.7–12.

Arsania River, 68 BC – see Artaxata, 68 BC.

Artaxata, 68 BC (Third Mithridatic War, Wars against Mithridates the Great) – In the summer of 68 BC, the Roman general Lucius Licinius Lucullus advanced into Armenia and crossed the Taurus River toward the capital city of Artaxata (Artashat). On the approach of Lucullus' legions, the Armenian king, Tigranes, brought out his army and encamped along the nearer bank of the Arsania River between the city and the advancing Romans. The king drew up his army for battle as the invaders neared the river. Despite a strong enemy presence, Lucullus boldly crossed the river with twelve cohorts and deployed the rest of his force in such a fashion as to prevent Tigranes from flanking the legionary elements fording the Arsania. Once over the river, the infantry detachments were immediately confronted with the potential danger posed by mounted Mardian archers and Iberian lancers operating in support of the main Armenian formation. These forces were quickly defeated in a brief skirmish with Roman cavalry, who then pursued the mercenary squadrons from the field. Following this initial engagement, Tigranes advanced against the legions at the head of his own cavalry. Impressed by the size and splendour of the Armenians, Lucullus recalled his cavalry in anticipation of an attack. With his army reassembled, the Roman commander suddenly took the initiative and launched a mounted charge against the enemy formation. The unexpected assault inspired a general panic among the Armenians, thereby permitting Lucullus to swiftly rout the entire army.

Plutarch, *Lucullus*, 31

Asculum, 279 BC (War with Pyrrhus) – This two-day battle between an Epirot invasion force led by Pyrrhus, king of Epirus, and two Roman armies commanded by the consuls Publius Decius Mus and Publius Sulpicius Severrio occurred near the southeastern Italian city of Asculum (Ascoli Satriano) in Apulia. At the time Pyrrhus' army arrived in southern Italy in 280 BC to support the city of Tarentum in its dispute with Rome, it numbered 3,000 horse, 20,000 infantry, 2,000 archers, 500 slingers, twenty war elephants and an advance contingent of 3,000 soldiers under Cineas. Of this initial force, Pyrrhus suffered approximately 7,000 casualties in his first engagement against the Romans at Heraclea that same year. His force now numbered 25,000 at Asculum with the inclusion of Italian allies. Against this threat, the Romans deployed approximately 40,000 infantry and allied horse. The rugged country where the engagement occurred initially proved more conducive to the flexible tactics of the legionary cohorts than those of the Epirot phalanx. Wooded terrain and a nearby river restricted Pyrrhus from fully deploying his cavalry and elephants to best advantage against consular forces, and the first day's action was largely a protracted but inconclusive struggle between Epirot and Roman infantry. Early on the second day, Pyrrhus dispatched elements of his army to seize the wooded ground where the previous day's fighting had

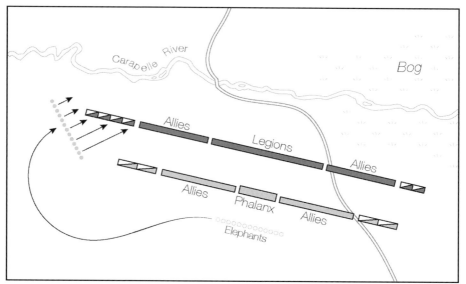

Battle of Asculum, 279 BC

occurred, forcing the battle into more open land where his phalanx, cavalry and elephants were at greater tactical advantage. Despite this relocation, the legions were still able to check the momentum of the Epirot infantry for several hours before a concentrated and overwhelming elephant charge disrupted the integrity of the Roman formation, forcing the consuls to abandon the fight and withdraw their armies from the field. The Romans suffered some 6,000 casualties and Pyrrhus' losses numbered 3,550.

Plutarch, *Pyrrhus* 15.1, 21.5–10; Dionysius of Halicarnassus, *Roman Antiquities*, 20.1–3; Frontinus, *Stratagems*, 2.3.21; John Zonaras, *Epitome of Histories*, 8.5; Paulus Orosius, *Seven Books of History against the Pagans*, 4.1; Titus Livius (Livy), *Summaries*, 13; Lucius Annaeus Florus, *Epitomy*, 1.13.9–10. Plutarch identifies the consuls at Asculum as Caius Fabricius, *consul* (278 BC), and Quintus Aemilius, *consul* (278 BC).

Asculum, 90–89 BC (Social War, Marsic War) – Following a failed attempt by Italian forces under the general Titus Lafrenius to trap Gnaeus Pompeius Strabo in the town of Firmum on the Adriatic coast, Pompey marched his legions approximately 25 miles southwest and invested the Picentine city of Asculum (Ascoli Piceno) in east central Italy. While the siege progressed, the Italian general Gaius Vidacilius arrived with a relief force of eight cohorts, breached the Roman lines and forced his way into the city. His efforts proved to be in vain, as the reinforcements failed to significantly alter the course of the siege. Recognizing that the loss of Asculum was inevitable, Vidacilius poisoned himself to avoid capture. Soon thereafter, Pompeius gained control of the city.

Appianus (Appian), *Civil Wars*, 1:47–48; Paulus Orosius, *Seven Books of History against the Pagans*, 5.18; Titus Livius (Livy), *Summaries*, 76.

Asio River, 82 BC – see Aesis River, 82 BC.

Astapa, 206 BC (Second Punic War, Wars against Carthage) – Following Scipio's victory at Ilipa, the general Lucius Marcius Septimus concentrated on the reduction of various tribes in south central Spain still resistant to Roman authority. After accepting the surrender of two cities south of the Baetis (Guadalquivir) River, Marcius moved against Astapa (Estepa), a community perennially loyal to Carthage and stringently opposed to Roman suzerainty. As the army prepared to lay siege, the men of the city suddenly rushed through the gates and attacked the Romans. After a fierce onslaught that drove back a detachment of cavalry and light infantry sent out to defeat the irregular force, the legions were able to check the assault when it reached the vicinity of the Roman camp. Even then the suicidal nature of the Astapians' attack initially proved a difficult challenge for the veteran legionaries. Despite the tenacity of the opposition, the overwhelming numerical superiority of the army finally permitted Marcius to extend his battle line and completely envelop the enemy. Encircled, but unwilling to surrender, the Astapians died to a man.

When the fighting eventually ended, the Romans entered the city, where they were stunned to find the bodies of the community's women and children, together with the peoples' accumulated material wealth, burning upon an immense pyre in the central marketplace. Following this grim discovery, the Romans withdrew from Astapa, having confiscated no slaves or booty.

Titus Livius (Livy), *History of Rome*, 28.22–23.4; Appianus (Appian), *Wars in Spain*, 6.33.

Astura River, 338 BC – As Rome prepared to move against the town of Pedum near Praeneste, a Roman army under the command of the *consul* Caius Maenius advanced southeastward into the Volscian lands. Near the Astura River southeast of Rome, the legions of Maenius surprised a combined army of Aricini, Lanuvini and Veliterni in the process of joining with a column of Antiate Volscians in anticipation of advancing to Pedum's aid. In the ensuing battle, the allied force, thrown into confusion by the sudden attack, was completely driven from the field.

Titus Livius (Livy), *History of Rome*, 8.13.1–5.

Athacus, 200 BC (Second Macedonian War, Wars against Macedon) – After an escalation in tensions between Rome and Macedon, the Senate dispatched an army to the Balkan Peninsula under the command of the *consul* Publius Sulpicius Galba Maximus. The expedition landed in Illyria in the autumn and almost immediately went into winter quarters. Early the following spring, before marching into Macedonia, the Romans dispatched a contingent of cavalry to ascertain the location of the Macedonian army under King Philip V. At the same time, the Macedonian ruler sent a squadron of horsemen westward to find Sulpicius' legions. The two cavalry forces eventually clashed in the territory of the Dassaretii. The struggle finally ended after several hours fighting, the Macedonians having suffered forty dead and the Romans thirty-five. The armies shortly converged in Macedonia near the community of Athacus. The king encamped his army of 20,000 infantry and 2,000 cavalry on a hill approximately a mile from the Romans. The opposing camps remained inactive for two days while each commander waited for the enemy to make the initial move. Sulpicius led his army onto the battlefield on the third day. Philip responded by sending out 700 lightly armed Illyrian and Cretan troops to engage in a round of hit-and-run skirmishes, but their efforts were thwarted by the spirited resistance of Roman cavalry and *velites*. Philip sent out all of his light infantry and cavalry two days later to again challenge their Roman counterparts. The efforts of the king's horsemen to lead the *equites* into an ambuscade failed when the *peltists* lying in wait attacked prematurely. The next day, Sulpicius again assembled his army in battle formation, introducing for the first time into a Roman tactical formation a detachment of war elephants, which he positioned ahead of his front line. The

Macedonians declined the offer of battle, and Sulpicius soon thereafter withdrew his forces to a new campsite at Ottolobum, 8 miles away.

Titus Livius (Livy), *History of Rome*, 31.34.7–36.4.

Athens-Piraeus, 86 BC (First Mithridatic War, Wars against Mithridates the Great) – In an effort to extend his power into Europe, King Mithridates VI of Pontus moved to subjugate Greece. He won the support of Athens following a popular revolt that toppled the city's oligarchic leadership. The successful takeover of government was orchestrated by Aristion, an Athenian statesman sympathetic to the Pontic monarch, and was soon reinforced by Archelaus, Mithridates' senior general, whose forces occupied Athens' primary port of Piraeus. In response to these sudden changes of circumstance, the Roman Senate dispatched Lucius Cornelius Sulla to Greece with five legions and support troops. Upon his arrival, Sulla marched his army into Attica and immediately began to invest the city and its three nearby harbours of the Piraeus. After all initial efforts to capture Athens failed, Roman forces briefly retired to Eleusis and Megara to build engines sufficient to breach the city walls. During this time, Sulla ordered the demolition of the Long Walls between Athens and the Piraeus to ensure the further isolation of both communities. Shortly thereafter, the legions resumed their general assault. Sulla ordered the construction of earthen ramps to permit siege machinery to draw near the city defences, but a renewed effort to penetrate enemy

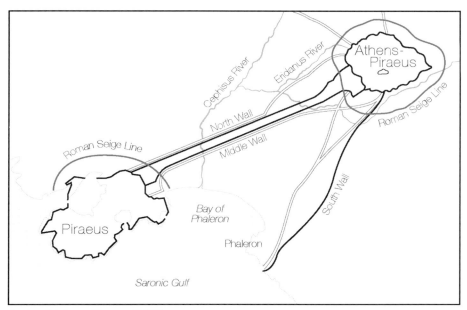

Battle of Athens-Piraeus, 86 BC

fortifications was capably repelled by appropriate countermeasures. Additional efforts to take Athens and the Piraeus by force were further hampered by the timely arrival by sea of Mithridatic reinforcements under Dromichaetes. As the assault wore on, the situation in the city and port became more desperate. Increasing food shortages contributed to widespread famine, and all efforts by Archelaus to deliver relief supplies to Athens were disrupted by Roman troops. To further exacerbate the conditions, Sulla ordered the complete circumvallation of the city to guarantee total isolation of the population. Starvation soon reduced the vitality of Athens' defence, permitting the legions to breach the outer walls at the Heptachalcum near the northwest part of the city and advance into the streets. Once inside, Sulla allowed his legions to sack the city, though issued strict prohibition against burning. Certain that defence of the port was now lost, Archelaus abandoned the Piraeus and withdrew his forces to Thessaly. Following the capture of Athens, Aristion and other authorites in the city were executed in retribution.

Plutarch, *Sulla* 12–14; Appianus (Appian), *Mithridatic Wars*, 28–40.

Atuatuca, 54 BC – see Aduatuca, 54 BC.

Aufidus River, 89 BC (Social War, Marsic War) – The Roman *praetor* Caius Cosconius retreated toward Cannae after his defeat at Canusium, relinquishing control of the town to its inhabitants and a victorius Samnite army commanded by Trebatius. Following the failed siege, Cosconius again engaged the Samnite army near the Aufidus (Ofanto) River. As the Samnites attempted a water crossing, the Romans under Cosconius suddenly surprised Trebatius and attacked. Caught at a disadvantage, the Samnites were routed with a loss of 15,000 men killed. The survivors took refuge in Canusium.

Appianus (Appian), *Civil Wars*, 1.52

Aurinx, 213 BC (Second Punic War, Wars against Carthage) – After the Roman victory at Munda, the Carthaginians withdrew with the Roman army in pursuit. Near the city of Aurinx, the two armies fought again. The depleted Punic force lost an additional 6,000 men. The addition of Gallic reinforcements recruited by Mago Barca, the brother of Hannibal, failed to reverse the situation and more than 8,000 Gauls fell to Roman arms, including the tribal princes Moeniacoeptus and Vismarus, with almost 1,000 captured. Three war elephants also perished in the fighting and eight were taken.

Titus Livius (Livy), *History of Rome*, 24.42.5–8.

Avaricum, 53–52 BC (Gallic War) – This siege marks one of the opening engagements in Caesar's campaign to suppress the Gallic revolt of 52 BC. After liberating the community of Cenabum (Orleans) from Gallic control, Roman forces crossed the Ligeris (Loire) River and moved southward toward

Avaricum (Bourges), the main stronghold of the Bituriges. As the legions advanced, a brief but sharp engagement ensued between elements of Roman cavalry and the vanguard of Vercingetorix's army near the fortified community of Noviodunum. Unhindered, Caesar continued his march on Avaricum. Ahead of the Roman formation, Gallic cavalry employed a scorched-earth strategy to deny forage and supplies to the invaders in an effort to force their withdrawal. The plan failed, and the legions initiated siege operations upon reaching the Biturigan capital. The Romans breached the city's defences after almost a month. Once inside Avaricum, the legionaries spared no one. Of the entire population of 40,000 men, women, and children, only 800 escaped the army's assault.

Julius Caesar, *The Gallic War*, 7.11–28.

Avus River, 198 BC – see Aous River, 198 BC.

Axinium, 153 BC (Numantine War, Wars in Spain) – After its defeat at Numantia (Garray), a Roman army led by the *consul* Quintus Fulvius Nobilior attacked a Celtiberian supply depot at the town of Axinium. The assault failed and Fulvius suffered numerous casualties, both dead and wounded.

Appianus (Appian), *Wars in Spain*, 9.47.

Axona River, 57 BC (Gallic War) – In the winter of 57 BC, Julius Caesar learned from his lieutenant Labienus that the Belgae of northern Gaul had formed a coalition of tribes hostile to Rome. In response, Caesar deployed eight legions and supporting auxiliaries to the Belgic frontier in preparation for a spring campaign. Once the weather improved sufficiently to ensure a good supply of forage for his cavalry, Caesar moved his army rapidly north toward a large concentration of several thousand Belgae massing north of the Axona (Aisne) River. Caesar's total command of some 60,000 men included six veteran legions – the Seventh, Eighth, Ninth, Tenth, Eleventh and Twelfth – and two newly mustered units from Italy, the *Legio XIII* and *XIV*. The unexpected speed of his march compelled the nearest tribe of Belgae, the Remi, whose territory lay south of the Axona, to immediately submit to Caesar. Quickly ascertaining that the large formation of Belgae warriors concentrated to the north had not fully assembled, Caesar determined to attack. He crossed the river 8 miles south of Bibrax, a town of the Remi, and secured control of a nearby bridge over the Axona by means of temporary earthworks and a detached force of 3,000 men under the command of Quintus Titurius Sabinus. Following a failed attempt by the Belgae to secure Bibrax by siege, the coalition army encamped within 2 miles of the Roman position on the north bank of the river. Given the nearness of the Belgic force, Caesar determined to offer battle with his six veteran legions, but a brook (the modern

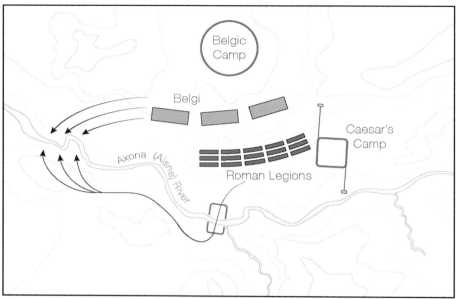

Battle of the Axona River, 57 BC

Miette) and surrounding marshland discouraged both armies from initiating a general engagement. Roman forces retired to camp following an indecisive skirmish between elements of cavalry. The withdrawal of Caesar's army from the field inspired the Belgae to attempt fording the Axona on the Roman left in an attempt to assault Titurius' command situated on the south bank of the river. Alerted to the Belgic movement, Caesar quickly led detachments of cavalry and light-armed troops across the bridge in a successful effort to cut off the enemy crossing. Intercepted while fording the river, an intense battle followed in which the Romans inflicted heavy casualties on the Belgae. The coalition tribes retired from the field and returned to their homelands, unable to achieve a victory over Caesar's army at the Axona River.

   Julius Caesar, *The Gallic War*, 2.5–10.

Baecor, 144 BC (Viriathic War, Wars in Spain) – At Baecor in southwestern Spain, a Roman army consisting of 15,000 infantry and 2,000 cavalry, under the command of the *proconsul* Quintius Fabius Maximus Aemilianus, overtook the Lusitanian leader Viriathus and a sizeable band of his warriors, and inflicted a final defeat on the enemy before ending the year's campaign. This last contest followed a more significant defeat of a Lusitanian army in the early spring. Fabius won a decisive victory in this previous clash; the first such Roman success in Spain for nine years. After routing Viriathus, Fabius subsequently captured two cities, permitting his troops to sack one and burn the other. Following the struggle at Baecor, the *proconsul* then wintered his army in Corduba (Cordoba) before relinquishing command to Quintus Pompieus Aulus the next year.

Appianus (Appian), *Wars in Spain*, 11.65

Baecula, 208 BC (Second Punic War, Wars against Carthage) – Concerned by the number of Iberian allies renouncing their allegiance to Carthage and joining the Romans, the Carthaginian general Hasdrubal Barca prepared to force a battle with the legionary forces of Publius Cornelius Scipio (Africanus). The two armies met near the town of Baecula in south central Spain. On approach of the Roman force, Hasdrubal repositioned the Carthaginian army on an elevated plain with a tributary of the Baetis River guarding its tactical rear. Any frontal assault against the Carthaginian position was now discouraged by the presence of a low ridge, which demanded an attacking formation climb in order to fully engage the Punic army situated on the plateau above. After surveying the enemy position, Scipio ordered his *velites* to attack Hasdrubal's light-armed infantry deployed along the ridge. The Roman advance was almost immediately hampered by a steep bank surrounding the plain, which formed an initial obstacle against any approach of the Carthaginians' front or flanks. The climb was made more difficult for the *velites* by the volume of missiles discharged from above, but once the Romans gained level ground they quickly scattered the enemy skirmishers, killing large numbers in the flight. Recognizing the acute danger of the situation, Hasdrubal quickly began the deployment of his main force. But but the intensity of the Roman action drove the remnants of the Punic light infantry back against his primary battle-formation of heavy infantry deployed on higher ground. As Hasdrubal worked to redress the situation on the plain above, Scipio ordered the remainder of his light infantry to continue to press the frontal assault while additional forces under Caius Laelius circled the plateau to attack the Carthaginian left flank. Scipio led a third concentration of men in a similar manner against Hasdrubal's right. Before the Punic commander could fully array his troops for battle, Laelius and Scipio initiated a simultaneous charge on both wings, collapsing the Carthaginian formation. The carnage within the enemy's ranks was compounded by the panic of Hasdrubal's elephants. Carthaginian losses amounted to 8,000 dead.

Polybius, *Histories*, 10.38.6–10.39; Titus Livius (Livy), *History of Rome*, 27.18.

Baetis River, 211 BC (Second Punic War, Wars against Carthage) – In an attempt to decisively end the fighting in Spain, the Roman generals Gnaeus and Publius Cornelius Scipio elected to divide their available forces into two armies: Publius to command two-thirds of the cohorts and allied troops in a campaign against the Punic commanders Mago and Hasdrubal, son of Gisgo;

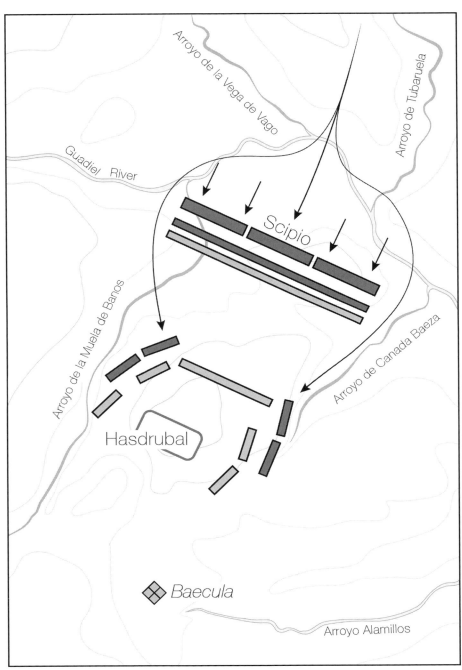

Battle of Baecula, 208 BC

and Gnaeus to lead the remaining third against Hasdrubal Barca. Publius advanced northeastward from the city of Amtorgis toward the upper Baetis (Guadalquivir) River, but was shortly detected by elements of cavalry under the command of the Numidian royal prince, Masinissa, an ally of Carthage. Thereafter, Publius' force was closely shadowed by the enemy in an effort to deny the Romans any opportunity to forage for provisions. While this harassment continued, the Romans learned of the approach of another Carthaginian ally, Indibilis, and an army of 7,500 Suessetani warriors. Alarmed at the danger should all three enemy formations converge at one time against his position, Publius chose to move against Indibilis in a night assault before the arrival of the larger Carthaginian force. In the engagement that followed, the two armies became embroiled in a running battle that attenuated both formations. The fighting intensified with the arrival of the Masinissa's Numidian cavalry, which quickly outflanked the Roman position and forced Publius to redeploy soldiers in an effort to counter the new attack. The tactical confusion inspired in the Romans by the nature of the fighting was further exacerbated with the sudden approach of the main Carthaginian army from the rear. Trapped by this superior force, the integrity of the Roman position began to erode. Following the death of Publius in the midst of some of the heaviest fighting, the entire Roman line was thrown into disorder and rapidly collapsed. Publius Scipio's entire command was destroyed in the rout which followed, with only a few survivors spared by nightfall.

   Titus Livius (Livy), *History of Rome*, 25.34; Appianus (Appian), *Wars in Spain*, 16.

Baetis River, 80 BC (War against Sertorius) – This battle was fought on the banks of the Baetis (Guadalquivir) River in south central Spain between the renegade Marian general Quintus Sertorius – in command of a composite militia force of legionary deserters, Roman refugees and Lusitanian volunteers – and at least two legions under Lucius Fufidius, the Roman governor of *Hispania Ulterior* (Western Spain). The talents of the veteran Sertorius resulted in the defeat of Fufidius' army and the death of some 2,000 soldiers.

   Plutarch, *Life of Sertorius*, 12.3.

Bagradas River, 255 BC (First Punic War, Wars against Carthage) – Following the Roman victory at Adys the previous year, a reconstituted Carthaginian army, now trained in Spartan battle tactics by the mercenary commander, Xanthippus – descended into the Bagradas Valley in the spring of 255 BC prepared to challenge a 30,000-man army under the leadership of Roman general Marcus Atilius Regulus. The Carthaginian force consisted of 12,000 infantry, 4,000 cavalry and a sizeable detachment of almost 100 war elephants. Xanthippus arrayed the elephants in a single line in front of the main Carthaginian phalanx. His mercenary units, together with a formidable

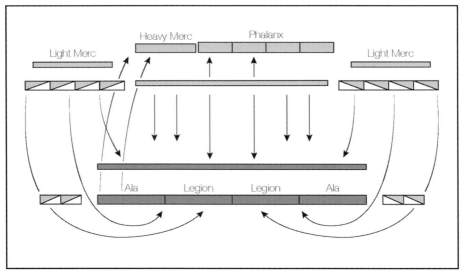

Battle of the Bagradas River, 255 BC

concentration of cavalry, were drawn up in front of the army's wings. In preparation for engaging the elephants, Regulus drew his legions in, narrowing the width of his front while redeploying the maniples to deepen the Roman formation. All available cavalry were then positioned on the infantry's flanks. Xanthippus opened the battle with an elephant charge that shattered the Roman centre. He simultaneously sent his mercenaries forward and ordered a charge of the Carthaginian cavalry that quickly drove off the Roman horse squadrons on both wings. Once the two armies joined, the Roman left succeeded in penetrating the mercenary detachments on the Carthaginian right and pressing as far as the Punic encampment. The depth of the Roman formation allowed the general integrity of the main body to remain intact until the Carthaginian cavalry wheeled inward to assault both the flanks and rear of the maniples. The overall constitution of the legions then began to erode under the pressure of the double envelopment, permitting the Carthaginians to complete the total destruction of the Roman army. Punic losses from the battle amounted to some 800 mercenaries, mostly killed during their engagement with the Roman left wing. Approximately 500 Romans were captured, including Regulus himself. An additional 2,000 legionaries, members of the maniples on the Roman left who were carried out of the battle by their pursuit of the defeated mercenaries, fled to the Roman held city of Aspis. The Roman dead numbered over 27,000, Xanthippus having never fully committed the main Carthaginian phalanx to the battle.

Polybius, *Histories*, 1.32–34; Appianus (Appian), *Punic Wars*, 3.

Bagradas River, 203 BC – see Campi Magni, 203 BC.

Bagradas River, 49 BC – Upon learning from a false report that the Numidian king, Juba, had withdrawn from the area with a sizeable portion of his army in order to address a regional border dispute in his kingdom, the Roman general Caius Curio dispatched his cavalry on a night march to surprise Juba's lieutenant, Saburra, and a detached force of Numidians encamped near the Bagradas (Medjerda) River in North Africa (Tunisia). Attacking in the early morning hours, the Roman cavalry overran the Numidian position, killing a large number of men. The cavalry prepared to return to camp following their success, but encountered Curio and the main body of Roman troops 6 miles from the army's *castrum* marching toward the river. Emboldened by the good report, Curio continued his advance toward Saburra, unaware that King Juba and his primary command were located only 6 miles from the Numidians. As the march resumed, Curio ordered the Roman horse to follow the legions toward the river. However, the weary cavalry failed to maintain contact with the advancing army. Near the Bagradas River, Curio observed the Numidian force withdrawing from the field and ordered his army in pursuit. After a 12-mile chase, exhaustion halted the legionary force, at which time Saburra wheeled the Numidians around in full battle formation and ordered his cavalry to attack the Roman line. The small number of cavalry still with Curio was insufficient to successfully check the assaults, and the Roman infantry faced a gradual envelopment by the enemy horse. Even as Roman casualties mounted, additional Numidian reinforcements sent by King Juba were arriving on the field. Sallies by individual cohorts proved ineffective, resulting in each unit being isolated and destroyed by Saburra's cavalry. A final desperate attempt by Curio to redeploy to high ground proved unsuccessful, and the entire army was destroyed piecemeal. The few survivors, almost entirely cavalry, fled to the safety of the five cohorts left by Curio to guard the Roman encampment.

Julius Caesar, *The Civil Wars*, 2.38–42; Appianus (Appian), *Civil Wars*, 2.45.

Baldano Valley, 153 BC, 23 August (Numantine War, Wars in Spain) – In a wooded river valley near the Durius (Duero) River in northern Spain, a Celtiberian coalition force of 20,000 foot soldiers and 5,000 horse, led by a Segedian named Carus, ambushed a 30,000-man Roman army under the command of the *consul* Quintus Fulvius Nobilior. As the Romans advanced through the defile, poor reconnaissance resulted in a surprise attack against them while still in marching order. Fighting through the dense forest after a protracted and desperate struggle against their attackers, the Roman infantry was finally able to assemble in battle order on open terrain with the cavalry in support. This defensive posture saved the army from complete destruction, but several thousand Romans died in the defeat. Celtiberian casualties were lighter, though Carus was slain in the final pursuit.

Appianus (Appian), *Wars in Spain*, 9.45.

Bantia, 208 BC (Second Punic War, Wars against Carthage) – This clash, though little more than a skirmish, resulted in the death of the veteran Roman general Marcus Claudius Marcellus during his fifth consulship. While encamped in the vicinity of Bantia (Banzi), near a Carthaginian army commanded by Hannibal Barca, Marcellus was killed in an ambuscade on the wooded heights leading to the village of Venusia (Venosa) on the Lucanian-Apulian border. Surprised by a force of Numidian cavalry, the *consul* died while fighting in the company of his Etruscan and Fregellean bodyguard. His fellow *consul*, Titus Quinctius Crispinus, was badly wounded in the encounter and ultimately succumbed to his injuries. The death of Marcellus was a significant loss for the Roman army because he was the first general capable of successfully challenging Hannibal on the battlefield.

Titus Livius (Livy), *History of Rome*, 27.26.7–27.14; Plutarch, *Marcellus*, 29.2–9; Appianus (Appian), *Hannibalic War*, 8.50.

Beneventum, 297 BC – see Maleventum, 297 BC.

Beneventum, 275 BC – see Maleventum, 275 BC.

Beneventum, 214 BC (Second Punic War, Wars against Carthage) – Having received orders from Hannibal to advance toward Campania, the Carthaginian general Hanno marched northward with an army of 1,200 mostly Numidian and Mari cavalry, and 17,000 infantry primarily recruited in the southern Italian regions of Lucania and Bruttium. Hanno's force was intercepted near the Campanian community of Beneventum by a Roman army of comparable size under the command of the *proconsul* Tiberius Sempronius Gracchus. Of the four legions in the service of Sempronius, two consisted entirely of slaves promised their freedom should they perform well against the Carthaginians. Both armies encamped near the town, Hanno close to the Cador River approximately 3 miles from Beneventum, and Sempronius within a mile of the enemy position. The armies joined in battle the following day. The action was stringently contested by each side, and the engagement remained undecided for several hours. An attempt by Roman cavalry to attack Hanno's flanks was successfully checked by the Numidians, and the fighting continued unabated. While the struggle remained in the balance, Sempronius sent word to the servile legions that freedom would only be granted should the army achieve victory. The Roman attack, now reinvigorated by this veiled threat, surged against the Carthaginian formation. The pressure proved irresistible, and all three Carthaginian lines collapsed sequentially. The Romans pursued the defeated survivors to their encampment and quickly overran the position. The victory was complete within a short time. Over 17,000 Carthaginians were killed or taken prisoner, and thirty-eight standards captured. Roman losses amounted to 2,000 men.

Titus Livius (Livy), *History of Rome*, 24.14–16.

Beneventum, 212 BC (Second Punic War, Wars against Carthage) – In order to garner a supply of grain for the city of Capua, whose leaders feared an imminent Roman siege, Hannibal instructed Hanno to lead a Punic army into the territory of the Bruttii. Establishing his camp 3 miles from the community of Beneventum, Hanno ordered the neighbouring peoples to deliver supplies of grain, with the guarantee of Carthaginian military escorts for all such endeavours. When apprised by the Beneventans of these activities, the *consul* Quintus Fulvius Flaccus quickly determined to lead his army into Campania and offer battle. The legions marched to Beneventum from near Bovianum in south-central Italy, entering the city under cover of darkness. Once there, the Romans learned that Hanno was presently away with a portion of his army procuring grain, and elected to exploit the opportunity by marching against the Punic encampment before dawn the following day. Burdened by the large number of unarmed civilians present, the Carthaginians were singularly ill-prepared to successfully address the sudden and unexpected arrival of Fulvius' legions, though the elevated location of the camp denied the Romans an easy victory. At daybreak, the legions launched a sustained assault, but the maniples were unable to breach the enemy's earthworks because of the steep approach. Hampered by the unfavourable terrain, and having suffered heavy casualties in the morning's action, Fulvius prepared to abandon the engagement but was persuaded by his officers and men to continue to press the attack. Rallied by the prefect Vibius Accaus, tribune Valerius Flaccus and centurion Titus Pedanius, the legions surged over the enemy defences and captured the camp. Some 6,000 Carthaginians were killed and over 7,000 captured in the fighting. Roman casualties were heavy but unspecified.

Titus Livius (Livy), *History of Rome*, 25.13–14.1–11.

Bibracte, 58 BC (Gallic Wars) – Following the battle at the Arar River, Caesar pursued the remainder of the Helvetii for two weeks before a shortage of provisions compelled the Romans to temporarily suspend the chase and march 18 miles to Bibracte, the chief town of the Aedui, to collect supplies. This action was interpreted by the Helvetii as a Roman retreat, and the Celtic force quickly turned in pursuit of the withdrawing legions. As Caesar moved toward Bibracte, the harassment of the Roman rearguard by bands of Helvetic warriors finally persuaded him to offer battle. Dispatching his allied

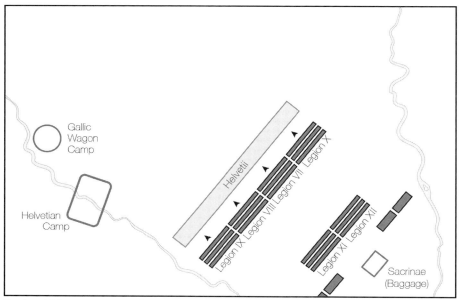

Battle of Bibracte, 58 BC (Phase 1)

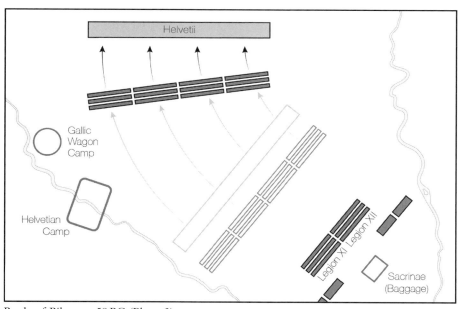

Battle of Bibracte, 58 BC (Phase 2)

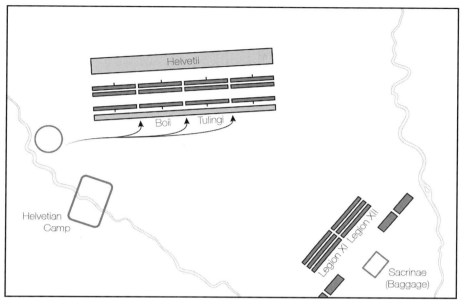

Battle of Bibracte, 58 BC (Phase 3)

cavalry to slow the Celtic advance, Caesar deployed his four veteran legions – the Ninth, Eighth, Seventh and Tenth – in battle formation (*triplex acies*) along the slope of a low hill. Behind these three lines of infantry he then stationed the recently recruited *Legio XI* and *Legio XII*, and all allied auxiliary troops. Finally, the legionaries' pack baggage was secured by entrenchment on the summit of the ridge. Opposite Caesar's position, the Helvetii prepared for battle. Once assembled in close formation, the numerically superior force of Celts moved against the front formation of Roman infantry. A volley of spears (*pila*) broke the momentum of this initial attack, and was quickly followed by a counter-charge of the legionary front line. After intense fighting, the Helvetii withdrew in an effort to disengage from the action, but the legions moved forward in an attempt to maintain contact with the enemy. This action by Caesar's cohorts provoked the Celtic rearguard of 15,000 Boii and Tulingi warriors to suddenly wheel and assault the legions' left flank and rear in an effort to check the Roman advance. Caesar quickly redeployed his third line of veteran cohorts to counter this fresh attack, while the first two lines of infantry continued to press the main force of Helvetii. The barbarian army was completely routed after several hours of bloody fighting. Following his victory, Caesar halted his army for three days to attend to his casualties before continuing the pursuit of the enemy.

Julius Caesar, *The Gallic War*, 1.23–26; Plutarch, *Caesar*, 18.2–5; Dio Cassius, *Roman History*, 38.32.4–33.6.

Bolae, 389 BC – Following the defeat of the Volscians at Lanuvium, the Roman dictator Marcus Furius Camillus moved against the Aequi, defeating their army at Bolae. The victory was total, Roman forces overrunning both the enemy's military encampment and city.

   Titus Livius (Livy), *History of Rome*, 6.2.14; Diodorus Siculus, *Historical Library*, 14.117.4.

Cape Bon, 255 BC – see Hermaeum, 255 BC.

Bon, 255 BC – see Hermaeum, 255 BC.

Bovianum, 298 BC (Third Samnite War, Samnite Wars) – In the beginning of 298 BC, envoys from Lucania appealed to the Roman Senate for aid against the Samnites, who had recently invaded their homeland in retribution for the Lucanians' refusal to join in an armed alliance against Rome. Having quickly entered into a treaty with Lucania, Rome dispatched *fetiales* to Samnium demanding the withdrawal of its army from Lucanian lands, but messengers intercepted the Roman priests and threatened the diplomatic party with bodily harm if it went before the Samnite council. Apprised of this hostile reaction to its overtures, the Senate compelled the people of Rome to declare war against Samnium. This action was soon followed by a Roman invasion of Samnium by legions under the command of the *consul* Gnaeus Fulvius Maximus Centumalus. Near the community of Bovianum (Boiano), Fulvius engaged and decisively defeated a Samnite army, and then followed this victory with the reduction and capture of the town itself.

   Titus Livius (Livy), *History of Rome*, 10.12.1–9.

Bovianum, 305 BC (Second Samnite War, Samnite Wars) – After a two-pronged invasion of Samnium by the Roman consuls Lucius Postumius Megellus and Tiberius Minucius Augurinus, the army of Minucius engaged a Samnite force near Bovianum (Boiano) in south-central Italy. After fighting a long and inconclusive battle, fresh legionary reserves led by Postumius unexpectedly arrived on the battlefield in late afternoon. Roman reinforcements quickly overran and destroyed the exhausted Samnite army, capturing twenty-one enemy standards.

   Titus Livius (Livy), *History of Rome*, 9.44.11–13.

Cabeirus, 72 BC (Third Mithridatic War, Wars against Mithridates the Great) – After driving the army of Mithridates VI Eupator, king of Pontus, out of Roman Bithynia, Lucius Licinius Lucullus invaded Pontus in the autumn of 73 BC and besieged the Black Sea ports of Amisus and Themiscyra, and the community of Eupatoria 40 miles inland. The following spring, Lucullus led his legions in pursuit of the great king himself, who had wintered with his army of 40,000 infantry and 4,000 cavalry near the city of Cabeirus. The Roman army crossed the inland mountains and debouched into the plain near the city, where it immediately encountered a strong concentration of enemy cavalry near the Lycus River. Unwilling to needlessly expose his infantry to sudden attack, Lucullus chose instead to withdraw his legions into the remote, wooded foothills overlooking Mithridates' position and await an opportunity for battle. With his camp in a secure location, Lucullus dispatched some ten cohorts to Cappadocia to procure a supply of grain for the army. The detachment was attacked soon after its departure in a narrow gorge by enemy cavalry, but the uneven ground and strict confines of the defile favoured the legionaries, who were able to assemble into battle-formation and completely shatter the assault, inflicting heavy casualties. A subsequent engagement fought under similar conditions also ended in Roman victory. Reports of these sudden and unexpected defeats so demoralized the main Pontic army that all discipline quickly degenerated into head-long, chaotic flight. Finding himself no longer in command of a viable fighting force, Mithridates ultimately elected to abandon the remnants of his army and withdraw into neighbouring Armenia, thereby conceding not only Cabeirus but temporarily relinquishing control of his entire kingdom to the Romans.

Plutarch, *Lucullus*, 15–19.1; Appianus (Appian), *Mithridatic War*, 79–81

Caiatia, 295 BC (Third Samnite War, Samnite Wars) – The legions' earlier victories at Sentinum and Tifernus Mons did not undermine the willingness of either the Etruscans or Samnites to continue prosecuting the war against Rome. In response to Samnite raids into a number of lands, including the territories of Formiae and Vescini, the Senate dispatched legionary forces led by the *proconsul* Lucius Volumnius Flamma Violens and *praetor* Appius Claudius to pursue and engage the interlopers. In the vicinity of the community of Caiatia in the Stellate district near the Volturnus River, the armies of Volumnius and Appius joined to confront the Samnite contingent. What followed was an intense struggle between the two hosts that only resulted in a Roman victory after heavy casualties were incurred by both armies. Samnite losses amounted to 6,000 killed and 2,700 captured. Roman dead totalled 2,700.

Titus Livius (Livy), *History of Rome*, 10.31.5–7.

Calagurris, 186 BC – In the vicinity of the community of Calagurris in the far north-central Iberian peninsula near the Ebro River, the Roman general Lucius Manlius Acidinus fought the last of two engagements against the Celtiberians. The first battle was an indecisive action. The Celts relocated their camp, but returned several days later with a sizeable number of reinforcements. The inclusion of additional manpower was to no avail. The Celtiberians were defeated following a spontaneous assault against the Roman position, with a loss of 12,000 warriors killed and another 2,000 captured. The Romans completed the victory by taking possession of the enemy's camp.

Titus Livius (Livy), *History of Rome*, 39.21.6–10.

Callinicus, 171 BC (Third Macedonian War, Wars against Macedon) – Near the Thessalian city of Larissa, a Roman force led by the *consul* Publius Licinius Crassus encamped in anticipation of offering battle to a Macedonian army under King Perseus. While the Roman commander was still in the process of developing a plan of action for the region, the Macedonian army was reported to be several miles away. Over the next few days, the king attempted to provoke a confrontation, and failing this elected to move his camp nearer the Roman *castrum* so that the two armies were only 5 miles apart. From there he advanced against the Roman position at dawn the following day. Less than half a mile from the enemy's fortifications, near a hill called Callinicus, Perseus assembled his cavalry and light infantry in full battle array. The Thracian Cotys, king of the Odrysae, and his tribe's cavalry were stationed on the left wing, supported by detachments of light infantry placed between the units of horsemen. Deployed on the right wing was the Macedonian cavalry led by Menon of Antigonea, with Cretan light troops under the charge of Midon of Beroea distributed among the squadrons. Posted next to the wings were the royal cavalry under Patrokles of Antigonea and mixed units of auxiliaries commanded by Didas, the governor of Paeonia. Positioned in the centre of the battle line was the king, together with the army's elite mounted squadrons including the royal horse guard, the *agema*. In response to this challenge, Crassus dispatched his cavalry with supporting elements of light-armed troops. Since the Macedonian phalanx was not present, the *consul* retained his legions and allied infantry inside the camp. Marshalled on the right wing was the army's full complement of Italian cavalry led by Caius Licinius Crassus. These squadrons were joined by the legions' *velites*. To the left, Marcus Valerius Laevinus commanded the allied Hellenic cavalry and light infantry, and in the centre were 200 Gallic cavalry and 300 Cyrtian auxiliaries. Posted beyond the left wing were 400 Thessalian horsemen, and placed between the camp and the Roman formation were additional forces under Eumenes and Attalus. Once the battle opened, a solid charge by Cotys' Thracians immediately broke the Italian allies, while Laevinus' Hellenes recoiled under Perseus' initial attack from the centre. As the Roman line collapsed into a headlong rout, the enemy's pursuit was partially checked by the Thessalian cavalry and Eumenes' auxiliaries, allowing the remainder of the forces to successfully escape. Meanwhile, the generals Hippias and Leonnatus moved the Macedonian phalanx forward, anticipating the king's need of heavy infantry, but Perseus elected instead to sound a general recall of his men. Roman dead amounted to 200 cavalry and almost 2,000 infantry, plus the loss of an additional 600 captured. Macedonian killed totalled only forty foot and twenty horse.

Titus Livius (Livy), *History of Rome*, 42.57.10–60.1; Plutarch, *Aemilius Paulus*, 9.2.

Camalatrum, 71 BC (War of Spartacus, Third Servile War) – The legions of the *propraetor* Marcus Licinius Crassus clashed near the community of Camalatrum with a division of Spartacus' servile army, led by Castus and Cannicus. The largely Gallic force was taken in the rear by twelve cohorts dispatched around a mountain by Crassus. The legionaries fell on the unsuspecting enemy with such force that the attack completely routed the Gallic masses, which then fled in total disorder.

Frontinus, *Stratagems*, 2.4.7.

Camarina 258 BC (First Punic War, Wars against Carthage) – During the sixth year of the war between Carthage and Rome, the *consul* Aulua Atilius Calatinus chose to attack Camarina (Camarana), a city located on the southwestern coast of Sicily, near the mouth of the Hipparis River. In order to reach the city, Calatinus recklessly decided to march his army into a narrow defile recently fortified by the Carthaginians. Once in the ravine, the Romans found themselves trapped in an ambuscade and in danger of being completely destroyed until a tribune, Marcus Calpurnius Flamma, and 300 chosen men successfully diverted the Punic assault by seizing a strategically sensitive knoll occupied by the enemy. The Roman occupation of the hill proved intolerable to the Carthaginians, who redirected their main attack against the small band of legionaries in a bid to recover the location. While the tribune and his men stubbornly bore the massed assault, Calatinus was able to successfully extricate the remainder of the army from the confines of the gorge. None of the 300-man force survived the battle. Only Flamma, gravely wounded and concealed among the corpses, escaped.

Paulus Orosius, *Seven Books of History against the Pagans*, 4.8.

Camerinum, 296 BC (Third Samnite War, Samnite Wars) – While encamped in Umbria, a Roman legion under the command of Lucius Cornelius Scipio Barbatus was attacked by a combined force of Samnites – under Gellius Egnatius – and Senonian Gauls. Faced by such overwhelming odds, Scipio sought to relocate the army to higher ground, but the attempt was blocked by Gauls already occupying the chosen hill. Unable to achieve the ridge, the legion was quickly surrounded. The now isolated Roman force was almost completely destroyed in the battle which followed.

Titus Livius (Livy), *History of Rome*, 10.26.7–11; Polybius, *Histories*, 2.19.5.

Campi Magni, 203 BC (Second Punic War, Wars against Carthage) – With the Roman destruction of the Carthaginian camp near Utica, the Punic general Hasdrubal, the son of Gisgo, immediately began amassing a new army in Carthage and the surrounding countryside. His ally Syphax, Numidian ruler of the Massaesylians, likewise escaped the disaster but chose instead to return to his capital of Cirta (Constantine). On his westward march, Syphax encountered 4,000 Celtiberian mercenaries recruited in Spain for Punic service. Within a matter of days, Hasdrubal joined with the Numidian monarch and repaired to a region known as the Great Plain (La Dakhla), the fertile 25-mile long valley of the Bagradas (Medjerda) River. The combined strength of the army was approximately 30,000. When the Roman commander Publius Cornelius Scipio (Africanus) received word of these events, he left sufficient land and naval forces to continue the siege of Utica and proceeded to the location of Hasdrubal's reconstituted army, approximately 80 miles to the southwest of the city. Scipio arrived in the valley five days later with a force of 15,000 men and temporarily established a hillside camp about 4 miles from the Numidian position. Both armies assembled on the plain for the next three days, but neither commander committed their main infantry divisions to action, preferring instead to permit only their cavalry and light troops to skirmish with the enemy until dusk. Scipio and Hasdrubal marched onto the plain in full battle-array on the fourth day. The Romans assumed their standard manipular formation, placing the *hastati* in the forward ranks, followed by the *principes*, with the *triarii* held in reserve. On the right wing, Scipio posted the Italian allied cavalry, and on the left the mounted squadrons under Masinissa, king of the Numidian Massylii. Across the plain, Hasdrubal positioned the Celtiberians in the centre facing the legions, with the Numidian horsemen of Syphax on the left wing and Carthaginian cavalry on the right. When the two sides clashed, Scipio's veteran cavalry immediately defeated both the Carthaginian and Numidian squadrons, exposing the flanks of Hasdrubal's infantry phalanx to direct attack. The Celtiberians made a determined stand despite the loss of cavalry support, refusing to surrender until the Romans had largely destroyed the entire mercenary band. Syphax and Hasdrubal both fled, pursued by elements of Numidian and Italian cavalry under Masinissa and Caius Laelius.

Titus Livius (Livy), *History of Rome*, 30.7–8; Polybius, *Histories*, 14.8.

Campus Martius, 390 BC – see Mount Marcius, 390 BC.

Campus Martius, 77 BC – Not long after the death of the former dictator Lucius Cornelius Sulla, the *consul* Marcus Aemilius Lepidus introduced a motion to overturn Sulla's legislation authorizing the confiscation of lands belonging to various Italian peoples. Because of his association with the Marian faction, the Senate feared a resurgence of civil war and demanded that Lepidus and members of both factions pledge not to resume the violent struggles. Frustrated, Lepidus soon quit Rome, raised an army and marched on the city. As he approached from the northwest, Lepidus' path was blocked by military forces marshalled under the command of his co-*consul* Quintus Lutatius Catulus. The armies collided near the Campus Martius, and after a short struggle Lepidus abandoned his attempt to enter Rome. He left Italy soon thereafter for the island of Sardinia, where he died from an unknown illness.

Appianus (Appian), *Civil Wars*, 1.107; Lucius Annaeus Florus, *Epitomy*, 2.11.6–7.

Campus Raudii, 101 BC – see Vercellae, 101 BC.

Cannae, 216 BC (Second Punic War, Wars against Carthage) – While Roman forces continued to successfully consolidate their control of north-eastern Spain and generate tribal unrest against the Carthaginians in the southern portions of the Iberian peninsula, a divided Senate debated how best to prosecute the war in Italy. Humiliated by a series of battlefield defeats, and dissatisfied with the strategy of attrition, recently implemented during the previous year by the former dictator Quintus Fabius Maximus, the Senate finally chose to deploy a massive army into the south of the Italian peninsula to directly confront the Punic general Hannibal Barca. The consuls Caius Terentius Varro and Lucius Aemilius Paulus commanded eight legions, consisting of some 80,000 men; the largest army ever recruited in Roman history. The two armies made contact 5 miles from the Adriatic Sea near the small town of Cannae, situated on the southern extremity of the Apulian plain and south of the Aufidus (Ofanto) River. The Carthaginian force numbered only 40,000 infantry and 10,000 cavalry, but consisted almost exclusively of battle-hardened veterans. By contrast, the thousands of soldiers under Paulus and Varro were largely untested levies, though some veteran consular troops were present from the previous year's campaigns. When the Romans arrived, the Carthaginians had already been present in the area for several days, with sufficient time to reconnoitre. Hannibal had initially encamped somewhat south of the town, but relocated to the northwestern bank of the river after learning of the Romans' approach. On reaching the vicinity of Cannae, the Romans established their main camp on the northwestern side of the Aufidus, approximately 2 miles northeast of the Carthaginian position. A second, smaller *castrum* was established on the southeastern bank near an important ford. Four days after sighting the enemy, Varro crossed the river at dawn and assembled the entire Roman army for battle facing southwest, his line extending from the Aufidus to the hill of Cannae. Hannibal shortly followed suit, sending his light infantry across first, followed by the rest of the army which forded the river at two points. As the Carthaginians reached the opposite bank, each division of infantry immediately assumed its place in the

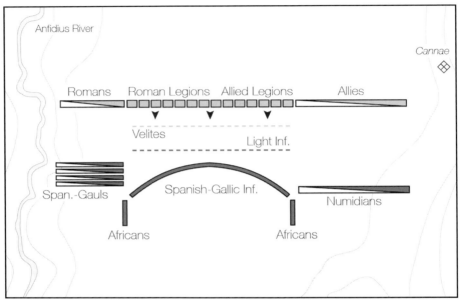

Battle of Cannae, 216 BC (Phase 1)

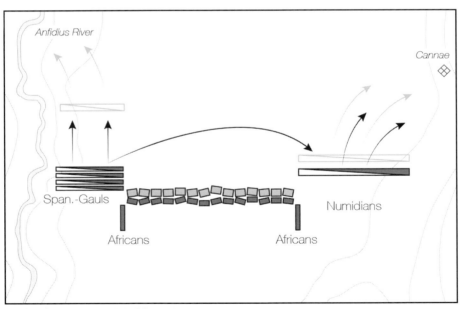

Battle of Cannae, 216 BC (Phase 2)

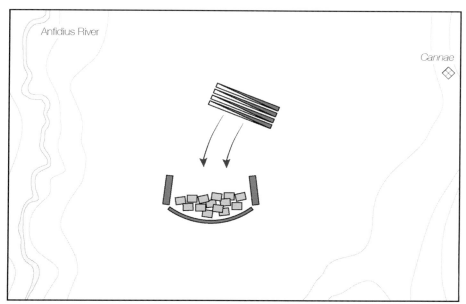

Battle of Cannae, 216 BC (Phase 3)

formation, while the cavalry ranged out to take up positions on the wings. Hasdrubal commanded the Spanish and Gallic heavy cavalry on the left near the Aufidus; Marharbal the Numidian light horse on the right. Hannibal arranged his Spanish and Gallic infantry *taxeis* in the centre in a crescent-shaped convex bowing outward toward the Roman maniples. Each end on this line had formations of African heavy infantry, largely equipped in Roman arms captured a year earlier at Trasimeno. He commanded the centre, and was joined there by one of his generals, Mago; another officer named Hanno led the right. Opposing the Carthaginians, Varro stationed Roman heavy cavalry under Aemilius Paulus on the right, facing the Spanish and Gallic horsemen. He deployed his amassed legions in the centre under the *proconsul* Cnaeus Servilius Geminius. On the left, the allied light horse, under Varro himself, faced the Numidians. The particular orientation of the opposing lines ensured that as the summer day matured, the prevailing winds swept hot clouds of blinding dust directly into the faces of the Romans. The battle began in mid-morning between the light infantry of both sides, followed by a strong charge of Spanish and Gallic cavalry against the Roman horse on the right. Because each body of riders was constrained by the river on one side and their respective infantry on the other, the oppugnant squadrons rushed head-on against each other. The resulting shock was violent and the fighting protracted, but the Romans inevitably gave way before the experience and numerical superiority of Hasdrubal's veterans. On the Roman left, the allied horsemen recoiled under the pressure of the Numidians' attack. In the meantime, the main infantry formations of the two armies collided in the centre. Though the Spaniards and Gauls offered stiff resistance, the inexorable pressure of the advancing legions gradually forced back the thin crescent line. As the Carthaginian centre began to fold inward, the Romans continued to push forward in an effort to split the enemy formation. The resulting penetration by the legions successfully drove Hannibal's centre backward, but also had the effect of placing the Romans squarely between fresh African divisions. The Punic heavy cavalry to the outside, at this point having completely overwhelmed the Roman right wing, pivoted right and charged the allied cavalry on the Roman left, already thrown into disorder by the Numidian attack. The collective result assured the complete rout of both Roman wings. As the Numidians went in hot pursuit of the fleeing remnants of the Roman cavalry, Hasdrubal again turned his heavy cavalry and immediately drove in the rear ranks of the Roman infantry. The assault only multiplied the scope of disaster befalling the legions; for while the cavalry battles were reaching their climaxes, Hannibal ordered the African heavy infantry on either side of the legions to attack. The thousands of Roman legionaries, already exhausted from their ongoing struggle with the now depleted Spanish and Gallic contingents, suddenly found themselves trapped between fresh formations of veteran troops and assailed from the rear by Hasdrubal's horsemen. Unable to escape the slaughter which followed, 50,000–70,000 Romans died, including the *consul* Aemilius Paulus, both former consuls Servilius and Marcus Atilius Regulus, eighty senators, twenty-nine military tribunes and two quaestors. Carthaginian losses amounted to less than 6,000 men.

Titus Livius (Livy), *History of Rome*, 42.42–49; Polybius *Histories*, 3.113–117.6; Plutarch, *Fabius Maximus*, 14–16; Appianus (Appian), *Hannibalic War*, 19–26; Cornelius Nepos, *Great Generals of Foreign Nations*, 23.4.4; Eutropius, *Abridgement of Roman History*, 3.10; John Zonaras, *Epitome of Histories*, 9.1.

Cantenna Mons, 71 BC (War of Spartacus, Third Servile War) –The Roman *propraetor* Marcus Licinius Crassus established two camps near Mount Cantenna, a short distance from the location of Spartacus and his slave army. Then at night he secretly gathered his entire army below the mountain while deceiving the enemy into believing that the larger legionary encampment remained occupied. Dividing his cavalry into two detachments, Crassus dispatched his lieutenant, Lucius Quintius, with one half of the horsemen to attack the main enemy division commanded by Spartacus. Meanwhile, he sent the rest to charge the German and Gallic contingents, and then by means of a feigned withdrawal, they were lured into an ambuscade. As intended, once the cavalry turned to flee, the Germans and Gauls recklessly pursued the riders directly into the awaiting legions, assembled in full battle formation at the base of the mountain. The Romans killed 35,000 men in the resulting struggle, including Spartacus' lieutenants, Castus and Cannicus.

Frontinus, *Stratagems*, 2.5.34; Paulus Orosius, *Seven Books of History against the Pagans*, 5.24; Titus Livius (Livy), *Summaries*, 97.

Canusium, 209 BC (Second Punic War, Wars against Carthage) – While the Roman *consul* Quintus Fabius Maximus Verrucosus pressed his attack against the Carthaginian stronghold of Tarentum (Taranto), the *proconsul* Marcus Claudius Marcellus led an army into Apulia in search of the Carthaginian general Hannibal Barca. On learning of the enemy's approach, the Punic commander withdrew from the open country around the town of Canusium (Canosa di Puglia) to higher, wooded terrain west of the Aufidus (Ofanto) River. The Romans went in pursuit, Marcellus electing to daily encamp near the enemy and offer battle each morning. In order to conserve his troops Hannibal repeatedly declined a general contest, but instead entered into a number of minor skirmishes using light infantry and cavalry. Finally recognizing that a major battle was unavoidable, the Punic general accepted the challenge. The resulting engagement lasted more than two hours. Both sides fought fiercely before the Carthaginians were able to gain advantage against the cavalry *ala* and allied infantry on the Roman right wing. As this portion of the front line began to weaken, Marcellus deployed the Eighteenth Legion in support, but the confusion created when the advancing maniples suddenly joined with the flagging troops resulted in a complete rout of the entire battle formation. The *proconsul*'s forces returned to their camp with a loss of 2,700 Roman and allied dead.

Titus Livius (Livy), *History of Rome*, 27.12; Plutarch, *Marcellus*, 25.2–4.

Canusium, 209 BC (Second Punic War, Wars against Carthage) – Following the Roman army's defeat near the town of Canusium (Canosa di Puglia) in southeastern Italy, the *proconsul* Marcus Claudius Marcellus upbraided his troops for their poor performance and then led the chastened but emboldened men onto the battlefield the next morning. In response, the Carthaginian general Hannibal Barca assembled his army into two lines, placing his Spanish veterans in the front. The Romans also arrayed in a *duplex acies*. In the front line, Marcellus deployed a cavalry *ala*, with the depleted allied maniples on the Roman left wing and the Eighteenth Legion to the right. He then stationed the second consular legion and the other allied legion in reserve. The *proconsul* personally led the centre, while his lieutenants Lucius Cornelius Lentulus and Caius Claudius Nero commanded the wings. Once the battle began, the fighting proved long, bitterly contested and inconclusive; which prompted Hannibal to finally order his war elephants into action. The inclusion of the large animals initially caused confusion within the ranks of the Roman formation, before the first maniple of the *hastati* pressed forward under its own initiative and disrupted the assault with a volley of javelins, driving the pachyderms off. As the animals turned in flight, other maniples joined in the attack. The wounded beasts, crazed with pain, dashed uncontrollably through the ranks of the Carthaginian lines, killing or injuring thousands. Seeking to exploit the moment, the Romans penetrated the broken Punic formation and completely routed the enemy from the field. Remnants of the defeated army fled to their camp, closely pursued by Roman cavalry. Total losses amounted to 8,000 Carthaginians and five elephants. Among the Romans, the two legions suffered 1,700 dead and the allies more than 1,300 killed.

Titus Livius (Livy), *History of Rome*, 27.13.11–14.14; Plutarch, *Marcellus*, 26.1–4.

Canusium, 89 BC (Social War, Marsic War) – After burning the south-eastern Italian town of Salapia and capturing nearby Cannae to the south, the Roman *praetor* Caius Cosconius besieged the community of Canusium, situated 14 miles inland from the Adriatic coast. As the investment progressed, a Samnite army soon arrived in relief of the town, forcing the Romans to engage in an intense battle. Both sides suffered very heavy casualties before the legions were finally driven off, retreating eastward toward Cannae.

Appianus (Appian), *Civil Wars*, 1.6.52.

Canusium, 83 BC (Roman Civil Wars) – Near the town of Canusium, the forces of Lucius Cornelius Sulla and Quintus Caecilius Metellus Pius fought a battle against an army led by the *consul* Caius Norbanus. After losing 6,000 men, the defeated Norbanus retreated across the peninsula to Capua. Sulla's forces suffered many wounded but only seventy dead.

Appianus (Appian), *Civil Wars*, 1.10.84.

Cape Bon, 255 BC – see Hermaeum Promontorium, 255 BC.

Cape Hermaeum, 255 BC – see Hermaeum Promontorium, 255 BC.

Cape Mercury, 255 BC – see Hermaeum Promontorium, 255 BC.

Capua, 212 BC (Second Punic War, Wars against Carthage) – Having dispatched their troops across the countryside of Campania, in an effort to destroy agricultural production in the immediate vicinity around the city of Capua, the Roman consuls Quintus Fulvius Flaccus and Appius Claudius Pulcher were surprised by an unexpected sally of Capuans, reinforced by Punic cavalry under the Carthaginian general Mago. A futile attempt by both consuls to reassemble their command in preparation for action resulted in the enemy overrunning the legionary battle line before it was fully formed. The suddenness of the assault resulted in over 1,500 Roman dead.

Titus Livius (Livy), *History of Rome*, 25.18.1.

Capua, 212 BC (Second Punic War, Wars against Carthage) – In order to provide protection from a Roman siege, a Carthaginian army under the leadership of Hannibal Barca marched westward from Beneventum to the Campanian city of Capua, located approximately 16 miles north of coastal Neapolis. Three days after his arrival, the Punic commander arrayed his army in battle formation in an attempt to provoke a general action, and the challenge was accepted. Once hostilities began, the Roman infantry was quickly subjected to intense pressure from Hannibal's army, particularly by elements of his veteran cavalry. This threat to the beleaguered cohorts was only relieved by a countercharge of Roman cavalry, which swiftly degenerated into an intense melee between opposing mounted squadrons. While the fighting raged, a Roman detachment commanded by the *quaestor* Gnaeus Cornelius was sighted in the distance by both armies. Unaware of the true identity of this approaching force, both commanders chose to abruptly terminate the engagement and retire to their respective encampments.

Titus Livius (Livy), *History of Rome*, 25.19.1–5.

Capua, 211 BC (Second Punic War, Wars against Carthage) – Still determined to reduce Capua by military force, the proconsuls Quintus Fulvius Flaccus and Appius Claudius Pulcher continued their investment of the Campanian city from the previous year. Two additional legions under the *propraetor* Caius Claudius Nero soon joined in the siege, for a total of six legions outside the city. This concentration of Roman power finally persuaded the Carthaginian commander, Hannibal Barca, to abandon his efforts to capture the citadel at Tarentum (Taranto) in southeastern Italy and march northward to the aid of his Capuan allies. Accordingly, he left his heavy infantry and most of his baggage in Bruttium and advanced toward Campania with a select force of some 35,000 light infantry and cavalry, and thirty-three war elephants. After several days' march, the Carthaginians arrived at a valley behind Tifata, a mountain overlooking Capua from the northeast, and encamped there before moving against the 60,000 Roman troops concentrated around the city. To further his cause, Hannibal secretly dispatched a messenger into the community to orchestrate a coordinated attack involving his army and the citizens of Capua, who were in turn supported by the resident Carthaginian garrison commanded by Bastar and Hanno. With this prearranged plan in place, the Punic host then marched around the base of Tifata Mons and descended onto the plain north of the city. Observing this movement, the *consul* Quintus Fulvius elected to cross over the siege works and marshal the army's legions ahead of the approaching Punic formation. The Romans were not yet fully prepared for action when the Carthaginians suddenly and unexpectedly charged the whole of the legionary line. This attack was joined by a simultaneous sortie from the Capuans inside the city. Caught off-guard by the swiftness of the two-fold attack, the Romans nonetheless managed to recover and assume a defensive posture. While Fulvius absorbed the brunt of the Punic offensive, Appius Claudius arrayed his forces facing the Capuans. Caius Claudius deployed the legions' cavalry along the highway leading to Suessula, and the legate Caius Fulvius Flaccus stationed the army's allied horse near the Via Appia in the direction of Casilinum. Once the antagonists closed ranks, Appius deftly turned the Capuan assault from the camp, but the *consul* Fulvius struggled to resist the pressure of the larger Carthaginian force led by Hannibal. Following intense fighting among the main body of Roman and Punic infantry, the Sixth Legion was driven back, permitting some Spanish troops and a trio of war elephants to penetrate as far as the breastworks of one Roman camp. Fulvius quickly rallied the *Legio VI*, and the maniples moved to close the breach. From atop the camp's earthworks, *velites* and reserve troops under the legates Lucius Porcius Licinus and Titus Popilius checked the momentum of the attack and slew the elephants, but the location where the animals fell inadvertently disrupted the Roman defences, allowing the Spanish detachment to force a passage into the encampment. For a time heavy fighting occurred over the bodies of the fallen elephants before the Romans finally succeeded in isolating and destroying the attackers. At the same time, on the other side of the camp, Appius pursued the retreating Capuans to the city's northwestern gate, but was forced to abandon the chase by the concentrated missile fire from ballistas and scorpions on the wall. With the Carthaginian and allied forces now largely repulsed, Hannibal decided to give up the assault, having lost 8,000 men in the course of the day's fighting. Capuan deaths totalled an additional 3,000. That night, under cover of darkness, the Punic general evacuated the area around Capua and marched on Rome.

Titus Livius (Livy) *History of Rome* , 26.5–6.13; Appianus (Appian) *Hannibalic War*, 6.38.

Carales, 215 BC (Second Punic War, Wars against Carthage) – The fragile state of Roman authority on the island of Sardinia ultimately persuaded the Senate to dispatch the *praetor* Titus Manlius Torquatus to aid the appointed magistrate, Quintus Mucius Scaevola, who was presently ill and unable to perform his duties. Manlius arrived with a force of 5,000 infantry and 400 cavalry to assist in the suppression of a native uprising led by a local leader named Hampsicora. Once ashore, Manlius armed the ships' crews, the *socii navales*, as infantry and then joined his forces with those Roman troops already on the island. Now in possession of an army of 22,000 infantry and

1,200 cavalry, the *praetor* prepared to prosecute his campaign. Manlius fought and won an initial clash with the Sardinians, but was soon faced with an expanded conflict after the arrival of a Carthaginian fleet commanded by Hasdrubal Calvus. Manlius shortly thereafter withdrew to the southern coastal city of Carales (Cagliari), providing Hampsicora the opportunity to join with the Punic expedition. Using the rebel leader as a guide, Hasdrubal began to devastate those lands belonging to Rome's allies on the island. This action quickly provoked the Romans to leave the protection of the city and confront the Carthaginian army. After engaging in a series of skirmishes near the two military camps, both armies finally committed to a pitched battle. The encounter lasted four hours and the outcome long remained uncertain, largely because of resistance offered by the Punic divisions. Finally, after all Sardinian opposition was completely broken, the Romans routed the Carthaginians. As Hasdrubal attempted to extricate his forces from the field, Manlius manoeuvred one flank of his army in order to block the enemy's retreat. The Punic host was trapped and largely destroyed. Some 12,000 Carthaginians and Sardinians died, and approximately 3,700 were captured, including Hasdrubal Calvus. Hampsicora committed suicide soon after.

Titus Livius (Livy), *History of Rome*, 23.34.10–16, 23.40–41.4.

Caravis, 179 BC (Wars in Spain) – Faced with a continuing insurrection in Spain, the Roman Senate dispatched a consular army under the command of Tiberius Sempronius Gracchus. Upon arriving in the peninsula, Gracchus immediately marched to the relief of the city of Caravis, a Roman ally besieged by a force of 20,000 Celtiberians. Recognizing that the community was on the verge of capitulation, the *consul* dispatched Cominius, a prefect of horse, to secretly cross the enemy's siege lines and carry word to the beleaguered population of the Romans' imminent arrival. Encouraged by this news, the townspeople continued to endure the investment for three more days. When the legionary forces arrived, the Celtiberians elected to retire. Around the same time, some 20,000 inhabitants of Complega arrived in Gracchus' camp feigning peace, but once there suddenly launched an attack against the unsuspecting Romans. In the midst of the assault, the *consul* ordered his men to abandon the camp to the enemy under the pretext of flight. When his troops were clear of the ramparts, Gracchus halted his army at some distance, redressed his maniples for battle, and counter-attacked. Preoccupied with plundering the deserted encampment, the Complegians were completely unprepared to resist the speed and strength of the Roman charge. Within a short time, most of the interlopers were killed and the camp firmly restored to the control of Gracchus.

Appianus (Appian), *Wars in Spain*, 8.43.

Carmone, 207 BC (Second Punic War, Wars against Carthage) – Near the town of Carmone (Carmona) located approximately 10 miles south of the Baetis (Guadalquivir) River in southern Spain, a Punic army of 70,000 infantry and 5,000 cavalry led by Hasdrubal Gisgo confronted a smaller Roman force of less than 25,000 men. Because of the size disparity between the two armies, the Roman general Publius Cornelius Scipio (Africanus) was initially content to skirmish with the Carthaginians, but diminishing supplies finally compelled him to force a general action. After ensuring that his soldiers were properly fed and armed, Scipio led the army out in battle formation; his lieutenants, Lucius Marcius and Caius Laelius, in command of the infantry, and Marcus Silanus at the head of the Roman horse. Because the camps were separated by only a mile, the Romans' advance quickly threatened the enemy camp, forcing the Carthaginians to rush to arms. Hasdrubal assembled his infantry, including the African phalanx, in the centre. On each flank he positioned cavalry; Mago and the Carthaginians to one side, and the Numidian light horse under their king, Masinissa, on the other. Once the two armies joined in battle, the Roman cavalry prevailed over the Numidians by denying them any opportunity to employ their traditional hit-and-run tactics. Closely pressed by the enemy, the African horsemen were unable to use their javelins to best effect and were eventually driven off. Likewise, the *equites* defeated Mago's heavy squadrons, but the Roman infantry was dangerously close to being overwhelmed by the larger Carthaginian formation. As the struggle continued, Hasdrubal slowly gained the advantage by reason of his superior numbers, giving Scipio no chance to turn the momentum of the contest in his favour. Finally, the Roman leader dismounted, and in a bold move calculated to rally his legions, seized an infantry shield and dashed into the space between the opposing battle lines, where he then called his men to rescue their commander. Shamed by their general, and in fear for his life, the maniples launched a furious charge against the enemy that broke the African formation and put the entire Punic army to flight. Carthaginian losses totalled 15,000; those of the Romans 800.

Appianus (Appian), *Wars in Spain*, 6.25.27.

Carmone, 152 BC (Lusitanian War, Wars in Spain) – Faced with ongoing revolt of the Lusitanians, Servius Sulpicius Galba, the *praetor* of *Hispania Ulterior* (Western Spain), assembled his army and travelled 60 miles by forced march to the vicinity of Carmone (Carmona), a city approximately 10 miles south of the Baetis (Guadalquivir) River in southern Spain. When scouts saw the enemy, Sulpicius determined to immediately bring the Lusitani to battle and ordered his legions into action, despite their extreme exhaustion after the day's journey. In the subsequent clash, the Romans successfully broke the ranks of the Lusitanian warriors, but were then recklessly ordered to pursue the fugitives despite the debilitating effects of the fatigue suffered by the entire army. When the retreating warriors recognized the weakened state of their pursuers, they stopped their flight and countercharged. Without the strength to capably repel the wave of tribesmen, approximately 7,000 Romans died in the attack. Galba and most of the cavalry fled to the safety of Carmone, where he collected the remnants of his legionary force.

Appianus (Appian), *Wars in Spain*, 10.58.

Carrhae, 53 BC June (Parthian Wars) – This battle was fought in north-western Mesopotamia near the town of Carrhae when a Parthian army of 10,000 cavalry – mostly mounted bowmen – led by the general Surena confronted seven Roman legions under the *triumvir* Marcus Licinius Crassus. The 40,000 Romans, overtaken on dry, open ground, were surrounded by the more agile cavalry and exposed to intense fire from the Parthian archers. Subsequent efforts by Crassus to resolve the situation through offensive action by light infantry failed; and a strong sally by a mixed formation of 6,000 Roman cavalry and infantry led by the *triumvir*'s son, Publius Licinius Crassus, ended disastrously when the formation was trapped by light and heavy Parthian horse and completely destroyed. The loss of this composite force now rendered the Roman position completely untenable, and the Parthian light cavalry subjected the imperiled legions to continuous attacks until evening. The dire situation compelled the shattered remnants of Crassus'

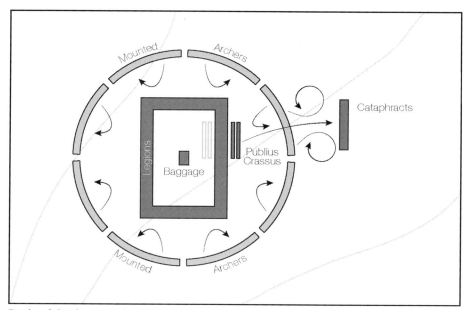

Battle of Carrhae, 53 BC

army to attempt a retreat under cover of darkness to the temporary shelter of Carrhae. The Parthians allowed the legions to withdraw, but resumed their pursuit the next morning, overrunning and killing some 4,000 Roman wounded left behind in the town by the desperate survivors. An additional four cohorts under the *legatus* Vargontinus, who became separated from the main body of troops during the night, were trapped on a low hill and destroyed almost to a man. Two nights later, the Romans initiated a final sustained withdrawal toward the western bank of the Euphrates River. This effort was accompanied by continual daylight assaults by the Parthian cavalry which slowed the retreat. Crassus' force was finally able to reach the temporary safety of the Armenian hill country of Sinnaca. There they were joined by 5,000 other survivors led by the *legatus* Octavius. A false offer by Surena to negotiate a Roman surrender resulted in the murder of Crassus. Afterwards, the Parthians hunted down the remainder of the expeditionary force as it sought to complete its escape. Approximately 20,000 Romans died in the encounter and 10,000 were captured. Only 10,000 Romans survived the flight into Syria, including Crassus' *quaestor*, Caius Cassius Longinus, who managed to flee earlier with 500 cavalry.

Plutarch, *Crassus*, 21.5–31; Dio Cassius, *Roman History*, 40.20–27; Strabo of Amasya, *Geography*, 16.1.23.

Carteia, 46 BC (Roman Civil Wars) – In Spain, the build-up of Caesarian forces alarmed Cnaeus Pompeius, the elder son of Caesar's former rival Pompey the Great, and he chose to retire with his army into the region of Baetica in the southern Iberian peninsula. This location thereafter served as a focal point for all who opposed the growing power of Caesar, including Sextus Pompeius, Titus Labienus and Pompey's *legatus* in Africa, Publius Atius Varus. The maritime traffic around the southern Spanish coast inevitably drew the attention of the Caesarians. Near the port of Carteia, situated on the Strait of Gibraltar, a fleet under the command of Caesar's general, Caius Didius, defeated a force of ships led by Varus. He at once fled to the safety of Carteia, and there blocked the mouth of the harbour with a row of sunken anchors in order to impair the approach of the enemy's vessels. The first of Didius' ships to attempt an entry into the harbour wrecked on the underwater obstacles, alerting the remainder of the fleet to the unseen impediment. With the threat from Didius temporarily allayed, Varus concentrated his forces against Ulia, the only city remaining in the region that was not in alliance with Cnaeus Pompeius.

Dio Cassius, *Roman History*, 43.31.3.

Carthage, 149–146 BC (Third Punic War, Wars against Carthage) – Following years of growing tensions between the city of Carthage and the neighbouring kingdom of Numidia, war erupted in 150 BC. The initiation of hostilities by the Carthaginians was a clear violation of the treaty concluded with Rome in 201 BC, and the Roman Senate promptly followed word of this transgression with a declaration of war against the Punic state. The next year, Roman legions began the investment of Carthage, but were unable to make significant progress toward the reduction of the great city until 147 BC. That year, the newly elected *consul*, Publius Cornelius Scipio Aemilianus, assumed the task of prosecuting the siege. He initially made little headway in the campaign to isolate the city, but was gradually able to employ sufficient manpower to construct the siege works necessary to successfully close off all means of egress and ingress. In early spring, Roman armies began the siege of the harbour of Cothon, as well as Byrsa, the strongest part of the city. With the capture of the inner harbour, Aemilianus concentrated his legions against the primary garrison. The Romans advanced against the citadel along three streets rising from the Forum. These avenues were lined on either side by multi-storey houses which provided the defenders with numerous locations from which to attack Aemilianus' infantry. The city surrendered after six days and nights of savage street-fighting in which large sections of the residential area were systematically burned or otherwise demolished by the legions. Once the 50,000 surviving inhabitants were removed, Aemilianus ordered the total destruction of Carthage.

Appianus (Appian), *Punic Wars*, 17–19.

Carthago Nova, 210 BC (Second Punic War, Wars against Carthage) – After assessing the high strategic value of the Spanish port of Novo Carthago (Cartagena) to the Carthaginians, Roman general Publius Cornelius Scipio (Africanus) formulated a daring plan to seize the city. Aware that the nearest Punic army capable of providing relief to the city was more than ten days away from the coast, Scipio prepared to prosecute a siege with an army of 25,000 infantry and 2,500 cavalry. Seven days after crossing the Ebro River, the legions approached Novo Carthago from the landward side, while a Roman fleet under Caius Laelius manoeuvred to blockade the city's harbour. A 1,000-man garrison commanded by the Carthaginian general Mago and several thousand armed civilians opposed the Roman attackers. Scipio established his camp to the north of the community opposite the sea because of the city's location on an isthmus. After fortifying his base on the outer side with a double line of entrenchments extending from shoreline to shoreline, he prepared his military and naval forces for a coordinated investment. The open ground between the Roman encampment and Novo Carthago was without fortification, providing his legions an unobstructed approach to the city. With everything in readiness the following day, he attacked with a select force of 2,000 infantry. Once the Roman assault began, a sudden sally by a detachment of armed citizens posted near the city's isthmian gate disrupted Scipio's efforts to quickly breach the defences. As the enemy pressed the attack, the Romans near the wall undertook a prearranged fighting withdrawal in order to lure the Carthaginians nearer the legionary camp. The fierce engagement was at first evenly matched, but as soon as the struggle drew close to the Roman *castrum*, Scipio decisively turned the battle to his advantage by the rapid injection of massive reinforcements, which served to overwhelm the Carthaginians and put them to flight. In the chaotic retreat which followed, many of the fugitives died during their flight to find shelter in the city or were trampled in their attempt to rush through the gate. Afterwards, the Romans successfully prosecuted the capture of Novo Carthago.

Titus Livius (Livy), *History of Rome*, 26.42–44.4; Polybius, *Histories*, 10.12.

Carystus, 173 BC – A large army of Ligurian tribesmen assembled near the city of Carystus in western coastal Cisalpine Gaul. The Roman Senate responded by sending an army under the command of the *consul* Marcus Popilius Laenas to quell the disturbance. As the Roman army drew into battle array outside the city's walls, the Ligurians left the safety of their ramparts and assembled into a line of battle in front of the gates. The resulting struggle lasted for more than three hours, and remained undecided until Popilius ordered his cavalry to intercede. The squadrons of horsemen simultaneously charged the enemy ranks at three separate points. In the midst of the fighting, a large concentration of the riders successfully penetrated the Ligurian centre and battled their way completely through the lines of opposing infantry, essentially splitting the enemy formation. This inspired widespread panic within the body of Ligurian warriors, immediately followed by the total collapse of all resistance. Some 10,000 Ligurians died in the battle or subsequent flight. Roman losses totalled over 3,000 men.

Titus Livius (Livy), *History of Rome*, 42.7.3–10.

Castrum Album, 214 BC (Second Punic War, Wars against Carthage) – A resurgence of Carthaginian power in southern Spain threatened to undermine Roman authority in *Hispania Ulterior* (Western Spain), forcing the Roman general Publius Cornelius Scipio to lead an army across the Iberis (Ebro) River in an effort to restore control in the region. Near the citadel of Castrum Album (Alicante), on the coast northeast of Carthago Nova (Cartagena), Scipio's column was repeatedly attacked by Carthaginian light cavalry. About 2,000 Romans died, mostly stragglers or members of foraging parties. Afterward, Scipio elected to withdraw his forces closer to peaceful territory.

Titus Livius (Livy), *History of Rome*, 24.41.1–4.

Castulo, 211 BC – see Baetis River, 211 BC.

Castulo, 208 BC (Second Punic War, Wars against Carthage) – While a Punic army led by Hasdrubal, son of Gisco, was seeking to subdue the territory of Lersa in Spain, a legionary force commanded by Publius Cornelius Scipio approached with the intention of bringing the Carthaginians to battle. On learning of the enemy's whereabouts, Hasdrubal promptly retreated to the city of Castulo and camped before its walls. Scipio followed, and the next day defeated the Carthaginian army, capturing the encampment and occupying the city.

   Appianus (Appian), *Wars in Spain*, 24.

Cauca, 151 BC (Numantine War, Wars in Spain) – Soon after arriving in Spain, the *consul* Lucius Licinius Lucullus made preparations for attacking the Vaccaei and Caucaei tribes without provocation or the endorsement of the Roman Senate. He invaded Celtiberian territory and crossed the Tagus (Tajo) River before encamping with his army near the city of Cauca (Coca), with the clear intention of making war. After enquiring into the reason why Licinius had encroached on their lands, the Caucaei rushed out from the protection of their walls and attacked some of the Roman foragers and wood-cutters roaming about the immediate countryside. This was soon followed by a pitched battle between Roman troops and lightly armed Caucaei warriors that remained unresolved until the Celtiberians were forced to retreat after exhausting their supply of missiles. As the Caucaei fell back, the Romans took advantage of a poorly executed withdrawal and killed approximately 3,000 warriors as they attempted to gain entry through the city gates. The following day, the city elders parleyed with Licinius in hopes of restoring peace. To this end, they readily complied with all of the consul's demands, including the admission of a Roman garrison to the city. Unknown to the Caucaei, Licinius was duplicitous in his negotiations, and, once inside, the 2,000-man detachment seized control of Cauca before opening the gates of the city to the remainder of the army. Shortly thereafter, the legions sacked the city and the entire male population of 20,000 was put to the sword.

   Appianus (Appian), *Wars in Spain*, 9.51.

Caudine Forks, 321 BC (Second Samnite War, Samnite Wars) – Five years after the renewal of war with the Samnites, two Roman consular armies were subjected to one of the most signal military humiliations in Roman history. In 321 BC, Samnite general Caius Pontius encamped his army near the village of Caudium (Montesarchio) in central Italy, and by ruse lured a consular force of 20,000 into a well-conceived trap. Dispatching ten soldiers in the guise of shepherds toward the Roman camp near Calatia, Pontius circulated a false story that a Samnite army was in Apulia besieging Luceria, a close ally of Rome, and was on the point of capturing the city. The desperate nature of the situation moved the Roman consuls Titus Veturius Calvinus and Spurius Postumius (Caudinus) to move their armies toward Apulia along a shorter, but more perilous route through the Caudine Forks east of Capua. This location consisted of a grassy plain between mountain ranges. Any traffic following this path was required to move through two deep, narrow passes situated on either end of the plain. The Romans entered by the western defile without incident, but as they prepared to exit through the eastern gorge discovered it blocked by boulders and felled trees. Prevented from going forward, the Romans attempted to retire through the first pass, but now found it closed by a similar barrier and Samnite troops. The following day, repeated efforts to breach the barricades by armed force failed, leaving Veturius and Postumius with no choice but to surrender. In the negotiations which followed, Pontius secured a peace from the Roman commanders by a solemn guarantee (*sponsio*), retained the consuls and leading officers as hostages and sent the entire defeated army under the yoke – a disgrace which later Romans never forgot.

Titus Livius (Livy), *History of Rome*, 9.2–6; Appianus (Appian), *Samnite History*, 4.2–6.

Caudium, 314 BC (Second Samnite War, Samnite Wars) – When the Samnites moved their forces near the town of Caudium (Montesarchio) in an attempt to seize Capua, the Romans responded by deploying two consular armies into the Caudium Valley to challenge the invaders. Within a short time, the opposing armies were camped near one another on the plain in anticipation of a decisive battle. After numerous skirmishes, the Samnite commanders grew impatient with the daily manpower losses accrued from such encounters and elected to assemble their entire army in an effort to provoke a major confrontation with the Romans. The co-consuls responded by deploying their legions on the field; Caius Sulpicius Longus in command of the right wing and Marcus Poetelius leading the left. The Samnite infantry, protected by squadrons of cavalry placed on each wing, opposed the Roman formation. On the Roman right, both armies were arrayed over a considerable stretch of ground, each side having attenuated its line to prevent an envelopment. By contrast, the Roman maniples positioned on the left were drawn up in close order, reinforced by auxiliary units. When the battle opened, Poetelius used the combined strength of these units on the left to immediately push the enemy back. Observing this contest, the Samnite cavalry advanced to the relief of their infantry on the right, but were suddenly subjected to a strong charge by Roman horsemen. The effect was to completely disrupt the cohesion of the Samnite formation. The force of the Roman cavalry attack carried everything before it, resulting in a rout of the Samnite right. At the same time, on the opposite flank, the Roman infantry were in a desperate state. Having been driven out of their original position in disorder, the legions were in danger of being completely routed. Despite the perilous nature of this situation, Sulpicius eventually rallied his troops, who were further emboldened by the Roman victory on the left. Accordingly, the integrity of the right flank stiffened and the maniples capably assumed the offensive and recovered lost ground, as the enemy grew less resolute. In the end, the Romans overwhelmed the entire opposing line, resulting in the loss of 30,000 Samnites captured or killed.

   Titus Livius (Livy), *History of Rome*, 9.27.

Chaironeia, 146 BC (War of the Achaean League) – A select detachment of a 1,000 Achaean troops, deployed in support of the Greek rebel *strategos* Critolaus, were as far as the Phocian town of Elateia when they learned of the Greek disaster at Scarpheia. The drastic turn of affairs prompted the Phocians to expel the entire force from the community for fear of Roman reprisals. As they were retreating south toward the Peloponnesus, the Achaeans were intercepted near Chaeroneia by a Roman army under the command of the *propraetor* Quintus Caecilius Metellus. The Romans completely destroyed the Achaean contingent in the resulting battle.

   Pausanias, *Description of Greece*, 7.15.5–6.

Chaironeia, 86 BC (First Mithridatic War, Wars against Mithridates the Great) – After a months-long siege, the Roman *consul* Lucius Cornelius Sulla finally wrestled control of Athens from pro-Mithridatic forces in the city and then successfully drove an army under the Pontic general Archelaus out of the Piraeus. These troops withdrew northward, where they rendezvoused with a second army sent by Mithridates which was moving south through Thessaly. Once assembled, Archelaus assumed command of the entire force of 120,000 men. After burning the Piraeus, Sulla pursued the enemy northward with a much smaller army. Marching into Boeotia, the *consul* joined with a legion-strength detached force under the command of his *legatus*, Lucius Hortensius. This move also allowed a sizeable portion of the Roman army to relocate into the fertile plains of central Greece, where supplies were more plentiful, and await an opportunity for battle. When the Pontic divisions reached the plains of Elatea ,they found Romans encamped on Philoboiotos, a heavily wooded hill located on the southern extremity of the expanse. After several days, the armies moved nearer the town of Chaironeia, southwest of Mount Parnassos. Sulla and Archelaus assembled their battle formations on a narrow plain divided by the Cephisos River. Sulla positioned his legions in the centre of the Roman line, and deployed squadrons of cavalry on both wings. The *consul* assumed personal command of the right, while his *legatus* Lucius Licinius Murena led the left. Several cohorts were held in reserve under the generals Hortensius and Galba on the heights behind the Roman line. Meanwhile, a small force of Chaironeians, dispatched earlier by Sulla, finally reached the crest of Mount Thurmium to the south of the town. There it surprised a detachment of Pontic soldiers. The unexpected attack killed 3,000 men and routed the remainder, whose disorderly retreat briefly caused confusion within the ranks of Archelaus' main battle line on the plain below. Sulla then moved the Roman line forward, intent on attacking the enemy while they were still constrained by poor terrain to their rear and flanks. Recognizing danger, Archelaus sent his cavalry against the Romans in an effort to slow the approaching legions and permit him time to debouch from the unfavourable location. The horsemen proved ineffective, and were soon driven back and shattered on rocky ground. An assault by sixty scythed chariots then followed, but the cars were channelled through gaps in the main Roman formation and their crews killed by light troops retained as the legions' rearguard. The delay which resulted from these two failed actions garnered sufficient time for Archelaus to properly array his phalanx before the opposing ranks of heavy infantry clashed. As fighting in the centre of the line intensified, Archelaus deployed his cavalry in an effort to extend the right wing beyond Murena. Sulla responded to this threatened envelopment by sending five cohorts under Hortensius to attack the Pontic right flank, a move that necessitated Archelaus redirect his 2,000 cavalry against the approaching detachment. With his superior numbers, he was quickly able to isolate the cohorts near a line of hills, forcing Sulla to redeploy his cavalry from the right to the left wing in order to rescue Hortensius. Observing this, the Pontic commander immediately sent his squadrons of horsemen against the now-depleted Roman right, even as Murena on the left was at the same time resisting a strong infantry attack led by Taxiles. Faced with simultaneous assaults on both ends of his line, the *consul* elected to send Hortensius and four cohorts to aid Murena while he returned to the right wing with the fifth, as well as two additional cohorts held in reserve. The speedy arrival of Sulla permitted the Romans to attack before Archelaus' column could fully organize on the left in support of those forces already engaged in the struggle. The unexpected swiftness of the attack threw the enemy into confusion, causing a collapse of the entire Pontic left wing. Sulla's victory on the right soon triggered a general rout of Archelaus' entire formation, which fled toward the Cephisos River and Mount Acontium. However, the fugitives' escape was slowed by rocky ground, permitting the Romans to overtake them near the Pontic encampment. In the slaughter which followed, all but 10,000 of Archelaus' soldiers died.

Plutarch, *Sulla*, 15–19; Appianus (Appian), *Mithridatic War*, 41–45.

Chalcedon, 74 BC (Third Mithridatic War, Wars against Mithridates the Great) – In the spring of 74 BC, Mithridates VI Eupator, king of Pontus, invaded the Anatolian kingdom of Bithynia, recently bequeathed to Rome by its last monarch, Nicomedes IV. The invasion was inspired by Mithridates' abject rejection of Rome's right of acquisition. He believed that the inter-lopers presented an acute strategic threat to regional interests. The Pontic ruler immediately moved his army against the town of Chalcedon, located on the southern mouth of the Bosphorus opposite Byzantium (Istanbul), where the *consul* Marcus Aurelius Cotta and many Roman refugees sought protection. An initial effort by a contingent of Roman troops – led by the naval prefect Nudus – to form a defensive line on the adjacent plain failed, and the entire force was overwhelmed by Mithridates' army and driven back against Chalcedon's gates. There, the men were refused ingress by guards, who feared the town would be overrun by the approaching enemy. Some officers, including Nudus, were hauled over the gates to safety, but the remaining Romans were slaughtered. Soon after this victory, Mithridates' fleet breached the harbour entrance, burned four ships and towed away an additional sixty. By the end of the day, Roman manpower losses amounted to 4,000 infantry and the entire complement of naval personnel aboard the captured vessels.

Appianus (Appian), *Mithridatic Wars*, 71; Titus Livius (Livy), *Summaries*, 93; Plutarch, *Lucullus*, 8.1–2.

Chaunus Mons, 179 BC – After having recently accepted the surrender of a number of Celtiberian towns, the outbreak of rebellion forced the *propraetor* Tiberius Sempronius Gracchus to return with his army in an effort to pacify several of those regions assumed to be at peace with Rome. The legions engaged a rebel army on Mount Chaunus in an inconclusive battle that resulted in heavy casualties on both sides. The Celtiberians elected to remain within their fortifications the following day, but were finally persuaded to open battle on the third day. The Romans proved victorious after a fierce struggle – 22,000 Celtiberians were killed and more than 300 captured. Roman losses are not recorded.

Titus Livius (Livy), *History of Rome*, 40.50.1–5.

Ciminian Forest, 308 BC – see Perusia, 308 BC.

Cirta, 203 BC (Second Punic War, Wars against Carthage) – Having escaped the Carthaginian defeat at Campus Magnus, the Numidian leader Syphax, king of the Massaesylians, fled to his capital of Cirta (Constantine), where he once again began to gather an army. The day following the battle, the Roman commander Publius Cornelius Scipio (Africanus) dispatched Masinissa, king of the Numidian Massylii, and Caius Laelius to the west with all of the army's Numidian and Roman cavalry and *velites* in pursuit of Syphax and the remnants of his force. The two cavalry forces clashed near the city. At first the superior numbers of Massaesylian horsemen provided Syphax an advantage and threatened to turn the battle against the Romans and their allies, but the interjection of the *velites* served to steady the battle line. Gradually, the coordinated tactics of the light infantry and cavalry shifted the momentum of the contest in favour of Laelius and Masinissa. While fighting continued, the arrival of Roman heavy infantry detachments further disheartened the enemy. Finally, after the capture of Syphax, who was thrown from his horse and overpowered by Masinissa himself, the Massaesylians chose to abandon the fight and fled westward across the Ampsaga (Rhumel) River, having suffered several thousand casualties. Roman dead amounted to 375, including 300 Numidians.

Titus Livius (Livy), *History of Rome*, 30.11–12.4; Appianus (Appian), *Punic Wars*, 5.26.

Cirta, 106 BC (Jugurthine War) – During the fifth year of war against the Numidian king, Jugurtha, the Roman *consul* Caius Marius concentrated his legions on the systematic reduction of several key enemy fortresses. The campaign climaxed with the capture of the king's primary treasure house, located on the Muluccha (Moulouya) River near the Mauretanian frontier. Marius then elected to retire to winter quarters in the vicinity of Cirta (Constantine), 600 miles to the east. The seizure of so vast a store of wealth drove the Numidian monarch to seek the military aid of his father-in-law, Bocchus I, king of Mauretania. Now strengthened by Moorish infantry and cavalry, Numidian forces struck the Roman column twice during its long march, the last incident occurring on the outskirts of the port city of Cirta. As the Romans drew near the coast, scouts informed Marius of the presence of enemy forces in every direction. Since the *consul* could not ascertain the exact location of Jugurtha's main body from the reports provided, he elected to maintain his legions in battle-readiness for whatever situation might present itself. Four individual columns of enemy troops closed in around the Romans, each column deployed separately by the Numidian king in order to increase the likelihood that at least one detachment would be able to deliver a surprise assault against the Roman rear. When the decisive battle finally came, Marius' *quaestor*, Lucius Cornelius Sulla, led several squadrons of Roman horse in a successful series of rolling charges against the Moorish cavalry. At the same time, Jugurtha led the largest division of Numidians against the main Roman formation. As the king concentrated his attack on the Roman front line, the Moorish infantry, under Bocchus and his son Volux, struck the Roman rear. The cohorts were hard-pressed by the simultaneous assaults and struggled to hold their ground, when Sulla's cavalry, having finally routed the Moorish horsemen, fell with tremendous force on the flank of Bocchus' unsuspecting infantry. The attack served to relieve pressure on the legions, and Marius' front line was soon able to turn the momentum of the battle against Jugurtha's cavalry and put the king to flight. Both monarchs escaped the disaster, though thousands of their men died in this final battle of the North African war.

Caius Sallusticus Crispus (Sallust), *Jugurthine War*, 101; Paulus Orosius, *Seven Books of History against the Pagans*, 5.15; Plutarch, *Sulla*, 3.1–3.

Cissis, 218 BC (Second Punic War, Wars against Carthage) – Near the community of Cissis, located north of the Iberus (Ebro) River in eastern Spain, a Roman army under the command of the general Gnaeus Cornelius Scipio engaged an enemy force led by the Carthaginian commander Hanno. In the resulting fight, 6,000 Punic soldiers died and 2,000 were captured, including their leader. The Romans plundered the opposing camp following this victory.

Polybius, *Histories*, 3.76.2–6; Titus Livius (Livy), *History of Rome*, 21.60.5–9.

Clastidium, 222 BC – Three years after the decisive defeat of the Gauls at the Battle of Telamon, Roman armies under the consuls Marcus Claudius Marcellus and Gnaeus Cornelius Scipio Calvus entered the Po Valley in an effort to drive the Celtic Insubres out of northern Italy. Near the confluence of the Padus (Po) and Adda rivers, the legions invested the Insubrian city of Acerrae, a community in Cisalpine Gaul on the banks of the Adda River, approximately 14 miles from Cremona. Unable to force an end to this siege of their tribal kin by direct military means, the Insubres, with the support of their allies the Gaesatae, chose instead to besiege the town of Clastidium, situated south of the Padus River in the territory of the Anares, in the hope of forcing the Romans to abandon their assault on Acerrae in order to aid the oppressed Anamarian community. Apprised of the situation, Marcus Claudius led a small mixed force of 600 light infantry and cavalry to the relief of the besieged town. As the Roman force drew near Clastidium, it encountered a sizeable Celtic army of some 10,000 Gaesatae, who promptly lifted their siege of the beleaguered village and advanced against the *consul* in battle formation. Claudius responded with a sudden strong charge of cavalry, which was initially resisted by the enemy but gradually succeeded in undermining the Celtic position through flank and rear assaults. Incapable of checking these mounted attacks, the integrity of the Insubrian formation eventually collapsed into a total rout. In the flight which followed, many Celts attempted to swim the Padus, while larger numbers of warriors were slain on the field, overtaken by pursuing Romans. Following this victory, Claudius reunited with Gnaeus Cornelius, who was by then fully involved in the investment of the Celtic city of Mediolanum.

Plutarch, *Marcellus*, 6.2–7.4; Polybius, *Histories*, 2.34.1–9.

Clupea, 208 BC – During the summer of 208 BC, Marcus Valerius Laevinus led a fleet of 100 ships from Lilybaeum in Sicily to North Africa, landing

80 miles east of Carthage at the town of Clupea, south of the Hermaeum promontory. The subsequent Roman raid on the surrounding countryside was quickly aborted with the unexpected approach of a Carthaginian fleet of eighty-three vessels. After recovering his foragers, Valerius put to sea and soon engaged the Punic warfleet not far from the African coast. The Carthaginian ships were driven off in the ensuing fight, with the loss of eighteen vessels captured. Following this victory, the Roman flotilla returned to Lilybaeum.

Titus Livius (Livy), *History of Rome*, 27.29.7–9.

Clusium, 296 BC – see Camerinum, 296 BC.

Clusium, 225 BC – Descending through Etruria, a Celtic army encountered a Roman legionary force near the town of Clusium, approximately 85 miles north of Rome and a short distance southwest of Lake Trasimenus (Trasimeno). Though the armies were in close proximity to one another, a serious engagement was avoided on the first day by the onset of darkness. The Celtic infantry withdrew north during the night toward the community of Faesulae on the north bank of the Arnus (Arno) River, the cavalry having been instructed to follow after daybreak. The enemy horse departed at dawn in the wake of the main van of Gallic troops; and having been observed, were pursued closely by the Roman army. As they followed in the train of the retreating cavalry, the legionary column was suddenly and unexpectedly attacked by the Celtic infantry lying in ambush. Intense fighting erupted and the field was stubbornly contested by both sides, but eventually the superior numbers of the enemy forced the Romans to retreat to a nearby hill, having suffered 6,000 dead. The Gallic warriors immediately sought to drive the survivors from their elevated position by direct assault, but were sharply repulsed. The action was temporarily broken off with sunset, each army anticipating a renewal of battle at daybreak. That evening, the Celts, as well as the beleaguered remnants of the Roman contingent, recognized a distant cluster of camp-fires as those of a second Roman army, commanded by the *consul* Lucius Aemilius Papus. Faced with this new danger, the Gallic leadership determined to refrain from further combat and retreat northward under cover of nightfall, following the coast of Etruria. The next morning, having safely retrieved the Roman survivors, Aemilius elected not to give chase to the Celtic army.

Polybius, *Histories*, 2.25–26.

Clusium, 82 BC (Roman Civil Wars) – A desperate battle was fought between the armies of Lucius Cornelius Sulla and the *consul* Gnaeus Papirius Carbo near the Etruscan town of Clusium. The struggle proved indecisive, lasting throughout the day and only ending because of darkness.

Appianus (Appian), *Civil Wars*, 1.89.

Clusium, 82 BC (Roman Civil Wars) – The 30,000-man consular army of Gnaeus Papirius Carbo was defeated by the legions of Gnaeus Pompey at Clusium in Etruria. Some 20,000 of Carbo's soldiers were killed in the struggle, the *consul* himself having previously fled to North Africa following the earlier defeat of his forces at Placentia in northern Italy.

   Appianus (Appian), *Civil Wars*, 1.92; Titus Livius (Livy), *Summaries*, 88.

Clusius River, 223 BC – The year after the Roman victory at Telamon in Etruria, the *consul* Caius Flaminius initiated a campaign against the powerful Insubres of Gallia Transpadana. The consular army crossed the Padus (Po) River near its confluence with the Adda, not far from the village of Cremona, in preparation for launching a campaign into the tribe's territories. Uncertain of the Gauls' strength, Flaminius determined to cautiously advance against the enemy from an unexpected direction. The legions marched by a circuitous route through the territory of the Cenomani and approached the lands of the Insubres from the northwest. Alerted to the arrival of the consular army, the Gallic chieftains mobilized approximately 50,000 warriors as part of an effort to force a decisive clash with the invaders. The Romans encountered the Insubres shortly after crossing the Clusius (Chiese) River. Sending his Cenomani allies back across the river, Flaminius ordered the destruction of all bridges in the immediate area, and then drew the legions into battle formation with the water situated behind them. The tribunes armed the front line of Roman infantry with the long spears of the *triarii* in order to break the momentum of the initial Gallic charge. Once the Insubres spent themselves on the first assault, the legionaries locked shields and launched an attack which routed the enemy. The Insubres suffered heavy casualties as a result of the encounter.

   Polybius, *Histories*, 2.32–33.

Coblenz, 55 BC – see Mosa River, 55 BC.

Colline Gate, 477 BC – see Porta Collina, 477 BC.

Comana Pontica 68 BC (Third Mithridatic War, Wars against Mithridates the Great) – As the Roman *legatus* Caius Valerius Triarius travelled through Pontus to join his superior, Lucius Licinius Lucullus, he learned that a Roman force under his fellow legate, Marcus Fabius, was presently besieged in the city of Cabira (Niksar) by the army of Mithridates VI. Hastily gathering a makeshift force, he marched to the relief of Fabius. Word of Triarius' unexpected approach alarmed the king, who mistook the advancing body of troops for a much larger Roman army, and elected to withdraw without offering battle. Once Cabira was out of danger, Triarius pursued the king southward as far as the city of Comana (Gumenek), where his forces encountered the Pontic army camped on the opposite bank of the Iris (Yesil) River. The king immediately ordered an attack when he observed the exhausted condition of the Romans. Gathering his soldiers, Mithridates led the main body of his army over the bridge at Comana, while a secondary column was sent to cross another bridge in an effort to attack the Roman flank. The resulting struggle proved long and difficult for the king's van, and no reinforcements were forthcoming after the second bridge collapsed under the weight of Pontic troops. Following lengthy fighting, neither side was able to claim a decisive victory and both commanders later elected to end the campaign and withdraw to winter quarters.

Dio Cassius, *Roman History*, 36.10–11.1.

Complega, 179 BC – While the Romans were encamped near the Iberian town of Complega, 20,000 inhabitants of the community – declaring their peaceful intentions – visited the army's *castrum*. The *propraetor* Tiberius Sempronius Gracchus willingly received them as guests, whereupon they suddenly attacked the camp, throwing everything into disorder. Under the *propraetor*'s leadership, the legions abandoned the camp and feigned flight, but suddenly turned and overran the *castrum*, surprising the Complegians while engaged in plundering, and killing most of them. Thereafter, Sempronius assumed control of Complega.

Appianus (Appian), *Spanish Wars*, 43.

Comum, 196 BC – The year after the defeat of the Insubres at the Mincius (Mincio) River, the Roman *consul* Marcus Claudius Marcellus again moved against the Insubres, this time in the district of Comum (Como). After crossing the Padus (Po) River, the Gauls launched a sudden preemptive attack against the approaching army. The speed of the charge drove the front line of the Roman formation backward. Fearing that his command was in danger of being defeated if he failed to act quickly, Marcellus deployed his entire complement of Latin cavalry together with a cohort of Marci and charged the enemy forces. The effort successfully checked the momentum of the Gallic attack and served to rally the the Roman infantry, who soon initiated a vigorous counter-attack. The offensive routed the Insubres, who fled the field in confusion, and Claudius followed the victory by capturing the enemy encampment and a significant store of booty. More than 40,000 of the defeated army died in the battle.

Titus Livius (Livy), *History of Rome*, 33.36.9–15.

Contrebia, 181 BC – The town of Contrebia surrendered to the legions of the *praetor* Quintus Fulvius Flaccus after a brief siege. He then billeted his army inside the community because of heavy rains. Soon afterward, a Celtiberian army, coming to the relief of the Contrebians and unaware that the

Romans were in the town, was completely caught off-guard by a sudden Roman sally in mass. Having approached the town in scattered groups, the Celtiberians were unable to mount any ordered resistance and were quickly overwhelmed. The defeat was total: 12,000 died in the rout and 5,000 were taken prisoner by the Romans.

Titus Livius (Livy), *History of Rome*, 40.33.

Coracesium, 67 BC – In response to the escalation of piracy in the Mediterranean, the Senate appointed Cnaeus Pompeius Magnus to oversee a major campaign to eradicate the threat. He assumed the task with great alacrity, and, supported by a substantial allocation of manpower and ships, immediately set about deploying his resources to best effect. He completely ended the danger of corsairs in western waters within forty days. Then, diverting the necessary men and materials into the eastern Mediterranean and Aegean seas, he directed the fleet's energies against the concentration of fortresses and citadels maintained by freebooters along the Cilician coast near the Taurus Mountains. The Roman campaign culminated at the promontory of Coracesium when Pompey's warships defeated a pirate fleet in a naval battle fought in the local harbour. Following this victory, he successfully besieged the town. Pompey's tenacity ultimately compelled the total capitulation of the buccaneers. When the great struggle ended after three months, Roman forces had seized several hundred ships, occupied numerous towns, fortresses and outposts, captured 20,000 pirates and killed at least 10,000 others in numerous battles and sea actions.

Plutarch, *Pompey*, 28.1–2; Appianus (Appian), *Mithridatic Wars*, 14.96.

Corfinium, 49 BC, 18–24 January, (Roman Civil Wars, Wars of the First Triumvirate) – Following Julius Caesar's night crossing of the Rubicon River with the Thirteenth Legion in mid-December, the *triumvir* marched southward along the Adriatic coast toward Brundisium. At the town of Corfinium, thirty-three cohorts under Gnaeus Pompey's associates, Domitius Ahenobarbus and Vibullius Rufus, made ready to oppose the approaching army. Nearing the community on 18 January, Caesar secured a bridgehead across the Aternus River before deploying his army in preparation for the town's investment. Caesar's force numbered approximately 20,000 men, including thirty cohorts of new levies, together with the Eighth, Twelfth and Thirteenth legions. The contravallation of Corfinium began almost immediately. On 24 January, after only a seven-day siege, the garrison mutinied, surrendering Domitius and his officers Vibullius, Sextus Quintilius Varus and Lucius Rubrius to Caesarian forces.

Julius Caesar, *The Civil Wars*, 1.16–23; Dio Cassius, *Roman History*, 41.10–11.

Corinth, 146 BC – see Leucopetra, 146 BC.

Cremera River, 478 BC – Owing to the frequent depredations directed by the Veientes against Roman territory, the Fabian clan volunteered to use its manpower to police the Veientine border on behalf of the Roman people. To this end the Fabii constructed a fort on the Cremera River, a small tributary of the Tiber River, located north of the city. The garrison's presence aggravated the people of Veii, who resolved to summon an army from Etruria and attack the Roman outpost. In response, legions were deployed under the *consul* Lucius Aemilius Mamercus to counter the threat. The two armies gathered near the fort. As the Veientes began to form their battle line, a sudden strong charge by Roman cavalry against one flank of the enemy formation irretrievably disrupted the Etruscan cause. Unable to stand their ground, the army was driven off and compelled to sue for peace.

   Titus Livius (Livy), *History of Rome*, 2.49.9–12.

Cremera River, 477 BC – The presence of Fabian clansmen to patrol Rome's border with Veii successfully reduced chronic raiding by the Veientes into outlying Roman territory. The frequent victories achieved by the Fabii over Veientine marauders not only angered the people of Veii, but caused the clan militia to become overconfident. This rashness proved detrimental. A numerically superior Etruscan formation ambushed the Fabii near the Cremera River. The clansmen formed into a tactical wedge and battled their way through the massed enemy, only to be encircled again, this time on the gentle slope of a hill. After an intense struggle, the entire Fabian force of 306 was killed and their fort captured.

   Titus Livius (Livy), *History of Rome*, 2.50; Dionysius of Halicarnassus, *Roman Antiquities*, 9.19–21.

Cremona, 200 BC – After the defeat of Hannibal the previous year in a decisive battle near the village of Zama in North Africa, and while Rome's attention was still focused on achieving victory over the Macedonians under King Philip V, a number of Gallic tribes – including the Boii, Cenomani and Insubres – suddenly attacked the Latin colony of Placentia in the Po Valley of northern Italy. Under the leadership of a Carthaginian general named Hamilcar, the Gallic force of 40,000 sacked the settlement and killed a considerable number of colonists before advancing against the colony of Cremona. Having learned of the fate of neighbouring Placentia, Cremona closed its gates and prepared for a siege while the provincial governor, Lucius Furius Purpurio, informed the Roman Senate of this fresh outbreak of violence and requested additional legions to be dispatched to the region. Following the arrival of a consular army, Lucius Furius moved the entire Roman force, including 5,000 Latin allies, to the vicinity of Cremona and prepared for action. The two opposing encampments were situated about a mile and a half apart. The Gallic army offered battle the following day. Lucius Furius responded by arraying his force with the allied contingents positioned in the front line and the two consular legions held in reserve. The Gauls opened the battle with an assault intended to overwhelm the Roman right, but the move was successfully checked. Failing in their initial attempt to disrupt the Roman formation, the Gauls then sought to envelop the Roman line with their superior numbers. Lucius Furius capably countered this man-oeuvre by deploying his legions on both flanks in order to extend his front line. Having stopped the momentum of the Gallic attack, and with the enemy line dangerously attenuated by the attempted envelopment, Lucius Furius quickly ordered the Roman and allied cavalry to charge the Gauls' flanks while his infantry pressed home a concerted assault in an effort to penetrate the enemy's centre. The move resulted in the complete collapse of the Gallic battle line. The legions overran the enemy encampment in the ensuing rout, with some 36,000 Gauls killed or captured, including Hamilcar.

Titus Livius (Livy), *History of Rome*, 31: 10, 21.

Croton, 204 BC (Second Punic War, Wars against Carthage) – Near the southern Italian coastal city of Croton, 7 miles northwest of the Lacinian promontory, the legions of the Roman *consul* Publius Sempronius Tuditanus engaged a Carthaginian army under the command of Hannibal Barca. The two armies fought a disorganized action in column while on the march, resulting in a confused tactical encounter. The battle ended with 1,200 Romans dead. The following night, Sempronius was joined by a second con-sular army led by Publius Licinius Crassus Dives. Encouraged by the addi-tional manpower, Sempronius arrayed his legion in battle formation, with those of Licinius held in reserve, and challenged the Punic force to battle. In the engagement that followed, Hannibal's army was routed with the loss of 4,000 killed and just less than 300 captured.

Titus Livius (Livy), *History of Rome*, 29.36.4–9.

Cuballum, 189 BC –A consular army under Cnaeus Manlius Vulso encoun-tered a force of Gallic cavalry while encamped near the Galatian fortress of Cuballum. The enemy unexpectedly attacked the Roman advanced guard, killing some men and throwing the rest into confusion. In response, the *consul* dispatched elements of his cavalry, who quickly routed the barbarian horse-men with considerable loss.

Titus Livius (Livy), *History of Rome*, 36.18.5–6

Cumae, 38 BC (Roman Civil Wars) – Despite an agreement at Misenum in 39 BC between Sextius Pompeius and the triumvirs Caius Octavius and Marc Antony that ended the former's naval blockade of Rome, the antagonists could not long avoid a resumption of war. All sides soon began to engage in provocative behaviour that threatened to undo the settlement. After the admiral Menodorus, Sextius' trusted governor of Sardinia, finally defected with his legions and fleet to Octavius, the war erupted afresh. Within a short time, Pompeius ordered those ships commanded by his new fleet admiral, Menecrates, to once again begin harassing the coast of Italy and intercepting grain transports sailing between North Africa and Rome. Octaviaus' fleet, under the joint command of Calvisius Sabinus and Menodorus, sighted the Pompeian flotilla near the Campanian coast around sunset one evening and elected to withdraw for the night to the relative safety of the Bay of Cumae (Bay of Naples). They assembled their ships for battle at dawn the following day near the city of Cumae on the northern coast of the bay. Drawing their vessels together in a crescent formation close to shore, the admirals awaited the arrival of the Pompeians. Not long after, Menecrates' squadron reached the location and immediately launched an assault. The initial attack sought to dislodge the Octavians from their defensive position in shallow water, but when this failed Menecrates resorted instead to pushing his adversaries back against the coastline. The tactic eventually succeeded in grounding some of Menodorus' and Calvisius' ships on the rocks. While the enemy was constrained by land on one side and his own craft on the other, Menecrates used his access to open water to rotate fresh vessels into the fighting. By this means he gradually wore down the opposition. The flagships of Menecrates and Menodorus were soon locked in a vicious struggle on the Pompeian left wing. This contest was fuelled by the mutual animosity long shared between the two admirals. Both ships were heavily damaged in the stubborn encounter, and Menecrates committed suicide after the capture of his *quadrireme*. In the midst of the fighting, Calvisius was able to separate some of the Pompeian ships from the main body and pursue them out to open sea, but his absence allowed Menecrates' warships, now under the command of Demochares, to concentrate on destroying the enemy vessels left behind. The eventual return of Calvisius put an end to this destruction, and likewise signalled an end to the engagement. Afterward, the Pompeians retired to Sicily, having inflicted serious damage to Octavius' fleet. Only one ship, that of Menecrates, was lost by the victors.

Appianus (Appian), *Civil Wars*, 5.81–83; Dio Cassius, *Roman History*, 48.46.5.

Curicta, 49 BC (Roman Civil Wars) – When Caesar decided to pursue Pompey's armies in Spain, he assigned the security of Illyria to his lieutenants, Publius Cornelius Dolabella and Caius Antonius; the former to secure the upper Adriatic Sea by means of a small fleet, and the latter employing military forces on the mainland. The responsibility of the two, especially Dolabella, was made extremely difficult by the presence of larger Pompeian fleets operating in the same waters under Marcus Octavius and Lucius Scribonius Libo. The circumstance proved untenable to both parties, and inevitably led to a decisive naval battle that ended in the defeat of Dolabella off Illyricum. This loss gravely imperilled the forces of Antonius, which were presently in residence on the island of Curicta (Krk) in the northern Adriatic Sea. Learning of his location, Octavius and Libo moved to blockade the coastal island and force the capitulation of the Caesarians. In order to achieve this, it was critical that the Pompeian fleets cut off Antonius' access to the Illyrian coast approximately a mile away. As the investment of Curicta wore on, the Caesarians lost support from the local population, further isolating the trapped army, which was suffering badly from a shortage of foodstuffs. In the midst of the siege, the Pompeians discovered three raft-loads of troops attempting to cross the channel between the island and mainland. After much trouble, two of the makeshift vessels managed to elude their pursuers, while a third carrying 1,000 auxiliaries from the town of Opitergium (Odenzo) in Cisalpine Gaul grounded in shallow water on the mainland coast and was surrounded by Pompeian troops. Unable to escape after a determined fight to avoid capture, the entire contingent committed suicide. Left with no hope of succour, Antonius ultimately surrendered his entire army on Curicta.

Lucius Annaeus Florus, *Epitomy*, 2.13.30–33; Dio Cassius, *Roman History*, 41.40; Marcus Annaeus Lucanus (Lucan), *Pharsalia* (*De Bello civili*), 4.402–581; Suetonius, *Julius Caesar*, 36. The accounts offered by Florus and Dio Cassius do not agree on the subject of the three rafts.

Cydonia, 69 BC (Third Mithridatic War, Wars against Mithridates the Great) – After authorities on Crete disdainfully rejected an initial overture by the Romans to desist from providing aid to pirates operating in the southern Aegean Sea, a second peace embassy likewise failed to stop the Cretans' provocative activities. A Roman army under Quintus Caecilius Metellus landed on the island in response, with the intention of ending the matter by force. Metellus defeated an army led by the Cretan leader Lysthenes near the port of Cydonia (Chania) on the northwestern coast. Following the surrender of the city by Panares, Metellus continued his campaign until the entire island was completely subdued.

Appianus (Appian), *Sicily and the Other Islands* (fragments), 6.1–2.

Cynoscephalae, 197 BC (Second Macedonian War, Wars against Macedon) – King Philip V of Macedonia and an army of 20,000 men clashed with a comparable Roman force under the *proconsul* Titus Quinctius Flamininus. The battle occurred following an unexpected encounter by advanced elements of both armies in fog on a low range of hills called Cynoscephalae. This initial skirmish steadily evolved into a larger engagement as both armies committed more troops to the struggle. A Roman force of 2,000 infantry and 500 horse, mostly Aeolian allies sent in relief, was itself driven back along with the hard-pressed advanced party by an opposing composite relief force of Thessalian and Macedonian cavalry, and mercenaries deployed by Philip. Having arrayed his legions south of Cynoscephalae, Flamininus moved the left half of the Roman main body toward the approaching Macedonian army, while holding the right wing with twenty war elephants in reserve. Philip, likewise pressed by the rapidly escalating nature of the engagement, advanced with only the centre and right wing of his phalanx completely assembled; the left, under his general Nicanor, having not fully deployed for battle. To the right of the Macedonian phalanx were deployed the army's supporting cavalry and light infantry, leaving the disarrayed Macedonian left flank fully exposed. Philip opened the battle with a phalanx attack from higher ground. The momentum of this assault initially drove back the Roman left, but broken ground further disrupted the cohesion of the Macedonian line, causing an attenuation of the entire phalangial formation, and permitting the legions and elephants of the Roman right under Flamininus to launch a charge which gained complete victory in that quarter. With the defeat of Nicanor's left now assured, a Roman tribune detached twenty maniples from the legions on the right and attacked the flank and rear of the remaining Macedonian formation. The assault shattered all Macedonian resistance on the right. Philip's defeat was total. Macedonian

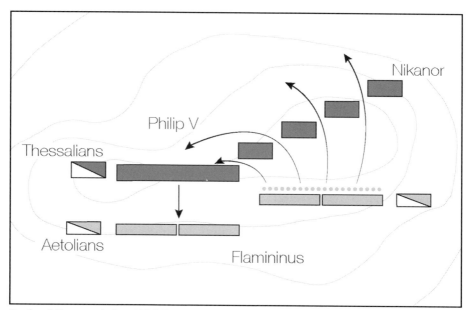

Battle of Cynoscephalae, 197 BC

losses amounted to 8,000 killed and 5,000 captured. Roman casualties numbered 700 dead.

Polybius, *Histories*, 18.18–27; Titus Livius (Livy), *History of Rome*, 33.7–10; Plutarch, *Flamininus*, 7–8.

Cypsela, 188 BC – After the completion of a successful campaign in Galatia, the Roman *consul* Cnaeus Manlius Vulso journeyed home to Italy in the company of his army. He employed the fleet of Eumenes II, king of Pergamum, to ferry the legions to Europe, and then elected to march overland through Thracia. Near the community of Cypsela, the army faced the task of traversing a narrow, rugged, 10-mile expanse of road surrounded by heavy forests. As a precaution against the possibility of attack by unseen enemies, the *consul* divided his command, placing half of his army in the van and deploying the remaining portion of his legionary infantry and ancillary forces some distance behind as a rearguard. In order to secure the army's material possessions, Manlius situated the baggage train between the two formations, including those carts carrying public money and booty. As the long column marched along the wooded track, a force of some 10,000 Thracian warriors suddenly launched an attack from the surrounding forest in an effort to isolate and plunder the army's baggage. When troops in the van and those approaching from the rear heard the tumult, both converged on the centre, but the narrow confines of the defile prevented the cohorts from properly forming into battle array. What followed was a disorderly struggle that continued unabated until dusk, when the Thracians elected to retreat after having secured sufficient spoils. The legions were again involved in a difficult battle the next day before finally crossing the Hebrus (Evros) River 30 miles north of the Aegean coastline, having suffered heavy casualties during two days of fighting.

Titus Livius (Livy), *History of Rome*, 38.40; Appianus (Appian), *Syrian Wars*, 43

Cyrnus River, 66 BC (Third Mithridatic War, Wars against Mithridates the Great) – Placing the affairs of Armenia in the charge of his legate Lucius Afranius, Gnaeus Pompeius marched in pursuit of Mithridates VI Eupator, king of Pontus, toward the Colchis. As his legions advanced through the mountains of the Caucasus, the lateness of the campaign season ultimately forced Pompey's army into winter quarters in the region of Caucasian Albania. The Romans were distributed in three camps under the authority of Pompey and his generals Metellus Celer and Lucius Flaccus. While the legions were encamped, the Albanian King Oroeses – who had earlier granted Pompey free passage through his territories – assembled a force of some 40,000 warriors and marched against Celer. At the same time he dispatched additional forces to prevent Pompey and Flaccus from sending aid to their beleaguered colleague. Artoces, king of Iberia (Georgia), provided thousands of additional troops in support of Oroeses, raising the total size of the barbarian army to perhaps 70,000. Despite such manpower, Oroeses' plan to overwhelm the Romans by means of surprise assault failed. Celer and then Flaccus in turn repulsed attacks directed against their encampments. Upon learning of the Albanian's actions, Pompey immediately moved his legions against the king. The two armies clashed near the Cyrnus River. Oroeses was badly defeated in the ensuing battle and sued for peace. Pompey then marched against the Iberians and in a single decisive engagement routed all opposition, killing 9,000 men and capturing an additional 10,000.

Dio Cassius, *Roman History*, 54; Plutarch, *Pompey*, 34; Appianus (Appian), *Mithridatic Wars*, 104.

Cyssus, 191 BC (War of Antiochus III) – As part of the ongoing struggle against the Seleucid King Antiochus III, a Roman fleet sailed into Aegean waters under command of the *praetor* Caius Livius Salinator. After taking on provisions at Chios, the Romans relocated to the Anatolian port of Phocaea, where they were soon joined by twenty-four decked warships and a slightly larger squadron of *pentekontors* under the command of Eumenes II, king of Pergamum. The flotilla headed for the coastal city of Corycus in Cilicia. The force included a total of 105 ships, including fifty *pentekontors*. On learning of the enemy's approach, Antiochus' admiral, Polyxenidas, departed from the harbour at Cyssus (Cesme) with a large fleet, including seventy decked craft and at least thirty *pentekontors*. Once in open water, he arrayed his command in a single line, the right wing extended toward the coast and the left out to sea, and advanced toward the oncoming ships. As the opposing lines drew closer, two Carthaginian warships ahead of the Roman formation clashed with three enemy vessels. One of the Punic ships was captured, being badly damaged in the struggle. Livius' flagship quickly arrived on the scene, and using grappling hooks, employed boarding crews to seize two of the attackers. While the *praetor*'s squadrons on the right wing began pressing their assault, Eumenes steered to the left in an effort to charge Polyxenidas' line of vessels on the right. The encounters soon grew into a single general engagement involving the total complement of both fleets. As the battle reached maturity, a few enemy ships on the left flank began to take flight, followed shortly by the entire wing. Not long after, those ships fighting Eumenes' vessels near the shore also began to retire. Following a futile chase after Polyxenidas' squadrons, the Roman and Pergamene ships finally ended the pursuit and retired to Corycus. The royal fleet suffered ten ships sunk and thirteen captured in the day's contest. Livius sustained the loss of only one Carthaginian craft.

Titus Livius (Livy), *History of Rome*, 36.43–45.4; Appianus (Appian), *Syrian Wars*, 5.22.

Cyzicus, 74 BC (Third Mithradatic War, Wars against Mithradates the Great) – Following his invasion of Bithynia, Mithridates VI Eupator, king of Pontus, besieged the port city of Cyzicus by land and sea. In response, the Roman general Lucius Licinius Lucullus encamped a short distance from the city near the village of Thracia with an army of five legions and 1,600 cavalry, and abruptly moved to disrupt the king's supplies in order to deny the enemy provisions. While the Cyziceans successfully resisted the king's efforts to breach the walls by siege machinery, the Romans steadily gained control of surrounding roads and land from which the Pontic army sought to garner materials. The diminishing foodstuffs eventually compelled Mithridates to dispatch a large contingent of his cavalry and supply animals, as well as many of his wounded infantry, to Bithynia in an effort to ease the consumption of his stores. However, this force was overtaken and destroyed by Lucullus as it sought to cross the Rhyndacus River. Undeterred, Mithridates continued to press forward with the investment of Cyzicus. With the onset of winter, the king's army was no longer supplied by sea, and the army gradually began to suffer from the effects of starvation and plague. These hardships, and the army's inability to capture the city, finally led Mithridates to abandon the siege. He fled by night with his fleet to Parius, while his army withdrew toward Lampsacus on the shores of the Hellespont. This latter force, inhibited in its journey by the rain-swollen Aesepus River*, was attacked by Lucullus. The Romans killed 20,000 enemy soldiers in the ensuing battle, and a large number were taken captive. The remainder of the Pontic army eventually reached Lampsacus, where it was briefly invested by legionary forces before being successfully extricated by Mithridates' fleet and transported to Nicomedia.

> Appianus (Appian), *Mithridatic Wars*, 72–76; Plutarch, *Lucullus*, 9–11; *or Granicus River, see Plutarch, *Lucullus*, 11.8

Dertosa, 215 BC – see Iberus River, 215 BC.

Dipo, 185 BC – see Toletum 185 BC.

Drepana, 249 BC (First Punic War, Wars against Carthage) – After more than fourteen years of war, only the Carthaginian-held western Sicilian ports of Lilybaeum (Marsala) and Drepana (Trapani) remained to be reduced by Roman siege. Having suffered heavy casualties in their ongoing investment of Lilybaeum, the *consul* Publius Claudius Pulcher redirected a portion of the Roman fleet – including newly arrived reinforcements from Italy – against Drepana, 40 miles to the north. Setting sail around midnight, the flotilla arrived off the coast opposite Drepana at daybreak. Observing the approaching enemy, Carthaginian commander Adherbal determined to put his ships to sea in an effort to avoid a blockade. As Claudius entered the harbour, expecting to cow the enemy by his bold attack, he was quickly taken aback by the action of the Punic squadrons, who dashed for the open sea and when clear of the harbour entrance immediately turned to face the coastline, arrayed line-abeam, with the clear intent of offering battle. The unforeseen move caught the *consul*'s fleet ill-prepared to accept the challenge, resulting in confusion and some damage to ships as various Roman vessels, suddenly coming about in the harbour, fouled their unsuspecting companions still seeking entry. When all eventually extricated themselves from the confined waters of the port, the Roman *quinqueremes* formed into a line near the shore, their prows facing the opposing formation of ships. Once battle was joined, the speed, agility and tactical advantage of the Punic craft proved decisive; while the location of the Roman vessels inshore restricted their ability to manoeuvre. After protracted fighting, the engagement turned against the Romans and Claudius promptly fled the struggle with thirty ships, electing to abandon the remaining ninety-three to the Carthaginians.

Polybius, *Histories*, 1.49–50; Diodorus Siculus, *Historical Library*, 24.1.5.

Dyrrhachium, 48 BC (Roman Civil Wars) – The ongoing conflict between the former political allies Gnaeus Pompeius Magnus and Caius Julius Caesar eventually moved from Italy to the eastern Adriatic coast near the city of Dyrrhachium. With Pompey's armies located in Macedonia, Caesar determined to move his forces into the region in order to further prosecute hostilities against his co-*triumvir*. The threat of intervention by a sizeable Pompeian fleet operating in the Adriatic forced Caesar to undertake a perilous winter crossing from Brundusium with seven legions and 600 cavalry during the January of 48 BC. The landing occurred north of Corcyra, where a 110-ship Pompeian fleet lay at anchor, unaware of Caesar's arrival. The audacity of the move was soon proven when Pompey's admiral, Marcus Calpurnius Bibilus, destroyed thirty of the transports on their return voyage. Outside Dyrrhachium, Caesar and Pompey camped opposite one another across the Apsus River. Here the opposing cavalry occasionally skirmished, but neither commander was yet willing to undertake a general engagement. The loss of transports alerted the Pompeians to Caesar's activities, making it impossible for him to move the remainder of his army from Italy. The situation now left Caesar isolated with a shortage of men and materials. All remained unchanged, and no more reinforcements were forthcoming, until the *legatus* Marcus Antonius braved a sea crossing, circumvented a Pompeian naval blockade and landed on the Epirotic coast north of Dyrrhachium with four legions and about 800 horse. Pompey attempted to prevent a juncture between Caesar and his lieutenant, but failing in that, retired to a position near the bay of Dyrrhachium. This placed him in a strong position to resist

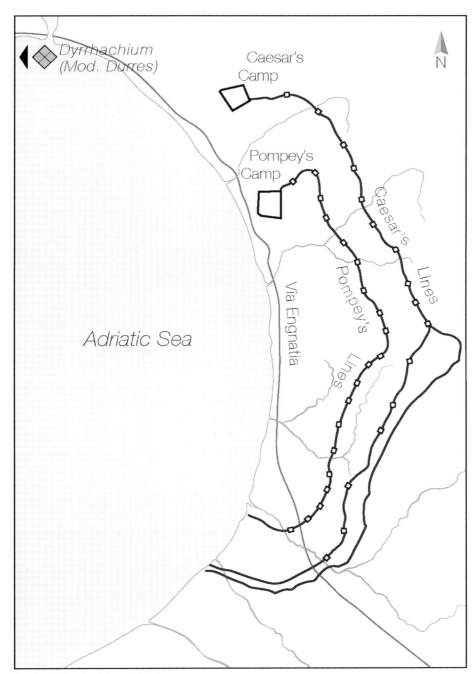

Battle of Dyrrhachium, 48 BC

Caesar, while at the same time allowing the ships of Bibilus' successor, Lucius Scribonius Libo, to resupply his army at will. Both armies settled into the new location over the next several weeks. Using the surrounding topography to his advantage, Caesar gradually extended siege lines around Pompey's encampment, which was located east-southeast of the community of Dyrrhachium. Pompey responded by constructing interior lines of contravallation which covered a circuit of approximately 15 miles. The armies were thereafter frequently engaged in skirmishing. As the investment continued, Pompey found it increasingly difficult to acquire the necessary water, supplies and fodder from the land still under his control. At the same time, such problems slowly abated for Caesar, in large part due to his access to the region's agricultural bounty. The growing shortages eventually forced Pompey to act. He relocated six legions and some light infantry from their positions along the northern defensive works, and attacked the uncompleted Caesarian lines to the south near the sea. Only the *Legio IX* under the *quaestor* Lentulus Marcellinus defended this location, and was insufficient to repel the coming mass assault. At daybreak, the Pompeian legions suddenly opened the battle by storming a section of earthworks near the coast that were guarded by only two cohorts of the Ninth. As the heavy infantry rapidly closed in from the north, the defenders were simultaneously subjected to withering missile fire delivered by light infantry moving against the defences on the south. In the midst of this fighting, some of the light troops also managed to penetrate an area of unfinished defences on the extreme left and take the beleaguered legion in one flank. Unable to effectively cope with the immense pressure of the Pompeian attack, the *Legio IX* disintegrated. The rout was checked near the camp of the Ninth by the arrival of twelve Caesarian cohorts under Marcus Antonius, followed shortly by the appearance of additional cohorts led by Caesar himself. These forces managed to contain the enemy assault, but were unable to recover lost ground. Pompey quickly secured control of the site by the construction of a strongly fortified *castrum*. Later that same day, Caesar attempted to redress the situation by capturing an older enemy encampment situated to the north of his opponent's new outpost. His effort to overrun this garrison with thirty-three cohorts ultimately failed when five legions redirected by Pompey launched a counter-attack from the new camp that successfully repulsed the Caesarian right wing. This failure on the right rippled down the entire length of Caesar's battle line and ultimately caused his left to likewise collapse in disorder and retreat. With his army now demoralized after two defeats, Caesar elected to lift the siege and withdraw from Dyrrhachium toward Thessaly. A total of 960 of his men died in the day's engagements. Pompey's casualties are not recorded by the sources.

Julius Caesar, *The Civil Wars*, 3.62–71; Appianus (Appian) *Civil Wars*, 2.60–62; Dio Cassius, *Roman History*; 41.50; Plutarch, *Caesar*, 30–32.

Ecnomus, 256 BC (First Punic War, Wars against Carthage) – After achieving a number of victories on land and sea, the Romans confidently prepared to expand the war by invading the African mainland and threatening Punic territory. Aware of Rome's intentions, the Carthaginians were equally determined to defeat any attempts to endanger their homeland. Thus, both sides prepared for a further intensification of hostilities. In early summer, a Roman fleet of 330 decked warships departed mainland Italy from Regium (Reggio di Calabria) and briefly put in at Messana (Messina) before continuing on to Ecnomus (Monte Cufino) on Sicily's southern coast. Once there, the ships rendezvoused with the Roman army in preparation for the expedition to North Africa. Unknown to the consuls Marcus Atilius Regulus and Lucius Manlius Vulso, a hostile force of 350 Punic vessels was presently at Heraclea Minoa, 35 miles west of their position. When everything was in

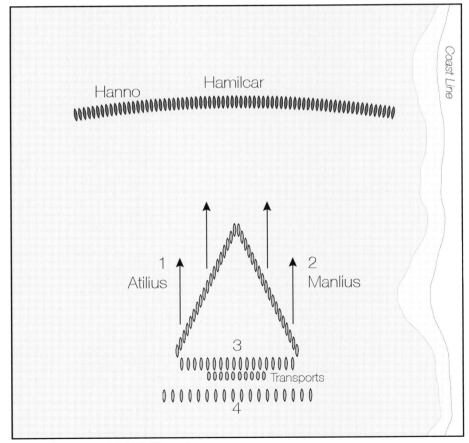

Battle of Ecnomus, 256 BC (Phase 1)

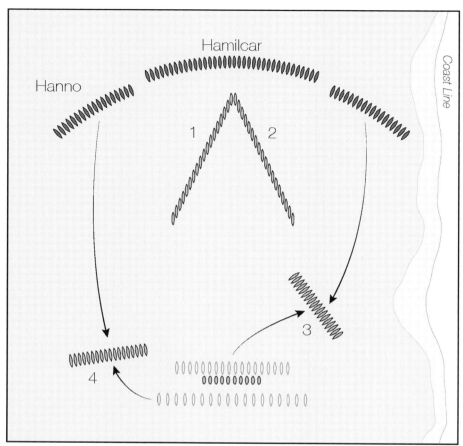

Battle of Ecnomus, 256 BC (Phase 2)

readiness, the Roman fleet put to sea. For defensive purposes, the Roman warships were arranged in a large triangular formation; the first and second squadrons forming the leading sides of the wedge with their ships *en echelon*, the third arrayed in a line at the base with the fleet's horse transports (*ιππηγοι*) in tow, and a fourth squadron of warships stationed in the rear with its line attenuated so that each end extended beyond the limits of the two preceding lines of craft. Sailing abreast of each other, and leading the Roman formation, were the two *hexereis* commanded by the consuls. As the entire formation steered southwestward toward the African coast, it was intercepted by the Carthaginians, who deployed their vessels in a single row – line-abeam – across the path of the approaching Roman host: the right wing was under the command of Hanno and the centre was led by Hamilcar. On the extreme left, extending toward the coastline, an additional line of Punic ships was situated

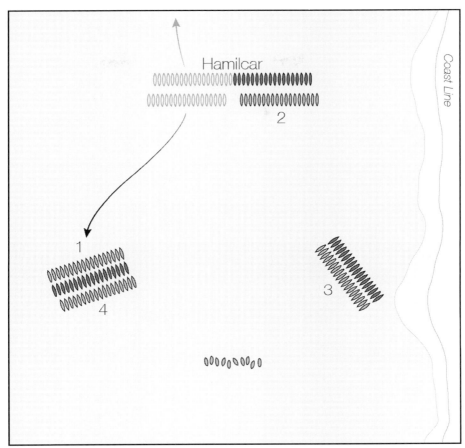

Battle of Ecnomus, 256 BC (Phase 3)

at a shallow angle to the rest of the fleet. The battle opened with a Roman attack against the opposing centre. When the *quinqueremes* of the two leading squadrons bore down on the enemy line, the ships of the Carthaginian centre withdrew in an attempt to draw the pair of approaching squadrons away from those at the back of the Roman formation. Once Hamilcar determined that the pursuing squadrons were sufficiently detached from the remainder of their fleet, he ordered his ships to turn and engage the enemy. Meanwhile, the ships of Hanno swept forward unmolested, skirted the Roman left flank and attacked the fourth squadron in the rear. At the same time, the Carthaginian vessels stationed on the far left charged against the third squadron towing the transports. As a result, the engagement devolved into three separate sea battles. Following protracted fighting, the consuls routed Hamilcar's squadron in the centre, and then Atilius turned his victorious ships against the

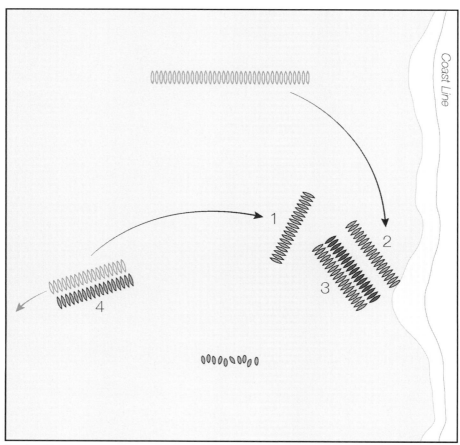

Battle of Ecnomus, 256 BC (Phase 4)

Punic craft presently assaulting the rear. Trapped between the warships of the fourth squadron and those of Atilius, Hanno elected to retreat. The first and second squadrons then collectively moved to relieve the beleaguered third squadron and claim the victory. At the end of the day's action, Roman losses totalled twenty-four ships, while the Carthaginians suffered thirty craft sunk and sixty-four captured in what was perhaps the greatest naval battle ever fought in the ancient world.

Polybius, *Histories*, 1.25.7–1.28.

Elinga, 206 BC – see Ilipa, 206 BC.

Elpeus River, 168 BC (Third Macedonian War, Wars against Macedon) – After three years of inconclusive war, Rome now shouldered the task of defeating Perseus, king of Macedon. Thus far they had failed to deliver a decisive blow to the Macedonian monarch. The victory of a Roman army at Phalanna in 171 BC was sufficient to force Perseus to retire into Macedonia, but three years later the king remained an untempered threat to Roman authority in the Balkan peninsula. By the spring of 168 BC, he and an army of 40,000 infantry and 4,000 cavalry were securely ensconced in a fortified encampment east of the village of Dius (Dio) on the banks of the Elpeus, a small river in northern Greece which flowed from the lower slopes of Mount Olympos and emptied into the Thermaicus sinus (Thermaic Gulf, Gulf of Salonika). To resolve the ongoing war, the Roman Senate dispatched the *consul* Lucius Aemilius Paulus, who soon advanced with his legions into Thessaly in mid-spring and camped on the southern bank of the Elpeus, opposite the Macedonians. Significant winter runoff negated any possibility of an imme-diate crossing, so each side waited in preparation for the inevitable clash. By late summer, the water flow had subsided enough to permit access to the far shore, but the banks of the river rose precipitously from the waters' edge, creating a difficult barrier for an army to cross. Compounding this risk was the rugged condition of the mile-wide riverbed; an area sufficient to permit tactical manoeuvre, but difficult for heavy infantry to traverse. Unable to prosecute a frontal attack without accruing heavy casualties, Aemilius elected to attempt outflanking the Macedonian position. Aware that the northern approaches to Mount Olympos were guarded by Macedonian garrisons at Petra and Pythios, the *consul* ordered his lieutenant, Publius Scipio Nasica, to lead a force of 8,000 Roman and allied infantry and 120 cavalry on a circuitous route along the southern base of Olympos to an unguarded pass through Perrhaedia on the western side of the mountain. This path would permit Scipio's troops to circumvent the headwaters of the Elpeus, on the eastern slopes of the mountain, and approach Perseus' encampment from the rear. In order to mask the movements of this mobilized column, Aemilius used diversionary engagements at the river to fix the attention of the king. For two days Roman *velites* skirmished with Macedonian light infantry in the open expanse of the dry river bed, and on the third day the *consul* refrained from battle and feigned preparations for a major assault using his legions. The magnitude of the threat forced Perseus to orient his army to receive the attack. While these events were going on, the king was suddenly alerted to Scipio's activities and sent a force of 10,000 mercenaries and 2,000 Macedonians under his general Milo with instructions to close all of the passes offering possible ingress to the Romans. These troops reached their appointed post but were surprised by Scipio and routed in a night action near Pythios. With his flank now decisively turned by Scipio's victory, Perseus elected to retire north toward Pydna. Aemilius went in pursuit, shortly joined by the troops of Scipio Nasica.

Titus Livius (Livy), *History of Rome*, 44.35.8–24; Plutarch, *Aemilius Paulus*, 13.4–16.5.

Emporiae, 195 BC (Wars in Spain) – Cognizant of the fact that the clashes at Turda and Iliturgi were representative of a growing insurrection in north-eastern Spain, the Senate dispatched the *consul* Marcus Porcius Cato to assume command of the war in *Hispania Citerior* (Eastern Spain). The army landed on the northern Iberian coast and encamped near the city of Emporiae (Ampurias). For weeks after his arrival, Cato led raids into the surrounding countryside in an effort to provide his soldiers with experience against the enemy. When he adjudged his forces to be in readiness, the army moved against a major encampment of hostile tribesmen located in the immediate vicinity of the Roman position. Marching under cover of darkness to a location near the enemy, the *consul* drew up his battle line at dawn, and then sent nine maniples near the fortifications of the Spanish camp in order to provoke the enemy to arms. Having successfully roused the opposition, the detachment then executed a feigned withdrawal to induce the Iberians to advance toward the main Roman formation. While the enemy spilled onto the battlefield and was still in disorder, Cato launched his attack. The cavalry rushed against both flanks, but was promptly repulsed on the right, causing a mild panic within the ranks of the Roman infantry stationed there. To stem this fear, the *consul* ordered six maniples to manoeuvre behind the Spanish right flank and threaten the enemy rear. This action served to steady the Roman right wing, but it still remained in danger of collapsing so long as the men were subjected to random missile fire from the opposing infantry. On the left and centre, the Romans slowly began to assert significant sustained pressure against the leading ranks of the enemy, who were still threatened by the half-dozen maniples to their rear. Gradually, a grim resolution translated down the entire length of the Roman line. Once the right wing finally came into direct contact with the Spanish left, the resulting hand-to-hand contest reinvigorated the confidence of the attending maniples and the entire formation stabilized. The battle now became a duel of stamina. Following prolonged fighting, the experienced Cato – with measured calculation – withdrew his exhausted front line of *hastati* and ordered reserve maniples to move forward. The sudden injection of fresh reinforcements permitted the Romans to launch an irresistible charge into the flagging ranks of the enemy. As the wedge-shaped formation of the *principes* bore into the centre of the opposing line, it completely shattered all Spanish resistance, triggering a rout. When the *consul* was satisfied that the enemy's resolve was irreparably broken on the battlefield, he ordered his second legion, which thus far had been withheld from the engagement, to aid in assaulting the enemy camp. The added strength of the additional legion helped to completely overwhelm all remaining Spanish defences. The encampment was taken with great slaughter and subsequently plundered. More than 40,000 Iberians died in the day's action.

Titus Livius (Livy), *History of Rome*, 34.13–15; Appianus (Appian), *Wars in Spain*, 8.40.

Eretum, 449 BC – Approximately 17 miles northeast of Rome, near the community of Eretum, the Sabines routed a Roman army commanded by the *decemvir* Quintus Fabius Vibulanus. The legions withdrew from Eretum under cover of darkness and re-established their camp near the Tiber River between the towns of Fidenae and Crustumeria. The Sabines shortly followed, but the Romans refused to engage the enemy on open ground, preferring to remain within the protected confines of the legionary camp.

Titus Livius (Livy), *History of Rome*, 3.42.3–4.

Erisana, 140 BC (Virathic War, Wars in Spain) – While continuing his pursuit of the Lusitanian leader Viriathus, the Roman *consul* Quintus Fabius Maximus Servilianus besieged the town of Erisana, one of the communities which had provided support to the rebel chieftain. As the Romans began to construct their lines of circumvallation, Viriathus and a portion of his army entered the town under cover of darkness. At dawn the following morning, they attacked and drove off the Roman troops excavating the trenches. In response, Servilianus assembled his army into battle formation. The Lusitanian chieftain willingly accepted the challenge and defeated the legions, driving them against some nearby cliffs. Trapped with no way to escape, the Romans accepted an offer to parley. In the resulting treaty, Viriathus demanded only that the Lusitanian people be recognized as *amici populi Romani* (friends of the Roman people), and Servilianus decreed that the Lusitani retain all of the lands they presently occupied. These provisions were later ratified by the Roman Senate, though incoming *consul* Quintus Servilius Caepio was instructed to renew the war.

Appianus (Appian), *Wars in Spain*, 12.69.

Faesulae, 225 BC – see Clusium, 225 BC.

Falernus Mons, 90 BC (Social War/Marsic War) – Near Mount Falernus in eastern Italy, a combined Italian army under the generals Titus Lafrenius, Gaius Vidacilius and Publius Vettius defeated the legions of the Roman legate Gnaeus Pompeius. Following this defeat, Pompey withdrew to the protection of the nearby Picentine city of Firmum.

Appianus (Appian), *Civil Wars*, 1.47.

Faventia, 82 BC (Roman Civil Wars) – Shortly before nightfall, Caius Norbanus and Gnaeus Papirius Carbo prepared to attack the Sullan forces of Quintus Caecilius Metellus Pius encamped in Faventia in far northern Italy. As the army advanced in the darkness toward Metellus' position, it became hopelessly disorganized while attempting to pass through some local vineyards. This vulnerability proved fatal, as the legions of Metellus inflicted a devastating defeat against the forces of Norbanus and Carbo. Approximately 10,000 men fell in the slaughter.

Appianus (Appian), *Civil Wars*, 1.91; Velleius Paterculus, *Roman History*, 2.28.1; Titus Livius (Livy), *Summaries*, 88.

Fenectane Plains, 339 BC – The Roman confiscation of land following the Battle of Trifanum in 340 BC inspired the Latins to resume hostilities the following year. Legions led by the *consul* Quintus Publius Philo defeated a Latin army and overran its camp in the Fenectane Plains.

Titus Livius (Livy), *History of Rome*, 8.12.4–5.

Ferentinum, 361 BC – Following the defeat of the Hernici near the town of Signa the previous year, the newly elected Roman consuls Caius Sulpicius Peticus and Caius Licinius Stolo renewed the war. Unable to find the Hernican army in the field, the legions marched southeast toward the city of Ferentinum, situated approximately 3 miles east of the Trerus River in central Italy. Once there, the army captured the city by assault.

Titus Livius (Livy), *History of Rome*, 7.9.1.

Fidenae, 437 BC – Following the appointment of the dictator Mamercus Aemilius Macerinus, the Senate aggressively prosecuted a war with the neighbouring communities of Fidenae (Castel Giubileo) and Veii who had earlier entered into an alliance against Rome. Under the capable leadership of the veteran commander Aemilius, the legions drove the enemy out of Roman territory; and crossing the Anio River, advanced north toward the town of Fidenae. The Fidenate and Veientine forces temporarily encamped on a hill between the river and town, and awaited the arrival of reinforcements from Falerii, an Italic city located north of Veii. Once the Faliscans crossed the Tiber River, all three parties relocated to an encampment outside Fidenae. Approximately 3 miles away, at the confluence of the two rivers, Aemilius elected to establish the Roman camp. Both armies assembled for battle on the intervening plain the following day. The Etruscan army was arrayed with the Faliscans on the left wing, the Fidenates drawn up in the centre and the Veientes formed on the right. The Roman battle formation was anchored by infantry on both wings, while the centre was held by a strong concentration of cavalry. The Romans opened the battle with a charge that collapsed the entire Etruscan line. In the struggle which followed, intense fighting swirled around the Veientine king, Tolumnius, until he was unhorsed and killed by the tribune Aulus Cornelius Cossus. The monarch's death was then followed by a complete rout of the enemy.

Titus Livius (Livy), *History of Rome*, 4.17.9–4.19.6.

Fidenae, 435 BC – A severe outbreak of pestilence completely disrupted daily life in Rome and the surrounding countryside. While the depressed conditions brought on by the epidemic discouraged the people and Senate from any immediate involvement in regional warfare, they did embolden armies from the neighbouring Etruscan communities of Fidenae (Castel Giubileo) and Veii to cross the Anio River and brazenly raid into Roman territory, almost to the outskirts of the city. In response, the dictator Quintus Servilius Priscus quickly levied an army and went in pursuit of the intruders. Near the town of Nomentum, about 13 miles northeast of Rome, his legions routed the Etruscan forces and pursued them to Fidenae. Though possessed of insufficient means to successfully prosecute a siege, Servilius determined to breach the town's defences by covertly constructing a tunnel into its citadel. In order to distract the Fidenates from discovering the mine, the legions encircled the town and launched a sustained assault. With the defenders preoccupied by continuous fighting, the Romans completed the underground passageway into the fortress and captured the community.

Titus Livius (Livy), *History of Rome*, 4.21.2–22.6.

Fidenae, 426 BC – Following a minor victory over a legionary army commanded by the military tribunes Titus Quinctius Poenus, Marcus Postumius and Caius Furius; the Veientes persuaded the people of Fidenae (Castel Giubileo) to join in a campaign against the Romans. Finding their lands once again threatened by enemies from the north, the Romans appointed Mamercus Aemilius Macerinus dictator. A veteran battlefield commander, Aemilius led his army across the Anio River and encamped a mile-and-a-half south of Fidenae. He then ordered one of his legates, Quinctius, to covertly lead a detachment to secure the ridge behind the town. The following day, the Etruscans assembled for battle, but the dictator hesitated in joining battle long enough to permit scouts to report the arrival of Quinctius at his clandestine location. Aemilius then gave the signal for the legions to form into line-of-battle on the nearby plain. As the two armies collided on the field, the Etruscan formation waivered at the first shock, but a sudden sally from inside the town by Fidenate civilians carrying firebrands temporarily distracted the Roman combatants. In the confusion of smoke and flames, the Roman left wing fell back. At almost the same instant, Aemilius, recognizing what was transpiring on the left, ordered reinforcements to redress the situation, and summoned Quinctius' force to launch an assault against the enemy's rear. While the infantry remained locked in a desperate struggle, a sudden improvised charge by Roman cavalry led by the *magister equitum* Aulus Cornelius further disrupted the enemy formation. At that moment, Quinctius' troops struck the Etruscans from behind. Caught between the two Roman lines, Fidenate and Veientine resistance collapsed. In the ensuing panic, refugees attempted to cross the Tiber River in their flight to Veii, or rushed headlong toward Fidenae. When the rout became irreversible and the enemy camp was successfully overrun, Aemilius ordered his army to assault the town. Fidenae was thoroughly sacked and the population sold into slavery.

Titus Livius (Livy), *History of Rome*, 4.31–34.4.

Fidentia, 82 BC (Roman Civil Wars) – Outside the town of Fidentia (Fidenza) in northern Italy, Marcus Terentius Varro Lucullus – one of Sulla's legates – with sixteen cohorts confronted a numerically superior force of fifty cohorts. In the ensuing battle, Lucullus defeated his challenger, killing 18,000 enemy troops and capturing their encampment.

Plutarch, *Sulla* 27.7–8; Titus Livius (Livy), *Summaries*, 88; Velleius Paterculus, *Roman History*, 2.28.1.

Firmum, 90 BC (Social War/Marsic War) – In the second year of the Social War, an Italian army under the command of Titus Lafrenius besieged the Roman forces of Gnaeus Pompeius in Firmum, a city in the coastal region of Picenum in eastern Italy. On learning of the approach of a second enemy force, Pompey determined to dispatch a portion of his command – under his lieutenant Publius Sulpicius – to assault Lafrenius' lines from the rear, while he himself led a simultaneous frontal attack in an effort to break out of the city. The Roman action resulted in bitter fighting which only abated after Sulpicius set fire to the Italian encampment. The incident quickly turned the momentum of the engagement in favour of the Romans, who pursued the remnants of the enemy army as it sought refuge in the neighbouring town of Asculum.

Appianus (Appian), *Civil Wars*, 1.47.

Forum Gallorum, 43 BC (Roman Civil Wars) – In the wake of Julius Caesar's assassination in the spring of 44 BC, the *consul* Marcus Antonius emerged as the leading political figure in Rome. As time progressed, Antony increasingly concluded that control of Cisalpine Gaul was in his own best interest as strategic security from future attacks by political opponents. Accordingly, Antony forced through the Senate passage of legislation stripping Decimus Brutus of the province's governorship. This action helped to further stimulate a growing power struggle among the Senate membership, particularly after the statesman Marcus Cicero called for an annulment of the measure in early 43 BC. In an effort to secure control of the region before the end of his consulship, Antony suddenly moved into the northern peninsula with two legions and trapped Brutus at Mutina (Modena). The Senate declared a state of emergency, and the new consuls, Aulus Hirtius and Caius Vibius Pansa, led armies in relief of Brutus. Hirtius' forces were the first to arrive and were soon joined by those of Caius Octavius. While Lucius

Antonius continued to press the investment of Mutina, Antony moved against Hirtius and Octavius. Several days of ineffectual skirmishing between the two sides followed before Antony drew off his forces under cover of darkness in order to attack Pansa, who approached from Bononia (Bologna) with four legions of recruits. Near Mutina, Pansa received Octavian's praetorian cohort and the Martian Legion as reinforcements. In marshland near the village of Forum Gallorum (Castelfranco) in the Padus Valley (Po Valley), Antony's two legions trapped Pansa's column in an ambuscade. At the onset of the battle, the praetorian cohorts of Antony and Octavius clashed atop an elevated roadway. Meanwhile, the Martian Legion divided into two halves and advanced against the Antonians situated in the marsh to either side. Pansa ordered the inexperienced levies to remain at the rear and not enter the action. As the day wore on, the battle gradually settled into three separate pockets of fighting. Amidst the quagmire, the opposing ranks of heavy infantry were unable to manoeuvre for tactical advantage and became locked in a savage hand-to-hand struggle. On the intervening causeway, Antony's praetorians finally succeeded in destroying Octavian's cohort after bitter resistance. Even after this loss, the Martian cohorts under Pansa – as well as those commanded by Octavian's lieutenant, Decimus Carfulenus – remained steadfast against the enemy until the *consul* was carried from the field severely wounded by a javelin. With Pansa injured, his army lost spirit and began to retreat in disorder, leaving Antony's veterans in control of the battlefield. Unknown to the exhausted victors, Pansa's fellow *consul*, Hirtius, was rapidly approaching the location with a fresh army in full battle array.

Appianus (Appian), *Civil Wars*, 3.67–69; Dio Cassius, *Roman History*, 46.37.5–6; Marcus Tullius Cicero, *Letters to His Friends*, 10.30.

Forum Gallorum, 43 BC (Roman Civil Wars) – The struggle between Marcus Antonius and the *consul* Caius Vibius Pansa near Forum Gallorum (Castelfranco) in the Padus Valley (Po Valley) drew the attention of the co-*consul* Aulus Hitrius, whose army lay about 7 miles northwest outside the city of Mutina (Modena). Upon learning of the ongoing engagement, Hirtius quickly moved toward the fighting but arrived too late to participate in the first action. As his two veteran legions* reached the vicinity of the clash, Hirtius' army, fully arrayed for battle, encountered the exhausted troops of Antony, flushed with victory but singularly unprepared for a second confrontation. Antony's army was virtually destroyed in the contest which followed.

Appianus (Appian), *Civil Wars*, 3.9.70; Dio Cassius, *Roman History*, 46.37.7–38.2; Marcus Tullius Cicero, *Letters to His Friends*, 10.30.4. *In his letter, Cicero's friend Sulpicius Galba refers to 'twenty veteran cohorts'.

Fucinus Lake, 89 BC (Social War/Marsic War) – In a clash near Lake Fucinus (Fucino lake bed), approximately 50 miles east of Rome, a Roman

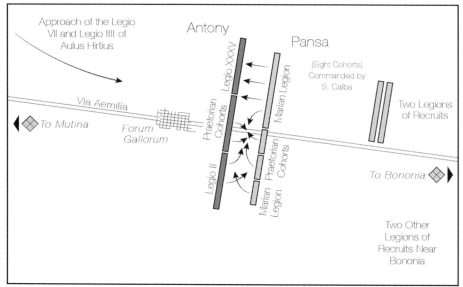

Battle of Forum Gallorum, 43 BC

army defeated a force of Marsi. During the struggle, the *consul* Lucius Porcius Cato was killed, possibly the victim of assassination by pro-Marian opponents. His lieutenant, Caius Gabinius, subsequently died storming the enemy's encampment.

Paulus Orosius, *Seven Books of History against the Pagans*, 5.18.

Garganus Mons, 72 BC (War of Spartacus, Third Servile War) – In the second year of the servile rebellion, a Roman consular army under Lucius Gellius Publicola defeated a 30,000-man slave army led by Crixus, a subordinate of the Thracian-born gladiator Spartacus, who was leader of the uprising in Italy. In the battle, which occurred near Mount Garganus in far southeastern Italy, Crixus and 20,000 of his men, mostly Germans, perished.

Paulus Orosius, *Seven Books of History against the Pagans*, 5.24; Appianus (Appian), *Civil Wars*, 1.117; Plutarch, *Crassus*, 9.7; Titus Livius (Livy), *Summaries*, 96.

Gaurus Mons, 343 BC (Third Samnite War, Samnite Wars) – Following an unwarranted attack by the Samnites against the Sidicini of Teanum, the Campanians became embroiled in a war with Samnium which climaxed with the devastating defeat of the Campanian army near Capua. Unable to resist the enemy with the flower of their soldiery now destroyed, the Campanians sought assistance from Rome. A subsequent senatorial embassy sent to Samnium failed to dissuade further assaults against Campania, provoking the outbreak of a general war. Once hostilities began, the Senate deployed both consular armies into the field; Marcus Valerius Corvus advanced into Campania, with a second legionary force under Aulus Cornelius Cossus entering Samnium. The *consul* Valerius encountered a sizeable force of Samnites near Mount Gaurus. The belligerents entered into a pitched battle after several days of skirmishing. The armies were evenly matched, and opposing infantry struggled savagely without result for most of the day. An attempt to force a decision on the field with an assault by Roman cavalry failed, compelling Valerius to order the legions to renew their attack against the enemy's front line. After hours of fighting, the Samnite centre finally wavered before collapsing entirely. Thousands of enemy levies were killed or captured by the pursuing Romans in the resulting rout.

Titus Livius (Livy), *History of Rome*, 7. 29.3–7, 7.32.1–6, 7.33.

Gereonium, 216 BC (Second Punic War, Wars against Carthage) – When the Roman Senate learned of the success achieved by the army's *magister equitum* Marcus Minucius Rufus in a skirmish against Carthaginian forces at Gereonium in Apulia, it took the extraordinary step of equally dividing *imperium* between the dictator Quintus Fabius Maximus and his lieutenant. Each general then assumed authority over two legions and their allied and Latin detachments; Minucius receiving charge of the first and fourth legions, and Fabius retaining command of the *Legio II* and *Legio III*. Afterward, the *magister equitum* chose to establish a separate camp approximately 1.5 miles from the dictator's position, thereby placing both Roman armies at an equal distance from the enemy compound near Gereonium. From the interrogation of prisoners, the Carthaginian general Hannibal Barca learned that Minucius possessed a rash and ambitious character, and he determined to exploit these reckless traits to best advantage. Under cover of night, he secretly concealed 5,000 men, both foot and horse, in shallow ravines and irregularities on open ground to the left of Minucius' encampment. At dawn the following morning, Hannibal ordered a small detachment of light troops to occupy a hillock between the Roman and Punic camps in an effort to provoke the *magister equitum* into action. When Minucius observed the enemy's movements, he dispatched some light infantry to contest the Carthaginians' possession of the knoll. Thereafter, each side repeatedly committed reinforcements to the growing skirmish until the Roman commander deemed the situation sufficiently volatile to order his legions to assemble for battle. Hannibal likewise chose to array his entire army on the field, even as cavalry from both sides clashed in strength near the summit of the hill. While the fighting intensified, additional Roman light infantry moved forward to join in the melee, but were repulsed by Carthaginian horsemen and driven from the height. As the *velites* fell back in disorder, they disrupted the ranks of cavalry and heavy infantry approaching from behind. Hannibal immediately sought to exploit the opportunity afforded by the situation and signalled those Punic troops lying in ambush to attack the legions. The unexpected assault, directed against both the flanks and rear of Minucius' formation, would have quickly proven decisive were it not for the timely arrival of the second Roman army. As the maniples of his beleaguered colleague reeled under the impact of the Carthaginian charge and were driven from the field, Fabius quickly advanced with his own fresh legions to redress the Roman battle line. Unwilling to engage this new threat, Hannibal abandoned his pursuit of Minucius' troops and retired to his encampment.

Titus Livius (Livy), *History of Rome*, 22.28–29.6; Polybius, *Histories*, 3.104–105.8.

Gergovia, 52 BC, spring (Gallic War) – In anticipation of engaging the Arvernian chieftain Vercingetorix, Julius Caesar advanced on Gergovia (Clermont) – the capital of the Arverni – with six legions. The Roman camp was situated on an elevated site south of a shallow lake and southeast of the hilltop settlement, so as to provide Roman forces with the easiest access to the plateau where the city lay. The Gallic army was likewise encamped near the city, with tribal detachments occupying all of the strategically important mountain heights in the immediate vicinity of the *oppidum* (settlement). In order to sever the community's access to a primary water source, two legions deployed under cover of darkness captured a strategically important hill position south of Gergovia. The site was then secured by the construction of a secondary camp and linked to the main *castrum* with a double trench. Legionary forces now possessed a more direct approach to the city. It was at this time that the integrity of Caesar's entire Gergovian campaign was threatened by an erosion of loyalty among some of Rome's Gallic allies, the Aedui. Leaving responsibility for the siege with his general Caius Fabius, Caesar advanced four legions and a strong contingent of cavalry against the Aeduan army situated approximately 30 miles distant. This show of force ended the mutiny, but during Caesar's absence the enemy launched a massive assault against the main Roman camp at Gergovia. An expeditious return of the four absent legions relieved the hard-pressed *castrum* and turned the attack, though the besieged cohorts suffered heavy losses. In preparation for a general assault of the city, Caesar deployed a large formation of mounted troops supported by a single legion, to make a demonstration southwest of the *oppidum*. Vercingetorix responded by drawing forces off Gergovia's southern perimeter to reinforce the southwestern defences. Having weakened the city's southern approaches by this feint, Caesar now secretly relocated his legions from the major *castrum* to the secondary camp, situated directly south of the depleted Gallic fortifications. Once in position, Roman forces initiated a total assault. Though executed in surprise, the momentum of the uphill attack faltered as it reached the walls of the *oppidum*, permitting Gallic contingents time to reinforce the threatened ramparts. Stiff resistance, coupled with the mistaken identification of Aeduan allies on the legions' right for formations of enemy, finally caused the Roman drive to collapse. As legionary forces fell back in disorder, the Tenth Legion and elements of the *Legio XIII* under the legate Titus Sextius effectively checked the Gauls' pursuit. This reverse ended Caesar's effort to take Gergovia. Roman casualties from this final engagement numbered 750 dead, including forty-six centurions.

Julius Caesar, *The Gallic War*, 7.45–56

Mount Gindarus, 38 BC (Parthian Wars) – When in early spring word reached the Roman general Publius Ventidius Bassus that a Parthian invasion of Syria was imminent, he sought by means of a ruse to delay the enemy long enough to permit his eight legions to assemble from their various encampments in Cilicia and Syria. A local noble named Channaeus, who was on friendly terms with Ventidius, unknowingly spread misinformation to Pacorus, son of King Orodes II, that persuaded the Parthians to cross the Euphrates River at a location far to the south of their usual bridgehead at the city of Zeugma (Belkis). The decision gave the Romans sufficient time to gather at Mount Gindarus and await the arrival of Pacorus' forces. The Parthians encountered no opposition either in crossing the river or on their subsequent northward march into the Syrian district of Cyrrhestica. As a result, they grew increasingly overconfident at the seeming weakness of the enemy. The two armies met at Gindarus. Pacorus observed Ventidius' *castrum* on the hill and immediately attacked with his cavalry, anticipating an easy victory. While the assault was underway, a sudden sally by Roman heavy infantry drove the squadrons of horsemen in confusion down the hill. The Parthians briefly regrouped at the base of Gindarus, but were soon put to flight by legionary cohorts and *auxilia*, especially slingers. Pacorus died in the fighting, along with a large number of his men. The remainder of his army retreated eastward beyond the Euphrates.

Strabo of Amasya, *Geography*, 16.1.28, 16.2.8; Plutarch, *Antony*, 34.1, *Crassus*, 33.5; Dio Cassius, *Roman History*, 49.19–20.3.

Glanis River, 82 BC (Roman Civil Wars) – As the general Lucius Cornelius Sulla advanced northward, intent on engaging the forces of the *consul* Papirius Carbo at Clusium in Etruria, he encountered on the banks of the Glanis River a detachment of Celtiberian cavalry sent by Roman praetors in Spain to aid consular forces. In the sharp action which ensued, fifty Iberian horsemen were killed, shortly followed by an additional 250 who deserted to Sulla's cause. In response to this betrayal, Carbo murdered the remaining Iberians in his army.

Appianus (Appian), *Civil Wars*, 1.89.

Granicus River, 74 BC (Third Mithridatic War, Wars against Mithridates the Great) – Following his failed siege of the Anatolian port city of Cyzicus, Mithridates VI Eupator, king of Pontus, departed with his fleet to Parion on the Hellespont and ordered his generals to lead the army to Lampsacus. Roman legions under the *consul* Lucius Licinius Lucullus surprised the retreating Pontic force on the banks of the Granicus River. In the ensuing battle, 20,000 of the king's men died and many were captured.

> Plutarch, *Lucullus*, 11.6; Appianus (Appian), *Mithridatic Wars*, 76.

Great Plains, 203 BC – see Campi Magni, 203 BC.

Grumentum, 215 BC (Second Punic War, Wars against Carthage) – Near the Lucanian community of Grumentum, a Roman army under the command of Tiberius Sempronius Longus defeated a Carthaginian force led by the Punic general Hanno. In the struggle, Roman troops killed more than 2,000 enemy soldiers and captured 280 others. Afterward, Hanno withdrew southward into the region of Bruttium, permitting the Roman *praetor* Marcus Valerius Laevinus to reassert Roman control over the Hirpinian towns of Vercellium, Sicilinum and Vescellium to the north of Lucania.

> Titus Livius (Livy), *History of Rome*, 23.37.10–13.

Grumentum, 207 BC (Second Punic War, Wars against Carthage) – While one Roman army marched from Rome northward toward Cisalpine Gaul to intercept a Punic invasion force from Spain, the *consul* Caius Claudius Nero moved his legions into the south of the peninsula to pursue a second Carthaginian army led by Hannibal Barca. The two armies met at the site of Grumentum, a Lucanian town located near the banks of the Aciris (Agri) River. Hannibal's camp was situated near the walls of the town, while the Romans established their *castrum* over a quarter of a mile away across a small plain. A line of barren hills was situated to the left of the Carthaginian position and on the right flank of the Romans. Because Nero's primary intent was to prevent Hannibal from moving north to join with the other Punic army, he was not inclined to force a major contest, but was instead content to allow his men to continually skirmish with the enemy. By contrast, Hannibal was determined to escape and march northward as soon as possible. This desire compelled him to frequently assemble his army for battle in hope of drawing his antagonist into a decisive contest. Nero declined to accept the challenge each time, but the eagerness of his opponent led the *consul* to prepare a trap. During the night, he sent a detachment of five cohorts led by the tribune Tiberius Claudius Asellus, and five maniples under the allied *praefectus* Publius Claudius, to cross the ridge and conceal themselves on the far side of the adjacent hills. Nero then drew up his army for battle the following morning. In their eagerness to come to blows with the enemy, a portion of the

Carthaginian army dashed onto the plain in a disorderly fashion, and Hannibal was not immediately able to restore discipline. The *consul* responded by ordering Caius Aurunculeius, *tribunus militum* of the *Legio III*, to attack the disorganized bands of cavalry and light infantry with the legion's contingent of horsemen. Before the enemy was able to properly organize against this initial threat, they were suddenly struck on the left by the First Legion and an accompanying cavalry *ala*. As Hannibal strained to array his divisions in proper order, the detached cohorts and maniples charged from their place of hiding and rushed against the Punic rear. The unexpected appearance of these troops from behind and to the left triggered a general panic within the ranks of the Punic levies. In the rout which followed, 8,000 Carthaginians died and more than 700 were captured. Nero's losses included about 500 Roman and allied dead.

   Titus Livius (Livy), *History of Rome*, 27.41–42.8.

Grumentum, 90 BC (Social War/Marsic War) – Legionary troops under the command of Licinius Crassus were defeated and driven into the Lucanian town of Grumentum by an Italian force led by Marcus Lamponius. Approximately 800 Romans died in the fighting.

   Appianus (Appian), *Civil Wars*, 1.41.

Gurasium, 391 BC – In a battle at Gurasium, a Roman army defeated a force of Volscians who suffered heavy casualties as a result of the encounter.

   Diodorus Siculus, *Bibliotheca historica*, 14.109.7.

Gytheum, 195 BC – Having learned that the port of Gytheum on the Gulf of Lycaonia was a central storage depot of Nabis, tyrant of Sparta; the Romans determined to concentrate naval and military forces against the town. With forty vessels, the Roman commander Lucius Quinctius Flamininus was soon joined by eighteen Rhodian warships and the allied fleet of King Eumenes of Pergamum. Together, the entire naval force proceeded to assault Gytheum from the harbour side. The work of battering rams finally succeeded in destroying a tower and portions of the harbour wall, and exposing the city to attack by Roman forces. The acute nature of the situation compelled Dexagoridas, one of two officers leading Gytheum's defence, to prematurely enter into negotiations for the city's surrender; but the effort was abruptly ended by his assassination at the hands of his co-commander, Gorgopas. As the allied war fleet continued to press its attack, the Roman general Titus Quinctius Flamininus suddenly arrived with 4,000 selected legionary troops to instigate a landward investment of Gytheum. Now thoroughly trapped by land and sea, Gorgopas finally handed the city over to the Romans with the proviso that he and his garrison be permitted to leave peacefully.

   Titus Livius (Livy), *History of Rome*, 34.26.11, 34.29.

Gytheum, 192 BC – Nabis, tyrant of Sparta, besieged the port of Gytheum on the Gulf of Lycaonia. In response, the Romans dispatched a warfleet for the protection of the city; but Philopoemen, *strategos* of the Achaean League, concerned that the deteriorating defence of Gytheum would be too far advanced for the Romans to successfully restore, immediately sent Achaean ships against the Spartans. The Achaean flotilla attacked the Spartan fleet in open water outside the city harbour. Leading the modest squadron of Achaean ships was Phiopoemen's flagship, an aged *quadrireme* whose keel was laid over eighty years earlier. The delapidated vessel could not endure the stress of the sea engagement and broke apart on first contact with a Spartan ship. The sudden loss of the flagship demoralized the remainder of the Achaean fleet and turned the battle in favour of Nabis. Philopoemen survived the encounter and escaped to Patrae.

   Titus Livius (Livy), *History of Rome*, 35.26.

Hasta, 186 BC – In southern Spain, approximately 30 miles northeast of Gades in the territory of Hasta, Caius Atinius engaged the Lusitanians in a pitched battle and defeated them with a loss of 6,000 warriors. The legions captured the town of Hasta after routing the enemy.

   Titus Livius (Livy), *History of Rome*, 39.21.1–3.

Hadrumentum, 46 BC (Roman Civil Wars) – Upon learning the whereabouts of the Senatorial forces commanded by the Pompeian general Quintus Metellus Pius Scipio, Caesar assembled an army of six legions and 2,000 cavalry and dispatched them to North Africa via Sicily. Shortly thereafter he departed from Rhegium, and after a brief call at Lilybaeum on the western tip of the island, continued on in the train of his fleet. Because of adverse weather in the Mediterranean, his ships were scattered, with the result that he arrived off the African port of Hadrumentum with only 3,000 infantry and 150 cavalry. Finding the town protected by 10,000 armed soldiers, Caesar determined that a successful assault was not possible with the small number of men presently available to him. Furthermore, he soon learned that heavy reinforcements of cavalry were approaching in relief of the community's garrison. Following failed negotiations with Scipio's lieutenant, Caius Longus Considius, Caesar prepared to abandon Hadrumentum. As his army retired from the camp in preparation for a march down the coast to the port of Ruspina, a strong contingent of Considius' troops made a sudden sally from inside the town, supported by a force of Numidian horsemen, and attacked the rearguard of the departing army. This action was capably disrupted by a gallant counter-charge from Caesar's small force of cavalry, who eventually succeeded in repulsing the larger formation. Thereafter, Caesar's force was periodically assailed by such tactics until a number of veteran cohorts were finally detached to reinforce the beleaguered rearguard and thereby permit a successful withdrawal.

Julius Caesar, *The African War*, 3–6; Appianus (Appian), *Civil Wars*, 2.95; Dio Cassius, *Roman History*, 42.58.4.

Heraclea, 280 BC (Wars of Pyrrhus) – Pyrrhus, king of Epirus, arrived in southern Italy following an appeal by the citizens of Tarentum for aid against the Romans, with whom they had recently gone to war. After an unexpected encounter with storms while crossing the Ionian Sea, Pyrrhus arrived on the peninsula with only a small force still intact, the remainder of the expeditionary fleet having been scattered as far south as Sicily and the Libyan Sea. Eventually, the Epirot monarch was able to assemble a sizeable force with the aid of his allies. Upon learning that a Roman army was approaching from the northwest under the leadership of the *consul* Publius Valerius Laevinus, and was presently ravaging Lucania, Pyrrhus advanced against the enemy, though his army was not yet fully assembled. Near the Siris (Sinni) River, between the communities of Pandosia and Heraclea, he encamped with the purpose of awaiting the arrival of his allies. When he learned that the Roman camp was pitched on the far side of the river, the king rode out to reconnoitre the enemy's position and then shortly withdrew after posting guards along the nearer bank; but the Romans were unwilling to delay battle until Pyrrhus' reinforcements arrived and soon began crossing the Siris at several points. In

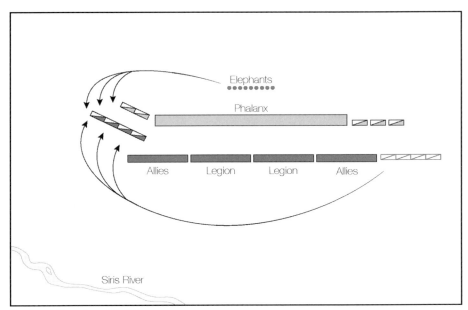

Battle of Heraclea, 280 BC

response, the king led 3,000 cavalry forward, hoping to overwhelm the Romans while they were still fording the river and in disarray. This effort ultimately failed, and he then ordered his infantry phalanx to assemble into battle formation and charge. The effect was to momentarily drive the legions back before they in turn mounted a counter-assault. The fortunes of the two armies thereafter fluctuated until Pyrrhus was able to rupture Laevinus' formation by a determined charge of war elephants. While the legions recoiled under the pressure of attack, the Roman cavalry proved completely ineffective after its horses panicked on encountering the large pachyderms. With the enemy thrown into disorder, Pyrrhus had his Thessalian cavalry charge the broken ranks. The attack proved decisive and the Romans were routed with great loss. Plutarch quotes conflicting mortality figures, noting Dionysius of Halicarnassus as recording the loss of 15,000 Romans and 13,000 Epirot and allied troops; and Hieronymus of Cardia mentioning only 7,000 and 4,000 respectively.

> Plutarch, *Pyrrhus*, 16–17; Titus Livius (Livy), *Summaries*, 13; John Zonaras, *Epitome of Histories*, 8.3; Paulus Orosius, *Seven Books of History against the Pagans*, 4.1; Lucius Annaeus Florus, *Epitomy*, 1.13.7–8; Sextus Julius Frontinus, *Stratagems*, 2.4.13.

Heraclea Minoa, 262 BC (First Punic War, Wars against Carthage) – While in the midst of a difficult five-month siege of the Sicilian town of Agrigentum, the Romans, weakened by disease and supply shortages, were suddenly faced with the arrival of a fresh Carthaginian army led by the general Hanno. Establishing a base at Herbesus in order to sever Roman supply lines, the Punic commander next moved to advance from Heraclea Minoa to the vicinity of Agrigentum with the remainder of his force, including fifty war elephants. Once on the march, he ordered his Numidian cavalry to move forward ahead of the main body of Carthaginian troops and approach one of two legionary camps surrounding the town in order to provoke Roman consuls Lucius Postumius Megellus and Quintus Mamilius Vitulus into action. Predictably, when the horsemen drew very near one of the camps, they were almost immediately attacked by Roman cavalry. As the *equites* charged headlong after the enemy riders, the Numidians deftly retreated toward the main body of the Carthaginian force. Once they reached the safety of their own lines, the Africans quickly wheeled round and encircled their pursuers. Trapped between Hanno's infantry and cavalry, the Roman horse suffered significant losses before fleeing survivors were able to reach the safety of their camp.

> Polybius, *Histories*, 1.18–1.4.

Heracleium, 38 BC – see Mount Gindarus, 38 BC.

Herculaneum, 293 BC – A Roman consular army under the leadership of Spurius Carvilius Maximus fought and defeated a Samnite force near the town of Herculaneum.* Though the engagement was protracted and resulted in greater battlefield losses for the Romans than the enemy, the *consul* was able to successfully contain and wear down the Samnites within Herculaneum before finally overrunning and capturing the entire community.

> Titus Livius (Livy), *History of Rome*, 10.45.9–11. *An unknown location not to be confused with the Roman town of the same name which was situated on the Bay of Naples, northwest of Pompeii.

Herdonia, 212 BC (Second Punic War, Wars against Carthage) – Upon learning that a poorly disciplined Roman army of some 18,000 men was situated near the Apulian town of Herdonia, a Carthaginian force led by Hannibal Barca moved toward the location in hopes of drawing the Romans into an unfavourable battle. Following his army's arrival near the enemy encampment, Hannibal perceived the undisciplined nature of the Romans. The legions' general, the *praetor* Gnaeus Fulvius Flaccus, was unable to exercise strict authority over his command, with the result that soldiers were eager for battle but too fractious to present a serious threat on the field. Hannibal, recognizing this vulnerability, prepared to exploit the situation to best effect. The next evening, under cover of darkness, he concealed 3,000 lightly armed troops in neighbouring farmhouses and surrounding woods and underbrush, and then ordered his brother Mago to covertly lead 2,000 cavalry away from the Punic camp and lie in wait for the outbreak of fighting the following day. At dawn, Hannibal arrayed his army in battle formation. In response, the Romans recklessly assembled their maniples, the first legion and an auxiliary force of equal size positioned in front, and a like formation consisting of a second legion and accompanying *auxilia* placed in reserve. Despite their tribunes' warnings that the forward line was both too long and dangerously attenuated, the infantry disregarded the officers' protests and entered battle. Predictably, on first contact the Roman line crumpled under the amassed weapons of the Carthaginian assault, and any hope of redressing the situation was completely lost when the previously hidden units of Punic infantry and cavalry launched a sudden attack against the unprotected rear and flanks of the legionary formation. The entrapped Roman army was completely destroyed in the resulting struggle. No more than 2,000 men escaped the carnage, Fulvius having already abandoned his command during the opening stages of fighting.

> Titus Livius (Livy), *History of Rome*, 25.20–21.

Herdonia, 210 BC (Second Punic War, Wars against Carthage) – While besieging the community of Herdonia in Apulia, the *proconsul* Gnaeus Fulvius Centumalus was caught off-guard by the unexpected arrival of Hannibal and a

Carthaginian army in full battle array. Fulvius responded by quickly muster-ing his army into battle formation, but the Romans were ill-prepared to resist such a hostile opponent. Hannibal ordered the Punic infantry to fully engage the legions, and directed a portion of his cavalry to sweep around the enemy flanks and charge the Roman rear while a second mounted force was to assault the enemy encampment. As the morning was foggy, Fulvius initially mis-judged the full scope of the Carthaginian action, thinking the cavalry then attacking the camp to be the full extent of the enemy force. When the entire Punic army finally closed with the assembled legionary infantry, the Romans swiftly found themselves surrounded. Posted in the front line with some mounted squadrons on the left, the Fifth Legion entered the battle with great confidence, but a furious charge of Numidian cavalry on the Roman rear quickly disrupted the Sixth Legion stationed in the second line. The momentum of this unexpected mounted attack penetrated to the forward ranks of Roman infantry and immediately threw the Fifth Legion into dis-order. Subjected to attack by Carthaginian forces from both sides, the cohe-sion of the Roman formation eroded. Some legionaries took flight, while many others were killed in the confused fighting which erupted at the centre of the battle. When the engagement finally ended, perhaps 13,000 Romans were dead, including Fulvius and eleven military tribunes.

Appianus (Appian), *Hannibalic War*, 8.48; Titus Livius (Livy), *History of Rome*, 27.1.1–13.

Hermaeum Promontorium, 255 BC (First Punic War, Wars against Carthage) – In early summer, a Roman fleet of 350 ships commanded by Marcus Aemilius Paulus and Servius Fulvius Paetinus Nobilior assembled for the purpose of rescuing the survivors of the Roman defeat at Bagradas, presently in the coastal town of Aspis after a failed Carthaginian siege to secure their capture. After departing Sicilian waters, the flotilla crossed to Libya, where it encountered 200 Carthaginian warships patrolling the North African coast in anticipation of the Roman fleet's arrival. Off the Hermaeum promontory (Cape Bon), the Roman vessels engaged and easily routed the Punic sail, capturing 114 enemy ships and their crews. Following this naval victory, the Romans recovered the remnants of the destroyed army at Apsis before returning to Italy, but an unexpected storm overtook the homeward fleet near Camarina, resulting in the destruction of all but eighty craft off the southeastern coast of Sicily.

Polybius, *Histories*, 1.36.5–12; Diodorus Siculus, *Historical Library*, 23.18.1; John Zonaras, *Epitome of Histories*, 8.14.

Himera, 260 BC – see Thermae, 260 BC.

Himera River, 211 BC (Second Punic War, Wars against Carthage) – Having finally captured the great city of Syracuse, Roman armies in Sicily now had only to overcome an intense pocket of enemy resistance in the vicinity of the city of Agrigentum (Agrigento), located near the island's south-western coast. In an effort to extinguish this threat, the Roman legate Marcus Claudius Marcellus deployed legions into the area against enemy forces commanded by the Carthaginian general Muttines and his co-commanders Epicydes and Hanno. Emboldened by Muttines' presence, the others elected to withdraw their troops from inside Agrigentum and encamp near the Himera River. The Romans established themselves approximately 4 miles away and awaited the enemy's next move. Muttines almost immediately ordered the harassment of Roman outposts across the river, and followed these actions by a larger assault the next day which forced Marcellus' legions to retreat inside their fortifications. In the midst of these events, Muttines was unexpectedly recalled to a military encampment at Heraclea Minoa to resolve a mutiny among a contingent of Numidian troops; he warned his two fellow generals not to engage the Romans in his absence. Contrary to his instruction, Epicydes and Hanno crossed the Himera and drew up their troops in battle formation. Marcellus responded by immediately ordering his legions to arms. It was at this time that a small body of Numidians broke away from the Carthaginian line and approached the Roman legate to inform him that they were in sympathy with their companions in Heraclea Minoa and would therefore not participate in the upcoming contest. As the Romans were encouraged by the withdrawal of these most feared horsemen, the enemy was equally demoralized by such a loss and also by the spectre that they might be attacked by their own cavalry. The subsequent inaction of the Numidians proved pivotal to the outcome of the battle, as the courage of the Carthaginian infantry gave way under the first shock delivered by the legions. With the Punic line broken, the struggle quickly turned into a complete rout and marked Marcellus' last signal victory in Sicily.

Titus Livius (Livy), *History of Rome*, 25.40.5–41.7.

Hippo Regius, 46 BC (Roman Civil Wars) – After the Battle of Thapsus, the Pompeian general Quintus Metellus Pius Scipio departed North Africa for Spain in a small fleet of ships. Also aboard the vessels were Publius Damasippus, Lucius Manlius Torquatus and Plaetorius Rustianus. While in the midst of the voyage, storms drove the craft near the African community of Hippo Regius and a hostile fleet under the command of a mercenary commander named Publius Sittius. In the ensuing action, Scipio perished and his ships, outnumbered and surrounded, were sunk.

Julius Caesar, *The African War*, 79–86; Dio Cassius, *Roman History*, 43.9.5; Appianus (Appian), *Civil Wars*, 2.14.100.

Ibera, 215 BC – see Iberus River, 215 BC.

Iberus River, 217 BC (Second Punic War, Wars against Carthage) – In early summer, the Punic admiral Himilco sailed from the Spanish port of Carthago Nova (Cartagena) with a fleet of forty warships, bound for the mouth of the Iberus (Ebro) River roughly 250 miles to the north. Marching along the coast in the company of the ships was an army led by the Carthaginian commander in Spain, Hasdrubal Barca. Suspecting the enemy of concentrating his forces at the Iberus, the Roman general Gnaeus Cornelius Scipio left the Roman-controlled port of Tarraco (Tarragona) and arrived near the entrance of the great river two days later. Anchoring about 10 miles from the Punic fleet, he waited for scouts to assess the enemy position before ordering an attack. The speed of his advance caught the Carthaginians off guard. Once the two fleets clashed, the fighting lasted only a short while before the Punic ships retreated to shore, their crews taking refuge with the army. The Romans boldly pursued the enemy vessels to the beach, and then towed away twenty-five ships which were deemed seaworthy. The victory provided the Romans with naval superiority along the entire length of the eastern Spanish coast.

Titus Livius (Livy), *History of Rome*, 22.19–20.3; Polybius, *Histories*, 3.95–96.6

Iberus River, 215 BC – In western Spain, the Roman generals Gnaeus Cornelius Scipio Calvus and Publius Cornelius Scipio combined their legions in an effort to stop the imminent departure of a Carthaginian expedition for Italy led by the veteran Punic commander Hasdrubal Barca. The opposing armies encamped near the Iberus (Ebro) River for several days in anticipation of battle. The close proximity of the two camps, situated only 5 miles apart, ensured repeated skirmishing before both armies finally elected to meet in a pitched struggle on the intervening plain. Upon reaching the battlefield, the Scipios formed the Roman infantry into a *triplex acies*, with *velites* placed at intervals between the maniples both before and after the standards. On the left and right flanks, squadrons of cavalry served to protect the legions from direct attack. Hasdrubal arrayed his Spanish infantry opposite the Roman front line, deployed the Carthaginians on the right wing and to the left the African foot and mercenary auxiliaries. On the extreme flanks he then placed his cavalry; Numidians on the right and other detachments of horsemen to the left. Once gathered on the field, the armies were evenly matched in every way but spirit. While the Romans were emboldened by the opportunity to fight on foreign soil and thereby protect their Italian homeland, the Punic army was equally disheartened at the possibility that a victory would result in a long and difficult campaign in a faraway land. The demoralization within the ranks of the Carthaginian forces became manifest in the opening clash of arms between the two opponents. An initial Roman charge quickly inspired the Carthaginian centre to retreat. The pressure of the legionary attack collapsed all resistance in the middle of the Punic line, splitting the formation and resulting in two separate pockets of fighting as the Carthaginian and African formations on the wings held their ground. The rout of the enemy centre provided the legions with numerical superiority, permitting them the means to press their attack against both of Hasdrubal's remaining divisions. The battle intensified as the African and Carthaginian troops fought desperately for survival against the unfailing pressure of the maniples. The danger to the trapped infantry was further assured when both the Numidian and Mauri cavalry on the flanks entirely failed to engage after the loss of the centre. Their sudden flight also drove off the army's detachment of war elephants. What followed was the complete destruction of those remaining elements of the Carthaginian army still on the battlefield. After witnessing the outcome of the engagement, Hasdrubal fled along with other survivors of the day's action. Punic losses amounted to no less than 25,000 dead.

Titus Livius (Livy), *History of Rome*, 23.28.7–29.15; Eutropius, *Abridgement of Roman History*, 3.11.

Ilerda, 49 BC (Roman Civil Wars) – Two days after Caesarian forces under Caius Fabius clashed with the troops of Lucius Afranius at the Sicoris (Segre) River, Caesar arrived on the scene with 900 cavalry and immediately proceeded to the outskirts of Ilerda (Lerida), an Iberian town in the province of *Hispania Citerior* (Eastern Spain). There he anticipated encountering the five legions and 5,000 cavalry of his Pompeian opponents, Afranius and Marcus Petreius. He established his camp approximately 670 yards from the enemy's position, and then proceeded to excavate trenches. Caesar attempted to occupy a low hill between Ilerda and the Pompeian encampment on the third day. This move threatened to block his adversaries from their store of supplies in the town and quickly led to a full-scale battle. Moving toward the location with three legions, Caesar deployed an advanced guard to occupy the hill; but Afranius' cohorts reached the place first, and with the aid of reinforcements, were able to secure control of the site. The enemy's use of unorthodox skirmishing tactics, acquired through frequent warfare with the Lusitanians and other tribes, caused considerable confusion within the ranks of Caesar's troops, forcing one of the beleaguered legions posted on the outside to withdraw to a nearby hill. As these troops fell back in disorder, Caesar moved the *Legio IX* forward to check the enemy attack and stop the retreat. The legion successfully drove back the Pompeian cohorts, but then recklessly pursued the fugitives too far, arriving at the base of the hill on which the town stood. The Ninth was then exposed to heavy missile fire from above. When it attempted to withdraw out of range, the cohorts of Afranius turned and counterattacked. As the fighting escalated, and additional Pompeian cohorts arrived through the town to support their exhausted companions, Caesar could only send limited aid to his beleaguered legion. The rugged topography surrounding the Ninth prohibited its reinforcement on either flank, and there was no room for cavalry to manoeuvre for effect. Five hours later, with their supply of *pila* and javelins expended, the men of the *Legio IX* launched a desperate frontal charge against the Pompeian forces. Though uphill, the assault carried all before it, driving the broken cohorts of Afranius and Petreius to the walls of Ilerda. The Ninth was able to properly extricate itself in the midst of this disorder. While the *Legio IX* descended the slope to safety, elements of Caesar's cavalry managed to ride between the two armies and provide the exhausted legionaries with rearguard support. Total casualties among Caesar's forces amounted to seventy killed and almost 600 wounded. Pompeian losses included over 200 dead.

   Julius Caesar, *Civil Wars*, 1.41–46

Ilipa, 206 BC (Second Punic War, Wars against Carthage) – With the aid of Mago, son of Hamilcar, the Carthaginian general Hasdrubal Gisgo gathered an army of 50,000–70,000 infantry, 4,000 cavalry and thirty-two war elephants and encamped on a small plain near Ilipa (Alcala del Rio), a town situated immediately west of the Baetis (Guadalquivir) River in south central Spain. When word reached the Roman commander Publius Cornelius Scipio (Africanus) regarding the size and location of the Carthaginian army, he quickly drafted additional levies from among his Spanish allies and then advanced into the region at the head of approximately 45,000 men. After arriving within sight of the enemy, the Romans immediately began construction of their camp, but were shortly attacked by Punic and Numidian cavalry under the command of Mago and Masinissa, ruler of the Massylii of eastern Numidia. Scipio anticipated the likelihood of such an assault, and when the African horsemen bore down on the partially completed encampment, they were suddenly charged by Roman cavalry concealed behind a nearby hill and forced to retreat with heavy losses. For several days thereafter, both commanders assembled their armies on the open plain, but committed only light infantry and cavalry to skirmishing actions. On each occasion Scipio permitted the Carthaginians to deploy first before leading his main body of troops out into battle formation; the legions formed in the centre and the Spanish allies on the wings. Hasdrubal likewise adopted the same tactical disposition, placing his Spanish mercenaries on both wings of the Carthaginian line and the African phalanx in the centre opposite the maniples of Roman heavy infantry. When, after several days, the Carthaginians continued to employ the same formation in anticipation that the Romans would do likewise, Scipio resolved to exploit the enemy's complacency and catch Hasdrubal unprepared for the actual engagement. The following morning, he altered the order of the Roman divisions and prepared to force a battle.

He instructed the tribunes to feed and assemble the army before daybreak, and contrary to ordinary practice, stationed the Spanish light infantry in the centre and placed the legions on both wings. Scipio quickly dispatched the *velites* and cavalry to harass the Punic camp, and then followed their departure by leading the infantry out in full battle array. The unexpected arrival of Roman cavalry in the pre-morning darkness roused the Punic encampment to arms. Alerted by the commotion outside the camp perimeter, Hasdrubal was startled to discover the entire Roman army so close at hand. He quickly assembled his forces according to their usual order. Before the Carthaginian and Libyan heavy infantry had completed preparations to meet the enemy, the African cavalry was already locked in a fierce battle – with the Roman horsemen and *velites* – that remained closely contested until Scipio sounded the recall, withdrawing both to a position behind his wings. The preliminary fighting now at an end, both armies positioned themselves for the main attack. When the two sides were less than a mile apart, Scipio ordered the Spanish troops in the centre to advance at a slow pace, while the legions posted on the wings moved forward with a faster step. Once the line began to bow inward to form a concave crescent, Scipio shifted the *velites* and cavalry to the extreme flanks. With the wings extended, they now advanced in column, the rest following obliquely. Near the point of contact, the Roman columns wheeled again to rejoin the main battle line. The entire Carthaginian formation was now in grave danger of being enveloped. While Scipio's Spanish contingents continued to refuse the Carthaginian centre, both wings simultaneously crashed into the Punic flanks at an acute angle. The attack proved irresistible. Roman heavy infantry drove into the more lightly armed Spanish mercenaries, just as the cavalry and *velites* charged the enemy horse stationed immediately beside the Carthaginian wings. As the flanks collapsed inward, Hasdrubal's war elephants – positioned near the mercenaries on the right and left – recoiled under the shock and panicked, creating even more carnage. At the same time, the African phalanx, held in check by the threat posed by the Roman centre, was unable to aid its Spanish allies and stood by helplessly as enemy maniples wrecked the mercenary divisions to either side. Gradually, the integrity of the entire Punic line started to give way under the pressure of the assault and the centre began to withdraw. The retreat was initially in good order, yet as the army grew aware of the battle's inevitable outcome, courage eroded within the Carthaginian ranks and the situation quickly collapsed into a complete rout. As the enemy fled from the battlefield, the victorious Romans went in pursuit, but a heavy rainstorm ended the day's action. The following day the chase resumed, and near the Baetis River the two armies clashed again. The Romans completely destroyed the remainder of the Carthaginian force in the resulting struggle. Scipio's lieutenant Marcus Silanus captured 6,000 fugitives soon thereafter. Hasdrubal escaped to Gades.

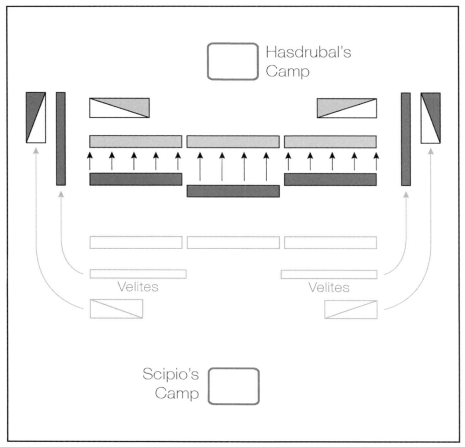

Battle of Ilipa, 206 BC

With the victory at Ilipa, Rome permanently ended Carthaginian rule of the Iberian peninsula.

Titus Livius (Livy), *History of Rome*, 28.12.10–16.10; Polybius, *Histories*, 11.20–23.

Ilipa, 193 BC (Wars in Spain) – The year following his praetorship in *Hispania Citerior* (Eastern Spain), the general Publius Cornelius Scipio Nasica engaged a numerically superior force of Lusitani returning home after an extended raid into Farther Spain. Burdened by their plunder and exhausted by the day's march, the tribesmen made a valiant stand against their attackers but were eventually worn down and defeated after five hours of fighting. In the battle and ensuing rout, 12,000 Lusitani died and an additional 540 were captured. Roman casualties included just seventy-three dead.

Titus Livius (Livy), *History of Rome*, 35.1.

Iliturgi, 215 BC (Second Punic War, Wars against Carthage) – Because of its recent alliance with Rome, the southern Iberian town of Iliturgi was besieged by a Carthaginian army led by Hasdrubal and Mago Barca – the brothers of Hannibal – and Hasdrubal, son of Bomilcar. The investment was disrupted by the arrival of Roman legions under the command of Gnaeus Cornelius Scipio Calvus and Publius Cornelius Scipio, who, after delivering grain to the beleaguered community, launched an assault against the largest of the three Punic camps outside the town. The attack provoked a general mobilization of those troops in the remaining two Carthaginian encampments. As Roman action progressed against the first camp, the 16,000 Romans quickly found themselves badly outnumbered by some 60,000 enemy soldiers. In the battle which followed, the legions made a determined stand against the larger force, and gained the victory after a desperate, protracted engagement. The Carthaginians were driven off, having lost more than 16,000 killed and 3,000 captured. Five Punic war elephants died in the fighting and seven were captured, along with 1,000 horses. By evening, the three enemy camps were also possessed by the Romans.

Titus Livius (Livy), *History of Rome*, 24.41.7–10

Iliturgi, 213 BC (Second Punic War, Wars against Carthage) – A Carthaginian army attempted to capture a Roman garrison in the town of Iliturgi, located on the left bank of the Baetis River in southern Spain. In order to relieve the situation, the Roman general Gnaeus Cornelius Scipio Calvus, leading a single legion, passed between the two Punic camps situated outside the community and fought his way into Iliturgi. The following day he launched a successful counter-assault against the besieging force, resulting in a total of 12,000 enemy dead and 1,000 captured during the two days of fighting. Unable to reduce the town, and now faced with the additional troops of Scipio, the Carthaginian army retired to the city of Aurinx.

Titus Livius (Livy), *History of Rome*, 23.49.5–11.

Iliturgi, 195 BC (Wars in Spain) – Following the end of his governorship, the *praetor* Marcus Helvius retired from *Hispania Ulterior* (Western Spain), accompanied by a guard of 6,000 troops provided by the new *praetor*, Appius Claudius Nero. Near the Iberian town of Iliturgi, the Roman detachment was attacked by a Celtiberian force of 20,000 warriors. In the ensuing battle, 12,000 Celtiberi were killed, the town captured and the adult population put to death.

Titus Livius (Livy), *History of Rome*, 34.10.1–2.

Ilorci, 211 BC (Second Punic War, Wars against Carthage) – While the Roman general Cnaeus Cornelius Scipio pursued a Carthaginian force under Hasdrubal Barca in eastern Spain, the latter was joined by two additional armies under the command of Mago Barca and Hasdrubal, son of Gisgo. Aware that he was now badly outnumbered, Scipio attempted to withdraw under cover of darkness, concerned that the presence of these new Punic forces signalled the defeat or destruction of a second Roman army under his brother, Publius. When the departure of the Romans became apparent the following morning, Hasdrubal dispatched his Numidian cavalry in pursuit and followed with the remainder of the army. The Numidians overtook the retreating enemy toward nightfall, and alternately attacked the rear and flanks of the column, forcing the troops to stop to repel the assaults. Thereafter, the Romans were repeatedly compelled to halt each time they attempted to continue the march. Finally, Scipio gathered his army and prepared to make a stand on a shallow hill near the town of Ilorci (Lorqui) on the banks of the Tader (Sequra) River, north of Carthago Nova (Cartagena). He formed his army into a hollow square, with the cavalry placed in the centre. Because the location was completely barren, and the hardness of the ground prohibited the construction of a trench and earthworks, the infantry erected a defensive barrier made of pack-saddles and baggage. When Hasdrubal arrived with the main Carthaginian van, his divisions easily approached the Roman position, where Punic soldiers managed with some difficulty to dismantle portions of the makeshift defences. The resulting gaps enabled the enemy to rush against the Romans from all sides. Trapped between the converging ranks of Carthaginian infantry, the Roman army was largely destroyed. Some of Scipio's men survived the struggle by fleeing to safety in the nearby forests, but the general died in the fighting along with most of his command.

Livy (Livy), *History of Rome*, 25.35–36.13; Pliny the Elder, *Natural History*, 3.9; for a discussion of the location of this battle, see G.K. Tipps, 'The Rogum Scipionis and Gnaeus Scipio's Last Stand', *The Classical World* Vol. 85, No. 2 (Nov–Dec. 1991), pp. 81–90.

Imbrinium, 325 BC (Second Samnite War, Samnite Wars) – During the Second Samnite War, while the dictator Lucius Papirius Cursor was in Rome, his Master of Horse – Quintus Fabius Maximus Rullianus – perceived an opportunity to initiate an offensive against the unwary Samnites. The legions encountered the enemy near the town of Imbrinium and entered into an intense struggle that only shifted in favour of the Romans when their cavalry – after repeated charges – broke through the Samnite ranks. With the opposing formation now in disorder, the legions pressed their assault through the ruptured line. Unable to redress the breach, the Samnites were defeated with a loss of 20,000 killed. The decision of Fabius to engage the enemy, though successful, was contrary to the direct orders of the appointed dictator. This momentarily generated a constitutional crisis in Rome. Lucius Papirius went on to defeat the Samnites following the controversy (8.36.8–9).

Titus Livius (Livy), *History of Rome*, 8.30.1–7.

Interamna Sucasina, 294 BC (Third Samnite War, Samnite Wars) – While one Samnite army campaigned against Roman forces in Apulia, a second attempted to capture the Roman colony of Interamna Sucasina located on the Via Latina. Unable to seize the settlement, the Samnites resorted to pillaging the surrounding countryside, driving off livestock and apprehending settlers. When the army began to withdraw in a disorganized column heavily laden with spoils, it unexpectedly encountered the legions of Marcus Atilius Regulus returning from Luceria to the southwest. In the brief struggle which followed, the Romans massacred the Samnites. Following the battle, Atilius restored the captives and their property to the land.

Titus Livius (Livy), *History of Rome*, 10.36.16–19.

Intercatia, 151 BC (Numantine War, Wars in Spain) – Following the sack of the Celtiberian city of Cauca (Coca) in north central Spain, the Roman *consul* Lucius Licinius Lucullus moved his army against the city of Intercatia (Villanueva del Campo), which provided refuge for more than 20,000 Celtiberian infantry and 2,000 cavalry. The *consul* invited the residents to accept the same type of pledge offered the Caucaei (when he had reneged on his promise and slain all the male population), but he was rebuked for his treachery. He then ordered his army to construct a siege line around the city, and repeatedly challenged the enemy to open battle. The Intercatians declined all offers of a decisive pitched engagement, but a returning detachment of Celtiberian horsemen, absent at the time the city was invested, remained outside the lines of circumvallation and subjected the Romans to constant harassment by night. This pattern of activity continued for a time, depriving the consular army of rest and compounding the hardship already resulting from a shortage of provisions. While the siege continued, the Romans finally succeeded in using their engines to topple a section of the city's wall. Legionary infantry quickly penetrated through the breach, but were overpowered and driven out after suffering heavy casualties. The following night, the Intercatians repaired the collapsed portion of the wall. Since both sides were severely debilitated by inadequate food supplies, and no resolution to the siege appeared imminent, Livinius' deputy, the *tribunus militum* Publius Cornelius Scipio Aemilianus, offered to conclude a treaty with a promise to uphold its provisions. The Celtiberians willingly agreed because Scipio was widely recognized to possess an honorable reputation. Soon afterward, Livinius abandoned his campaign against the Intercatii and directed his forces to the city of Pallantia (Palencia).

Appianus (Appian), *Wars in Spain*, 9.53–54.

Intibili, 215 BC (Second Punic War, Wars against Carthage) – In the wake of its failed siege of Iliturgi, the Carthaginian army withdrew to the nearby town of Intibili, shortly followed by Roman legions under the command of Gnaeus Cornelius Scipio Calvus and Publius Cornelius Scipio. There the two armies once more assembled into battle formation, and the Romans again defeated the Punic force with heavy losses, including more than 13,000 dead and over 2,000 captured. Nine elephants were also taken by the Romans.

> Titus Livius (Livy), *History of Rome*, 23.49.12–14.

Italica, 75 BC (Roman Civil Wars, War with Sertorius) – Near the community of Italica (Santiponce), approximately 6 miles northwest of Hispalis (Seville) in southwestern Iberia, a Sertorian army led by the *quaestor* Lucius Hirtuleius engaged Roman legions under the *proconsul* Quintus Caecilius Metellus Pius. The battle proved a decisive victory for the Romans and resulted in the deaths of 20,000 enemy troops. Hirtuleius fled to Lusitania and Metellus marched northward to confront Sertorius.

> Titus Livius (Livy), *Summaries*, 91; Paulus Orosius, *Seven Books of History against the Pagans*, 5.23.

Itucca, 142 BC (Virathic War, Wars in Spain) – In an effort to recover the city of Itucca (Martos) from the Lusitanian leader Viriathus, the *consul* Quintius Fabius Maximus Servilianus led an army of 18,000 infantry and 1,600 cavalry toward the Baetican community. In his haste to reach the city, Servilianus divided his force into divisions and advanced with only a portion of his army, intending that the remainder follow once additional reinforcements arrived. As the lead column of Roman troops progressed toward Itucca, Viriathus attacked with 6,000 warriors. Maintaining their poise, the Romans capably turned the enemy assault, and the Lusitanian chieftain shortly thereafter withdrew from the field. When the rest of the legionary army finally caught up with Servilianus' vanguard, the *consul* established his camp and then made preparations to pursue the rebel leader. With his overall command strengthened by the addition of two fresh legions and their accompanying allied troops, as well as a contingent of ten war elephants and 300 Numidian cavalry sent by Micipsa, king of Numidia, Servilianus confidently began the hunt for his elusive opponent. The Romans advanced against the Lusitanians and defeated them near Itucca, but the disorderly pursuit which followed provided Viriathus with the opportunity to counter-attack. While the *consul*'s troops continued their chase, the Lusitani rallied, killing some 3,000 Romans. The rest of Servilianus' force then retreated to their encampment, which was soon subjected to attack. The assault lasted until evening, though hostile incursions continued intermittently until the Romans resolved to retire to the safety of Itucca.

> Appianus (Appian), *Wars in Spain*, 12.67.

Janiculum Hill, 476 BC – Undeterred by their defeats at the Temple of Spes and the Colline Gate, the Veientes began pillaging Roman territory. In an effort to end these depredations, the Senate dispatched a Roman army under the *consul* Spurius Servilius Structus. The enemy proved elusive, in part because of their determination not to be drawn into a set-piece battle. Smarting from a successful Roman ambush, the Etruscans finally crossed the Tiber River in retaliation and attacked Servilius' camp. The Veientes suffered heavy casualties in the unsuccessful assault, and were forced to retire across the river to Janiculum Hill immediately west of Rome. The attack prompted Sevilius to cross the Tiber in pursuit and encamp beneath the hill. The following day, the legions attempted to capture the enemy position atop the Janiculum, but were thoroughly repulsed. Only with the arrival of Sevilius' co-*consul*, Aulus Verginius Tricostus Rutilus, were the Romans able to successfully overrun the Etruscan camp. Trapped by two consular armies, the Veientes were badly defeated, much of the enemy force being slaughtered in the final struggle.

Titus Livius (Livy), *History of Rome*, 2.51.4–9.

Jerusalem, 63 BC – While the Roman general Cnaeus Pompeius Magnus was preoccupied with the restoration of order in post-Seleucid Syria, he was asked in 64 BC to resolve a dispute in neighbouring Judaea between Hyrcanus and his younger brother Aristobulus, the sons of the ruling Hasmonean house. Before the Roman *proconsul* could render a decision in the thorny issue, Aristobulus abruptly withdrew to the mountain fortress of Alexandreium to the west of the Jordan Valley. This provocative action incited Pompey to march south from Damascus toward the stronghold, crossing the Jordan River near Scythopolis and halting at Coreae to the immediate northeast of Alexandreium. Aristobulus relinquished control of the mountain outpost after protracted negotiations and withdrew toward Jerusalem, followed closely by the Roman army. At Jericho, the Hasmonean prince finally surrendered to Pompey's arbitration in the matter and offered to pay tribute; but upon learning of this decision, his followers refused to admit the Romans into Jerusalem. Aristobulus was promptly taken into custody and the legions prepared to besiege the city. Aristobulus' supporters withdrew into the Temple Mount when the investment began. The battle for the city was stubbornly fought by both sides throughout the late summer. In September or early October, during the third month of the siege, the Romans were finally able to breach the walls at two separate locations: to the southwest of the Temple Mount, above the Tyropoeon Valley; and on the north side at the Baris fortress. Savage fighting continued inside the precinct until the cohorts, with the aid of Jewish reinforcements loyal to Hyrcanus, were eventually able to overcome all resistance. Approximately 12,000 of Aristobulus' men died in the struggle. Roman losses proved negligible, though the legions suffered a large number of wounded.

Flavius Josephus, *Jewish War*, 1.7.141–151; Flavius Josephus, *Jewish Antiquities*, 14.4.54–71.

Jerusalem, 57 BC (Jewish Revolt) – While the Romans were still embroiled in affairs in Judaea following Pompey's capture of Jerusalem in 63 BC, Alexander, the older son of Aristobulus II – the now deposed Hasmonean ruler and high priest – raised a revolt with the intention of toppling his pro-Roman uncle, Hyrcanus II, from the high priesthood. Collecting 10,000 infantry and 1,500 horsemen from the Judaean countryside, Alexander set about fortifying Alexandreium, a stronghold near the mountains of Arabia. He likewise seized the fortresses of Hyrcania and Machaerus. In response, Aulus Gabinius, the *proconsul* of Syria, descended on the country to quell the rebellion. Once in Judaea, the Romans were reinforced by Jewish forces led by Pitholaus and Malichus. Gabinius sent his lieutenant, Marcus Antonius, and a body of troops, including cavalry, ahead of the main column. The two sides met in pitched battle near Jerusalem. Alexander's army was unable to resist the opposing assault, suffering the loss of 3,000 dead and 3,000 captured. The survivors and their captain fled to Alexandreium following the defeat. Soon thereafter, Gabinius besieged the mountaintop fortress and eventually forced Alexander to capitulate.

Flavius Josephus, *Jewish War*, 1.8.160–163; Flavius Josephus, *Jewish Antiquities*, 14.5.82–85.

Kydonia, 69 BC – see Cydonia, 69 BC.

Lake Trasimeno, 217 BC – see Trasimeno Lake, 217 BC.

Lake Vadimon, 310 BC – see Vadimonis Lake, 310 BC.

Lake Vadimon, 283 BC – see Vadimonis Lake, 283 BC.

Lanuvium, 389 BC – Forced to repel Etruscan and Volscian threats in the immediate wake of the Gallic sack of Rome the previous year, a Roman army under the leadership of the dictator Marcus Furius Camillus marched against an army of the Volsci encamped near the community of Lanuvium, approximately 18 miles south of Rome. Alarmed at the approach of a force commanded by Camillus, the Volscians surrounded their camp with earthen fortifications reinforced by a log barricade around the outside perimeter, and prepared for a Roman assault. After observing the enemy's defences, the dictator ordered a portion of the barricade set ablaze. The subsequent confusion created in the enemy camp by smoke and flames from the conflagration permitted the Roman infantry to easily breach both the barricade and inner ramparts, and quickly rout the Volscian defenders.

Titus Livius (Livy), *History of Rome*, 6.2.

Laodicea, 42 BC (Roman Civil Wars) – In the wake of Caesar's assassination in the spring of 44 BC, political authority in the Roman state was temporarily thrown into chaos. Both the allies of the murdered dictator and the tyrannicides manoeuvred for political control and to secure themselves in preparation for civil war. In Rome, the *consul* Marcus Antonius quickly emerged as a leading figure in the affirmation or redistribution of authority in Italy and the provinces. To that end, he permitted Publius Cornelius Dolabella to assume the governorship of Syria as Caesar had wished, but that allocation was shortly challenged when the Senate granted Caius Cassius Longinus authority to seize the province following Dolabella's murder of Caius Trebonius, one of the assassins. While in Cilicia consolidating his authority among the local population, Dolabella was confronted by Cassius near the Syrian port of Laodicea (Latakiyah) and thoroughly defeated. Shortly thereafter, the victorious legions besieged Dolabella and the remnants of his army in the coastal city. Though he now lacked adequate military forces to confront his enemy, Dolabella still possessed some foreign naval support, including ships sent to him by the Egyptian queen Cleopatra VII. This advantage was quickly lost with the arrival of an opposing fleet under Lucius Murcius Staius, whose vessels sailed boldly into the harbour of Laodicea, defeated those ships sent against them and proceeded to blockade the port. Unable to escape, and suffering from a shortage of provisions for his troops, Dolabella chose to kill himself rather than be betrayed to his enemy.

Dio Cassius, *Roman History*, 47.30.1–5.

Larissa, 171 BC – see Callinicus, 171 BC.

Lauron, 76 BC (Roman Civil Wars, War with Sertorius) – Soon after arriving in Spain, the *proconsul* Cnaeus Pompeius Magnus confronted the forces of the Roman rebel general Quintus Sertorius, while the latter was in the midst of besieging Lauron, a town in Hispania Terraconensis near the coast. Pompey intended to force his opponent to abandon the assault completely, but he first sought to thwart Sertorius' efforts to capture a nearby strategic hill. His attempt failed, and Sertorius was able to seize the knoll and thereby position his forces between the town and Pompey's legions. Satisfied that he had trapped his enemy between the walls of Lauron and his own army, the *proconsul* failed to recognize the presence of 6,000 hostile troops still occupying Sertorius' former camp to his rear. Their location made it impossible for him to assault the main body of the enemy or attempt to relieve the town for fear of being surrounded. Snared by his own tactical blunder, and Sertorius' cunning, Pompey was forced to stand by helplessly while the town was systematically reduced.

> Plutarch, *Sertorius*, 18.3–6, *Pompey*, 18.3; Paulus Orosius, *Seven Books of History against the Pagans*, 5.23.

Lautulae, 315 BC (Second Samnite War, Samnite Wars) – As the theatre of war shifted northwestward from Samnium and Apulia into Latium, Roman and Samnite armies concentrated in the region of Sora, a Volscian community in the Liris River valley which had recently allied with the Samnites after massacring the Roman colonists in the city. The two armies met in the vicinity of Lautulae, a town situated to the west near the Tyrrhenian coast. In the battle which followed, neither side gained a decisive victory – though the Roman army appears to have suffered more in the fighting, having at one point apparently experienced panic and flight in a portion of its ranks – before nightfall put an end to the action. After the clash, the Roman dictator Quintus Fabius Maximus Rullianus assumed a defensive posture within the safety of the army's marching camp while an account of the engagement was relayed to the Senate. Counted among the Roman casualties suffered in the day's action was the *magister equitum* Quintus Aulius Cerretanus.

> Titus Livius (Livy), *History of Rome*, 9.23.1–5; Diodorus Siculus, *Historical Library*, 19.72.6–7.

Lautulae, 315 BC (Second Samnite War, Samnite Wars) – After a failed encounter with the Samnites near Lautulae the Roman dictator Quintus Fabius Maximus Rullianus kept his army safely within the confines of the legionary camp for several days in order to permit the soldiers to recuperate from fighting. When word reached Rome concerning the outcome of the contest and the death of the *magister equitum* Quintus Aulius Cerretanus, the Senate dispatched a fresh army under the newly appointed Master of the Horse, Caius Fabius Ambustus, brother of the dictator. Rullianus prepared for battle upon learning of the approach of the relief army. He related the details of his plan to Ambustus, who thereafter concealed his army at some distance in expectation of a signal to action. The dictator then assembled his legions into battle formation and ordered the Roman camp burned – the awaited indication for the second army to attack. As Rullianus' infantry closed with the Samnites and disrupted their ranks in the first assault, the *magister militum* suddenly charged against the enemy rear. In the resulting struggle, the two Roman armies trapped and destroyed the flower of the Samnite host.

> Titus Livius (Livy), *History of Rome*, 9.23.6–16.

Lemnos Island, 73 BC (Third Mithridatic War, Wars against Mithridates the Great) – In an effort to resume the war against the Pontic king, Mithridates VI Eupator, the Roman general Lucius Licinius Lucullus assembled a war fleet at the Hellespont before proceeding southward against a group of enemy ships operating off the Anatolian coast. Shortly after its arrival off the Troad, the Roman fleet captured thirteen ships commanded by Isodorus which were part of a larger fifty-ship flotilla sailing between the harbour of the Achaeans and the island of Lemnos (Limnos) to the west. Lucullus immediately took up pursuit of the remaining vessels, eventually forcing them to seek refuge on the small barren island. Once there, the king's ships stubbornly refused to be drawn into battle. Thwarted by his opponents' determination to remain safely beached, Lucullus finally resolved to put soldiers ashore on the far side of the island with the intention of driving the recalcitrant enemy to sea. The resulting infantry assault eventually forced the Pontic fleet to abandon the island, at which point it was immediately assailed by awaiting Roman squadrons. Subjected to the relentless attacks of Roman *triremes*, and suffering severe manpower losses, Mithridates' ships scattered in open flight. The Pontic commanders Alexander and Dionysius were soon captured, along with the rebel generals Marcus Varius and Marcus Marius.

Plutarch, *Lucullus*, 12; Appianus (Appian), *Mithridatic Wars*, 77.

Leontini, 214 BC (Second Punic War, Wars against Carthage) – Following the death of the Syracusian tyrant Hiero II in 215 BC, his grandson Hieronymus rejected his predecessor's twenty-two-year alliance with Rome and opened negotiations with the Carthaginian envoys Hippocrates and Epicydes. Within a few short months, pro-Roman sympathizers assassinated the young king and reasserted their power in the city, forcing the Punic agents to take refuge in Leontini (Lentini), a community located northwest of Syracuse and overlooking the Plain of Catana. There, the Carthaginians persuaded the Leontinians to massacre a nearby detachment of Roman guards. In response, the Roman *praetor* in Sicily, Marcus Claudius Marcellus, accompanied by his *legatus* Appius Claudius Pulcher, attacked Leontini with three legions. Storming the walls from two sides, the army breached the city's defences at the first assault. Afterward, the *praetor* ordered the execution of 2,000 Roman deserters seized there.

Titus Livius (Livy), *History of Rome*, 34.30.1–6; Plutarch, *Marcellus*, 14.1–2.

Letum et Ballista, 176 BC – The year after a Roman defeat of the Ligurians at the Scultenna (Panaro) River, the tribes again rose up in revolt. Still chaffing from the previous year's loss against the *consul* Caius Claudius Pulcher, and unwilling to again provide Rome's legions the advantage of level terrain, the rebels decided to occupy two mountains, Letum and Ballista, in the territory of Mutina (Modena) in Cisalpine Gaul. In response, the *consul* Quintus Petilius Spurinus requested that Claudius, now a *proconsul*, meet him at a location called Campi Macri, in the vicinity of the Ligurian stronghold.

The two armies were soon joined by the *consul* Caius Valerius Laevinus and his legions. Once there, Claudius turned command of his army over to Petilius, and the consuls then distributed these legions and supporting auxiliary forces between their two armies. From Campi Macri, the Roman forces approached the Ligurian position from different directions. Petilius opened the attack. Encamped with his men near the base of the mountains and facing the adjoining saddle ridge, the *consul* split his forces into two columns and assaulted the twin heights simultaneously. The troops under his personal leadership advanced quickly without significant opposition, but the enemy soundly repulsed the other contingent. Observing the second line falter and begin to retreat, Petilius crossed over on horseback and rallied the soldiers, but was killed with a javelin in the midst of the fighting. Some of the soldiers immediately concealed the *consul*'s body, cognizant that knowledge of his death could demoralize the ranks, while the remainder of the army continued to press the attack, unaware of their leader's demise. Eventually, the infantry and cavalry overcame all resistance and seized control of the mountains and col. Approximately 5,000 Ligurians died. Roman losses amounted to only fifty-two men, Valerius' legions having apparently never entered the struggle.

Titus Livius (Livy), *History of Rome*, 41.18.1–13.

Leucae, 130 BC – Upon the death of Attalus III, king of Pergumum, in 133 BC, the monarch bequeathed his entire kingdom to the Roman people, but authorities in Italy were slow to secure control of the region because of domestic political turmoil in Rome. The delay permitted Aristonicus, illegitimate half-brother of the deceased king, to attempt to seize the Pergamene throne. The Senate responded to this threat by sending an army to Asia Minor under the leadership of the *consul* Publius Licinius Crassus Mucianus. There, Crassus secured the support of several regional kings, including King Nicomedes II of Bithynia, the Pontic ruler Mithridates V, Pylaemenes of Pyphlagonia and King Ariarathes V of Cappadocia. The two armies met in the vicinity of Leucae, a small town located near the city of Phocis (Foca) some 40 miles north of Smyrna (Izmir). Crassus was killed and the army routed with heavy losses in the resulting battle.

Paulus Orosius, *Seven Books of History against the Pagans*, 5.10; Eutropius, *Abridgement of Roman History*, 4.20; Titus Livius (Livy), *Summaries*, 59.

Leucopetra, 146 BC (War of the Achaean League) – When the leadership of the Achaean League learned of the defeat and death of Critolaus at Scarpheia, it appointed the Achaean *strategos* Diaeus to assume command of the league's army. Aware of the magnitude of the danger posed by the Romans, the general enlisted thousands of Achaeans and Arcadians of military age, as well as freed slaves, to form an army of roughly 14,000 infantry and

600 cavalry. He then dispatched 4,000 men under Alcamenes to garrison the city of Megara some 30 miles away, and ordered his lieutenant to attempt to check the approach of the Roman army before it reached Corinth. After capturing the city of Thebes, the legions of the *propraetor* Quintus Caecilius Metellus marched southward, passing through northern Attica before moving toward the Corinthian isthmus. When the army approached Megara from the northeast, the Achaeans immediately abandoned the city and withdrew, leaving the way to Corinth undefended. The Megaran citizens surrendered their city to Metellus without resistance. On approaching the isthmus, the *praetor* made a last attempt to restore peace before the advent of hostilities, but the Greeks rejected all efforts at negotiation. Around the same time, the leading elements of a Roman invasion fleet arrived under the command of the *consul* Lucius Mummius. While the *consul* awaited the arrival of his remaining transports, Metellus was ordered to return to Macedonia. The expeditionary force consisted of 23,000 infantry and 3,500 cavalry. As a precaution, Mummius stationed Italian and auxiliary troops at a forward outpost about a mile away from the Roman earthworks, but an early morning attack by the Achaeans forced the advanced party to abandon its position. This initial contest preceded a general action between the armies on open ground outside Corinth. As the opposing lines moved closer, the Achaean cavalry abruptly fled the field without making contact with the Roman horse. By contrast, the infantry battle proved to be a protracted struggle despite the pressure exerted on the enemy by the maniples, and remained undecided until a select detachment of 1,000 legionaries outflanked the Achaeans. This assault fatally disrupted the integrity of the enemy formation and resulted in a complete rout. That night, the remnants of the Achaean army and much of the Corinthian population fled the city. Three days later, Mummius sacked and burned Corinth.

Pausanias, *Description of Greece*, 7.16.1–9; Lucius Annaeus Florus, *Epitomy*, 1.32.4–5; Sextus Aurelius Victor, *Lives of Illustrious Men*, 60; Paulus Orosius, *Seven Books of History against the Pagans*, 5.3; Titus Livius (Livy), *Summaries*, 52.

Lilybaeum, 218 BC (Second Punic War, Wars against Carthage) – The capture of three Carthaginian ships in the Straits of Messina by the Syracusian tyrant Hiero II alerted the Romans to the presence of a Punic naval force operating north of the island of Sicily with the intention of capturing the Roman-controlled port of Lilybaeum (Marsala). The remaining seventeen warships of the enemy fleet, still present in the waters around the Lipara Islands, awaited the arrival of an additional thirty-five *quinqueremes* from Carthage before moving against the western Sicilian city. Learning of this threat, the Roman *praetor* in Sicily, Marcus Aemilius Lepidus, immediately warned Lilybaeum and other cities in the vicinity to remain alert to the danger. The threat was soon fully revealed by moonlight when lookouts spotted the approach of the invasion fleet as it bore down on the port under cover of darkness. When the Carthaginians spied signal fires burning atop watchtowers along the coast, they realized their plan had been foiled and prepared for a naval battle the following day. At dawn, the Punic craft withdrew into open sea, shortly followed by the Roman *quinqueremes* from the harbour. The encounter proved to be a contest between the heavier Roman warships, which sought to overpower the enemy by boarding, and the more agile Carthaginian ships, that manoeuvred for tactical advantage in order to disable their opponents. The Romans managed to isolate and capture seven enemy vessels before putting the remainder to flight, having suffered no losses themselves.

Titus Livius (Livy), *History of Rome*, 21.49–50.6.

Lipara, 260 BC (First Punic War, Wars against Carthage) – Learning that a Roman fleet of seventeen ships was sitting at anchor in the port town of Lipara on the island of Lipara (Lipari), the Carthaginian general Hannibal Gisco sent a force of twenty ships under the command of the Carthaginian senator Boodes, from the Sicilian port of Panormus (Palermo), to capture the vessels. Approaching the town under cover of darkness, the Punic fleet blockaded the harbour, trapping the enemy ships and forcing their capitulation. The Roman commander, Gnaeus Cornelius Scipio Asina, likewise surrendered.

Polybius, *Histories*, 1.21.3–8.

Lipara, 252 BC (First Punic War, Wars against Carthage) – Having failed three times in 260, 258 and 257 BC, to capture the port of Lipara on the island of Lipara (Lipari), the Romans again attempted the reduction of the community, this time under the leadership of the *consul* Caius Aurelius Cotta. After acquiring ships from Hiero, king of Syracuse, the *consul* deployed a legionary force on the island and charged the tribune Quintus Cassius with prosecuting the siege. The officer was further ordered to refrain from engaging the Carthaginians in battle. Ignoring these instructions, Cassius eventually attempted the capture of the town by direct assault, but failed after Roman forces were repelled with heavy losses. For his disobedience, Aurelius removed the tribune from his command. The *consul* later seized Lipara by investment and massacred it occupants.

Polybius, *Histories*, 1.39.13; John Zonaras, *Epitome of Histories*, 8.14; Diodorus Siculus, *Historical Library*, 23.20.

Litana, 216 BC (Second Punic War, Wars against Carthage) – In the spring, the *praetor* Lucius Postumius Albinus marched northward into Cisalpine Gaul at the head of a 25,000-man army which included two Roman legions and numerous allies. The purpose of the campaign was to create a diversion of sufficient intensity to compel the Gauls to recall their troops from Carthaginian service in southern Italy. Near the town of Mutina (Modena), and northwest of Bononia (Bologna), Postumius and his army entered the great forest of Litana, unaware that the Boii had prepared an elaborate trap for the Roman column. All along the highway which passed through this dense stand of forest, the Gauls had cut a large number of trees in such a way that they would topple if pushed. The Boii lay in hiding on the edge of the forest in anticipation of springing the ambush. Once the Romans entered the woods, the Gauls overturned the outermost trees, causing a chain reaction which trapped the army inside the forest under tons of falling tree-trunks, branches and debris. The vast majority of the men were either crushed to death under the tangle of material or slain by the Boii. Some of the Romans at the front of the column avoided the avalanche of trees behind, but were blocked from crossing a nearby river bridge by a force of armed Gauls. Left with no option, the Romans attempted to fight their way through the mass of warriors, but all were either killed or captured. Among the thousands of Roman dead was the *praetor*, whose severed head later served to adorn a sacred temple of the Boii.

Titus Livius (Livy), *History of Rome*, 23.24.6–13.

Litana, 195 BC, summer – Near the forest of Litana, northwest of Bononia (Bologna), the Roman *consul* Lucius Valerius Flaccus defeated a force of Boii tribesmen. The battle resulted in some 8,000 Gallic dead. The remainder of the Gauls was compelled to return to their homeland following the defeat.

Titus Livius (Livy), *History of Rome*, 34.22.1–3.

Locha, 204 BC (Second Punic War, Wars against Carthage) – After devastating the North African town of Locha, Roman and Numidian troops resumed their ravaging of the surrounding countryside. In an effort to defeat these forces, the Carthaginian general Hasdrubal, son of Gisgo, prepared an ambuscade, sending Mago, his master of horse, to attack the Romans in front while he fell on the enemy from behind. Confronted in such a manner; the Roman *proconsul* Publius Cornelius Scipio (Africanus) and Masinissa, king of the Massylian Numidians, divided their forces in an effort to repel the simultaneous assaults. In the resulting battle, Hasdrubal lost 5,000 men and an additional 1,800 were captured.

Appianus (Appian), *Punic Wars*, 8.15.

Locri, 208 BC (Second Punic War, Wars against Carthage) – During the summer, the consuls Titus Quinctius Crispinus and Marcus Claudius Marcellus ordered Lucius Cincius to sail from Sicily with his fleet and besiege the southern Italian coastal town of Locri (ruins of Locri Epizefiri), which was held by the Carthaginians. An attempt to deploy additional Roman man-power by land from Tarentum was stopped when Punic forces ambushed a detachment near the community of Petelia. Following the death of Marcellus and serious injury to Crispinus in the skirmish near Bantia, Hannibal marched southeastward toward the Bruttium peninsula in order to raise the siege of Locri. Ahead of his infantry column, the Punic general dispatched the Numidian cavalry to advance as quickly as possible to the aid of the beleaguered town. When Mago, the commander of the garrison at Locri, learned of the approach of the Numidian horse, he led a sudden, unexpected sally against Cincius. As both armies were of roughly equal size, the battle remained undecided until the arrival of the Numidians. The sight of the African horsemen – and their fearsome reputation – alarmed the Romans. Faced with the anticipated arrival of Hannibal's entire army, the Romans abandoned the siege, leaving their engines, and departed by sea.

Titus Livius (Livy), *History of Rome*, 27.26.3, 27.28.13–17; Plutarch, *Marcellus*, 29.1.

Locri Epizephyrii, 208 BC – see Locri, 208 BC.

Longula, 482 BC – Following a failed battle against the Volsci outside the city of Antium (Anzio), the *consul* Lucius Aemilius Mamercus relocated his army to a hill near the town of Longula. Still flush with victory, the Volscians pursued the retreating legions to the new location. An initial attack against the Roman camp failed, largely due to a stubborn defence by *triarii* and cavalry, the latter being compelled by the rugged terrain to fight on foot. Over the following days, the Volsci repeatedly assembled in hope of battle, but Aemilius refused to accept each challenge, partly because of extensive manpower losses accrued at Antium. While both armies prepared for a major struggle, Aemilius' co-*consul*, Caeso Fabius, dispatched reinforcements. These units, travelling through the mountains largely under cover of darkness, successfully reached the beleaguered force and entered the Roman camp undetected. When the Volscians again elected to assault the encampment, they were unexpectedly subjected to an intense attack from the legions. Concentrated missile fire, together with a strong frontal charge by the reinvigorated ranks of the Roman infantry, routed the Volsci with heavy losses.

Dionysius of Halicarnassus, *Roman Antiquities*, 8.85.4–86.

Luceria, 294 BC (Third Samnite War, Samnite Wars) – When word reached the Romans that the city of Luceria was under siege by the Samnites, the *consul* Marcus Atilius Regulus led an army to the relief of the beleaguered community. The two armies met near the Lucerine frontier, and the Romans were beaten. The loss demoralized the Romans, who were unaccustomed to defeat. The camp remained agitated throughout the following night from fear of imminent attack and anxiety over the possibility of having to fight the enemy again the next day. Despite their victory, the Samnites were also hesitant to engage the legions a second time and preferred to retire at first light. This intention was made more difficult, however, by the fact that the only road leading out of the area passed directly by the Roman *castrum*. When the Samnites began to withdraw at dawn, the Romans misinterpreted their intentions and concluded that the enemy was marching to attack the camp. Atilius quickly ordered his troops to arm and assemble for battle outside the ramparts, but the men remained dispirited from the previous encounter and were reluctant to fight another pitched battle with the same foe. The insubordinate behaviour of the infantry threatened to undermine the integrity of the entire army, and compelled the *consul* to declare that he would sooner charge the enemy alone than cower behind the camp's defences and await an assault. Shamed by Atilius' words, the army arrayed for battle, much to the regret of the Samnites, who were no more eager to renew the struggle than their opponents. Once both armies formed their battle lines, neither side made any immediate move to initiate the contest, and only advanced out of fear that should one retire the other side would attack. The fighting lacked energy when the battle commenced, and an attempt by Atilius to turn the encounter to his favour failed when a Roman cavalry charge went awry, causing the infantry to take flight toward the camp. The enemy pursued only a short distance, permitting the *consul* to check the rout by deploying a mounted guard to block entry into the *castrum*. He then proceeded to harshly castigate the men. At the same time, the remainder of the cavalry gathered round and levelled their spears at the mass of legionaries, compelling the maniples to resume battle. The legions again advanced against the awaiting divisions of Samnites, this time forcing their adversaries to retreat after only a short clash. The fugitives briefly rallied around their store of baggage, but were soon overwhelmed by a simultaneous assault of infantry and cavalry. As the legions executed a holding attack, the squadrons of horsemen assailed the enemy's rear. Few managed to escape. Roman dead amounted to 7,800, while Samnite losses totalled 4,800 killed and 7,800 captured. The prisoners were stripped and sent under the yoke.

   Titus Livius (Livy), *History of Rome*, 10.35–36.15.

Lyco, 190 BC – Near the Iberian community of Lyco, in the lands of the Bastetani, a Roman army led by Lucius Aemilius Paulus was badly defeated by a force of Lusitani warriors. Some 6,000 legionaries were killed, while the remainder of the command was driven back into the army's marching camp. Continued enemy assaults against the ramparts of the encampment were repelled with difficulty, ultimately compelling Aemilius to order the withdrawal of the Roman cohorts by forced marches into less hostile territory.

   Titus Livius (Livy), *History of Rome*, 37.48.7–9.

Lycus River, 72 BC, spring (Third Mithridatic War, Wars against Mithridates the Great) – In the spring of 72 BC, the Roman general Lucius Licinius Lucullus renewed his campaign against the Pontic king Mithridates VI Eupator, who had wintered with his army near the city of Cabeirus in the Lycus River valley. When weather finally permitted, Lucullus and his legions crossed the inland mountains and descended onto the plain near the city. The arrival of the Romans prompted Mithridates to offer battle, and he crossed the Lycus River and readied his forces for action. Among the king's troops were some 4,000 light and heavy horse. A cavalry engagement followed, and the Romans were put to flight. The defeat persuaded Lucullus to move his army into the surrounding hill country in order to neutralize the Pontic king's numerical advantage in cavalry.

Plutarch, *Lucullus*, 15.1–3

Magaba Mons, 189 BC – Following the previous day's cavalry skirmish, the Roman *consul* Cnaeus Manlius Vulso advanced against a substantial enemy force positioned on Magaba Mons, located east of the city of Ancyra in central Anatolia. Having already fought a series of engagements against Gallic tribes in the region, including the battle at Olympus Mons, Manlius moved to end all remaining tribal opposition in northern Galatia by means of a decisive action. After two days of reconnaissance, the *consul* divided his army into four columns and prepared to ascend the mountain. The enemy was formidably arrayed. The centre consisted of 50,000 Tectosagi and Trocmi warriors. On the left wing, 4,000 additional troops were positioned under the Cappadocian leader Ariarathes and the Paphonlagonian prince Morzius. Lastly, protecting the right flank of the Gallic line was a large concentration of 10,000 cavalry, forced to dismount and fight because of the rugged terrain. Manlius initiated the assault by ordering two of his infantry columns to climb the central portion of the mountain, and placed some of his light-armed troops in the van with a large supply of weapons. At the same time, the *consul* instructed the remaining columns to scale the sides of the mountain in order to attack the enemy's flanks. As the main company of Roman troops approached the formation of Tectosagi and Trocmi, the light infantry discharged a heavy volley of missiles which quickly caused the Gallic centre to collapse, shortly followed by a complete rout of the entire army. In the following pursuit, 8,000 Gauls died. Soon thereafter, tribal ambassadors sued for peace.

Titus Livius (Livy), *History of Rome*, 38.26–27; Appianus (Appian), *Syrian Wars*, 42; Lucius Annaeus Florus, *Epitomy*, 1.27.5.

Magnesia, 190 BC (War against Antiochus III) – Following years of growing tension between Rome and the Seleucid Empire of King Antiochus III the Great of Syria, an attempt by the latter to expand his power in the eastern

Mediterranean resulted in war. Entering into an alliance with the Aetolian League, Antiochus invaded Greece in 192 BC. In response, Rome mobilized for war, fearing an alliance between Syria, Macedon and Carthage. At Thermopylae two years later, Roman legions under Acilius Manius Glabrio decisively checked Antiochus' conquest of the peninsula. The Seleucid king's defeat was soon followed by a Roman invasion of Asia Minor. At Magnesia, northeast of Smyrna in Asia Minor, Antiochus assembled an army of 70,000 near the Hermus River. In the centre he placed his 16,000-man Macedonian phalanx. This was divided into ten sections of 1,600 men each, and interspersed between each was a detachment of two war elephants. Stationed on both flanks and to the front were sizeable formations of cavalry. On the right side of the phalanx, the king deployed 500 Gallograecian horsemen, 3,000 cataphracti and several hundred riders of the royal *agema*. On the left was an assorted force of cavalry anchored against the phalanx by 1,500 Gallograecians. Arrayed in front of these was a sizeable concentration of scythed chariots. The Roman force of 30,000 was under the command of Lucius Cornelius Scipio (Asiaticus) and his *legatus* Caius Domitius Ahenobarbus and included 20,000 Roman and Italian legionaries, each legion arranged in a *triplex acies*. Domitius deployed the infantry on the left against the river Phrygius, a tributary of the Hermus, with large contingents of cavalry positioned to the right of this main legionary formation. The battle opened on the

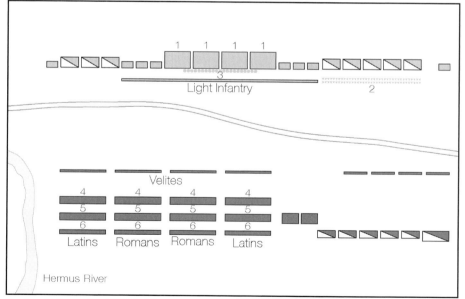

Battle of Magnesia, 190 BC (Phase 1). (1=Phalangites; 2=Chariots; 3=Elephants; 4=Hastati; 5=Principes; 6=Triarii)

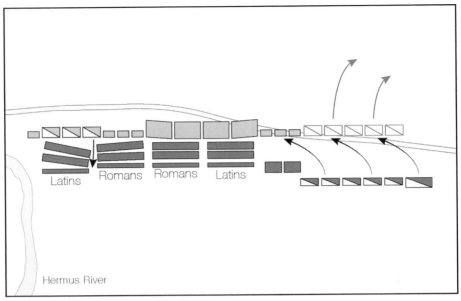

Battle of Magnesia, 190 BC (Phase 2)

Roman right with a charge of light infantry followed by squadrons of cavalry, led by Rome's ally, Eumenes II, king of Pergamon. As Eumenes' forces drove in Antiochus' left wing, scattering the latter's mounted squadrons and chariots, the legions attacked the phalanx. At the same time, the Syrian cavalry, led personally by Antiochus III, penetrated the Roman line nearest the river, scattered four troops of horse and momentarily endangered Scipio's left flank and *castrum*. Stout resistance by cohorts defending the Roman camp, together with a mounted countercharge by Attalus, the brother of Eumenes, checked the king's attack. Syrian resistance began to erode under pressure from the Roman assault. The phalanx, now devoid of its mounted contingents, was soon trapped by Roman and allied cavalry and broken apart. The destruction of the phalanx preceded the complete collapse of Antiochus' entire army. In the ensuing rout, 50,000 Syrians and supporting troops were killed or captured. Antiochus fled the field.

Appianus (Appian), *Syrian Wars* 30–36; Titus Livius (Livy), *History of Rome*, 37.37.9–44.2.

Magnesia ad Sipylum, 190 BC – see Magnesia, 190 BC.

Maleventum, 297 BC (Third Samnite War, Samnite Wars) – In an attempt to prevent the Apulians from providing the Samnites with military aid during a Roman invasion of Samnium, the *consul* Publius Decius Mus encamped his army near the town of Maleventum in southwestern Italy. Apart from successfully disrupting efforts by the two Italic armies to join together in resisting the Roman incursion into Samnium, Decius induced the Apulians into open battle and defeated them with a loss of 2,000 dead. Following this victory, Decius led his legions into Samnium where, together with a second army under fellow *consul* Quintus Fabius Maximus Rallianus, the Romans decisively overran the territories of the Samnites after a four-month campaign.

Titus Livius (Livy), *History of Rome*, 10.15.1–2

Maleventum, 275 BC (Wars of Pyrrhus) – From his Sicilian campaign, the Epirot king Pyrrhus returned to Italy at the request of the Samnites to continue the war against the Romans. He arrived by sea at Tarentum in southern Italy with 20,000 infantry and 3,000 cavalry, and immediately acquired additional forces from the Tarentines. Having assembled his forces, Pyrrhus marched toward the district of Samnium in south-central Italy, intent on engaging one of two consular armies presently operating in the southern portion of the peninsula. As he pushed northwestward, the Epirot ruler, in an effort to avoid facing the combined strength of both Roman armies, dispatched elements of his command into Lucania to delay the second *consul*, Lucius Cornelius Lentulus Caudinus, from immediately offering reinforcements to his colleague. Pyrrhus then led the remainder of his army against the legions of the more experienced *consul* Manius Curius Dentatus, now encamped near the town of Maleventum. These legions, awaiting the arrival of aid from Lentulus, were unaware of the approaching enemy. Pyrrhus attempted to surprise the unsuspecting Curius by a night assault, but was badly delayed in his approach by rugged, heavily wooded terrain. The arrival of daylight found the Epirot army still in the surrounding hills and its position fully revealed to the Roman encampment on the plain below. As the leading elements of the Epirot force began to emerge from the treeline into open ground, Curius attacked, routing the advanced formations of the enemy and driving the main van of Pyrrhus' army onto the open plain. Both armies then entered into a general engagement. As the action evolved, the legions slowly gained overall tactical advantage, but were suddenly overpowered on one quarter of the battlefield by Pyrrhus' war elephants. This swift reversal compelled the *consul* to order an attack by legionary reserves presently guarding the Roman encampment. An unexpected discharge of javelins from these fresh reinforcements disrupted the elephant assault, and drove the confused animals back into the ranks of Epirot infantry. The resulting havoc within the enemy formation shifted the momentum of the struggle decisively in favour of the legions, who quickly routed Pyrrhus' army from the field.

Plutarch, *Pyrrhus*, 24.4–25; Eutropius, *Abridgement of Roman History*, 2.14; Paulus Orosius, *Seven Books of History against the Pagans*, 4.2; John Zonaras, *Epitome of Histories*, 8.6; Dionysius of Halicarnassus, *Roman Antiquities*, 20.10–12; Titus Livius (Livy), *Summaries*, 14; Lucius Annaeus Florus, 1.13.11–13.

Manlian Pass, 180 BC – Because of the delayed arrival of his appointed replacement from Rome, the *propraetor* of Nearer Spain, Quintus Fulvius Flaccus, initiated a campaign against those peoples in the remote interior of Celtiberia which had yet to surrender to Roman authorities. Leading an army out of winter quarters and into the unconquered territory, the legions proceeded to devastate the countryside. Rather than demoralizing the inhabitants, the assault provoked the people to arms. In the midst of these events, Flaccus received word of his successor's imminent arrival and ordered an immediate withdrawal of all Roman forces from the region. The return march carried Flaccus and his command through the Manlian Pass (Jalon Valley). A Celtiberian army lay in ambush there, emboldened by the belief that the Roman retreat was inspired by fear of the native uprising. At dawn, the Roman column entered the pass and was suddenly attacked on two sides. The *propraetor* quickly checked the panic in the army's ranks by an appeal to discipline. He ordered the legates and tribunes to assemble the men under their standards and prepare for action, even as fighting erupted on the extreme flanks of the battle line. Within moments, both armies were fully engaged. The legions and Latin allies capably repelled the assault, but the provincial auxiliaries were unable to hold their position and struggled to maintain the composition of the Roman line. When it was apparent to the Celtiberi that they could not disrupt the integrity of the enemy's centre by any other means, they assembled into a wedge formation and attacked. The offensive proved irresistible and was at the point of completely rupturing the legionary line when a sudden charge by Roman cavalry shattered the integrity of the entire enemy formation. Once the squadrons of riders cleared the mass of barbarian infantry, the horsemen wheeled around and again drove through the startled ranks of the Celtiberi. The carnage wrought by the attacks panicked the survivors, who were unable to recover before another charge by fresh squadrons of allied cavalry devastated the battered remains of the once-formidable body of warriors. The Romans slaughtered the remnants of the defeated army as the wedge disintegrated. Casualties resulting from the battle included 17,000 Celtiberian dead and 472 Romans. The Latin allies lost an additional 1,000 soldiers and provincial auxiliary troops of approximately 4,000 men.

Titus Livius (Livy), *History of Rome*, 40.39–40.

Marcius, 390 BC – see Mount Marcius, 390 BC.

Martius, 390 BC – see Mount Marcius, 390 BC.

Martius, 77 BC – see Campus Martius, 77 BC.

Massilia, 49 BC (Roman Civil Wars, Wars of the First Triumvirate) – During Caesar's absence in Spain, a naval engagement occurred between a squadron of seventeen Massilian ships and other smaller craft, led by the

Pompeian commander Lucius Domitius Ahenobarbus, and a force of twelve Caesarian vessels commanded by Decimus Brutus. The Massilian galleys were manned by seasoned oarsmen, supported by archers and auxiliary Albici. The Roman ships, though fewer in number and lacking experienced crews, carried volunteer detachments of veteran centurions and front-line infantry-men, or *antesignani*. The battle was fought near an island (Rattonneaux) opposite the port of Massilia (Marseille). As the engagement began, the Massilians, possessing faster, more nimble vessels, deployed their battle line in an attempt to surround the larger, slower Roman flotilla; and failing that, to attack individual galleys with several of their own ships, or cripple them by the shearing away of oars. The skillful handling of the Messilian craft initially permitted them to evade the dangers of ship-to-ship shock action with their bigger opponents, but Domitius' vessels were eventually forced into close fighting by the persistent efforts of Brutus' crews to secure the enemy ships to their own by means of grappling irons. Once ensnared, Roman infantry quickly boarded and subdued the Massilian ships; capturing some, sinking others and driving the remainder into the harbour. Domitius' losses amounted to nine ships, including those captured.

   Caesar, *The Civil Wars*, 1.56–58; Dio Cassius, *Roman History*, 41.21.3.

Mediolanum, 222 BC – In an effort to completely extinguish a Gallic threat in northern Italy, the Roman consuls Marcus Claudius Marcellus and Gnaeus Cornelius Scipio Calvus led legions into the Padus (Po) Valley. After capturing the city of Acerrae by siege, a consular formation led by Gnaeus Cornelius pursued a force of retreating Gauls to the community of Mediolanum (Milan) in the territory of the Insubres, but shortly withdrew without offering battle in order to again rendezvous with the legions of Marcus Claudius. As Cornelius' cohorts began their return march to Acerrae, the Gauls unexpectedly left the protection of Mediolanum and attacked the Roman rearguard, throwing a portion of the force into disarray. The *consul* quickly rallied the scattered elements of the guard in order to redress the situation, and ordered legionary detachments ahead of the main van to fall back as reinforcements. Intense fighting ensued and continued unabated for some time before Gallic resistance finally collapsed. Once the defeated remnants of the Celts were thoroughly scattered and driven into the surrounding mountains, Cornelius turned his cohorts against Mediolanum and captured the city by assault.

   Polybius, *Histories*, 2.34.9–15.

Mediolanum, 194 BC – The Cisalpine Gallic tribe of the Boii, led by Dorulatis, incited the Insubres to renounce their recent peace with Rome and take up arms. In response, the *proconsul* Lucius Valerius Flaccus marched Roman legions into the Padus (Po) Valley, where they engaged a combined

Insubrian-Boiian army near Mediolanum (Milan). The Gauls were defeated in the battle with a loss of 10,000 warriors.

Titus Livius (Livy), *History of Rome*, 34.46.1.

Mellaria, 80 BC (War against Sertorius) – At the invitation of Lusitanian ambassadors, the Roman rebel general Quintus Sertorius prepared to cross the Straits of Hercules (Straits of Gibraltar) from Mauritania with 2,600 Roman legionary deserters and 700 Libyans in order to lead the Iberians in their struggle against Rome. When he learned of the plan, the Roman *legatus* Caius Annius Cotta* deployed his fleet in an attempt to stop Sertorius from reaching the European mainland, but his ships were defeated by Sertorius in a naval battle in the straits near Mellaria, approximately 45 miles southeast of Gades (Cadiz). This marked the first in a series of clashes between Sertorian and Roman forces over the next six years.

Plutarch, *Sertorius* 12.1–3; *possibly Lucius Aurelius Cotta.

Messana, 264 BC (First Punic War, Wars against Carthage) – Soon after the outbreak of regional hostilities in Sicily between the Syracusans under King Hiero II and a group of Campanian mercenaries called Mamertines – who had years earlier seized control of the Greek coastal colony of Messana (Messina) – both Carthage and Rome became embroiled in the dispute. As the war broadened, a Carthaginian army eventually joined with the Syracusans in the siege of the port city. The advent of Punic forces in the struggle was soon followed by the arrival of Roman legions under the *consul* Appius Claudius Caudex, who landed in Sicily with the intention of aiding the Mamertines. After crossing the Straits of Messana from Italy at night and entering the city, the *consul* attempted to negotiate with the besieging parties, but his efforts were rejected. Regarding it as prudent to avoid being trapped in Messana, Claudius determined to draw the Syracusans into a struggle. Hiero accepted the challenge and both armies assembled for battle outside the city. After a lengthy clash, the Romans finally succeeded in driving the enemy back to their camp. That evening, the king abandoned the siege and withdrew to Syracuse with his army.

Polybius, *Histories*, 1.11.9–15; John Zonaras, *Epitome of Histories*, 8.9.

Messana, 264 BC (First Punic War, Wars against Carthage) – Following the defeat at Messana (Messina) of a Syracusan army under King Hiero II, the Roman *consul* Appius Claudius Caudex arrayed his army in formation the next morning in an attempt to draw out the Carthaginians, the other hostile army presently besieging the city. The Punic force accepted the offer of battle, was defeated and withdrew in disorder to neighbouring communities. The Roman legions led by Appius thereafter felt at liberty to begin a campaign to devastate the Syracusan territories preparatory to initiating a total siege of Syracuse proper.

Polybius, *Histories*, 1.11.12–12.4; John Zonaras, *Epitome of Histories*, 8.9.

Metaurus River, 207 BC, 23 June (Second Punic War, Wars against Carthage) – The Carthaginian loss at Baecula in south central Spain finally convinced Hasdrubal Barca that the peninsula must be abandoned to Roman forces, and in the autumn of 208 BC, he led his army into southern Gaul, intent on an invasion of Italy the following year. He crossed the Alps in the spring of 207 BC after wintering in Transalpine Gaul. The crossing proved uneventful, and he descended into the valley of the Padus River (Po Valley) without opposition. His intent was to provide support for his brother, Hannibal, and to that end he marched toward southern Italy by way of the *Via Flaminia*, following the Adriatic coast. After crossing the Metaurus (Metauro) River, Hasdrubal advanced as far as the coastal city of Sena Gallica (Senigallia), where he encountered the legions of the *consul* Marcus Livius Salinator and the *praetor* Lucius Porcius Licinus. Neither side sought battle and both armies eventually settled into camps about half a mile apart near the banks of the Sena (Cesano) River. Soon afterward, the Punic commander dispatched messengers down the peninsula to locate Hannibal and arrange a meeting of the Carthaginian armies in the Ager Gallicus in eastern Umbria, but the riders were captured near Tarentum. The local *propraetor* immediately sent the expropriated information to the *consul* Caius Claudius Nero, who was presently encamped near Hannibal at Canusium (Canosa di Puglia) in southeastern Italy. When he learned of the Carthaginians' intentions, Claudius formulated a plan to fatally undermine the proposed union of the Punic armies. Apprising the Senate of his actions, the *consul* left the preponderance of his command in its present location in order to hold Hannibal in check, and then led a select force of 6,000 infantry and 1,000 cavalry on a forced march to the north, covering some 250 miles in six days in order to reinforce the legions of Livius. Since it was vital that he execute the plan as covertly as possible, so that his intentions were not revealed to the enemy, Claudius departed Apulia under cover of darkness, and later entered the camp of his co-*consul* after nightfall. To further ensure that Hasdrubal would not detect the presence of the reinforcements, Livius' troops shared their camp with Claudius' legionaries rather than expand the size of the *castrum*. In a war council the following day, Claudius rejected the suggestion to postpone the battle so as to provide his men with rest, and pressed for an immediate confrontation. Delay, he argued, endangered the army outside Canusium should Hannibal discover his absence and launch an attack against the depleted legions. As the Roman and Carthaginian forces deployed for battle, Hasdrubal keenly deduced the presence of the additional maniples and ordered a recall of his men. That evening, the Punic army relocated some 15 miles north to a new location along the banks of the Metaurus, but was unable to ford the river without the aid of local guides. Subsequent efforts by scouts to identify an adequate crossing in the darkness failed, and the army became lost on un-known ground. Hasdrubal's inability to find a way across the Metaurus per-mitted the consular legions time to overtake the Carthaginians. Accompanied by cavalry, Claudius intercepted the exhausted column at dawn approximately 3 miles from the coast. These squadrons were shortly joined by light infantry under Porcius. As the Romans began to launch skirmishing attacks against the weary army, Hasdrubal attempted to establish a camp, but the sudden arrival of the legions in full battle array instead forced him to hastily assemble the Punic divisions into line-of-battle along the south bank of the river. On the left wing he positioned the Gauls behind a projecting hillock, and on the right his veteran Spanish troops. The centre was held by the army's Ligurian allies, and ahead of this formation Hasdrubal placed a line of ten war elephants for the purpose of disrupting those ranks of Roman heavy infantry under the command of the *praetor*. On the right wing Claudius gathered his select force of 7,000 men, but was hindered in his ability to readily engage the enemy by the uneven terrain. To the left, Livius formed his legions against the Spanish phalanx led by Hasdrubal. It was here that the battle opened. From the very beginning, the fighting in this location proved particularly savage. Because

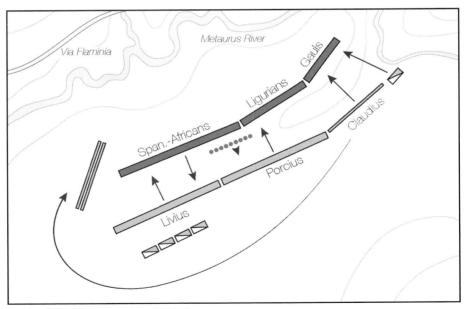

Battle of the Metaurus River, 207 BC

the open ground provided a natural arena for contending infantry, fighting gradually expanded to include both the Ligurians and their opposing legions. The carnage was further exacerbated by the elephants, which soon roamed uncontrollably between the two battle lines. For some time the struggle remained inconclusive, until Claudius – whose legionaries had yet to gain the upper hand against the Gauls – finally assumed the initiative and detached a number of maniples from the right wing and led them behind the formations of Porcius and Livius. Once his forces attained the extreme left of the Roman line, they immediately charged the Spanish veterans. This sudden influx of additional troops collapsed the Carthaginian right flank. The loss of the phalanx quickly inspired a general rout of the entire Punic army. Ancient sources record Carthaginian losses between 10,000–56,000 dead, including Hasdrubal. Roman losses totalled only 2,000. The defeat was decisive and destroyed any remaining possibility of Hannibal winning the war in Italy.

Titus Livius (Livy), *History of Rome*, 43–49.7; Polybius, *Histories*, 11.1,3; Appianus (Appian), *Hannibalic War*, 8.52; John Zonaras, *Epitome of Histories*, 9.9; Eutropius, *Abridgement of Roman History*, 3.18.

Mevania, 308 BC (Second Samnite War, Samnite Wars) – After learning that a large army composed of Umbrians and Etruscans threatened to march on Rome, the Senate dispatched envoys to the *consul* Quintus Fabius Maximus Rullianus, directing him to discontinue operations in Samnium if possible and march his legions into Umbria with all speed. In response, Fabius quickly moved his army northward, and by forced marches arrived near the town of Mevania, situated southeast of Purusia (Perugia), near the Etrurian border. Umbrian forces were gathered here in preparation for war. A second consular army under Publius Decius Mus encamped east of Rome and south of the Anio River, near the community of Gabii, in order to intercept all hostile forces moving southward into Latium. The Umbrians were momentarily unnerved by the unexpected arrival of Fabius, who was thought by the enemy to be heavily embroiled in the war in Samnium, but they soon recovered their courage and launched an immediate offensive against the Romans while the latter were preoccupied with entrenching their camp. Surprised by the attack, Fabius speedily assembled his soldiers, who charged the enemy of their own volition. Choosing to employ brute force rather than edged weapons, the Romans overpowered the Umbrians and forced them into submission by means of sheer physical intimidation. When the contest finally ended, the number of enemy prisoners detained by the legions far exceeded those which had died in the day's fighting. The battle, unique for the manner in which the Romans subdued the Umbrians, was nevertheless a signal victory which served to end the war.

Titus Livius (Livy), *History of Rome*, 9.41.8–20.

Milvian Bridge, 77 BC – see Campus Martius, 77 BC.

Mincius River, 197 BC – Once again faced with disturbances among the Gallic tribes of northern Italy, the Senate dispatched Roman armies northward to suppress the uprisings. While his co-*consul* advanced toward Genoa in the west, Caius Cornelius Cethegus and his legions followed the *Via Flaminia* toward the lands of the Insubres. Dissension among the Gauls had weakened the alliance between the Insubres, Boii and Cenomani, providing the Romans greater opportunity to successfully prosecute the campaign. These disagreements finally led the Boii to abandon their support for the insurrection and return home, and weakened the existing bonds of trust shared between the two remaining allies. The Romans established their camp approximately 2 miles downstream from the enemy's position, on the banks of the Mincius (Mincio) River. On arrival, Cornelius learned that the leadership of the Cenomani had not approved of their warriors' involvement in the revolt, and obtained a pledge from tribal elders that the young men would not actively participate in the approaching clash, and might in fact aid the Romans on the battlefield, should opportunity permit. On the day of the engagement, the two armies assembled in preparation for hostilities. The Insubres, suspecting duplicity on the part of their allies, placed the Cenomani in reserve behind the main battle line. When the fighting began, the Gallic ranks almost immediately crumpled under the Roman assault, possibly due to a Cenomani attack directed against the enemy's rear. Losses among the Insubres totaled 35,000 dead and 5,200 captured. Similarities between Livy's description of this battle and his record of the earlier contest at Cremona in 200 BC suggest that the separate accounts describe the same battle.

> Titus Livius (Livy), *History of Rome*, 32. 30. Regarding Livy's conflicting accounts, see Livy, *History of Rome*, Sage trans., volume IX, fn. 2, Loeb ed., 1985, pp. 246–47.

Morbihan Gulf, 56 BC (Gallic War) – The detention of Roman tribunes sent to collect grain from the Celtic tribes of the Esubii, Curiosolites and Veneti forced Julius Caesar to prepare his army to take punitive action. Aware that the primary instigators of the trouble were the Veneti, a maritime people whose *oppida* were concentrated around the tidal estuaries along the coast of Brittany, he instructed his *legati* to immediately begin the construction of warships on the Liger (Loire) River, and the drafting of able seamen from Provence. The Veneti soon learned of the Romans' preparations and promptly started to recruit Celtic allies from among the Osismi, Lexovii, Namnetes, Ambiliati, Morini, Diablintes and Menapii, as well as auxiliaries from the tribes in Britannia. In an effort to check any further spread of the rebellion, Caesar sent his *legatus* Titus Labienus with a substantial force of cavalry into the lands of the Treveri near the Rhenus (Rhine) River, and twelve cohorts under the general Publius Crassus into Aquitania. He then dispatched three full legions to the territories of the Venelli, Curiosolites and Lexovii to block their junction with the Veneti. When spring arrived, Caesar left Illyria and re-joined his armies in Gaul. While he marched his legionary forces overland toward the lands of the Veneti, his new fleet and its accompanying allied Gallic ships advanced by sea. Most of the tribe's *oppida* occupied eminences in and around the Morbihan Gulf. The extreme tidal variations and strong currents at this location created a difficult challenge for the Roman invaders. Some strongholds were accessible at low tide, but completely cut-off from the mainland when the sea rose. Moreover, the tribe's many flat-bottomed ships were of oaken construction, making them both ideal for traversing the treacherous waters and virtually impervious to ramming. The craft were rigged almost exclusively with sail, and sported high prows and sterns in order to better weather the region's rough seas, rendering their overall height taller than that of the Roman galleys. The Romans possessed only the advantage of speed and oarsmanship. As Caesar's flotilla entered the gulf, it faced an opposing fleet of 220 ships. The Roman naval commander, Decimus Junius Brutus Albinus, was somewhat perplexed as to the appropriate tactics to employ under such circumstances, but ultimately settled on the technique of severing the enemy's halyards by means of grappling hooks mounted on long poles. With the Gallic vessels rendered immobile, it was then simply a matter of boarding the stricken ships. When the fighting began, the Romans successfully implemented this plan, tearing down the yards and surrounding each hapless craft with two or three of their own. Following the loss of several of their ships, the Veneti began to retreat when the winds suddenly went calm, stranding the entire fleet in the open waters of the gulf. The Romans thereafter seized the Gallic vessels and their crews one by one. After several hours, the engagement ended with nightfall. Caesar's victory was total.

Julius Caesar, *The Gallic War*, 3.12–14.

Mosa River, 55 BC (Gallic War) – In the autumn of 56 BC, two German tribes, the Usipetes and Tenchtheri, crossed the Rhenus (Rhine) River into Gaul after being driven westward by the more powerful Suebi. Marching with eight legions, together with Gallic infantry and 5,000 cavalry, Julius Caesar crossed the Mosa (Meuse) River in an effort to block the tribes' advance. Following an initial parley with the Germans, Caesar moved his army approximately 4 miles from the river to a second water source. In so doing, his cavalry were unexpectedly attacked by 800 German horsemen and driven off with a loss of seventy-four men. This seemingly blatant violation of a truce angered Caesar, who determined to punish the Germans for the transgression. He immediately assembled his army into battle-readiness, arranging the legions into three columns, with the Gallic cavalry in the rear. Moving quickly against the German camp, which was located near the confluence of the Mosa and Rhenus rivers, the Romans burst in upon the unsuspecting tribesmen with devastating force. The warriors had no time to form ranks or even attain their weapons before the Romans had largely overrun the encampment. Fighting occurred for a time among the carts and baggage-wagons of the tribes, but the Germans were unable to check the progress of the legions. Panic soon swept through the masses of non-combatants, and thousands of women and children began to flee in all directions. Caesar responded by ordering his cavalry to overtake the fugitives. The sounds of the resulting massacre caused all German resistance to swiftly collapse, and suddenly the entire host of the Usipetes and Tenchtheri were racing to the banks of the rivers, pursued by the Roman army. There, trapped between Caesar's cohorts and the deep waters of the two rivers, the combined populations of both tribal nations were largely destroyed.

Julius Caesar, *The Gallic War*, 4.4–15.

Mount Marcius, 390 BC – Recognizing the weakened state of the Romans after their defeat at the Allia River and the subsequent occupation of Rome by the Gauls, the Volscians sought to exploit the situation by a declaration of war. To address the threat, the Romans dispatched an army under the command of military tribunes, but it was soon besieged by a combined force of Volsci and Latins near Mount Marcius. Due to the acute danger which this larger force posed to the deployed legions, an additional army was sent in relief, led by Marcus Furius Camillus, appointed dictator for a third time. Departing at night, Camillus guided his troops on a long march around the mountain in order to avoid hostile detection, and then established his camp directly behind the enemy position. Once the location was properly fortified, the dictator revealed his presence by the illumination of numerous campfires. The sudden turn of events served not only to embolden the trapped legions but compelled the Latins and Volscians to strengthen their position through the construction of a wooden palisade. Observing this activity among the enemy, Camillus determined to launch an assault the following morning. The Romans initiated an attack against the enemy camp at daybreak. When the engagement began, a portion of the troops launched fire-tipped missiles against the Volscians' position. The prevailing wind, made increasingly strong by the rising sun, quickly spread the flames throughout the wooden structure. Unable to extinguish the growing conflagration the Latins and Volscians were finally forced to flee the protection of the palisade, only to rush headlong into Camillus' awaiting army assembled in full battle array. Almost all of the fugitives were killed in the ensuing struggle.

Plutarch, *Camillus*, 34; Diodorus Siculus, *Historical Library*, 14.117.1–3.

Mount Tabor, 55 BC (Jewish Revolt) – When Aulus Gabinius, the *proconsul* of Syria, was distracted by the prospect of war with Parthia, Alexander, the older son of the Aristobulus II, the Hasmonean ruler and high priest of Judaea, led a revolt against Roman authority in the region. Gathering an army of 30,000 men, Alexander fought the Romans near Mount Tabor and was beaten, suffering 10,000 killed in the battle. The remainder of the Jewish host was put to flight.

   Flavius Josephus, *Jewish War*, 1.8.175–177, *Jewish Antiquities*, 14.6.101–102.

Mount Tifata, 83 BC – see Tifatum Mons, 83 BC.

Muhlhausen, 58 BC – see Vosegus, 58 BC.

Munda, 213 BC (Second Punic War, Wars against Carthage) – Following a failed attempt to capture Iliturgi, the Carthaginian army relocated to Munda. Here, a Roman army led by Gnaeus Cornelius Scipio Calvus attacked the Punic force. The ensuing battle lasted four hours and resulted in some 12,000 enemy killed, 3,000 captured and thirty-nine war elephants slain. Despite such successes, the legions prematurely broke off the action following the wounding of Scipio.

   Titus Livius (Livy), *History of Rome*, 24.42.1–4

Munda, 45 BC, 17 March (Wars of the First Triumvirate) – This was the decisive battle of Julius Caesar's Spanish campaign against the sons of Pompey the Great (Cnaeus Pompeius Magnus). After two previous encounters with Pompey's oldest son, Cnaeus Pompeius, at the Baetis River and Soricaria, Caesar sought to bring the younger Pompey to battle. In mid-March, Pompeius withdrew his legions toward Carteia and encamped the army of 45,000 under the walls of Munda, a Spanish hill town in south-central Spain. Caesar moved his army of 40,000 to within 5 miles of the Pompeian position and entrenched on 16 March. This action compelled Pompey to array his command for battle in the pre-dawn hours of 17 March. The infantry were drawn up at a distance from the town, though near enough that the elevated nature of the terrain and close proximity of the community's fortifications provided the army ample protection. Flanking this main formation of thirteen legions were cavalry and 6,000 light troops, together with an equal number of auxiliaries. Having learned of Pompeius' preparations, Caesar assembled his army into three lines (*triplex acies*). On the right was stationed the *Legio X*. The Third and Fifth legions were deployed on the left with the remainder of the army's eighty cohorts, auxiliaries and 8,000 cavalry. Between the two opponents was a rolling plain of approximately 5 miles. Pompey's unwilling-ness to descend from his protected hillside position caused the Caesarian formations to undertake an advance. The two opposing lines closed on the lower slope of the hill. Caesar's cohorts, already hampered by the uphill assault, wavered even more when struck, first by a devastating volley of *pila* and then a downhill countercharge by Pompey's legionaries. After both armies had exhausted their reserves, the engagement degenerated into hours of close-range combat. Gradually, resistance on the Pompeian left began to erode under sustained pressure from the Tenth Legion, forcing the redeployment of a legion from the right to reinforce the failing left. Recognition of this movement now compelled elements of Caesarian cavalry to assault the depleted right wing of Pompey. With intense pressure maintained by Caesar's army at all points along the enemy front, Pompeius' line broke and was put to flight toward Munda, pursued by Caesar's horse. Some 30,000 Pompeians were slain in the ensuing rout, including Titus Atius Labienus and Publius Attius Varus. Cnaeus Pompeius was himself ultimately captured and executed.

Appianus (Appian), *Civil Wars*, 2.104–105; Dio Cassius, *Roman History*, 43.36–38; Plutarch, *Caesar*, 56.1–5; Julius Caesar, *The Spanish War*, 28–31.

Muthul River, 108 BC (Jugurthine War) – The defeat and humiliation of a Roman army the previous year by the Numidian king Jugurtha moved the Senate to again deploy legions into North Africa. Responsibility for prosecuting the war fell to the senior *consul*, Quintus Caecilius Metellus (Numidicus). The arrival of thousands of Roman troops near Utica and the loss of at least one of his strongest cities left Jugurtha with no option but to seek battle when presented the right opportunity. From the inland market city of Vaga (Beja), Metellus marched deeper into the arid reaches of the interior in a campaign to destroy all opposition in the country. The Roman column descended through a range of low mountains to the dry plain below, some 20 miles from the Muthul River. As the legions picked their way over the rugged ground, Metellus was unaware that a large concentration of Jugurtha's army awaited his arrival on a nearby slope. The Numidian cavalry and a select portion of the infantry led by the king himself were partially concealed within a stand of scrub and low trees, while a short distance away his lieutenant, Bomilcar, stood ready with the remainder of the Numidian foot, along with a large contingent of war elephants. The insufficient shrubbery on the hillside soon revealed to the *consul* the presence of the ambuscade, and he immediately ordered the Romans to stop and assembled into battle formation. The legions formed three lines facing the enemy, and the army's slingers and archers were interspersed among the maniples. On each wing, Metellus positioned his squadrons of horsemen. Once arrayed, he wheeled the entire formation to the left so that the left wing now formed the vanguard of the column, and the right, under the command of the *legatus* Caius Marius, the rearguard. Anticipating that the enemy might harass the army's rear in an effort to impede its march toward water, he deliberately moved the column forward in increments according to the dictates of the terrain. Because their progress would be necessarily slow, Metellus sent forward one of his *legati*, Publius Rutilius Rufus, with a detachment of *auxilia* – both light infantry and cavalry – to prepare an encampment near the river. He then brought Marius forward to command the heavy infantry in the centre. When the legions had moved sufficiently down the mountain, Jugurtha sent a force of 2,000 infantry to occupy the ground over which the Romans had marched in order to deny Metellus a possible avenue of retreat. The king then opened the battle with a furious charge against the rear and flanks of the enemy column. From the beginning, the Roman infantry struggled under the swift and agile attacks of the Numidian horse, while the Roman cavalry could provide nothing more than temporary relief from the incessant harassment. Jugurtha's horsemen retreated with each sally by the *equites*, only to regroup and again charge once Metellus' riders withdrew. As the day wore on, both armies grew fatigued under the hot sun. Despite the dangers inherent in such a running battle, the *consul* used his army's discipline to good effect and restored order within the maniples as soon as exhaustion slowed the enemy's attacks. When it became evident that night was approaching, Metellus gathered his weary heavy infantry for one final offensive, this time against the main body of Numidian infantry on an adjacent hill. The attack proved irresistible. As the four legionary cohorts drove forward, they swept all before them. Once the enemy was dispersed beyond reconstitution, the Romans resumed their march toward the Muthul. Meanwhile, across the plain, Bomilcar led his forces against the troops of Rufus. The two sides clashed near the Roman camp. In the midst of the contest, while opposing contingents fought each other among the dense vegetation near the river, the war elephants became entangled in the trees branches and were easily surrounded or driven off by the *auxilia*. Deprived of the beasts' support, the Numidians lost courage and fled. Four elephants were captured and forty slain. That night Metellus reunited his command on the banks of the Muthul River.

Caius Sallusticus Crispus (Sallust), *Jugurthine War*, 48–53.

Mutina, 193 BC – While one consular army battled the Ligures near Pisa, a second legionary force under the command of the *consul* Lucius Cornelius Merula resumed the war against the Boii. Two legions, together with supporting allies, marched northward into the enemy's territory. Once there, the Roman troops began plundering the countryside in an effort to incite a pitched battle, but the Boii declined to risk a single decisive confrontation. When the land was sufficiently devastated, the *consul* ordered the army to withdraw west toward the city of Mutina (Modena), located in the southern Padus (Po) River Valley. The departure of the Romans was shortly followed by the Boii, who hoped for an opportunity to steal past the enemy column and prepare an ambuscade. That night, the Boii secretly bypassed the Roman encampment and occupied a defile along Cornelius' line of march. There they laid a trap in anticipation of the legions' arrival the next day. Upon breaking camp the following morning, the *consul* dispatched cavalry to reconnoitre ahead of the army. The scouts soon discovered the location of the enemy and reported the information to Cornelius, who immediately ordered the *triarii* to secure the column's baggage within the protection of an earthen rampart. He then proceeded against the Boii with the remaining two lines of infantry in battle formation. When the Gauls learned that their plan had been foiled, they too assembled for action. The Romans opened the contest by deploying the allied cavalry and irregular infantry on the left against the Gallic line, while holding the legions in reserve. Cornelius then moved the legions' cavalry into open ground beyond the centre of fighting and directed the tribunes Quintus Minucius and Publius Minucius to await his signal to attack. The initial assault soon proved insufficient to overcome the strength of the Boii, and word reached the *consul* that the Roman front was in imminent danger of collapsing. In response, he sent the second of his two reserve legions forward to temporarily relieve the allied troops. Once the line was stabilized, other auxiliary units were relocated from the right to replace the legionary maniples, who then resumed their place in reserve. Intense fighting continued throughout the hot day as the Gauls stubbornly resisted a number of assaults. When the *consul* was finally assured that the strength of the enemy was largely depleted by the long contest, he moved to resolve the impasse by a charge of allied cavalry. As the horsemen swept in, supported by the legionary squadrons under the Minucii, the impact of the mounted assault completely disrupted the exhausted Gallic formation. The Boii immediately attempted to reform their line but were hindered by the presence of the cavalrymen. Before the enemy was able to fully recover, they were suddenly confronted by the undiminished power of the legions, which had at last joined in the battle. The arrival of these fresh reserves irreparably shattered the opposing line. The Roman cavalry hotly pursued the broken army from the field. Some 14,000 Boii died and 1,092 were captured. Roman and allied fatalities amounted to more than 5,000, including four allied praefects and two tribunes of the Second Legion.

Titus Livius (Livy), *History of Rome*, 35.4–5.

Mutina, 72 BC (War of Spartacus, Third Servile War) – After soundly defeating the consular armies of Lentulus and Gellius in central Italy, the Thracian gladiator Spartacus led his slave army toward the Padus (Po) Valley in anticipation of marching northward across the Alps to freedom. Upon reaching the plain of the Padus, Spartacus descended from the Appenine range and entered Cisalpine Gaul. There he encountered the Roman garrison at Mutina (Modena), under the command of the *proconsul* Caius Cassius Longinus. The forces of the Thracian completely routed the two Roman legions in the battle which followed.

Lucius Annaeus Florus, *Epitomy*, 2.8.10

Mutina, 43 BC, 14 April (Roman Civil Wars) – The Roman general Marcus Antonius followed his loss at Forum Gallorum by withdrawing with the remnants of his army to Mutina (Modena) to await the capitulation of Decimus Brutus, his besieged opponent in the city. Because the troops of Decimus were near starvation, his fellow generals Aulus Hirtius and Caius Octavius wanted to bring Antony to battle as quickly as possible. Since Antony would not readily abandon his siege lines to accept battle, they re-directed their attack against a weaker portion of his works in an effort to draw him from his defences. Deploying only their cavalry to harass the enemy while they prepared their legions for the decisive assault, the generals were able to exert enough pressure on Antony to finally compel him to fight. He responded to the mounted attack by sending his own horsemen into action, while at the same time readying two legions for the anticipated engagement. In response, Hirtius and Octavian quickly moved their legions into position, and then charged. The abruptness of the assault did not allow Antony time to bring up additional legions, and Octavian was able to carry the day. Hirtius was killed while attempting to overrun the opposing encampment. Octavian briefly secured control of Antony's *castrum* before a successful counter-attack forced him to retreat. The two armies then remained under arms throughout the following night. After this loss and the previous defeat at Forum Gallorum, Antony rejected the counsel of friends and elected to lift the siege and withdraw toward the Alps.

Plutarch, *Antony*, 17.1; Appianus (Appian), *Civil Wars*, 3.71–72; Dio Cassius, *Roman History*, 46.38.5–7.

Mylae, 260 BC (First Punic War, Wars against Carthage) – Soon after learning of the capture of Gnaeus Cornelius Scipio and his fleet at Lipara (Lipari), Caius Duilius, the general in command of Roman forces in Sicily, turned the authority of his legions over to the army's tribunes and joined the Roman war fleet as it prepared to put to sea in search of the Carthaginian flotilla. Because the Punic warships were superior in speed and agility, the Romans equipped their vessels with a grappling device called a *corvus* (raven), which served to secure a Roman ship to an enemy craft, thereby permitting Roman marines to board the opposing vessel and overwhelm its crew. Learning that the Carthaginians were plundering the territory around the port of

Mylae on the northeastern tip of Sicily, the Romans moved against the enemy with a force of 120 ships. When the Carthaginians sighted the approaching fleet, Punic commander Hannibal put to sea with 130 vessels and immediately steered toward the Roman squadrons. The Carthaginians confidently bore down on the enemy craft, but were soon alarmed to find their ships affixed to the Roman vessels by the *corvii* and boarded by marines. In the hand-to-hand fighting which followed, the Romans captured fifty enemy ships and forced the remainder to retire. In defeating Hannibal at Mylae, Caius Duilius secured the first great naval victory in Roman history.

Titus Livius (Livy), *Summaries*, 17; Polybius, *Histories*, 1.22–23; John Zonaras, *Epitome of Histories*, 8.11; Diodorus Siculus, *Historical Library*, 23.10.

Mylae, 36 BC (Roman Civil Wars) – After concluding that a concentration of Pompeian ships at Pelorum (promontory of Punta del Faro), Mylae (Milazzo) and Tyndaris (Tindari) on the northeastern coast of Sicily was an indication that his opponent Sextius Pompeius was present, Octavian sailed to Vibo Vilentia (Vibo Valentia) on the Italian mainland to collect three legions in preparation for attacking Tauromenium (Taormina). He left his fleet in the charge of his trusted commander, Marcus Vipsanius Agrippa. After occupying the island of Hiera, Agrippa planned to attack a Pompeian fleet of forty ships under Demochares which was presently anchored at Mylae. Upon receiving word of the developing situation, Pompeius sent forty-five ships led by Apollophanes to Demochares, and arranged to quickly follow in person with an additional seventy. Agrippa sailed before dawn from Hiera with half of his ships, intending only to engage a detachment of ships commanded by Papias, but was surprised to observe the larger complement of ships under Apollophanes and Pompeius. After sending word to Octavian regarding the changed circumstances, he arrayed his *quinquiremes* in the centre of his developing battle line and then summoned the remainder of his ships from Hiera. As the fleets began to assemble for battle, it became apparent that Pompeius possessed lighter, more manoeuvrable vessels, primarily *quadriremes*, while Agrippa benefitted from a number of larger, heavier craft equipped with *corvi*. In the resulting battle, both navies acquitted themselves well, but the imminent arrival of Agrippa's reinforcements from Hiera persuaded Pompeius to order his fleet to retire in late afternoon. Agrippa was forced to abandon his pursuit when the more shallow-drafted Pompeian ships took refuge among some area shoals. Both fleets suffered considerable damage. Five of Agrippa's ships were sunk in the confrontation, while his opponent lost a total of thirty. The battle was largely inconclusive, but the inability of Pompeius to replace his destroyed craft would prove decisive at Naulochus.

Appianus (Appian), *Civil Wars*, 5.105–108; Dio Cassius, *Roman History*, 49.2–4.1.

Myndos, 42 BC (Roman Civil Wars) – Near the port of Myndos (Gumus-lik), located on the Carian coast northwest of the city of Halicarnassus, a force of thirty-three Rhodian ships commanded by Alexander and Mnaseas sailed against a larger Roman war fleet in the service of Caius Cassius Longinus. The battle proved a contest of strength versus agility, as the lighter Rhodian vessels sought to use their speed and manoeuvrability to best advantage against their heavier and more numerous opponents. Using their numerical superiority, Roman squadrons eventually succeeded in surrounding the Rhodians, thereby eliminating their ability to turn and dart through the opposing battle line. Once the enemy was effectively contained within a narrow space of water, the heavy Roman vessels were largely impervious to ramming attacks, while the greater momentum of Cassius' ships inflicted significant damage to the lighter craft. Following intense fighting, two Rhodian ships floundered after being rammed, three were captured with their crews and the remainder fled to Rhodes with battle damage. Cassius witnessed the entire fight from a nearby mountain. Soon afterward, his legions and fleet captured the city of Rhodes.

Appianus (Appian), *Civil Wars*, 4.9.71.

Myonessus, 190 BC (War against Antiochus III) – While the Roman navy at Samos prepared to sail north to the island of Chios in order to replenish its depleted stores of supplies, the fleet's commander, the *praetor* Lucius Aemilius Regillus, received word that the anticipated supply ships from Italy were delayed in their arrival to the island because of storms. At about this same time, he also learned through informants that the community of Teos (Sigacik), located on the Anatolian coast to the north of the Myonnesus Promontory, had offered the king's fleet under Polyxenidas a generous supply of stores and wine. As Aemilius led his ships together with an accompanying Rhodian squadron northwest toward Chios, he suddenly altered course toward Teos, determined to acquire the provisions by either consent of the Teans or by seizure. The Romans arrived at the city the next day. Porting his ships in the more confined harbour called Geraesticus, the *praetor* dispatched troops to plunder the surrounding countryside. While Aemilius was preoccupied with matters in Teos, the royal fleet put to sea from Colophon and sailed north toward the southern shore of the promontory to a concealed anchorage off a small island called Macris. From there, Polyxenidas hoped that by stealth his vessels might have the opportunity to trap the Roman fleet in the harbour, but Aemilius unknowingly foiled this plan when he relocated the Roman squadrons to the other Tean harbour facing the sea in order to better load the collected supplies. While the transfer of cargo from the shore was ongoing, a peasant arrived at Teos and informed Aemilius that an unknown fleet had been anchored for two days off Macris, and was presently making preparations to return to sea. The *praetor* immediately suspected the enemy, and ordered the Roman ships out of port as soon as each had recovered its crew. When the Rhodians heard the news, their commander, Eudamus, also led his twenty-two ships away from the coast and cleared the vessels for action. The entire Roman flotilla successfully reached deeper water after some initial confusion. As the craft moved into open sea, the enemy was sighted beyond the promontory to the south, advancing in a long column, two ships abreast. When the approaching fleet spotted the Romans, its vessels quickly turned to form a battle line, even as the *praetor*'s warships assembled their own formation facing the enemy. The length of the king's line on the left wing threatened to envelop the Roman right until Eudamus, perceiving the danger, brought his vessels forward to lengthen Aemilius' front. The royal fleet consisted of eighty-nine ships, including two outfitted with seven banks of oars. In addition to the Rhodians, the *praetor* commanded fifty-eight craft. Once battle was joined, Polyxenidas' ships immediately manoeuvred to avoid the Rhodians' vessels, each of which carried an iron canister filled with a flammable mixture suspended from the prow. These efforts to evade Eudamus' *trireme*s fatally undermined the strength of the left wing. After some time, Aemilius' warships successfully penetrated the enemy centre, further weakening the integrity of the entire opposing formation. The collective actions served to trap perhaps two-thirds of the king's ships between the Roman and Rhodian squadrons. This disastrous turn of events compelled Polyxenidas and his right wing to abandon the struggle and take flight to Ephesus. The Roman fleet remained intact when the engagement finally ended, while the Rhodians lost only a single ship to seizure. Enemy losses totalled thirteen captured and twenty-nine burned or sunk. This sea battle, together with an earlier victory by the Rhodians at Side, established Roman naval superiority for the duration of the war.

Titus Livius (Livy), *History of Rome*, 37.27–30; Appianus (Appian), *Syrian Wars*, 5.27; Lucius Annaeus Florus, *Epitomy*, 1.24.12.

Naulochos, 36 BC, 3 September (Roman Civil Wars) – The persistent contest between Caius Octavius and Sextius Pompeius that had first begun at Scyllaeum six years earlier reached its climax in a sea battle off the Sicilian coastal city of Naulochos. Outmatched on land by the superior number of legions commanded by his opponent, and suffering from a shortage of supplies brought on by the enemy's occupation of towns which provided him support, Pompey finally decided to gamble everything on a major naval engagement between his fleet and the forces of Octavian. The two antagonists clashed in a decisive battle near the northern coast of Sicily between Naulochos and the anchorage of Mylae (Milazzo). Each side possessed 300 ships, fully equipped for sea action. The *legatus* Marcus Vipsanius Agrippa commanded Octavian's squadrons, while Pompey assumed personal charge of his own vessels. Once the battle commenced, Agrippa's heavier warships employed grappling devices to seize enemy ships prior to their boarding by detachments of soldiers. Octavian ultimately gained the victory after a long, intense struggle. Twenty-eight Pompeian ships were sunk, seventeen escaped and the remainder were captured. Agrippa lost a total of three ships. Sextus Pompey fled eastward to Messana with the remnants of his fleet. Shortly afterward, his *legatus* Tisienus Gallus surrendered the entire army on Sicily.

Dio Cassius, *Roman History*, 49.9–11.1; Appianus (Appian), *Civil Wars*, 5.118–121; Suetonius, *Augustus*, 16.

Nepheris, 149 BC (Third Punic War, Wars against Carthage) – During the first months of the Roman siege of Carthage, the *consul* Manius Manilius led an expedition against Nepheris, the mountain stronghold of the Punic commander Hasdrubal. Among the tribunes accompanying Manilius on the march, Publius Cornelius Scipio Aemilianus was alone in expressing reservations over the dangers of prosecuting a campaign in the rugged, mountainous terrain against an opponent who possessed superior knowledge of the land and environment. The army prepared to traverse a deep river bed when it was within 600 yards of Hasdrubal's position. Scipio recommended the Romans withdraw, and await a better time and opportunity to attack. The other officers disagreed with this proposal, and likewise scorned his suggestion to construct a fortified camp in the event that it became necessary to retreat. Manlius also dismissed Scipio's concerns as overly cautious and pressed forward with the assault. The Romans encountered the enemy on the opposite side of the river. Both armies suffered serious losses in the battle before the Carthaginians elected to withdraw to the security of their camp. Now fully appreciative of the dangers inherent in continuing the campaign, the *consul* determined to seek refuge on the other side of the river. The Carthaginians struck again while the Romans were attempting to ford the channel. The attack caught the cohorts ill-prepared for battle, and they suffered additional heavy casualties. In an effort to relieve the pressure on Manilius' infantry, Scipio gathered 300 horsemen and initiated a counter-attack. Dividing the cavalry into two groups, he assailed the enemy with a series of alternating hit-and-run charges. The continuous attacks ultimately compelled the Punic forces to turn against their antagonists, thereby permitting the Roman infantry to complete their escape. All four cohorts reached the safety of the far bank, cut off from the main body of Manilius' troops when the battle began and unable to reach the river. These were now gathered on the crest of a hill and surrounded by Carthaginians. Scipio immediately selected some squadrons of cavalry and rushed to their aid. Once these reinforcements reached the location of the fighting, they seized some high ground adjacent to the trapped infantry. The enemy troops quickly understood that they were at risk of a mounted attack, abandoned the siege and returned to Nepheris. The four cohorts were then able to escape.

Appianus (Appian), *Punic Wars*, 102–104; Titus Livius (Livy), *Summaries*, 49.

Nepheris, 147 BC (Third Punic War, Wars against Carthage) – During the early winter, the Roman general Publius Cornelius Scipio Aemilianus focused his army on the fortified city of Nepheris and its attending military camp as part of a final campaign to destroy Carthaginian power in North Africa. Determined to eliminate Nepheris as a source of support for Carthage, Aemilianus sent a portion of his army southwestward from the outskirts of the capital and around the Lake of Tunis in order to reach the Punic garrison, which was situated in difficult terrain near the outlying port. Once there, he established his encampment about a quarter of a mile from the enemy ramparts and assigned the prosecution of the siege to his *legatus* Caius Laelius and the Numidian prince Gulussa. The *consul* then returned to Carthage and allowed his two lieutenants to begin the investment of the camp. When the Roman forces at Nepheris successfully breached a portion of the breastworks between two defensive towers, Aemilianus arrived to assume responsibility for the final assault. Using a select force of 4,000 soldiers, he positioned three-quarters of the men in preparation for a frontal attack and covertly stationed the remaining 1,000 *milites* in the enemy's rear. The *consul* then took the troops assigned to the main assault and arrayed them in detachments, one behind the other, in order to overwhelm the defenders at the point where the ramparts were demolished. Aemilianus' effort to force an entry into the camp was vigorously resisted by the Carthaginians and served to distract the Punic army and its commander, Diogenes, from immediately detecting the smaller contingent of Romans scaling the palisade from behind. The unexpected discovery of legionaries inside the defensive works panicked some of the African troops, who suddenly fled the encampment. Their escape was shortly followed by a complete rout of the entire garrison. Gulussa quickly gave chase with his Numidian cavalry and war elephants, inflicting a tremendous slaughter on the fugitives. Approximately 70,000 died in the pursuit, including a great number of non-combatants. Captives totalled 10,000, with only about 4,000 survivors managing to elude their attackers. The city of Nepheris also succumbed to a Roman siege twenty-two days later.

Appianus (Appian), *Punic Wars*, 18.126; Titus Livius (Livy), *Summaries*, 51.3; John Zonaras, *Epitome of Histories*, 9.30.

New Carthage, 210 BC – see Novo Carthago, 210 BC.

Nicopolis ad Lycum, 66 BC (Third Mithridatic War, Wars against Mithridates the Great) – When Cnaeus Pompeius Magnus arrived in Asia Minor to resume the war against Mithridates VI of Pontus, he benefitted greatly from the successful work of his predecessor, the Roman general Lucius Licinius Lucullus. At the time of Pompey's campaign into Armenia the Pontic king was situated in the Lycus valley with an army of only 30,000 infantry and 2,000 cavalry. The Roman column approached the region from Cilicia to the south. The armies made initial contact near Mount Dasteira. The king initially occupied the heights with his whole army, but deeming the place vulnerable because of a lack of available water for his men and horses, removed the army to the plain below. The Romans promptly relocated to the abandoned site, and after some effort managed to find water by sinking wells. Now ensconced on high ground, Pompey settled into a forty-five-day siege of the king's camp before Pontic forces were able to slip away under cover of darkness. The legions swiftly went in pursuit in an attempt to overtake Mithridates' army before it had an opportunity to cross the Euphrates River. The two armies camped in close proximity to each other near the head of the valley, neither electing to take any immediate action. At midnight, the Romans formed into battle array and advanced against the Pontic position in a pre-emptive move intended to prevent the king escaping again. Mithridates responded by ordering his generals to assemble the men for battle. After some initial hesitation following the detection of activity outside the enemy camp, Pompey ordered his cohorts to attack. A low moon behind the approaching army confused the enemy as to the number and composition of their attackers, while helping the Romans to clearly identify the target of their assault. Once their missiles were exhausted, Pompey's forces then charged the opposing battle-formation. Pontic resistance eventually disintegrated into general panic under sustained Roman offensive pressure. The king fled to Sinora, after cutting his way through the Roman formation with some 800 cavalry. Roman losses totalled 1,000 wounded and less than 100 killed. Enemy dead from the battle and subsequent pursuit amounted to perhaps 40,000. Sometime later, near the site of the great clash, Pompey founded the city of Nicopolis (Purkh) in memory of his victory.

Plutarch, *Pompey*, 32.1–7; Paulus Orosius, *Seven Books of History against the Pagans*, 6.4; Dio Cassius, *Roman History*, 36.48–49; Appianus (Appian), *Mithradatic Wars*, 99–100. In their accounts, the descriptions of the battle offered by Dio Cassius and Appian differ markedly from those provided by Plutarch and Orosius.

Nicopolis ad Lycum, 47 BC (Roman Civil Wars) – In 48 BC, the kingdoms of Lesser Armenia and Cappadocia were threatened by the expansionist aspirations of Pharnaces II, king of Bosphorus Cimmerius. The crisis compelled Deiotarus, king of Armenia Minor and tetrarch of Galatia, to appeal on behalf of both realms for aid from Cnaeus Domitius Calvinus, Julius Caesar's appointed representative in Asia Minor. After a Roman order to withdraw from Armenia Minor was ignored by the Bosphoran ruler, Domitius moved against Pharnaces in the autumn of 48 BC. Domitius' force consisted of one Roman legion, the *Legio XXXVI*, one native legion from Pontus and two additional legions supplied by Deiotarus and trained in Roman arms. Roman command was further strengthened by additional auxiliary troops from Cilicia and 200 horse. The two armies engaged near the Armenian community of Nicopolis ad Lycum (Purkh). Domitius deployed his forces with the Thirty-sixth Legion arrayed on the right flank, the Pontic on the left and the two legions of Deiotarus formed in the centre along a narrow front. The remaining elements of cavalry and auxiliary infantry were positioned on both wings. Against this Roman formation, Pharnaces constructed two ditches 4ft deep extending perpendicularly from the town's walls, between which he deployed his entire infantry. The Bosphoran phalanx extended fully between the trenches, with both flanks and the centre reinforced by three lines of reserves. Squadrons of cavalry were then stationed beyond the linear works on each wing. Once battle was joined, the *Legio XXXVI* on the right quickly shattered the Bosphoran cavalry and drove it against the walls of Nicopolis before pivoting to strike the enemy rear. However, all tactical advantage gained by the Thirty-sixth was soon lost when the Pontic legion on the left was repulsed and then completely routed, along with Deiotarus' two legions in the centre. The victorious Bosphoran right and centre then turned the flank of the Thirty-sixth Legion, which quickly formed into a defensive circle and retired from the field in good order. With this defeat, Roman losses amounted to 259 legionaries from the *Legio XXXVI* and the almost total destruction of the three native legions under Deiotarus' command.

Julius Caesar (Aulus Hirtius), *The Alexandrine War*, 34–41.

Nilus River, 47 BC (Roman Civil Wars, Alexandrian War) – After the murder of Pompey the Great in Egypt in 48 BC, the Roman *consul* Julius Caesar became embroiled in that country's affairs, including a dispute between King Ptolemy XII and his sister and co-ruler, Cleopatra VII. This involvement eventually led to the outbreak of war. When hostilities began in Alexandria, Caesar quickly recognized the need for reinforcements and requested aid from his ally, Mithridates of Pergamum. In the early spring of 47 BC, Mithridates and a substantial army arrived in Egypt following a long overland march from Syria. The force consisted of Syrian, Cilician and Arab contingents, along with some 3,000 Jewish troops under Antipater of Jerusalem. Once across the Sinai Peninsula, Mithridates seized the city of Pelusium, located on the eastern bank of the Nilus (Nile) River near the Mediterranean coast. He then turned southward in anticipation of fording the river near

Memphis some 140 miles away, before turning north and following the west bank to Alexandria, thereby circumventing the treacherous Delta. An advance force of Egyptian troops attacked Mithridates' encampment near the Nilus, but was repulsed. He then counter-attacked, badly defeating the enemy. News of the Egyptian loss prompted Ptolemy to confront Mithridates with the remainder of his army and a large fleet, in a second attempt to stop the Asian ruler. Around the same time, Caesar departed Alexandria with most of his legionary forces, leaving an adequate garrison to hold the city while he sought to join with Mithridates. He sailed west along the seacoast and, at an unknown location, put his army ashore. The Romans then proceeded south-eastward across the desert, staying to the west of Lake Mareotis. Following several days' march, the cohorts finally joined with the army of Mithridates. Caesar immediately assumed overall command and advanced against Ptolemy, whose army was camped several miles away beside the Nilus River on a point of high ground surrounded by difficult terrain, including marshland. As the approaching Roman and allied contingents neared the king's position, they encountered a mixed detachment of Egyptian cavalry and light infantry, intent on stopping the *consul*'s forward progress at a high-banked canal. Using a makeshift bridge, Caesar's infantry managed to cross the water-course in the face of this resistance, and with a body of German auxiliary horsemen over-whelmed the enemy, who suffered heavy losses in the encounter. Once across the canal, Caesar encamped at some distance from Ptolemy's location. The following day, his soldiers seized a strategically valuable fort built by the Egyptians in a small village near the king's encampment. The capture of this outpost allowed the Romans to move directly against the enemy's main fortifications from two sides. An initial effort to breach the ramparts near the Nilus failed after the assaulting troops found themselves on unfavourable ground and subjected to concentrated missile fire from both the king's camp and nearby ships. While this fight continued, Caesar redirected certain cohorts against an elevated section of the defences abandoned by the Egyptians when the assault began. This second attempt successfully overcame the entrenchments, allowing the Romans to completely penetrate the camp. The Egyptian army of Ptolemaeus XII was largely destroyed during the battle, the king himself drowning in the great river during the ensuing flight.

Julius Caesar (Aulus Hirtius), *The Alexandrian War*, 26–31; Josephus, *Jewish Antiquities*, 14.133–136.

Nola, 216 BC (Second Punic War, Wars against Carthage) – Immediately after his crushing victory at Cannae, Carthaginian general Hannibal Barca marched out of Apulia into Samnium, staying only briefly before advancing into Campania with the intention of attacking Neapolis (Naples). Unable to secure control of the city because of its fortifications, he remained in the district for some time, systematically reducing the region around the great port by force or negotiation. When the Carthaginians finally reached the town of Nola, approximately 12 miles east of Neapolis, they found a sizeable Roman garrison in control of the community. The *proconsul* Marcus Claudius Marcellus occupied the town with a force of two legions, but was aware that a portion of the population wished to seize control of Nola and deliver it into Hannibal's possession. Alerted by the senators of the town that the citizens intended to carry out their plan when the Romans marched out to offer battle, Marcellus apportioned his forces to ensure the town was made secure and that his intentions were not conveyed to the enemy. Dividing his army, he posted troops at each of the three gates facing the Carthaginian encampment, and then deployed additional forces to protect the army's baggage. Marcellus stationed select detachments of legionaries and cavalry by the middle gate, while positioning his recruits, *velites* and allied horsemen at the two remaining locations. The citizens were forbidden access to either the walls or gates of the town until the day's action was complete. Meanwhile, Hannibal's army remained in battle-readiness until late afternoon. Concluding that the Romans were again refusing battle, as they had done on previous days, he ordered some of his soldiers to return to camp and collect siege machinery. He then moved the rest of the Punic line closer to the walls in a last demonstration intended to inspire capitulation, when the Roman army suddenly sallied through the middle gate. The speed of the assault threw the entire Carthaginian centre into confusion. Hannibal attempted to redeploy his infantry to best tactical advantage while still in this state of disorder, but more Roman soldiers charged through the side gates and attacked the enemy's flanks. The cumulative effect of the onset was to rout the Punic army from the field. Roman losses amounted to 500 killed, while the Carthaginians suffered between 2,800 and 5,000 dead.

Plutarch, *Marcellus*, 10–11; Titus Livius (Livy), *History of Rome*, 23.16.

Nola, 215 BC (Second Punic War, Wars against Carthage) – Still determined to capture the Roman-held town of Nola, Carthaginian general Hannibal Barca once more moved against the Campanian community, located about 12 miles east of the port of Neapolis (Naples). After failing to secure control of the town by treachery, he invested Nola, an action that provoked the *proconsul* Marcus Claudius Marcellus to leave the safety of the town walls and offer the Carthaginians battle. The ensuing struggle was bitterly contested, and remained undecided when a heavy thunderstorm suddenly interrupted the fighting and compelled both sides to retire from the field; the Romans into the town and the Punic forces to their encampment approximately a mile away. Incessant rain the following day discouraged both armies from leaving the protection of their fortifications. Hannibal sent out some of his forces to plunder the immediate countryside on the third day. When Marcellus saw that the Carthaginians were no longer in readiness to fight, he marched through the gates of the town and assembled his troops in preparation for battle. Hannibal quickly responded to the challenge, and both armies converged on the open plain between Nola and the Punic camp. The struggle was bloody, and continued unabated for several hours before the Carthaginians finally withdrew to the safety of their stronghold. Less than 1,000 Romans died in the battle, while the enemy suffered more than 5,000 killed and 600 captured. The legions apprehended two war elephants and four others were slain in the action.

Plutarch, *Marcellus*, 12.2–3; Titus Livius (Livy), *History of Rome*, 23.44–46.7.

Nola, 214 BC (Second Punic War, Wars against Carthage) – After plundering the lands around the southern Italian port of Neapolis (Naples), Carthaginian general Hannibal Barca attempted a third time to reduce the nearby town of Nola by siege. The magistrates in the city requested aid from the Roman *consul* Marcus Claudius Marcellus. Travelling from Cales to Suessula in response to the plea for help, Marcellus led an advance force of 6,000 infantry and 300 cavalry to secure the town and protect the local government from the hostility of the townspeople who were opposed to Rome. He then ordered *propraetor* Marcus Pomponius Matho to march the remainder of the army from its camp near Suessula to Nola, and be prepared for battle. Before the Carthaginian army reached the town, Marcellus dispatched Caius Claudius Nero with a select detachment of cavalry through the eastern gate under cover of darkness, and ordered the officer to circumvent the approaching column and assume a position behind the enemy. The next day, Marcellus assembled his army before the walls of the town and the two sides joined in battle. The *consul* was unable to use the detached force to his advantage because it failed to reach its assigned station in time to contribute to the engagement. The assembled legions eventually secured control of the battlefield after struggling at length against the Carthaginians. Punic forces retired to their encampment, having suffered 2,000 dead. Roman losses totaled less than 400 killed. Marcellus again offered battle the following day, but Hannibal declined to leave his camp. The Carthaginians abandoned their attempt to seize Nola and marched southeast to the town of Tarentum (Taranto) on the evening of the third day.

Titus Livius (Livy), *History of Rome*, 24.17; Eutropius, *Abridgement of Roman History*, 3.12.

Nola, 89 BC (Social War/Marsic War) – A Roman army under Lucius Cornelius Sulla encountered an Italian force led by Lucius Cluentius while campaigning in the region around Mount Vesuvius. The two armies clashed twice near the Pompeian hills, each winning a battle but neither able to claim a decisive victory. Following his defeat in the second of the engagements, Cluentius prudently elected to withdraw some distance from the enemy's position, but considered the battlefield loss only a temporary setback. After receiving Gallic reinforcements, he relocated his troops near the Roman camp with the intention of provoking another confrontation with the legions. As the two armies prepared for a third clash, a preliminary contest between a pair of champions representing the opposing armies ended when the Roman soldier killed his much larger Gallic challenger in single combat. The Gaul's death served as the catalyst for a wholesale flight of the entire army. His fellow tribesmen, stunned and demoralized by the unexpected turn of events, promptly abandoned the field in panic, leaving the centre of Cluentius' battle line substantially weakened. Their retreat soon inspired the remainder of the army to flee in disorder to the nearby community of Nola. Sulla ordered his army to give chase when the enemy dashed to safety. Overtaken by cavalry, 3,000 Italians died before reaching the safety of the walls. As the fugitives neared the town, the Nolans opened only a single gate, fearing that the Romans would also rush in. The resulting bottleneck permitted the pursuers to trap the Italians outside the town. The Romans killed about 20,000 men, including Cluentius, in the disaster which followed.

Appianus (Appian), *Civil Wars*, 1.50; Eutropius, *Abridgement of Roman History*, 5.3; Paulus Orosius, *Seven Books of History against the Pagans*, 5.18

Noreia, 113 BC – Upon learning of a massive migratory body of Cimbri and Teutones in the regions of Illyricum and Noricum, the Senate moved to dispatch an army to deter the movement of these peoples into Italy. The *consul* Cnaeus Papirius Carbo marched northward to secure control of the nearest Alpine crossing and thereby deny the Germans access to the Po Valley. When the *consul* informed their leaders that they had encroached upon lands whose peoples were considered friendly to the Senate and people of Rome, the Germans declared their willingness to cease plundering the territories. Carbo persisted in his hostility despite these overtures. His provocative behaviour eventually forced a battle near Noreia in which the Romans were badly beaten. The destruction of the consular army only ended with the onset of darkness and a violent, early evening thunderstorm. The Germans continued into Gaul.

Appianus (Appian), *Gallic History* (fragments), 4.13; Titus Livius (Livy), *Summaries*, 63; Strabo of Amasya, *Geography*, 5.8.

Noviodunum, 52 BC (Gallic War) – After capturing the towns of Vellaunodunum and Cenabum (Orleans), the Roman *proconsul* Caius Julius Caesar besieged Noviodunum, a stronghold of the Bituriges, located in central Gaul. This action moved Vercingetorix, chieftain of the Arverni and leader of the Gallic tribal coalition, to lead his army in relief of the fortified town. The approach of Vercingetorix's mounted vanguard emboldened the residents, who promptly abandoned ongoing peace talks with Caesar, closed the gates of their community and rearmed themselves. The *proconsul* responded by dispatching some squadrons of Gallic cavalry against the advancing enemy force. When his native auxiliaries failed to put their opponents to flight, he sent roughly 400 German horsemen in support. These troops proved overwhelming and Vercingetorix's cavalry fled the field, having suffered heavy casualties in the fighting. Caesar afterward accepted the surrender of Noviodunum and then marched against the city of Avaricum, the main stronghold of the Bituriges.

  Julius Caesar, *The Gallic War*, 7.12–13.

Numantia, 153 BC, September (Numantine War, Wars in Spain) – Shortly after his defeat in the Baldano Valley, the Roman *consul* Quintus Fulvius Nobilior moved his army against the Celtiberian community of Numantia (Garray) on the upper Durius (Duero) River in northern Spain. He camped approximately 3 miles from the city, where he was soon joined by 300 Numidian horsemen and ten war elephants, sent to him by Masinissa. When all was in readiness, Fulvius advanced against the enemy, which was assembled for battle outside the walls. As the two armies came face to face, the Roman formation suddenly divided, revealing the line of elephants. The unexpected sight of the strange animals panicked the Celtiberians warriors, who immediately fled to the safety of Numantia. The Romans shortly followed, leading the large beasts up to the very walls of the city. While Fulvius confidently continued to prosecute the fighting, the momentum of the struggle abruptly altered in favour of the besieged when a large stone fell from atop the battlements and struck an elephant's head, injuring the pachyderm, which quickly and indiscriminately turned upon the men around it. The animal's cries agitated its companions, which likewise ran amok, trampling and tossing the nearest soldiers. The uncontrollable brutes then wrecked the integrity of the entire Roman battle formation, as the adjacent files of legionaries and light troops scattered in an effort to escape the rampage. The Numantines suddenly sallied out in pursuit as the enemy fled from the field in disorder. In the chaotic fighting which followed, 4,000 Romans died as well as three elephants. Celtiberian fatalities amounted to about 2,000 men.

  Appianus (Appian), *Wars in Spain*, 9.46.

Numantia, 133–132 BC (Numantine War, Wars in Spain) – Since the attempt by Quintus Fulvius Nobilior to capture Numantia in 153 BC, nine other Roman magistrates had sought to conquer the city without success. Twenty years of humiliation finally persuaded the Senate to waive the traditional restrictions prohibiting an individual from holding two consulships

within a ten-year period and appoint Publius Cornelius Scipio Aemilianus Africanus as *consul* of *Hispania Citerior* (Eastern Spain). Upon his arrival in Spain, Scipio restored discipline to the ranks of a Roman army long demoralized by defeat. Once he considered everything prepared, he invested Numantia. Rather than challenging the citizens to open battle, as some of his predecessors had sought to do, the *consul* elected to besiege the city and starve the occupants into submission. To this end, he enclosed the city in a siege line approximately 6 miles in length, and beyond these excavations constructed a second ditch complete with fortifications and towers to retard assaults from the outside. Mounted atop these defensive towers were catapults and *ballistae*, and distributed along the length of the siege lines were some 60,000 Roman and allied troops. As the months passed, the population inside the city began to suffer badly from the effects of the siege, the hardship of incarceration being made more difficult by famine and plague. The Numantines made attacks at several points along the ramparts in order to relieve their suffering, but they were unable to overcome the Roman defences. After fifteen months, the city finally surrendered. With the capture of Numantia, all of Spain, except the tribal regions in the north, was subjugated to Roman rule.
    Appianus (Appian), *Wars in Spain*, 15.90–96.

Numistro, 210 BC (Second Punic War, Wars against Carthage) – The *consul* Marcus Claudius Marcellus advanced into northern Lucania at the head of a Roman army and engaged a Carthaginian force commanded by Hannibal Barca in an inconclusive battle near the community of Numistro. The legions of Marcellus encamped on level ground in the immediate vicinity of the town and near the Punic army's position on a low hill. The *consul* initiated the confrontation by leading his army onto the field in battle formation, and Hannibal readily answered the challenge. Having anchored his left wing on Numistro itself, Marcellus opened the battle with the First Legion accompanied by a cavalry *ala* on the right. Arrayed with its right wing situated against the base of the hill, the Punic army entered the struggle led by concentrations of Spanish heavy infantry and Balearic slingers, shortly followed by the injection of Punic war elephants. The fighting lasted for several hours before the Third Legion rotated forward to replace the exhausted legionaries of the First. At the same time, the left *ala* relieved those Roman cavalry squadrons deployed on the right at the beginning of the battle, and Hannibal likewise withdrew his spent divisions and moved fresh troops into the front line. These movements preceded a rejuvenated round of fighting that lasted until nightfall and left the confrontation undecided when both armies finally elected to retire due to darkness. The next morning, Marcellus advanced his legions onto the battlefield and remained there throughout the day, but

Hannibal refused to accept the challenge. On the third day, the Romans awoke to find the enemy camp abandoned. Leaving a small garrison in Numistro to care for the Roman wounded, the *consul* departed in pursuit of the Carthaginian army.

Plutarch, *Marcellus* 24.4–6; Titus Livius (Livy), *History of Rome*, 27.2.1–10.

Ocile, 153 BC (Lusitanian War, Wars in Spain) – After rising up against the Romans, the Lusitanians of western Hispania – led by their general Caucaenus – invaded the territory of the Cunei, a Roman subject people, and assaulted the cities of Conistorgis and Ocile in the extreme southwestern Iberian peninsula. Upon receiving word of the incursion, Lucius Mummius, the Roman *praetor* of *Hispania Ulterior* (Western Spain), advanced into the region with a force of 9,000 infantry and 500 cavalry. By the time the legions arrived in support of their allies, the first city had fallen to the attackers and the second was presently under siege. The Romans immediately engaged the marauders, killing perhaps 15,000 Lusitani who were pillaging the territory. Mummius then forced the tribesmen to lift the siege of Ocile, and followed this with the destruction of an additional band of Lusitani attempting to escape the district with plunder seized in the campaign.

Appianus (Appian), *Wars in Spain*, 10.57

Octodurus, 57 BC (Gallic War) – With campaigns against the Nantuates, Veragri and Seduni successfully completed, Caesar's lieutenant Servius Sulpicius Galba led his small army – consisting of the *Legio XII* and mounted *auxilia* – into winter quarters at Octodurus (Martigny), an *oppidum* of the Veragri located in the Rhone valley. The *legatus* stationed two cohorts down-river in the territory of the Nantuates and then settled the remainder of the legion in town. The Dranse River bisected the community, and Galba elected to assign the Gauls to the part of town on the opposite bank, while his cohorts established themselves in the other half once the residents relocated. The Romans then set about fortifying the site with trenches and earthen walls. Several days later, Galba's scouts reported the Gallic part of the town abandoned and the heights above occupied by a large concentration of Seduni and Veragri, clearly intent on renewing hostilities. In addition, the passes leading into Octodurus were blocked by tribesmen. Short of provisions, and forced to defend an unfinished camp, the undermanned legion prepared to receive the enemy. In a sudden rush, the amassed body of warriors charged the Roman defenes from all sides. The legionaries offered a stubborn defence, but after six hours of continual fighting the cohorts were exhausted and their store of missiles depleted. Aware that the legion's only chance now lay in breaking through the massive cordon of Gauls surrounding the camp, the *primipilus* and a military tribune persuaded Galba to allow the army to sally against the unsuspecting enemy. When all was in readiness, the cohorts made a simultaneous sortie through the gates of the *castrum*. The force and speed of the attack caught the Gauls completely unprepared, and they were not able to resist the Roman onslaught. In the resulting struggle, the *Legio XII* and its supporting *auxilia* slew 30,000 Gallic warriors and put the remainder to flight.

Julius Caesar, *The Gallic War*, 3.1–6.

Olympus Mons, 189 BC – Faced with the recalcitrance of the Celtic Tolostobogii, Trocmi and Tectosagi, the Roman *consul* Cnaeus Manlius Vulso moved to suppress all tribal opposition in northern Galatia by military means. The Tolostobogii occupied the barren slopes of Mount Olympus, a summit in the Olympus Range of central Anatolia. Due to the nature of the terrain, Manlius anticipated the Celts avoiding close hand-to-hand fighting and accordingly assembled an assortment of missiles, including javelins, spears and shot. Following a brief cavalry skirmish on the first day, the *consul* prepared to scale the mountain in order to force a decisive confrontation. After studying the topography, Manlius judged that his best option was to divide his infantry into three columns for the ascent; he would lead the main legionary force up the southern side of the mountain following the most gradual slope to the summit, while his lieutenants, Lucius Manlius Volso and Caius Helvius, were to simultaneously advance along the steeper and more difficult southeastern and northwestern approaches. Likewise, the auxiliary infantry under Attalus was also divided into three sections and ordered to scale the summit; while the accompanying contingent of auxiliary horse, together with the army's war elephants, remained on the plain below with instructions to render aid where practical. A forward detachment of 4,000 Gauls on a hill overlooking the legions' line of march blocked the primary movement from the south, ensuring that initial contact was made by Roman skirmishers deployed ahead of the leading cohorts. As Manlius' *velites*, Cretan archers and slingers engaged the Tolostobogii, the accuracy of their fire soon threw the enemy into retreat toward the central Gallic position on the summit. The Romans continued their advance and the main body of legionary infantry was shortly reinforced by the approach of Lucius Manlius and Caius Helvius, whose columns now fell in behind that of the *consul* after failing to find accessible approaches to the top of the mountain. Manlius briefly rested the army before initiating the final assault against the Gauls. Once the cohorts resumed their march, the light-armed skirmishers encountered a dense concentration of Celtic warriors arrayed outside their fortifications. The exposed location of the Gallic formation subjected the Tolostobogii warriors to an intense barrage of Roman missiles, which forced a disorganized retreat inside the compound. All enemy resistance suddenly collapsed as the Romans rushed forward. In the rout which followed, thousands of Tolostobogii, including women and children, scrambled down the precipitous slopes of Mount Olympus with legionary and auxiliary infantry in close pursuit. As the scattered survivors reached the plain below, the cavalry took up the chase without succour and completed the destruction of the Tolostobogii. At least 40,000 Celts were killed or captured: the prisoners were sold to neighbouring tribes.

Titus Livius (Livy), *History of Rome*, 38.19–23; Appianus (Appian), *Syrian Wars*, 42; Lucius Annaeus Florus, *Epitomy*, 1.27.5

Orchomenos, 86 BC (First Mithridatic War, Wars against Mithridates the Great) – The year following his consulship, the Roman general Lucius Cornelius Sulla crossed the Adriatic Sea and landed in Epirus with an army of approximately 30,000 men in order to prosecute a war against the Pontic king Mithridates VI. Once his five legions reached southern Greece, Sulla invaded Attica and brutally reduced the city of Athens by siege for its alliance with Pontus. He then moved his forces northward into western Boeotia, where he destroyed a massive Pontic army at Chaeronea (Heronia). From there, Sulla pursued the defeated remnants approximately 5 miles eastward to a broad plain below the hillside city of Orchomenos, situated between the Cephisus (Kifissos) River and its smaller tributary, the Melas. Approximately 10,000 survivors of the Chaeronean disaster and their general Achelaus were soon joined by another Pontic army, recently arrived from Asia and consisting of 80,000 troops, including numerous squadrons of horsemen. In an effort to both circumvallate the enemy encampment and hamper the cavalry's access to the open plain, Sulla immediately began construction of several 10ft-wide trenches near the enemy's camp. These excavations were soon interrupted by a mounted attack, which scattered the Roman labourers as well as those troops drawn up to guard them. With some difficulty, Sulla managed to rally the fugitives and lead a counter-assault – reinforced by two cohorts from his right wing – which overwhelmed the enemy. Later that same day, Archelaus again launched an attack, but the offensive failed and the Pontic army was forced to retreat behind its own earthworks. The Romans resumed building their network of trench fortifications the next day, an untenable situation for Archelaus which finally motivated the general to lead most of his forces onto the surrounding plain in a determined effort to avoid being trapped. Sulla quickly accepted the offer of battle and the Romans completely routed their opponents from the field. Losses to the Pontic army amounted to 15,000 men, of which two-thirds were cavalry.

Appianus (Appian), *Mithridatic Wars*, 7.49; Plutarch, *Sulla*, 21.

Ottolobum, 200 BC (Second Macedonian War, Wars against Macedon) –
Near the town of Ottolobum, a Roman consular army led by Publius
Sulpicius Galba Maximus engaged a force of 20,000 infantry and 2,000
cavalry under Macedonian ruler Philip V. After receiving word from scouts
that Roman work parties were gathering grain from fields surrounding the
small community, the king moved to isolate the foragers and deployed some
of his cavalry and light infantry to block all roads leading to the enemy
encampment. He then sent the remainder of his force to destroy the workers
in an attempt to disrupt Sulpicius' collection of food supplies. The king's
horsemen and auxiliaries soon began hunting down the widely scattered
groups of men, killing many. Some survivors eventually managed to escape the
disaster and reach Sulpicius. The *consul* immediately responded by dispatching
his cavalry to aid the beleaguered foragers, and followed shortly with the
remainder of the army. When the mounted squadrons reached the area where
the attack was occurring, they dispersed in an effort to rescue their fellow
Romans. As a result, fighting quickly erupted in various locations across the
countryside, particularly near the central road leading to the Roman *castrum*,
where a sharp exchange occurred between disorganized elements of Roman
cavalry and Philip's royal guard supported by Cretan auxiliaries. The enemy
soon forced those Romans fighting near the highway to fall back toward their
camp, hotly chased by Macedonian horsemen. As Sulpicius' riders fled their
pursuers, both unexpectedly met the approaching legions. Emboldened by
the presence of reinforcements, the Roman cavalry suddenly wheeled around
and charged their Macedonian adversaries. The new circumstances immediately reversed the outcome of the battle. In the disorderly retreat which
followed, many of Philip's guardsmen were killed in flight or overtaken after
they became mired in nearby swamps. When the fighting ended, 200
Macedonians were dead and an additional 100 captured. Among those who
narrowly escaped was the king himself.

   Titus Livius (Livy), *History of Rome*, 31.36.5–37.12.

Panormus, 251 BC – Aware that the Roman troops were still very hesitant to
engage the Carthaginians after their disastrous encounter with war elephants
at the Bagradas River five years earlier, the Punic general Hasdrubal advanced
confidently against Roman forces occupying the Sicilian port city of Panormus (Palermo). Marching 55 miles northeast from the city of Lilybaeum
(Marsala), the Carthaginians encamped on the border of the city's territory in
anticipation of confronting the legionary forces of the *consul* Lucius Caecilius
Metellus. When the Romans failed to immediately offer battle, Hasdrubal
ordered his army to descend through the Orethus Pass and destroy the wheat
crop surrounding Panormus in an effort to provoke the legions into action.

Caeclius did not immediately respond, but waited until the enemy had crossed the Orethus River with their war elephants before dispatching light troops to harass the enemy vanguard and attack the animals with javelins. This activity soon inspired a charge from the pachyderms that compelled the light infantry to withdraw to the safety of a pre-constructed ditch near the city walls. From here they resumed their harassing fire. When the elephants next charged the trench, they came too near the walls and were suddenly subjected to an additional hail of missiles from the ramparts and from reinforcements deployed near the ditch. The combined attacks served to panic the beasts, which then turned and charged into the ranks of their own troops. Upon seeing the enemy thrown into such confusion, Caecilius ordered his legions to assault the flank of the Carthaginian line. The manoeuvre completely shattered the enemy formation. The Romans captured ten elephants and their drivers in the subsequent rout.

Polybius, *Histories*, 1.40.1–15; John Zonaras, *Epitome of Histories*, 8.14; Diodorus Siculus, *Historical Library*, 23.21; Lucius Annaeus Florus, *Epitomy*, 1.18.27.

Pedum, 358 BC – When the Romans learned that the Gauls were encamped in the vicinity of Pedum, the *consul* Caius Platius Proculus – acting with the support of the Senate – appointed Caius Sulpicius Peticus dictator. The war proved a lengthy affair, prolonged by the dictator's determination to weaken the Gallic force by attrition. Content to let the depletion of supplies force the Gauls to withdraw, Sulpicius was ultimately compelled to seek battle when his legions demanded he pursue hostilities. The night before the planned engagement, the dictator accordingly ordered the army's contingent of almost 1,000 muleteers to arm themselves and then remove the pack-saddles from their animals before leading the beasts into the wooded mountains above the Roman camp. Once there, they were to await his signal to attack. A hundred cavalrymen accompanied the men. Sulpicius arrayed his legions and horsemen along the lower slopes at dawn the following morning. When the Gauls saw the Romans begin their descent to the plain, they rushed against the enemy before the signal was given by their generals. The Gallic right wing struck the Roman left hard. The violent force of the attack was only blunted because the dictator was present on the left to both encourage and berate the maniples, who soon rallied and drove back the enemy in disarray. Before the Gauls on the right were able to reconstitute their formation and counter-attack, the Roman cavalry under the *magister equitum* Marcus Valerius swept in and put the enemy to flight. When Sulpicius saw the Gallic right begin to waver under the mounted charge, he redirected those legions on the left against the opposing left wing. The manoeuvre compelled the Gauls there to undertake a disorderly retreat toward their camp, where they were swiftly confronted by the victorious Roman cavalry still flushed from their defeat of the Gallic right. The cavalry completely scattered the remnants of the barbarian army. The surviving Gauls fled into the forests and mountains, where they were overtaken and slaughtered by the awaiting muleteers.

Titus Livius (Livy), *History of Rome*, 7.14.6–15.8.

Pedum, 338 BC – In order to conclude the previous year's campaign against the Pedani, which was disgracefully abandoned by the former *consul* Tiberius Aemilius Mamercinus, the Senate deployed an army under the consuls Lucius Furius Camillus and Caius Maenius. Aware that a siege of Pedum was imminent, other Latin tribes attempted to provide aid to the city. Support from the nearby communities of Praeneste and Tibur successfully arrived, but reinforcements sent by the Aricini, Lanuvini, Veliterni and Antiate Volsci were intercepted and thoroughly routed near the Astura River by legions under Maenius. Camillus then defeated the Tiburte army near Pedum, during which the Pedani sallied from the city in an unsuccessful effort to provide support for the Tiburtes. After this victory, the *consul* completed the capture of Pedum by siege that same day.

Titus Livius (Livy), *History of Rome*, 8.13.1–8.

Perusia, 310 BC – see Sutrium, 310 BC.

Perusia, 308 BC (Second Samnite War, Samnite Wars) – The Roman *consul* Quintus Fabius Maximus Rullianus fought and defeated remnants of the Etruscan army near Perusia, a city in central Italy east of Lake Trasimeno. His subsequent preparations to invest the city were stopped when representatives surrendered Perusia.

Titus Livius (Livy), *History of Rome*, 9.40.18–20; Diodorus Siculus, *Historical Library*, 20.35.1–4.

Petelia, 208 BC (Second Punic War, Wars against Carthage) – In an effort to recapture the Carthaginian-held town of Locri, located in the extreme south of Italy on the Bruttium peninsula, the consuls Titus Quinctius Crispinus and Marcus Claudius Marcellus ordered the Roman garrison at Tarentum to dispatch a detachment of troops to the coastal community. This deployment did not go unnoticed, and the Punic general Hannibal, made aware of the Roman plan by informants from the port of Thurii, sent 3,000 cavalry and 2,000 infantry to the hill of Petelia in order to ambush the force during its march to Locri. Caught by surprise, about 2,500 Romans were killed and some 1,500 captured, while the remainder scattered in disorganized flight back to Tarentum.

Plutarch, *Marcellus*, 29.1; Titus Livius (Livy), *History of Rome*, 27.26.4–6.

Petelia, 71 BC (War of Spartacus, Third Servile War) – Spartacus, leader of a slave rebellion in Italy, marched his 120,000 followers southward from the region of Lucania to the relative safety of the Petelian mountains in Bruttium. He was followed closely by two Roman forces, one of which was led by the *quaestor* Scrophas. When Spartacus unexpectedly turned and attacked his pursuers near Petelia, both opposing armies were repulsed with losses. These successes filled the slave army with over-confidence, inspiring his followers to demand Spartacus retrace their passage through Lucania to the north and lead them against the legions of Marcus Licinius Crassus.

Plutarch, *Crassus* 11.4–5.

Phalanna, 171 BC (Third Macedonian War, Wars against Macedon) – After gathering the harvest near the Thessalian town of Crannon (Kranno), the Roman army relocated approximately 16 miles north to the region around Phalanna (Falanna), a village situated outside the city of Larissa. When the Macedonian king Perseus learned that foraging parties were scattered throughout this area and were without the protection of an armed guard, he led 1,000 cavalry and 2,000 Thracian and Cretan light troops to attack the enemy. The speed of the column's approach caught the Romans by surprise, and the king was able to seize 1,000 grain-laden wagons and some 600 men, while killing numerous foragers roaming the countryside. Perseus then directed his forces against the nearest Roman guard unit, an 800-man detachment under the command of the tribune Lucius Pompeius. As the Macedonians bore down on the Roman contingent, Pompeius withdrew to the safety of a nearby hill rather than allow his troops to be overtaken on open ground. Perseus surrounded the knoll with his light infantry and then ordered the enemy position assaulted from all sides while his archers and slingers provided suppressive fire. The effectiveness of the attacks gradually undermined the physical stamina and morale of the Romans. Regardless of the tactical disposition assumed by the legionaries, they could not capably repulse the enemy. The beleaguered force still refused to surrender, despite suffering serious casualties. By this time, reports of the guard's predicament reached the Roman *consul* Publius Licinius Crassus, who soon marched to the relief of the trapped men with the army's cavalry, light auxiliaries and *velites*. He also ordered the legions to follow as quickly as possible. On witnessing the approach of this force, Perseus summoned his Macedonian phalanx, but it failed to arrive before Crassus joined battle. The king's forces were badly mismatched against the Romans and soon retreated, having lost over 300 men in the melee, including twenty-four from the king's own royal cavalry, the *agema*. After driving off the enemy and rescuing Pompeius' command, Crassus elected not to give chase. A more serious battle apparently occurred sometime afterward, resulting in 8,000 Macedonian dead and 2,800 captives. Roman losses totalled more than 4,300.

Titus Livius (Livy), *History of Rome*, 42.65–66.

Pharos, 219 BC (Second Illyrian War, Illyrian Wars) – In early summer, the Senate deployed a Roman army under the *consul* Lucius Aemilius Paulus to move against Demetrios – ruler of the island of Pharos (Hvar) off the coast of Illyria (Croatia) – because of treaty violations and continued depredations against Illyrian cities subject to Rome. After quickly reducing a formidable stronghold at Dimale (Krotina) by siege, Aemilius sailed against Demetrios and his 6,000-man garrison at Pharos (Stari Grad), the major city on the island of the same name. Learning that the local fortress was both well supplied and heavily defended, the Roman commander devised a plan to lure his opponent from the citadel. Sailing to the island at night, the general put the majority of his troops ashore in a heavily wooded area. With twenty ships, Aemilius and a smaller Roman contingent sailed into the harbour near the city at dawn the following day. On observing the size of the attacking force, Demetrios grew overconfident in his ability to easily eject the intruders and sallied from the protection of his redoubt against those Romans disembarking in the harbour below. Despite their numerical advantage, the Illyrians could not dislodge the legionary force and the struggle grew violent, forcing the Greek ruler to summon reinforcements. The intensity of the battle ultimately moved Demetrios to commit his entire garrison to the action. While the fighting continued, the main Roman force suddenly appeared, occupied a hill between the city and harbour and cut off enemy troops from the safety of their fortress. The Illyrians immediately turned to face this larger threat, paused long enough to reconstitute their ranks, and advanced to battle in good order. Seeing the approaching formation, the Romans on the hill assembled their maniples and charged. The impact of the downhill assault, combined with an attack against the enemy rear from Roman detachments still fighting in the harbour, proved devastating. The Illyrians were soon routed from the field. Now without an army, Demetrios fled to the court of Philip V of Macedon.

Polybius, *Histories*, 3.18–19.8.

Pharsalus, 48 BC (9 August) 29 June (Roman Civil Wars, Wars of the First Triumvirate) – This was the climactic battle in the Roman civil war between Caius Julius Caesar and Cnaeus Pompeius Magnus for supreme power in Rome. Following his defeat at Dyrrachium, Caesar moved his legions into eastern Greece in anticipation of again engaging the forces of Cnaeus Pompeius. Pompey's army of 45,000 was encamped on a low hill south of the Enipeus River, northeast of the community of Pharsalus. Having moved

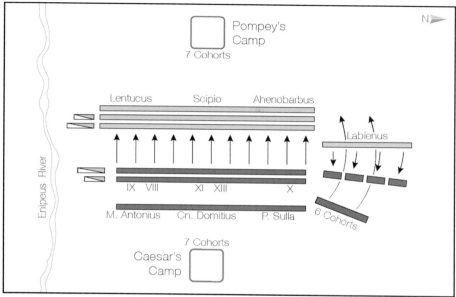

Battle of Pharsalus, 48 BC

his army of 22,000 southeastward from the Adriatic coast, Caesar established his camp some distance west of Pompey's position and daily drew up his command in hope of bringing the latter to battle. Pompeius responded cautiously to Caesar's demonstrations, but was finally compelled to act on 29 June. The Pompeian army assembled on open ground between the opposing camps. The right wing, consisting of veteran Cilician and Spanish troops, was anchored on the steep and uneven banks of the Enipeus in order to prevent possible envelopment. The Syrian legions under Quintus Caecilius Metellus Pius Scipio Nasica were deployed in the centre. Pompey and Lucius Domitius Ahenobarbus were positioned on the left with *Legios I* and *III*, both formerly Caesarian legions. This exposed flank was supported by archers, slingers and a substantial formation of cavalry under Titus Atius Labienus. A further 110 cohorts were deployed between the centre and wings as additional reinforcement. In response, Caesar arrayed his eighty cohorts in three lines, placing the Tenth Legion on the right wing under the command of Publius Cornelius Sulla and the badly depleted *Legio IX* – reinforced by the Eighth Legion – on the left, led by Marcus Antonius. Cnaeus Domitius Calvinus commanded in the centre. Caesar stationed a small mounted complement to the right of the *Legio X*. In order to further protect his right flank from envelopment by cavalry, he consolidated six cohorts from his third line to form a detached fourth line. Once battle opened, Caesar advanced his first two lines only, holding his third and detached fourth in reserve. With the approach of Caesar's army, cavalry and archers on the Pompeian left launched an intense and sustained attack which broke the Caesarian horse. As Pompey's cavalry then prepared to deploy by contingents in an assault on the flank and rear of the exposed legions, Caesar's reserve detachment suddenly and unexpectedly initiated a furious attack which completely shattered the Pompeian horse. This rout permitted the reserves to then entrap and slaughter the accompanying archers and slingers before completing an envelopment of Pompey's legionary lines. While this attack on the Republican flank and rear intensified, Caesar committed his third line to the struggle, held in reserve until now. This sudden injection of fresh cohorts broke Pompey's front line. All enemy resistance collapsed under the acute weight of Caesar's final assault. Pompeius fled the field with his army in disarray.

> Caius Julius Caesar, *The Civil Wars*, 3.84–98; Marcus Annaeus Lucanus (Lucan), *Pharsalia*, 7. ver. 214–679; Appianus (Appian), *Civil Wars*, 2.70–82; Dio Cassius, *Roman History*, 41.53–61.1; Velleius Paterculus, *Roman History*, 2.52.1–3; Plutarch, *Pompey*, 68–72, *Caesar*, 42–45; Eutropius, *Abridgement of Roman History*, 6.20; Sextus Julius Frontinus, *Stratagems*, 2.3.22.

Philippi, 42 BC, 3 October (Roman Civil Wars, Wars of the Second Triumvirate) – A year after the assassination of Julius Caesar, the Second Triumvirate of Marcus Aemilius Lepidus, Caius Octavius (now formally recognized as Caius Julius Caesar) and Marcus Antonius assumed office. From the very beginning, their authority within the Roman state was threatened by the presence of powerful naval and land forces in Asia Minor under the command of Republican conspirators Marcus Junius Brutus and Caius Cassius Longinus. In the summer of 42 BC, while Lepidus remained in Italy with fifteen legions, Octavian and Antony crossed the Adriatic Sea from Brundisium to Dyrrhachium with twenty-eight legions and advanced against the Republican forces which were already moving through Thrace into Macedonia. Brutus and Cassius established their camps on elevated ground near the town of Philippi, 11 miles from the Aegean coast in north central Macedonia. The two *castra* were situated approximately a mile apart on either side of the *Via Egnatia*, which served as the main highway from Dyrrhachium to Anatolia, and were linked by a line of fortified works. A system of mountains to the immediate right of Brutus, and a swamp extending between Cassius' position and the sea, rendered the encampments unassailable by flank assault. Brutus and Cassius possessed nineteen understrength legions and 20,000 cavalry. Antony arrived in the vicinity of Philippi in early October and camped approximately a mile (eight *stadia*) from the enemy's position on a low plain. Like Brutus and Cassius, Antony and Octavian led nineteen legions, though each was at full strength, and 13,000 cavalry. The triumvirs arrayed their legions and offered battle following some preliminary skirmishing by cavalry, but the challenge was not accepted. Aware that Antony's

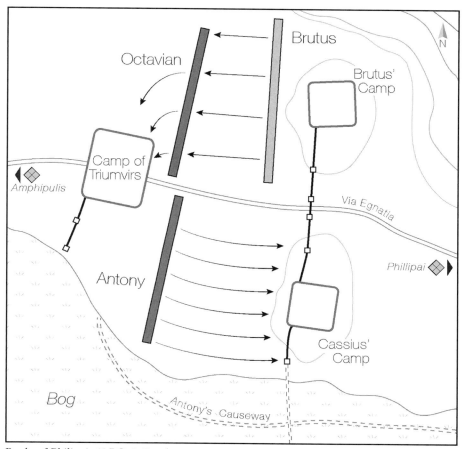

Battle of Philippi, 42 BC, 3 October

immediate supplies were approximately 40 miles away in Amphipolis, and that additional foodstuffs were unavailable from the territories under the control of the Triumvirate, Brutus and Cassius deliberately avoided a decisive fight for several days to force the depletion of Antony's provisions. Recognizing this logistical weakness, Antony moved to force a decisive confrontation by seeking to affect a passage through the marsh in order to sever the Republicans' supply lines. For ten days, Antony sought to distract Brutus and Cassius from his true intentions by daily assembling the legions for battle, while at the same time secretly deploying a portion of his force to construct a causeway through the swamp. After crossing the marsh, Antony's troops quickly built a series of redoubts to threaten the enemy position. Cassius responded to this new danger by constructing a wall from his camp to the sea, which severed the marshland path and thereby isolated the redoubts from

Antony's main position. Antony attempted to redress this circumstance by a forceful assault against Cassius' fortifications, and was answered by a sudden charge of Brutus' infantry against the legions of Octavian. In the battle which followed, Antony's soldiers successfully breached the wall and overran the Republican camp, while his main legionary forces defeated those of Cassius, killing some 8,000 men. Simultaneously, Brutus' legions routed Octavian's entire command, shattering three legions, inflicting heavy casualties and capturing three eagles before completely overwhelming the *castra* of both triumvirs. The battle ended in stalemate as both armies achieved a partial victory on the battlefield. Cassius committed suicide in the wake of his defeat. Octavian suffered perhaps 16,000 dead and narrowly avoided capture.

Plutarch, *Antony*, 22.1–3, *Brutus*, 40.10–45.2; Appianus (Appian), *Civil Wars*, 4.107–112; Dio Cassius, *Roman History*, 47:42–46; Eutropius, *Abridgement of Roman History*, 7.3.

Philippi, 42 BC, 23 October (Roman Civil Wars, Wars of the Second Triumvirate) – Following Marcus Antonius' victory over Caius Cassius Longinus at Philippi in early October, the army of Antony and Caius Octavius remained encamped at the battlefield in anticipation of a subsequent clash with the remaining Republican army, commanded by Marcus Junius Brutus. The two armies fought a bitter hand-to-hand struggle toward the end of the month. On the left, the triumvirs' legions were driven back in disorder by the pressure of Brutus' infantry and elements of cavalry. However, this success was almost simultaneously tempered by the desperate situation in Brutus' centre and on the left, which was dangerously attenuated in an effort to extend the left wing so as to prevent the enemy turning the army's flank. The extension weakened Brutus' battle line, rendering his legions susceptible to a sustained attack by Antony's infantry arrayed in the center and on the right. After intense fighting, the Republican centre collapsed quickly followed by an erosion of the left wing, the loss of which permitted a complete envelopment of the right, where Brutus was situated. Now encircled, the remnants of his army fought desperately but were finally routed. Brutus escaped in the flight that followed, only to later commit suicide. This second engagement marked an end to all serious military resistance to the triumvirate of Antony, Octavius, and Marcus Aemilius Lepidus.

Plutarch, *Antony* 22.4, *Brutus*, 49; Appianus (Appian), *Civil Wars*, 4:107–112; Dio Cassius, *Roman History*, 47.48.4–49.3; Eutropius, *Abridgement of Roman History*, 7.3.

Phintias, 249 BC (First Punic War, Wars against Carthage) – Unaware of the Roman disaster at Drepana, *consul* Lucius Junius Pullus sailed from Italy with a sizeable flotilla of freight transports and escort ships to deliver provisions and supplies to the Roman army presently besieging the port of Lilybaeum in far western Sicily. He rendezvoused with additional ships already operating in Sicilian waters at Messana (Messina), and then turned south

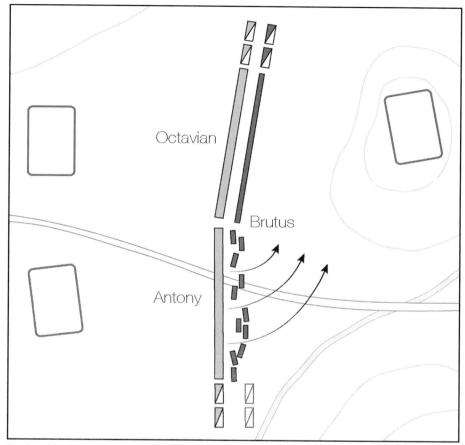

Battle of Philippi, 42 BC, 23 October

toward Syracuse and the Pachynus Promontory with a total combined fleet of 120 warships and 800 transports. Junius sent most of his fleet ahead under the command of his *quaestores classici*, while he remained in Syracuse to collect additional supplies and grain from Rome's allies on the island. The Roman fleet encountered a Carthaginian squadron under the command of Carthalo near the southern Sicilian town of Phintias, situated on the eastern bank of the Himera (Salso) River where it flows into the Mediterranean. The Punic vessels sank fifty transports and seventeen warships, and damaged thirteen other *quinqueremes*. Junius later arrived with additional warships, but the entire fleet was largely destroyed in a sudden terrible storm near the coast of Camarina. Only two of the 105 warships survived the tempest, including the one carrying the *consul*, but the entire complement of freighters was lost. The Carthaginian fleet, which had earlier fled to eastern Sicily ahead of the storm, was unharmed. In his account of the Roman fleets' destruction, Polybius makes no reference to a naval battle.

Diodorus Siculus, *Library of History*, 24.1.7–9; Polybius, *Histories*, 1.52.4–54.8.

Phoenicus, 190 BC (War of Antiochus III) – In order to both gain the support of the Lycians of southern Anatolia and prevent an enemy fleet in Cilicia from joining with the navy of Antiochus III in Ephesus, Roman *praetor* Lucius Aemilius Regillus dispatched a small force of ships from Samos to Patara, the chief city of the country. Because of its diplomatic nature, the expedition was led by the *propraetor* Caius Livius Salinator and consisted of two Roman *quinqueremes*, seven Rhodian *quadriremes* and two *pentekontors* from Zmyrna. Unable to reach the harbour because of inclement weather, the eleven-ship flotilla abandoned Patara and put in at the nearby port of Phoenicus (Finiki), located on the southern Anatolian coast across from the island of Rhodes. Alarmed by the approach of Livius' ships, the civilian population of the town and local garrison loyal to Antiochus seized the cliffs overlooking the harbour. The hostile reception forced the *propraetor* to deploy a detachment of light-armed auxiliaries to harass the Lycians. Tensions quickly escalated when larger numbers of the population came out of Phoenicus, forcing Livius to lead out his marines, the naval allies and the entire complement of oarsmen. The resulting battle ended when the Lycians were routed and driven into the town, but not before slaying a number of Romans, including Livius' lieutenant, the *legatus* Lucius Apustius. The Romans and allies returned to their ships and left Patara after this incident, electing to abandon the campaign in Lycia.

Titus Livius (Livy), *History of Rome*, 37.16.

Phraaspa, 36 BC – see Phraata Atropatene, 36 BC.

Phraata Atropatene, 36 BC (Wars against Parthia) – Impatient to prosecute the war against Phraates IV, king of Parthia, Roman *triumvir* Marcus Antonius chose to lead his exhausted army out of Armenia and invade Media. Antony advanced rapidly against the royal city of Phraata, located in the province of Atropatene (eastern Azarbaijan), with a massive army that included 60,000 Roman infantry, 10,000 Iberian and Gallic cavalry, 6,000 horse and 7,000 foot led by the Armenian ruler Artavasdes, and 30,000 allied troops, consisting of both cavalry and light infantry. The speed of his march necessitated that Antony abandon his slower wagon train and allow the transports to follow with the army's siege machinery as swiftly as possible. He placed these under the authority of his *legatus*, Oppius Statianus, and provided a substantial escort of several thousand men. When Phraates learned of this, he sent a large detachment of cavalry against the lagging column. The wave of horsemen swept in and destroyed the engines, killing Statianus and some

10,000 soldiers in the process. Word of this loss reached Antony and the army besieging Phraata. As a result, Artavasdes shortly abandoned the Roman cause and retired homeward with his forces. The Parthians arrived outside the city while Antony was still preoccupied with the investment. Aware that any inaction against this new danger, especially when coupled with the earlier news of Statianus' disaster and the departure of the Armenian contingent, would threaten to demoralize his army, Antony led ten legions, three praetorian cohorts and his complete complement of cavalry out to forage in hopes of enticing Phraates to a battle. After advancing a day's march from his main camp, the *triumvir* recognized that the Parthians were beginning to surround his army in preparation for a major attack, and accordingly feigned a retreat. As the Roman army marched past the enemy troops, who were assembled in a crescent-shaped line, the cavalry suddenly wheeled at Antony's signal and charged the Parthian formation. The legions and light infantry quickly followed suit. The sudden mass assault caught Phraates' army completely unprepared. The din raised by the approaching cohorts panicked the Parthian horses, causing the ranks to collapse in total disarray before the armies had even joined in battle. Despite the determined pursuit which followed, the Romans were only able to collect thirty prisoners. Parthian losses amounted to no more than eighty men. Antony's casualties in this second engagement went unrecorded, but were apparently negligible.

Plutarch, *Antony*, 38–39; Dio Cassius, *Roman History*, 49.25–26.2.

Pisae, 192 BC – A Roman army led by the outgoing *consul* Quintus Minucius Thermus clashed with a substantial force of Ligurian tribesmen in the vicinity of Pisae (Pisa). The enemy was completely routed with a loss of 9,000 killed. The remainder fled to their camp, which was afterward assaulted by the Romans until nightfall. That night, the Ligures abandoned the struggle and withdrew under cover of darkness. Minucius' troops entered the compound at dawn the following day, pillaged the remains and then initiated a campaign to reduce the Ligurian lands.

Titus Livius (Livy), *History of Rome*, 35.21.7–10.

Pistoria, 62 BC (Catiline Conspiracy) – Following two failed attempts to win election to the consulship in 63 and 62 BC, the Roman patrician Lucius Sergius Catilina conspired to overthrow the government in Rome and seize power. The *consul* Marcus Tullius Cicero eventually revealed evidence for the plot to the Senate, and Catiline's fellow conspirators were arrested and subsequently executed. Away in Etruria (Tuscany) when the conspiracy collapsed, Catiline attempted to flee with a small army of followers into Transalpine Gaul, but was blocked from doing so by a trio of legions under Quintus Caecilius Metellus Celer. This turn of events forced Catiline to come about and face a second, larger pursuing army led by the *consul* Caius Antonius Hybrida. About 18 miles northwest of the town of Florentia (Florence), at the base of the Appennine Mountains near the village of Pistoria (Pistoia), Catiline's force prepared to challenge the legions of Antonius, which were commanded in the battle by the *consul's legatus*, Marcus Petreius. Catiline placed eight cohorts in battle array, with his remaining troops held in reserve behind the front line. The right wing was placed in the charge of his veteran centurion Caius Manlius. Across the field, Petreius assembled his veteran cohorts in line of battle, and likewise established his reserves in the rear. The consular forces were the first to advance, immediately followed by the Catilinarians. Once the armies drew near enough to permit the opposing skirmishers to engage, heavy infantry charged from both sides. The resulting struggle proved extremely bloody. When the battle appeared to shift in favour of Catiline after intense fighting, Petreius directed his praetorian cohort against the enemy's centre. This attack was shortly accompanied by a simultaneous assault on the Catilinarians' flanks, which served to put the entire enemy formation to flight, leaving only Catiline and a determined corps of troops to carry on the fight. After more savage hand-to-hand combat, the contest finally ended with the deaths of Catiline and all 3,000 of his men. Antonius' losses are unknown, but his army did accrue heavy casualties.

Appianus (Appian), *Civil Wars*, 2.7; Dio Cassius, *Roman History*, 37.39–40; Caius Sallusticus Crispus (Sallust), *War with Catiline*, 56–61.

Placentia, 82 BC (Roman Civil Wars) – A Sullan army under the leadership of Marcus Terentius Varro Lucullus defeated a detachment of troops loyal to the *consul* Gnaeus Papirius Carbo near the community of Placentia (Piacenza) in the Po Valley. The demoralizing effect of this defeat compelled Carbo to abandon his army presently deployed around the Etruscan community of Clusium and flee to North Africa.

Appianus (Appian), *Civil Wars*, 1.92.

Pometia, 502 BC – Two Latin colonies, Pometia and Cora, rejected their alliance with Rome and joined with the Aurunci, a rustic Italic people situated in Campania between the Volturnus River and Tyrrhenian Sea. In reply, the Senate deployed an army to invade Auruncan territory. The legions, who offered no quarter on the battlefield, overwhelmed the Aurunci and indiscriminately massacred all prisoners. The next year, the consuls Opiter Verginius Tricostus and Spurius Cassius Viscellinus moved against the colony of Pometia. Following a failed attempt to capture the community by direct assault, the Romans initiated a siege. In desperation, the Aurunci unexpectedly sallied from the town gates armed with firebrands and destroyed or damaged much of the Roman machinery and mantelets (screens to protect soldiers from missiles). This material destruction was accompanied by numerous Roman casualties, including one *consul* who was seriously injured after being thrown from his horse. The disaster compelled the legions to withdraw, but before the end of the year a reinvigorated army returned to resume the investment of Pometia. As the Romans prepared to launch an attack against the walls of the town, the citizenry suddenly elected to surrender. Capitulation did not avoid retaliation. For its role in the rebellion, the community was destroyed, its leaders executed and the colonists sold into slavery.

   Titus Livius (Livy), *History of Rome*, 2.16–17.1–6.

Pontevert, 57 BC – see Axona River, 57 BC.

Porta Collina, 477 BC – Following an indecisive engagement near the Temple of Spes on the outskirts of Rome, a second battle between the Etruscans and Romans was fought at the *Porta Collina*, a gate in the Severan wall located on the northeastern approach to the city. In this confrontation the Roman army, commanded by the *consul* Caius Horatius Pulvillus, gained a narrow victory and thereby eliminated the threat of siege to the capital.

   Titus Livius (Livy), *History of Rome*, 2.51.2–3; Dionysius of Halicarnassus, *Roman Antiquities*, 9.24.4.

Porta Collina, 360 BC – A union of the neighbouring Tiburtes with a large band of invading Gauls from the north exposed the entire region around Rome to raids and devastation. As depredations continued in the districts of Labici, Tusculum and Alba, the Senate instructed the *consul* Caius Poetelius Libo Visolus to lead a Roman army against the town of Tibur 17 miles east of Rome on the Anio River. At the same time, Quintus Servilius Ahala was appointed dictator to address the greater threat presented by the Gauls. Instructing Poetelius to use his own consular army to contain the Tiburtes, Servilius deployed his legions in an effort to confront the Gallic force. The two armies joined in battle near Rome's northeastern gate, the *Porta Collina*. After a long struggle in which heavy casualties were accrued by both sides, the defeated Gauls finally fled eastward in hope of procuring safety at Tibur. As they neared the community, an attempt was made by the Tiburtes to assist the Gauls, but it was turned back by Poetelius' army, and the Gallic survivors were driven through the gates and confined inside the town.

   Titus Livius (Livy), *History of Rome*, 7.11.3–8.

Porta Collina, 211 BC (Second Punic War, Wars against Carthage) – After abandoning his effort to relieve the city of Capua from a Roman siege, Punic general Hannibal Barca marched northward into Latium. By directly threatening the city of Rome, he hoped to draw the proconsular armies of

Quintus Fulvius Flaccus and Appius Claudius Pulcher away from the Campanian community. Rather than advancing toward the city along the more coastal highway, the *Via Appia*, the Carthaginian army followed the *Via Latina* situated further inland. This particular path afforded Hannibal's troops the opportunity to plunder the agricultural lands south of the Tiber River. Once Punic forces reached the vicinity of Rome, they encamped approximately 8 miles away from city in the Pupinian district west of the town of Tusculum. From here, Hannibal's Numidian light horse ranged throughout the immediate region terrorizing the local population, which had been abruptly dislocated from the land by the army's arrival. Unknown to Hannibal, the *proconsul* Quintus Fulvius – recently departed from Capua – approached Rome by way of the more westerly *Via Appia* and entered the city through the *Porta Capena* on the southeastern side with an army of 15,000 infantry and 1,000 cavalry. Then crossing through the centre of the city, they encamped outside the northeastern walls between the *Porta Esquilina* and the *Porta Collina*. The consular armies of Caius Fulvius Centumalus and Publius Sulpicius Galba established their camps in the same locality shortly thereafter. Meanwhile, the Carthaginians relocated to a point near the Anio River some 3 miles from Rome. Hannibal then led a detachment of 2,000 Numidian horsemen to reconnoitre as far as the Temple of Hercules near the *Porta Collina*. The brazenness of this act provoked Flaccus to dispatch a force of 1,200 Numidian deserters against their former comrades. The interlopers were driven off after a brief, sharp cavalry battle. Three days later, following two failed attempts to enter into a decisive battle against the Romans, the Carthaginian army retired southeastward along the *Via Valeria* toward the coastal city of Tarentum.

Titus Livius (Livy), *History of Rome*, 26.10.3–9; Appianus (Appian), *Hannibalic War*, 6.40.

Porta Collina, 82 BC (Roman Civil Wars) – With Lucius Cornelius Sulla's forces apparently gaining the ascendancy in the ongoing struggle in Italy, the Marians joined with the Samnites, who were led by Telesinus, and the Lucanians under Lampronius. The new allies, still bitterly antagonistic toward Sulla after events of the recent Social War, amassed a large army of 70,000 men and marched to Praeneste to relieve the besieged Caius Marius the Younger. As Telesinus approached the town, he learned that his troops were in danger of being trapped between the armies of Sulla and Pompey, and diverted the army's course of march toward an undefended Rome. Upon arrival, the Italians camped northeast of the city, a short distance from the Colline Gate. When Sulla learned of Telesinus' intentions, he dispatched a detachment of 700 horsemen under his lieutenant, Balbus, to ride with all speed and harass the enemy until the remainder of the Roman army arrived to offer battle. Around midday, Sulla's legions reached the city and encamped close to the *Porta Collina* near the Temple of Venus. Both armies quickly began to arm and the two sides clashed in the late afternoon. On the Roman right, the infantry under Marcus Licinius Crassus soundly defeated the opposition, but the Italians completely overwhelmed Sulla's cohorts on the left wing. The contest remained undecided with the onset of darkness. As a result, savage fighting continued throughout the night. The battle was over by daybreak the following morning, by when most of the Samnite and Lucanian forces were destroyed. The estimated number of dead totalled 50,000, and Sulla ordered an additional 8,000 Samnite prisoners massacred. Telesinus died in the struggle. Lampronius escaped, and the Marian generals Marcius and Caius Carrinas were captured and executed on the third day.

Eutropius, *Abridgement of Roman History*, 5.8; Paulus Orosius, *Seven Books of History against the Pagans*, 5.20; Plutarch, *Sulla*, 29–30(1); Appianus (Appian), *Civil Wars*, 1.93; Velleius Paterculus, *Roman History*, 2.27.1–3; Titus Livius (Livy), *Summaries*, 88; Lucius Annaeus Florus, *Epitomy*, 2.9.23.

Praaspa, 36 BC – see Phraata, 36 BC.

Privernum, 357 BC – A Roman army commanded by the *consul* Caius Marcius Rutulus advanced into the territory of the Privernates, and after pillaging the countryside, moved against the town of Privernum, approximately 70 miles southeast of Rome between the Liris River and Tyrrhenian coast. Anticipating the approach of the invading army, the Privernates encamped before the walls of their community within a network of strong entrenchments and prepared to offer resistance. Undeterred by this show of force, Marcius quickly initiated an assault that completely routed the enemy. As the Roman army prepared for a general investment of the town, the residents surrendered.

Titus Livius (Livy), *History of Rome*, 7.16.3–6.

Protopachium, 88 BC (First Mithridatic War, Wars against Mithridates the Great) – For Lucius Cassius, the Roman governor in Asia, and his legates, the defeat of their ally Nicomedes III of Bithynia at the Amnias River was sobering evidence of the acute military threat posed by their new opponent, Mithridates VI of Pontus. At a stronghold called Protopachium, a Pontic army under Neoptolemus overtook a Roman force of 40,000 infantry and 4,000 cavalry commanded by the *legatus* Manius Aquillius – 10,000 Romans died and 300 were captured in the resulting battle. Mithridates released the prisoners unharmed soon afterwards. Following defeat, Manius escaped to Pergamum.

Appianus (Appian), *Mithridatic Wars*, 19.

Pydna, 168 BC (Third Macedonian War, Wars against Macedon) – During the fourth year of the Roman war against the Macedonian king Perseus, a legionary army arrived in Macedonia under the leadership of the

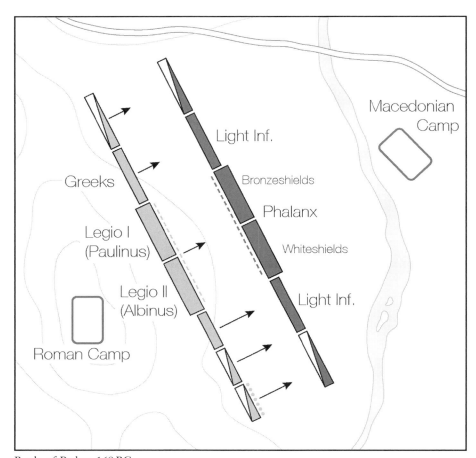

Battle of Pydna, 168 BC

consul Lucius Aemilius Paulus. After defeating Perseus at the Elpeus River, the Romans pursued the Macedonian army northward. The two armies encamped on opposite banks of a shallow river near the port of Pydna, on a narrow coastal plain northeast of Mount Olympus. Each side deployed detachments to protect the camp because of the proximity of the enemy. A mule broke loose from its Roman handlers and bolted for the river around three o'clock in the afternoon on the second day. A trio of soldiers promptly pursued the animal into the water, and a confrontation with some of Perseus' Thracians followed at the water's edge. The fighting swiftly escalated into a set-piece battle between the contending armies. Paulus assembled his battle line around the two consular legions, placing the first opposite the Macedonian *strategia* known as the *chalcaspides* 'Bronzeshields', and the second, under the command of the ex-*consul* Lucius Postumius Albinus, facing the *strategia* called *leucaspides* 'Whiteshields'. Contingents of allied infantry were arrayed on the wings, including Latins, Italians and Greeks. Paulus stationed heavy and light cavalry on the extreme flanks. Perseus likewise adopted a conventional tactical arrangement. After using the *strategiai* to form his phalanx in the centre, he stationed light infantry units across from Paulus' allied contingents. Lastly, squadrons of Macedonian and Thracian cavalry protected the flanks of the infantry line. Once the fighting began on the Roman right, the *consul* moved forward a detachment of war elephants, reinforced by the Latin cohorts. Joined with a solid attack by the supporting infantry, the resulting elephant charge proved irresistible and successfully repulsed the Macedonian left. Toward the centre, where the main contest was unfolding, the legions had a more difficult time and were largely powerless against the phalanx. Amassed behind a formidable wall of levelled spears, Perseus' phalangites forced the Roman heavy infantry to give ground. This situation did not alter until the Macedonian formation attempted to traverse uneven ground. The broken topography disrupted the cohesion of the phalanx, allowing the individual Roman cohorts to exploit the resulting gaps in the enemy ranks. The fighting fragmented when Paulus' infantry penetrated the Macedonian lines. Incapable of repelling the attacks of the more dexterous cohorts, the phalanx collapsed. Perseus' army died in vast numbers all across the battlefield. Approximately 20,000 Macedonian and allied troops died in the battle, and some 11,000 were captured. The engagement lasted only an hour, but pursuit of the fugitives did not end until sunset. King Perseus and the cavalry on the Macedonian right survived, escaped and fled to the safety of the Pierian forest. Roman dead numbered around 100.

Titus Livius (Livy), *History of Rome*, 44.40–42; Plutarch, *Aemilius Paulus*, 16.4–22.1; Frontinus, *Stratagems*, 2.3.20.

Pydna, 148 BC (Fourth Macedonian War, Wars against Macedon) – While the Romans were preoccupied with affairs in the central Mediterranean, a sizeable portion of the Balkans again flared into revolt, this time led by a royal pretender named Andriscus, a native of the Anatolian city of Adramyttion (Edremit). Calling himself Prince Philip, the son of the deceased Macedonian king Perseus, he assembled an army from among various peoples in the region, including the Thracians, and proceeded to spread dissent throughout much of Macedonia and Thessaly. An initial Roman effort to suppress the growing rebellion ended in disaster when an army under the *praetor* Publius Iuventius was all but destroyed by Andriscus' forces. The death of Iuentius and the near annihilation of his cohorts awakened the Romans to the magnitude of the danger, and they dispatched a second army to Macedonia, this time under the command of the *praetor* Quintus Caecilius Metellus. The Romans were again defeated near the port of Pydna, this time in a minor cavalry action. The victory emboldened Andriscus, who soon afterward divided his forces into two sections; one to remain on guard against the Romans, and a second to raid into Thessaly. Metellus, immediately recognizing the error in his opponent's tactical judgment, moved his legion against Andriscus and joined battle. The Romans overpowered the enemy phalanx in the resulting contest. The decisiveness of the *praetor*'s victory quickly convinced the remainder of the rebel army to capitulate.

John Zonaras, *Epitome of Histories*, 9.28; Lucius Annaeus Florus, *Epitomy*, 1.30; Titus Livius (Livy), *Summaries*, 49–50.14, 52.7; Velleius Paterculus, *Roman History*, 1.11; Polybius, *Histories*, 36.10, 36.17.13.

Quiberon Bay, 56 BC – see Morbihan Gulf, 56 BC.

Raudian Plain, 101 BC – see Vercellae, 101 BC.

Raudine Plain, 101 BC – see Vercellae, 101 BC.

Lake Regillus, 496 BC (Latin War) – Rome's rejection of the Tarquin dynasty of kings in 509 BC was soon followed by a growing rivalry between the new Republic and an alliance of Latin states concerning the status of Roman authority in Latium. When war finally erupted over the question of territorial control, the Tarquinii joined with the Latin League in a final bid by the royal family to recover the throne. Near Lake Regillus, 14 miles southeast of Rome, an army of 23,700 infantry and 1,000 cavalry under the Roman dictator Aulus Postumius Albus Regillensis engaged a numerically superior Latin force of 40,000 foot and 3,000 horse. The *magister equitum* Titus Aebutius Elva commanded the Roman left wing, the *consul* Titus Verginius Tricostus Caeliomontanus the right, while the centre was led by Postumius himself. Opposing the Roman right wing were the Latins under the leadership of the Tarquin prince Sextus. The centre was led by a second prince, Titus Tarquinius, and the right wing by the Tusculan general Octavius Mamilius. The fighting was embittered by the presence of the Tarquinii, particularly that of the 90-year-old ex-king Tarquinius Superbus. Both Aebutius and Mamilius were wounded in the struggle, along with many nobles on either side. The Latin battle line began to waver after much intense fighting. Mamilius responded by ordering detachments of Roman exiles into action, both cavalry and light infantry. These fresh reinforcements in turn caused the legionary line to falter. Recognizing that the Roman formation was now in imminent danger of collapse, Postumius ordered his own elite guard of cavalry – together with an additional squadron of horsemen led by the legate Titus Herminius – to manoeuvre behind the Roman battle line and kill any soldiers attempting to abandon the ranks. This threat served to check the army's flight, and it abruptly turned to resume its assault against the enemy with renewed vigour. Supported by Roman cavalry, who dismounted at one point to reinforce the exhausted infantry, the legions made a final rush that completely routed the opposition. In their ardour, the victorious Romans quickly overran the Latin encampment, forcing the enemy to entirely abandon the field. Over 30,000 Latins died in the battle, which ended forever the Tarquinii's efforts to restore the Roman monarchy.

> Titus Livius (Livy), *History of Rome*, 2.19–20; Lucius Annaeus Florus, *Epitomy*, 1.5.1–4; Dionysius of Halicarnassus, *Roman Antiquities*, 6:4–12.

Rhodanus River, 218 BC (Second Punic War, Wars against Carthage) – In the spring, Punic general Hannibal Barca departed Spain with 40,000 infantry and 6,000 cavalry, crossing the Iberus (Ebro) River in mid-July and transversing the Pyrenees before moving into southern Gaul. Near the Rhodanus (Rhone) River, a 500-man Numidian scouting-party, dispatched by Hannibal to patrol south of the Carthaginian crossing point, encountered a Roman reconnaissance force of 300 horsemen travelling north from a camp near the mouth of the river. A sharp engagement followed that ended with the Numidians being put to flight, having lost about 200 men. Roman dead included 140 riders, some of which were Gallic allies. This was the opening battle between Roman and Carthaginian forces in the Second Punic War.

> Titus Livius (Livy), *History of Rome*, 21.29.1–4; Polybius, *Histories*, 3.45.1–2.

Rhodanus River, 121 BC – Having been badly beaten by the Romans at Vindalium, the Allobroges gained the support of the Arverni, a powerful Celtic tribe located in central Gaul. Joined by the Allobrogian warriors, the Arvernian king Bituitus was able to muster an army of 180,000 men. Near the confluence of the Rhodanus (Rhone) River and its tributary, the smaller Isara (Isere) River; the Celtic army clashed with the legions of the *consul* Quintus Fabius Maximus. The Allobroges and Arverni suffered heavy casualties in the resulting defeat, and those losses were further magnified when a temporary bridge constructed by Bituitus across the Rhodanus collapsed under the weight of the fleeing tribesmen, drowning thousands more in the flowing waters. Celtic dead totalled between 120,000 and 150,000. This defeat permanently broke the power of the Arverni, who were until that time one of the leading tribes in Gaul.

> Paulus Orosius, *Seven Books of History against the Pagans*, 5.13; Titus Livius (Livy), *Summaries*, 61; Lucius Annaeus Florus, *Epitomy*, 1.37.4.

Rhodes, 42 BC (Roman Civil War, Wars of the Second Triumvirate) – After the repair of his ships following the engagement at Myndus, Caius Cassius Longinus led his entire force to Loryma on the Asiatic mainland. From there, his lieutenants Fannius and Lentulus employed transports to carry the legions across to the island of Rhodes, while he personally advanced against the port with a fleet of eighty ships. Once in position, he invested the city by land and sea. The Rhodians prepared to offer resistance but were, in fact, completely unprepared to endure a sustained siege. As a result, the city of Rhodes soon surrendered without serious incident.

Appianus (Appian), *Civil Wars*, 4.72.

Rhyndacus River, 74 BC (Third Mithridatic War, Wars against Mithridates the Great) – Following the investment of the Anatolian port city of Cyzicus by Mithridates VI Eupator, king of Pontus, Roman *consul* Lucius Licinius Lucullus relocated his army to the nearby village of Thracia in order to control the roads and land from which the Pontic king might acquire provisions for his army. Lucullus possessed 30,000 infantry and 2,500 cavalry, a force insufficient to challenge the much larger army presently engaged in the siege, but of satisfactory size to disrupt the flow of materials to those attacking the city. Mithridates grew increasingly frustrated with his generals' inability to capture the city as the operation progressed and his store of supplies diminished. While Lucullus was away, Mithridates continued to prosecute the assault against Cyzicus, but used the opportunity to dispatch into Bithynia almost all of his cavalry, supply and draft animals, and wounded in order to conserve the army's provisions. On learning of this, Lucullus led his cavalry and ten cohorts of infantry in pursuit of the retiring enemy detachment. He successfully overtook the Pontic force at the Rhyndacus River, despite snow and bitter cold. In the following battle, the Romans inflicted heavy casualties, in addition to capturing 15,000 men, 6,000 horses and a large number of supply animals.

Appianus (Appian), *Mithridatic Wars*, 75; Plutarch, *Lucculus*, 11.1–3.

Rome, 88 BC (Roman Civil Wars) – The growing personal hatred between Caius Marius and current *consul* Lucius Cornelius Sulla evolved once again into a politically divisive dispute, this time over the Senate's selection of a commander for an upcoming campaign against Mithridates VI Eupator, king of Pontus. Driven by social bias against the plebeian Marius, the senators awarded the coveted position to Sulla in recognition of his battlefield contributions during the recently ended Social War. Soon afterward, a tribune named Publius Sulpicius Rufus persuaded the *Comitia Tributa* to pass a law stripping Sulla of leadership in the approaching war and awarding it to his rival. In response, Sulla marched on Rome with six legions, intent on forcing a reinstallation of his appointment. On reaching the city, Sulla secured control of the *Porta Esquilina* and the adjoining Servian Wall with a single legion, while a second, led by his co-*consul* Quintus Pompeius Rufus, assumed possession of the *Porta Collina* to the north. Southwest of the Esquiline Gate, Sulla stationed a third legion at the *Pons Sublicius*, which crossed the Tiber River near the Janiculum Hill, and deployed a fourth contingent of legionaries to guard the city walls. With the remaining two legions, Sulla entered

Rome in flagrant violation of ancient law which prohibited armed troops within the city. Faced with this massive show of force, Marius and Sulpicius hastily assembled a body of armed followers near the Esquiline Forum. Here, the two sides clashed. After lengthy fighting, Sulla's legions began to waiver, compelling the *consul* to enter the struggle personally in order to rally his men. At the same time, he ordered reinforcements from his camp and directed other troops to follow the Suburran road and attack the opposition's rear. The addition of these fresh reserves finally forced the Marians to flee the city. Following his victory, Sulla distributed guards throughout Rome and established martial law, marking the first violent entry of a Roman army into the Sacred City.

Appianus (Appian), *Civil Wars*, 1.58; Plutarch, *Sulla*, 9.5–7, *Marius*, 35.5.

Rusellae, 294 BC (Third Samnite War, Samnite Wars) – After defeating the Volsinienses in central Etruria, Roman *consul* Lucius Postumius Megellus led his legions northwestward into the territory of Rusellae (Roselle). The army devastated the surrounding fields, provoking the people to take up arms. In the battle which followed, 2,000 Etruscans were captured and a somewhat lesser number killed during the fighting around the walls. Afterward, the Romans seized the city.

Titus Livius (Livy), *History of Rome*, 10.37.3.

Ruspina, 46 BC (Roman Civil Wars) – With his *castrum* properly entrenched to the west of the North African coastal city of Ruspina (Monastir), Julius Caesar led a portion of his army inland to forage. Scouts alerted him of the enemy's approach when he was some 3 miles from camp and a growing dust cloud identified their location in the distance. Caesar had in his company three legions, 400 cavalry and 150 bowmen in light marching kit. Uncertain of the enemy's numbers, Caesar moved his archers and horse squadrons forward and instructed the infantry cohorts to assemble for battle. As the Pompeian forces drew closer, it became apparent that his army faced a vastly larger opponent. The opposing commander, Caesar's former lieutenant Titus Labienus, arrayed his forces in a single line of extraordinary length, with the intention of enveloping the smaller Caesarian formation once the fighting began. Caesar faced 44,000 heavy infantry and 10,500 horse. In addition, mixed among the approaching line of cavalry was a sizeable concentration of Numidian light infantry. To effectively counter Labienus' tactical arrangement, Caesar was obliged to assemble his thirty cohorts into a single line, and place the horse squadrons on both wings. Caesar then deployed his archers in front of his battle line and instructed his horsemen to guard against being enveloped by their more numerous counterparts once the fighting began. Both wings of enemy cavalry extended their line, forcing Caesar's horsemen to attenuate their formation in order to avoid being surrounded. In the meantime, the opposing centres were almost upon each other when the cavalry of Labienus' composite division suddenly dashed forward and discharged their javelins into the leading ranks of legionaries. The cohorts immediately moved against their mounted attackers, but the horsemen as quickly retired through the ranks of the Numidian light infantry. These soldiers then delayed the Roman infantry long enough to permit the riders to regroup for another charge. When the cavalry returned, they in turn provided relief for their foot companions. By means of these innovative tactics, Caesar's cohorts suffered numerous casualties at the hands of the enemy, particularly when they rushed forward beyond the safety of the Roman line. As the battle matured, Labienus was able to exploit his advantage in numbers in order to completely surround Caesar's army. Cut off from any escape, the Caesarians were corralled into a circle, where they remained frustrated by their inability to engage the elusive enemy in a hand-to-hand contest. Aware that the situation would only continue to deteriorate unless some action was taken to extricate the trapped units, Caesar ordered alternate cohorts to about-face, and then each to position its back against its neighbouring cohort. Once this was accomplished, those cohorts on the flanks then forced a lateral extension of the Caesarian line by pushing outward to the left and right. This action, together with the resulting fighting, split the enemy circle at both locations, effectively creating two Pompeian battle lines. Caesar at once ordered both of his fronts to charge the enemy. The vigour of the simultaneous assaults completely routed the forces of Labienus. With the opposition put to flight, Caesar gradually retired to the safety of his camp, all the while maintaining his cohorts in battle array. Labienus resumed the attacks while the Caesarians were still in the middle of the plain, following the arrival of Marcus Petreius and Cnaeus Piso with 1,600 Numidian horsemen and additional infantry. These reinforcements caused Caesar to again order his army to turn and face their antagonists. After subjecting the beleaguered formation of soldiers to continuous hit-and-run attacks, Labienus' forces were suddenly charged by some of the exhausted cohorts. The unexpected assault drove the Pompeians off the plain and behind some high ground. Following a short pause atop the shallow knoll, Caesar withdrew to the safety of his fortifications. Libienus departed shortly thereafter.

Julius Caesar (Aulus Hirtius), *The African War*, 12–18.

Sabis River, 57 BC (Gallic War) – After settling affairs with a number of Belgic tribes following a clash at the Axona River the previous winter, Caesar moved his army against the Nervii, a formidable tribe of Belgae whose lands were situated east of the Schelde River in northern Gaul. Along with the Nervii, the Atrebates, Viromandui and Aduatuci were prepared to resist the

Roman incursion. Caesar entered Nervian territory with eight legions and a sizeable force of *auxilia*, including archers and cavalry. Following a march of three days, he learned from prisoners that a large Belgic army was 10 miles away on the opposite bank of the Sabis (Selle) River awaiting the arrival of the Romans. The Aduatuci had not yet arrived. Because he was so near the enemy, Caesar prudently placed his six veteran legions, the *Legio VII, VIII, IX, X, XI* and *XII*, in light field order at the front of the column, followed by the army's baggage-train, and finally the two new Thirteenth and Fourteenth legions as a rearguard. Once they were near the river, the Romans began to establish their camp on a low hill. On the opposite bank, a screen of enemy cavalry posts occupied a brief expanse of open ground along the Sabis. Behind these, approximately 160 yards from the river in a dense stand of woods atop a shallow knoll, lay hidden the entire Belgic army. While Caesar's cohorts worked to construct the *castrum*, his cavalry crossed the river, accompanied by slingers and archers, and engaged the enemy horsemen. After a brief skirmish, the Belgic riders retired into the tree line, leaving the Roman *auxilia* alone on the field. During this entire episode, the excavation of the camp had continued unabated, and work was still ongoing when the baggage caravan finally reached the site of the encampment. Its arrival served as the signal for the entire mass of Belgic warriors to rush against the Roman position. The sudden assault caught the Romans completely unprepared. The charge easily scattered the cavalry and light auxiliaries across the river. In one seemingly fluid movement, the formation of Belgae swept over the open land between the forest and river, forded the shallow water-course, ascended the hill and crashed into the Roman camp and its occupants, who were still preoccupied with entrenching the fortifications. The speed of the attack offered the cohorts no time to properly assemble, forcing the soldiers to gather under the nearest standard. In the midst of the crisis, the Roman cause was assisted by both the experience and instilled discipline of the men, and by the presence of the *legatii*, each of whom Caesar had forbidden to leave their command during the camp's construction. As the fighting intensified, each legion deployed according to the immediate terrain and the unfolding circumstances on that part of the battlefield. On the extreme left flank, the *Legio X*, together with the Ninth Legion, used the momentum afforded by their occupation of high ground to charge into the Atrebates and drive them into the river. The tribesmen suffered heavy casualties as they attempted to retreat to the opposite bank. The two legions gave pursuit, and when the enemy turned to again offer resistance, the cohorts resumed the battle and put the Atrebates to flight. Likewise, in the centre, the *Legio XI* and *Legio VIII* broke the opposition of the Viromandui and pushed them to the banks of the Sabis. The Roman attack stalled to the right. The Twelfth Legion, joined on the extreme right flank

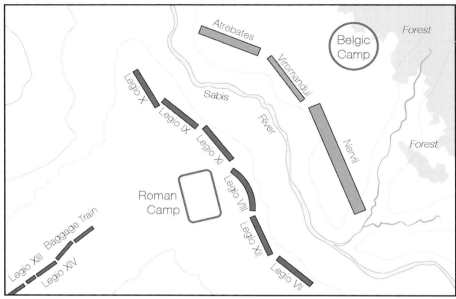

Battle of the Sabis River, 57 BC (Phase 1)

by the *Legio VII*, was hard-pressed by the Nervii. The inability of these two legions to force back the Belgic left created a gap in the Roman line. In addition, the intensity of the enemy attack in that quarter resulted in heavy casualties for the men of the *Legio XII*, and so compressed the legion that the Nervian chieftain, Boduognatus, was able to drive a massed column of warriors through the opening between the Twelfth and Eighth. The attack threatened not only to overrun the Roman camp located behind the legionary line, but envelop the right flank of the *Legio VIII*. Despite its best efforts, the exhausted Twelfth continued to struggle futilely against the Nervii, and was in danger of imminent collapse. Perceiving the threat, Caesar ordered the tribunes of the legion – together with those of the badly harassed Seventh – to gradually draw the two formations together and then pivot to the left against the enemy. These actions collectively served to redress the flagging right flank, while at that moment the *Legio XIII* and *Legio XIV*, forming the rear-guard of the marching column, finally reached the scene of fighting. The arrival of these two fresh legions on the crest above the *castrum*, together with a sudden charge of the Tenth Legion from its place atop the enemy hill across the river, worked to reinvigorate the entire army and thereby turn the momentum of the battle. The Romans surged forward against the remaining Belgae. Even so, the Nervii resisted with obstinate courage, unwilling to concede any ground. Their determination, and the grim intention of the legions to gain the victory, resulted in the near destruction of the entire

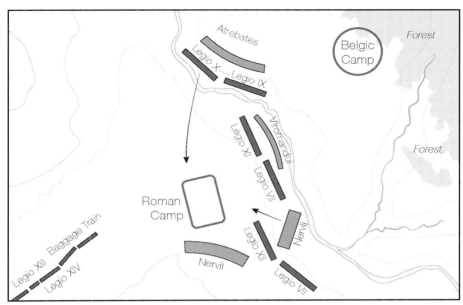

Battle of the Sabis River, 57 BC (Phase 2)

Nervian army. Thousands died in the fighting. When they learned the outcome, the Aduatuci returned to their homeland.

Julius Caesar, *The Gallic War*, 2.15–29; Appianus (Appian), *Gallic History* (fragments), 1.4; Plutarch, *Caesar*, 20.4–10.

Sacriportus, 82 BC (Civil Wars) – At Sacriportus, near the community of Signia (Segni), approximately 30 miles southeast of Rome, Caius Marius the Younger challenged Lucius Cornelius Sulla to battle. The engagement followed a protracted period of minor skirmishing as Sulla attempted to escape several opposing armies which blocked his march through Latium. He permitted his exhausted legions to pitch camp following an end to several hours of inconclusive fighting. The Marian forces attacked while the soldiers were in the midst of their work, hoping to take the disorganized cohorts by surprise. The assault inflamed Sulla and his men, who responded with an irresistible charge that smashed into the opposing formation. As the consul's left wing began to waiver during the fighting, five infantry cohorts and two squadrons of cavalry suddenly deserted to Sulla. This loss signalled the defeat of the Marian force, which thereafter collapsed in complete disorder and fled to the nearby town of Praeneste (Palestrina) to the northwest. As the leading remnants of Marius' shattered army arrived outside the walls of the community, the Praenestines offered them shelter, but then unexpectedly closed the gates in alarm as the bulk of the survivors were seen approaching the town's fortifications with Sulla's cohorts in close pursuit. Trapped between the town and the victorious legions of Sulla, the remains of the Marian army were essentially destroyed, though the *consul* was lifted over the ramparts to safety using ropes. Approximately 20,000 Marian troops lay dead as a result of the day's action, with an additional 8,000 captured. Sulla's fatalities amounted to only twenty-three men. In the aftermath of the fighting, he ordered the execution of the entire Samnite contingent detained.

Plutarch, *Sulla*, 28.4–8; Appianus (Appian), *Civil Wars*, 1:87; Velleius Paterculus, *Roman History*, 2.26.1; Titus Livius (Livy), *Summaries*, 87; Lucius Annaeus Florus, *Epitomy*, 2.9.23.

Saguntum, 75 BC – see Segontia, 75 BC.

Salonae, 48 BC (Roman Civil Wars) – As part of the growing struggle between Julius Caesar and Cnaeus Pompeius Magnus, the Pompeian admiral Marcus Octavius attempted to persuade the residents of the Dalmatian coastal town of Salonae (Split) to renounce their support for Caesar. This population staunchly refused to do, thereby compelling Octavius to place the city under siege. Constructing five camps around Salonae, he proceeded to subject the community to both blockade and siege. After a time, the length of the investment caused the attackers to grow careless. Secretly assembling their forces inside the town, the occupants of Salonae suddenly launched an assault against the nearest camp, overrunning the location before continuing against a second enemy encampment. In turn, the local residents captured each Pompeian camp until Octavius was left with no other option but to abandon the siege and flee with the remainder of his forces. After putting to sea, the admiral led his ships southeast along the Adriatic coast to Dyrrhachium (Durres), where Pompey was presently residing with his legions.

Julius Caesar, *The Civil Wars*, 3.9.

Salonae, 47 BC (Roman Civil Wars, Alexandrian War) – The continuing difficulties which the *propraetor* Quintus Cornificius suffered at the hands of the Pompeians in Illyria ultimately moved Julius Caesar to dispatch Aulus Gabinius to the region with reinforcements. Once there, his efforts were badly hampered by a scarcity of local resources and the winter weather. The poor climatic conditions and supply shortages forced the Romans to frequently assault towns and enemy strongholds, and in so doing Gabinius sustained a number of reverses. The apparent weakness of his forces eventually emboldened the enemy to attack his army while it marched toward the port city of Salonae (Split). In the battle, Caesar's lieutenant lost more than 2,000 men, including thirty-eight centurions and four military tribunes. Casualties incurred by the opposition are not recorded.

Julius Caesar (Aulus Hirtius), *The Alexandrian War*, 43.

Salonae, 47 BC (Roman Civil Wars, Alexandrian War) – While Julius Caesar's lieutenant Aulus Gabinius was in Illyria, the Pompeian admiral Marcus Octavius, operating a fleet off the coast, attempted to seize the port city of Salonae (Split) by siege, but was repulsed by local forces with the aid of the Caesarians. Gabinius, with the support of the Salonians, attacked the enemy's fortifications at midnight. The assault was swift, and many of Octavius' men died while still asleep. Within a short time, the Caesarians had captured both the camp and harbour, temporarily forcing Octavius to abandon his investment of the city.

   Dio Cassius, *Roman History*, 42.11.

Saltus Manlianus, 180 BC – see Manlian Pass, 180 BC.

Sambre River, 57 BC – see Sabis River, 57 BC.

Sapriportis, 210 BC (Second Punic War, Wars against Carthage) – Two years after the Carthaginian siege began, the Roman-held citadel in Tarentum (Taranto) continued to endure the blockade, but a dwindling store of provisions made the garrison's capitulation a certainty unless relief came soon. While the situation remained dire, the Roman *praefectus* Marcus Livius Macatus refused to surrender in anticipation of supplies eventually arriving from Sicily. As the long-awaited convoy of cargo vessels finally departed the island and skirted the southern Italian coast, it acquired an escort fleet of twenty ships out of the port of Regium (Reggio), commanded by Decimus Quinctius. Not anticipating trouble, the flotilla approached their destination under sail. Off the coast near Sapriportis, about 15 miles from Tarentum, the Romans were unexpectedly intercepted by twenty Tarentine warships led by the admiral Democrates. A sudden drop in the wind permitted Quinctius time to take down his vessels' rigging and prepare the fleet for battle. When the distance sufficiently narrowed between the antagonists, the two lines of ships raced headlong against the other, each pressing a head-on attack. The engagement which followed was heavily contested, the opposing craft so closely drawn together as to permit intense ship-to-ship fighting. In the midst of the action, the struggle climaxed between the first pair of vessels to clash; the quinquereme of Quinctius and a *trireme* commanded by a Tarentine officer named Nico. During the contest, a spear thrust killed the Roman commander, whose death was shortly followed by the capture of his ship when a second enemy *trireme* joined in the fight. The loss of their flagship caused the remainder of the Roman war fleet to immediately retreat in disorder. Once the battle was seen to be lost, the transports – which had remained on the periphery of the engagement – abandoned all hope of reaching Tarentum and put out to open sea.

   Titus Livius (Livy), *History of Rome*, 26.39.1–19.

Saticula, 343 BC (First Samnite War, Samnite Wars) – When peace negotiations failed between Rome and Samnium, the Senate elected to declare war and shortly thereafter dispatched two armies into the field. One force, under the leadership of the *consul* Marcus Valerius Corvus, advanced into Campania, while a second pair of legions marched into Samnium under the co-*consul* Aulus Cornelius Cossus Aruina. Near the city of Saticula in south-central Italy, the second army narrowly avoided a Samnite ambuscade, saved in large part by the actions of a select force of 3,000 legionaries under the tribune Publius Decius Mus. That night, the detachment boldly attempted to rejoin with their fellow Romans by passing stealthily through the Samnite encampment. When the effort failed, and an alarm was raised among the sleeping enemy, Decius' men stirred such panic and confusion in the camp that all were able to escape unscathed. Upon safely arriving in the Roman compound the following morning, the tribune recommended to Cornelius that the entire army quickly mount a surprise assault against the Samnites while the enemy was still in a state of disorder following the events of the previous night. The legions were immediately armed and led to battle. After advancing through the surrounding forests undetected, the Romans launched a sudden attack against the unsuspecting enemy. Many Samnites were driven off in the melee which followed, but thousands of others fled to the safety of their camp. The pursuing legions quickly overran the enemy stronghold, and soon thereafter executed some 30,000 enemy prisoners before retiring from the immediate region.

Titus Livius (Livy), *History of Rome*, 7.34–36.

Saticula, 316 BC (Second Samnite War, Samnite Wars) – Following the resumption of hostilities with the Samnites, the Roman dictator Lucius Aemilius Mamercus Privernas and his *magister equitum* Lucius Fulvius besieged the Campanian city of Saticula. In response, the Samnites concentrated a large army near the community in order to relieve their allies. As the investment progressed, the Satriculani unexpectedly initiated an intense sally from their gates that was simultaneously accompanied by a concerted attack of the Samnites. Anticipating such a possibility, Aemilius earlier arrayed his legions so as to face both the city and the enemy camp. As fighting quickly unfolded on the two fronts, the dictator elected to stall the Samnite assault by means of a holding action, and concentrated his maniples on successfully driving the Satriculani back into the town. Once this was accomplished, Aemilius turned the full might of his legions against the Samnite army. The enemy formation collapsed and fled the battlefield in disorder after long, intense fighting. The Samnites withdrew that night, permitting the Romans to resume their siege uninterrupted.

Titus Livius (Livy), *History of Rome*, 9.21; Diodorus Siculus, *Historical Library*, 19.72.4.

Saticula, 315 BC (Second Samnite War, Samnite Wars) – In an attempt to divert the attention of the Senate from the siege of Plistica, a town allied with Rome, a Samnite army again encamped near the community of Saticula, located approximately 23 miles northeast of Neaopolis on the border between Samnium and Campania. In answer to this provocative action, the dictator Quintus Fabius Maximus Rullianus proceeded to the Campanian town with a newly levied legionary force. Once encamped near the Samnite army, Fabius' command was repeatedly harassed by enemy horsemen riding up to very walls of the Roman *castrum*. The brazen nature of the taunting finally moved the *magister equitum* Quintus Aulius Cerretanus to lead his squadrons of cavalry in a sudden counter-attack. The charge proved successful, but both Aulius and the Samnite general were killed in the subsequent melee. Thereafter, a savage hand-to-hand fight developed when both the Roman and Samnite cavalry dismounted in an effort by each to recover the body of their respective commander. The Romans finally drove off the Samnites, who soon withdrew and returned to the siege of Plistica.

Titus Livius (Livy), *History of Rome*, 9.22.

Satricum, 386 BC – Having learned that the people of Antium, a community along the shores of the Tyrrhenian Sea, were arming themselves in preparation for war against Rome, and recruiting support from among their fellow Volsci as well as the neighbouring Latini and Hernici, the Senate dispatched an army under the command of the veteran general Marcus Furius Camillus to confront the enemy force currently assembling in the town of Satricumm some 38 miles south of Rome. Upon seeing the superior size of the enemy, Roman levies expressed apprehension about the approaching battle, but Camillus quickly rallied the legions and attacked. The strength of the first Roman assault, and the presence of the now legendary and feared Roman commander, caused the Antiates' resistence to waver. Despite the growing panic within the enemy's ranks at the sight of Camillus, the right wing held fast and was close to carrying the field against the Roman left when Marcus Furius intervened personally and helped to reverse the fighting in favour of the legions. The victory of Camillus' left wing caused a general rout of the enemy's formation, but all subsequent pursuit by the Romans was prematurely interrupted by a sudden rainstorm. That evening, the Hernici and Latini abandoned the fight and returned to their homelands, forcing the Antiates to shut themselves inside Satricum and prepare to resist a Roman siege. The following day, after a brief demonstration by Camillus' troops, the town was captured along with the entire force of Volsci.

Titus Livius (Livy), *History of Rome*, 6.7–8.

Satricum, 381 BC – Angered by Praeneste's support of the rebellious Roman colony of Velitrae, the Senate and people issued a declaration of war against the city, located 22 miles southeast of Rome in the Apennine foothills. The next year the Praenestini joined with the Volsci to attack the Roman colony of Satricum, then further enraged the Romans by abusing the population following its capture. The Senate responded by marching four consular legions to the relief of Satricum. Command of the 16,000-man force was given to two tribunes, Lucius Furius Medullinus and the veteran general Marcus Furius Camillus. Following the army's arrival near Satricum, the enemy assembled for battle and advanced to the very breastworks of the legionary camp, confident that its superior numbers would overcome the Roman threat. Despite this overt challenge, Camillus refused to be prematurely drawn into an engagement. Indignant at their elder commander's decision, the legionaries – led by the headstrong young Furius – dismissed the caution of Camillus and arrayed the army for battle. In the struggle which followed, the Romans initially pushed the enemy back, but a feigned retreat by the Volsci toward their encampment drew the legions into an unfavourable position where they were subjected to a sudden attack by additional enemy troops held in reserve. Camillus, witnessing the rout, rallied the legions before the camp gates and then reformed the army into battle line. The sight of the reconstituted formation compelled the enemy to abandon the attack. On the following day, Camillus led the Romans into battle against the Volsci, who were driven from the field with heavy losses.

Titus Livius (Livy), *History of Rome*, 6.22–24; Plutarch, *Camillus*, 37.

Satricum, 377 BC – In an effort to address the threat posed by the presence of Latin and Volscian armies encamped near Satricum, legions were dispatched under the tribunes Publius Valerius Potitus Publicola and Lucius Aemilius Mamercinus. Observing the enemy in a strong position, the Romans immediately attacked. As the engagement progressed, the fighting gradually began to favour the Romans when a sudden rainstorm ended all combat. The battle was renewed the next day. This second struggle proved difficult for the legions, particularly against the Latin army, whose long association with Rome ensured it was properly schooled in battlefield discipline. The fighting remained inconclusive until a concerted charge by Roman cavalry disrupted the enemy line. The infantry surged forward in the confusion, driving the Latins and Volscians back and irrevocably shifting the momentum of the battle in favour of the legions. The routed enemy fled for the safety of Satricum 2 miles away, but was overtaken by the cavalry, who slaughtered large numbers of fleeing soldiers. Unable to find protection in their own camp, which had been overrun and sacked, the Volscian and Latin survivors of the battle took temporary refuge in the town before slipping away under cover of darkness to the community of Antium.

Titus Livius (Livy), *History of Rome*, 6.32.5–9.

Satricum, 346 BC – Upon learning that the Volscians of Antium were attempting to agitate the Latin peoples toward war with Rome, the Senate dispatched an army under the *consul* Marcus Valerius Corvus to suppress the threat before it reached maturity. Valerius marched with his legions 38 miles south of Rome to the community of Sarticum, and there encountered a sizeable force of Antiates and other Volscians, mustered earlier in anticipation of Roman action. As the legions prepared to take the town by general assault, the Volsci garrison of 4,000 soldiers and all of the civilian citizenry abruptly surrendered. Following the confiscation of booty, the Romans burned the town, sparing only the temple of Mater Matuta.

Titus Livius (Livy), *History of Rome*, 7.27.5–8.

Saturnia, 82 BC (Roman Civil Wars) – Near the town of Saturnia in Etruria, 20 miles inland from the Tyrrhenian Sea, a force under the command of Lucius Cornelius Sulla defeated a detachment of enemy troops.

Appianus (Appian), *Civil Wars*, 1.89.

Scarpheia, 146 BC – The history of injustices committed by Romans in their efforts to subjugate the Balkan Peninsula exacerbated the circumstances in 147 BC that led to the outbreak of war with the Achaean League. Following a failed diplomatic mission to resolve a growing dispute between the league and Rome, the Senate ordered the *consul* Lucius Mummius (Achaicus) to lead an invasion force against the Greeks. At the same time, the Roman *propraetor* Quintus Caecilius Metellus marched his legions southward from Macedonia through Thessaly, following the northern shore of the Gulf of Lamia (Malian Gulf). To the southwest near the head of the gulf, the Achaean leader Critolaus besieged the town of Heracleia (Iraklia) for its unwillingness to support the league. When his scouts suddenly reported that the Roman army was across the Spercheius (Sperhios) River to the immediate north of the town, Critolaus hastily withdrew southeastward through the Thermopylai pass toward Locris. The legions overtook the fleeing Greeks and forced them into battle near the town of Scarpheia. Metellus quickly gained the victory, killing numerous league soldiers in the course of the struggle and capturing approximately 1,000 more. Critolaus was not found, and no extant sources record his ultimate fate.

Pausanias, *Description of Greece*, 7.15.2–4.

Scirthaea, 103 BC (Second Servile War) – To Sicily, where a slave uprising had rapidly evolved into a major insurrection, the Roman Senate dispatched a

16,000-man army led by the *propraetor* Lucius Licinius Lucullus. A servile force of 40,000 under the leadership of a slave and self-styled king called Tryphon opposed the Romans. The two armies met near Scirthaea in western Sicily. After an initial period of skirmishing, the two armies joined in a major engagement. Both sides suffered many casualties during the lengthy struggle, and many Romans died fighting a detachment of 200 cavalry obedient to a rebel general named Athenion. The battle hung in the balance for a long time until serious wounds forced Athenion to retire. Thereafter, fearing his death, many the slaves grew disheartened and were soon routed from the field. Tryphon escaped with the survivors, leaving behind no fewer than 20,000 dead.

Diodorus Siculus, *Historical Library*, 36.7–8.4.

Scodra, 168 BC (Third Macedonian War, Wars against Macedon) – The formal conclusion of a treaty of alliance between Perseus, king of Macedon, and the Illyrian king Gentius only served to magnify the existing threat posed by these monarchs to Roman interests in the Adriatic and Greece. In February 168 BC, in an effort to address the Illyrian danger, the Roman *praetor* Lucius Anicius Gallus advanced against Gentius' capital of Scodra (Shkoder), located 20 miles from the Adriatic coast between the Oriundes (Drin) River and Labeate Lake. In a bold move calculated to provoke a reaction from the enemy, Gallus ordered his army to advance in battle formation to the very walls of the city. Gentius responded to the challenge by rashly ordering an attack. When the king's forces sallied from the city gate, they were quickly defeated on open ground by the awaiting Romans. As a gesture of magnanimity, shortly after the fighting ended, the *praetor* granted Gentius a requested three-day truce. After initially resisting capitulation, the Illyrian ruler finally surrendered when it became apparent that he possessed no other recourse. The entire Illyrian campaign had taken Gallus less than thirty days to complete.

Titus Livius (Livy), *History of Rome*, 44.31.

Scotussa, 197 BC – see Cynoscephalae, 197 BC.

Scultenna River, 177 BC – Following the recommendation of the Senate, the Roman *consul* Caius Claudius Pulcher led several legions to aid the *praetor peregrinus* Tiberius Claudius Nero – garrisoned at Pisae (Pisa) with a single legion – in subduing the Ligurians of northwest Italy. The consular army engaged and defeated an enemy force of several thousand warriors on the open plains near the Scultenna (Panaro) River. Ligurian losses amounted to some 15,000 killed and more than 700 captured. Roman casualties are not recorded.

Titus Livius (Livy), *History of Rome*, 41.12.7–10.

Scyllaeum Promontory, 42 BC – Following Sextus Pompeius' seizure of Sicily from local Roman authorities in 43 BC, the triumvirs Marc Antony, Lepidus and Octavian were forced to tolerate his naval supremacy over the central Mediterranean Sea while they concentrated on the defeat of Caesar's assassins in Macedonia. Once Brutus and Cassius were beaten at Philippi the following autumn, Octavian turned his attention toward Pompeius. Aware that Sicily also provided sanctuary for a number of his political opponents, Octavian sent his lieutenant, Salvidienus, with a fleet to destroy Sextus Pompeius. The two sides joined in battle off the promontory of Scyllaeum (Scilla) near the northern entrance to the Sicilian Straits (Stretto di Messina). Pompeius' lighter ships quickly proved faster and more agile than those commanded by his opponent, whose vessels handled poorly in the strong currents and heavy waves. The Roman crews' inexperience in the rough waters of the straits likewise proved to be a liability in the struggle. After extensive fighting, Salvidienus elected to break off the engagement around sunset, having been worsted in the day's action. As the Roman ships withdrew, Pompeius declined to give chase, his fleet having suffered significant damage. Pompeius retired to secure anchorage in Sicily, while the Romans sought safety in the port of Balarus, facing the straits. Salvidienus sought the opportunity there to repair his crippled ships and await the arrival of Octavian.

Appianus (Appian), *Civil Wars*, 4.9.85.

Segontia, 75 BC (War against Sertorius) – The armies of the *proconsul* Quintus Caecilius Metellus Pius and Cnaeus Pompeius Magnus clashed with an army under the command of Quintus Sertorius near the Iberian town of Segontia. After an intense battle lasting from noon until nightfall, Sertorius gradually began to gain advantage in the struggle, defeating Pompey and inflicting heavy casualties before driving his attack toward Metellus. The *proconsul* was wounded in the midst of the fighting. The injury to their commander enraged Metellus' legions, which immediately launched a vicious counter-assault against Sertorius' forces. The charge drove the Iberians back, forcing Sertorius to retreat from the battlefield. Roman losses totalled 6,000 men, including the death of Pompey's *legatus* Caius Memmius. Sertorius suffered 3,000 dead, and his lieutenant Marcus Perperna an additional 5,000 killed in the contest against Metellus.

Plutarch, *Sertorius* 21.1–3; Appianus (Appian), *Civil Wars*, 1.8.110.

Seguntia, 75 BC – see Segontia, 75 BC.

Segovia, 79 BC (War against Sertorius) – After earlier defeating a Roman army at the Anas (Guadiana) River, Sertorius' lieutenant – the *quaestor* Lucius Hirtuleius – achieved a second victory over legionary forces led by Lucius

Thorius Balbus at Segovia, a small community 15 miles east of Corduba (Cordoba). Thorius was killed in the battle.

Plutarch, *Sertorius* 12.4; Lucius Annaeus Florus, *Epitomy*, 2.10.6–7.

Sentinum, 295 BC (Third Samnite War, Samnite Wars) – A short time after the Senonian Gauls destroyed a Roman legion at Camerinum (Camerino), the consuls Quintus Fabius Maximus Rullianus and Publius Decius Mus led a 40,000-man army against an alliance of Umbrians, Etrurians, Samnites and Gauls concentrated in northern Umbria. The expeditionary force consisted of four legions, a strong contingent of Roman cavalry, 1,000 Campanian horsemen and thousands of additional allied and Latin troops. To protect Rome from the threat of attack during the consuls' absence, two other Roman armies were stationed immediately outside the city toward Etruria; one in the Faliscan district to the north and the other across the Tiber River in the vicinity of the Vatican. Command of these forces was handed to the propraetors Gnaeus Fulvius and Lucius Postumius Megellus. The consular legions came upon the enemy near the community of Sentinum (near Sassoferrato), 110 miles northeast of Rome. The Romans found the Etruscans and Umbrians camped apart from the Gauls and Samnites. The consuls soon learned from deserters that the purpose of this arrangement was to allow the latter pair to prosecute the battle, while the former attacked the Roman camp. Fabius, aware that the enemy's numerical superiority provided them the means to carry out their intentions, moved to thwart the plan. Writing to Fulvius and Postumius, the propraetors were instructed to initiate a diversionary campaign into Etruria in order to draw off the Etruscan and Umbrian forces around Sentinum. The ploy worked, and the consuls immediately moved to provoke a confrontation with the remaining enemy divisions. The two armies finally met in battle following three days of skirmishing. The Samnites arrayed on the left wing opposite the First and Third legions under Fabius, while the Gauls to the right faced the maniples of the Fifth and Sixth led by Decius. Fabius held a portion of his command in reserve when the battle opened, intending to exhaust the enemy before committing fresh reinforcements. By contrast, Decius attacked with his entire force in an attempt to overwhelm the enemy in the first encounter. When the Roman initiative stalled on the left, Decius ordered his cavalry to break the impasse. Two separate charges successfully drove back the Gallic cavalry, but the momentum of the last attack carried the Roman horsemen deeply behind the enemy's front line, where they became isolated among companies of reserve infantry. Before the riders were able to extricate themselves from the perilous situation, they were subjected to a violent countercharge by Gallic chariots which completely scattered the Roman cavalry and penetrated into the legionary ranks. As the chariots disrupted the cohesion of the maniples on the Roman left,

Gallic infantry attacked the disorganized consular troops, putting some to flight. After witnessing the chaos occurring within his own lines, Decius invoked the intercession of the Roman gods as his father had done forty-four years earlier during the battle at Veseris. Employing the help of the attending *pontifex* Marcus Livius, Decius completed the solemnity and then charged directly into the midst of the enemy. His sacrificial act served to rally the left wing, which was simultaneously joined by reserve forces sent over by Fabius. At the same time, those legions on the right also received the support of reinforcements. Now reinvigorated by additional manpower and inspired by the courage of the slain Decius, the entire Roman line exerted new pressure on the enemy front. The legions to the left resumed their attack on the Gallic formation, while the maniples under Fabius surged once more against the exhausted Samnites. The infantry attack on the right was then accompanied by a charge of Roman cavalry against the enemy's left flank. The cumulative effect routed the Samnites. The sudden loss of their allies on the right compelled the Gauls to compress their formation into a *testudo*. This closely packed phalanx proved formidable and finally compelled Fabius to attempt outflanking the opposing line using both the Campanian horse and the *principes* of the *Legio III*. Once this mixed detachment successfully enveloped the *testudo*, a well-executed cavalry assault thoroughly disrupted the integrity of the enemy's rear, permitting the legionaries to attack the Gauls piecemeal. In the rout which followed, the Romans seized the Samnite camp after a brief struggle. Roman dead amounted to 7,700. Gallic and Samnite losses totalled 25,000 killed and 8,000 captured.

Polybius, *Histories*, 2.19.6; Titus Livius (Livy), *History of Rome*, 10.27.8–10.29.

Sicoris River, 49 BC (Roman Civil Wars) – Marching ahead of Caesar's main column as it advanced toward Spain from southern Gaul were three legions under the command of his lieutenant, Caius Fabius. After securing control of the passes over the Pyrenees Mountains, Fabius descended to the eastern bank of the Sicoris (Segre) River and there constructed two bridges, 4 miles apart. Having exhausted his available supplies, he dispatched foraging parties across the river. At the same time, this area was also being combed by foragers sent out by the Pompeian generals Lucius Afranius and Marcus Petreius, whose five legions and 5,000 cavalry were encamped a short distance away near the community of Ilerda (Lerida). As a result, cavalry skirmishes frequently erupted between the opposing sides. While Fabius remained in place, Caesar approached from the north with the remainder of the army. While two of Fabius' legions were across the Sicoris to provide additional protection to the foragers, a sudden storm destroyed the nearest bridge, leaving the legions isolated and unable to receive support from a large force of cavalry preparing to cross over. The trapped legions quickly drew the attention of the Pompeians. Afranius immediately marched against them with four legions and the entire complement of cavalry. The Caesarian *legatus* in charge of the isolated legions, Lucius Plancus, responded to the impending attack by gathering his forces on a slight hill and drawing the cohorts into battle formation. On reaching the location, Afranius launched a series of infantry and cavalry assaults against Plancus, which only ended when two additional legions, deployed by Fabius when the crisis began, were seen approaching in the distance. Caesar's legions suffered serious losses in the fighting at the Sicoris River.

Julius Caesar, *The Civil Wars*, 1.40; Appianus (Appian), *Civil Wars*, 2.42; Dio Cassius, *Roman History*, 41.20.1–2.

Signia, 362 BC – Following a declaration of war against the Hernici, Lucius Genucius Aventinensis – seeking to be the first plebeian *consul* to conduct a successful military campaign under his own auspices – unwittingly marched a Roman army into an ambush. Genucius was killed in the ensuing battle and the remnants of his defeated legions besieged within their own encampment near the Latin community of Signia (Segni). Given the dire circumstances resulting from the engagement, the patrician Appius Claudius Crassus was appointed dictator and quickly led a second army in an invasion of Hernician territory. Before the arrival of these reinforcements, the Hernici attempted to capture the trapped legions by means of an assault against their camp, but were thrown back in confusion when the legate Caius Sulpicius instigated an unexpected sally from inside the fortifications. The relief column finally reached the beleaguered forces of Sulpicius, then promptly moved against the Hernici. The two armies clashed on a large 2-mile plain located between the opposing camps. The outcome of the battle remained far from certain for some time. Despite repeated charges by Roman cavalry, all efforts to penetrate the enemy line failed because of a stern defence centered around eight elite units of Hernici foot. The fighting continued unabated until a determined surge by the legions exerted sufficient pressure to force the entire enemy line to waver before collapsing in total flight. The Romans thereafter pursued the Hernici to their camp but refrained from a protracted assault because of the onset of darkness. Claudius found the enemy camp abandoned the following day. Both sides suffered significant casualties in the contest, Roman losses amounting to a quarter of the army's infantry.

Titus Livius (Livy), *History of Rome*, 7.6–8.

Signia, 82 BC – see Sacriportus, 82 BC.

Silarus River, 71 BC (War of Spartacus, Third Servile War) – This was the decisive battle in the long struggle of Roman authorities to defeat a rogue slave army in Italy under the leadership of Spartacus, an escaped Thracian gladiator. The battle near the boundary between Lucania and Campania was the culmination of a long series of unsuccessful efforts by Rome to end the servile revolt by military means. In 73 BC, near the base of Mount Vesuvius, Spartacus defeated the first of several armies deployed to stop him. The rebels defeated a force of 3,000 militia troops under the leadership of Clodius Glaber. This loss was compounded by Spartacus' seizure of large quantities of arms and armour after the battle. Largely in response to the failure of this initial effort, the Senate deployed two full legions of militia under the command of the *praetor* Publius Varinus in what proved another failed campaign to stop the slave army. Early losses were accrued by Varinus' junior commanders near Mount Vesuvius, where Furius suffered the near total destruction of a 2,000-man militia detachment, and not far away in Herculaneum, in another battle that resulted in the annihilation of a column of troops led by Cossinius. Finally, Varinus' entire command was badly defeated in Lucania, with a smaller detached force under Gaius Thoranius later destroyed in Campania. Frustrated by these events, the Senate dispatched four consular legions into the field during the spring of 72 BC, resulting in the defeats of the consuls Lucius Gellius Publicola and Gnaeus Cornelius Lentulus Clodianus, plus the *praetor* Quintus Arrius. This trio of losses was followed by the destruction of a 10,000-man army under Caius Cassius in northern Italy. Compelled by the inability of any armies to thus far stop Spartacus, the Roman government sent out eight legions under the leadership of the *praetor* Marcus Licinius Crassus. Crassus resumed the Roman pursuit of the servile army as it traversed the length of Italy from north to south, finally inflicting a sharp but inconclusive defeat on Spartacus in the region of Lucania. Continuing southwestward, Spartacus finally reached the coastal city of Rhegium in a desperate but futile attempt to hire a fleet of ships to transport the slaves to Sicily. Seeing an opportunity, Crassus attempted to trap Spartacus in the toe of Italy through the construction of an extensive ditch spanning the entire 32-mile width of the Bruttium peninsula, but Spartacus was able to break through the Roman lines and return to Lucania. Alarmed, the Senate now took the extraordinary step of recalling the veteran combat legions of Gnaeus Pompey from Spain and those of Lucius Lucullus from Asia Minor. Pressured politically to resolve the matter before the imminent arrival of the overseas legions, Crassus once again marched after the slave army. As Spartacus' enormous band turned toward the heel of Italy and its major port of Brundisium, the ex-gladiator suddenly learned of the landing of Lucullus in the coastal city. Trapped by Lucullus' legions in Brundisium and the approaching army of Crassus from the west, Spartacus determined to offer battle. Before reaching the main rebel army, Crassus smashed a substantial force of Gallic and German auxiliaries, killing roughly 30,000. The *praetor* then moved his legions toward Spartacus' encampment, which was situated at the head of the Silarus (Sele) River. The

Roman army consisted of about 40,000 men, while the full contingent of slaves numbered perhaps 100,000, including women and children. The battle which followed claimed thousands of Roman casualties, including 1,000 dead, but resulted in the total destruction of the entire servile army. The survivors from among the thousands of slaves who perished beneath Roman swords were later hunted down mercilessly by the legions of Pompey, and 6,000 of those captured were crucified along the entire 132-mile length of the *Via Appia* between Capua and Rome. The defeat of Spartacus marked an end to the last significant slave revolt in the Roman world.

> Plutarch, *Crassus*, 8–11.7; Paulus Orosius, *Seven Books of History against the Pagans*, 5.24; Appianus (Appian), *Civil Wars*, 1.116–120; Lucius Annaeus Florus, *Epitomy*, 2:8.5–14; Titus Livius (Livy), *Summaries*, 95–97.

Silipa, 206 BC – see Ilipa, 206 BC.

Sinnaca, 53 BC – see Carrhae, 53 BC.

Solonium, 61 BC – A revolt among the Allobriges – a Celtic tribe whose lands lay between the Rhone River and Lake Geneva in the northeastern district of Gallia Narbonesis – led the provincial governor Caius Pomptinus to dispatch legionary forces under the legates Lucius Marius and Servius Galba to suppress the uprising. The two generals crossed the Rhone and devastated the territory of the Allobriges before moving against the city of Solonium. Once there, the Romans defeated the opposition in battle and burned a portion of the town, but were prevented from its complete capture by the unexpected arrival of Celtic forces under the Allobrigian chieftain Catugnatus. Upon learning the results of the campaign, Pomptinus soon returned with his entire army and successfully reduced Solonium, but failed to capture the tribal leader.

> Dio Cassius, *Roman History*, 37.48.

Sotium, 56 BC (Gallic War) – While Julius Caesar was away in Illyria, the Veneti, a powerful Gallic tribe located on the coast of southern Brittany, stirred up trouble against the Romans. Once he returned to Gaul, Caesar sent Publius Licinius Crassus to Aquitania to ensure that the southern tribes provided no aid or reinforcements to the rebels. Consisting of legionary cohorts and auxiliary infantry and cavalry, the army crossed the borders of the Sotiates. Upon learning that their lands had been invaded, the tribesmen prepared an ambuscade for the Roman column in a valley near the town of Sotium (Sos). The Gauls opened the encounter with a cavalry attack, hoping to use their horsemen to lure the Romans into the trap. When Crassus' horsemen proved superior in the struggle and gave chase, they were ambushed by thousands of amassed warriors, who easily scattered the Roman riders before joining battle with the awaiting cohorts. The tribesmen fled the battlefield following a long and savage contest in which the Sotiates suffered heavy casualties. Crassus then pursued the fugitives to Sotium and proceeded to reduce the *oppidum*.

Caius Julius Caesar, *The Gallic War*, 3.20–21; Dio Cassius, *Roman History*, 39.46.1–2; Paulus Orosius, *Seven Books of History against the Pagans*, 6.8.

Sparta, 195 BC – The withdrawal in 197 BC of the eastern Peloponnesian city of Argos from the Achaean League prompted the Roman war against Nabis, tyrant of Sparta. Following the Argives' departure from the league, the city-state sought protection from the Macedonian king, Philip V. Unable to provide Argos with such a guarantee because of his ongoing struggle with Rome, Philip handed the city over to the temporary protection of Nabis (Livy, 32.38.2). Following a successful prosecution of the Second Macedonian War which ended with the defeat of Philip at Cynoscephalae, Roman general Titus Quinctius Flamininus prepared to intervene in the matter of Argos. Flamininus summoned a council of Greek delegates to Corinth, at which war against Nabis was decided for his unwillingness to relinquish Argos to the Achaean League. From their base at Elateia in central Greece, Flamininus ordered his legions to move southward into the Peloponnesus. Along the march they were joined by 11,000 allied Achaeans. After a brief show of force outside Argos, the Roman commander turned the entire army toward Lacadaemonia in preparation for assaulting the city of Sparta, considered by Flamininus to be the primary objective of the campaign. As the Romans advanced beyond Mount Parthenius, Macedonian and Thessalian reinforcements arrived, raising the total number of troops under Flamininus to around 50,000. Advanced elements of the army began construction of a camp once they were near the city, but were suddenly thrown into confusion by the unexpected attack of enemy auxiliary troops. The situation was quickly recovered by the arrival of the legions, whose leading cohorts immediately entered into the battle and drove off the attackers. The following day, as Flamininus moved his army along the Eurotas River outside Sparta, a strong contingent of the tyrant's mercenaries attacked the Roman rearguard commanded by Appius Claudius. Anticipating such an action, the trailing detachments swiftly wheeled about and deployed into battle formation. A general engagement followed. The enemy line eventually collapsed after intense fighting, resulting in a total rout of the entire army. In the following pursuit, most of those fleeing the field were killed or captured. The defeat was further assured with the systematic destruction of the countryside surrounding the city by Roman and allied Greek forces. Flamininus besieged Nabis in Sparta before the end of the year, and forced the Lacadaemonian tyrant to surrender following a protracted investment. In the subsequent settlement, Nabis was stripped of all his foreign possessions, though left in control of the city proper.

Titus Livius (Livy), *History of Rome*, 34.22–40.

Temple of Spes, 477 BC – On the outskirts of Rome near the Temple of Spes, an army under the *consul* Caius Horatius Pulvillus engaged an invading force of Etruscans which had recently crossed the Tiber River after destroying a contingent of Roman troops recruited from the Fabian clan near the Cremera River. The battle proved indecisive, and was almost immediately followed by a struggle outside the Colline Gate which finally stopped Etruscan encroachment on the city.

Titus Livius (Livy), *History of Rome*, 2.51.2–3; Dionysius of Halicarnassus, *Roman Antiquities*, 9.24.4.

Spoletium, 82 BC (Roman Civil Wars) – In central Italy on the plain of Spoletium, Sullan forces under the command of Gnaeus Pompeus and Marcus Licinius Crassus killed some 3,000 men under Gnaeus Papirius Carbo and besieged the Cinnan forces under Caius Carrinas. In response, Carbo deployed reinforcements to Carrinas, but this movement was discovered by Lucius Cornelius Sulla, who ambushed the relief column, killing about 2,000 men.

Appianus (Appian), *Civil Wars*, 1.90.

Stratonicea, 130 BC – The death of Publius Licinius Crassus Mucianus and destruction of his consular legions at Lencae was soon followed by the arrival of a second Roman army in Asia Minor under his successor, Marcus Perperna. The *consul* located his adversary Aristonicus, an illegitimate half-brother of the deceased Pergamene ruler Attalus III, and his army near the community of Stratonicea in southwestern Anatolia. There, Perperna routed the enemy. The general and the remnants of his defeated army took refuge inside the city, but were ultimately forced to surrender after a protracted siege.

Paulus Orosius, *Seven Books of History against the Pagans*, 5.10; Eutropius, *Abridgement of Roman History*, 4.20; Titus Livius (Livy), *Summaries*, 59.

Sucro River, 75 BC (War against Sertorius) – With the advent of spring in 75 BC, Quintus Sertorius and Gnaeus Pompeius Magnus resumed their war, the former marching with Marcus Perperna from Lusitania, and the latter leading his armies out of the Pyrenees Mountains. The two adversaries met near the Sucro (Xucar) River in the southeastern Iberian peninsula. Pompey was eager to engage Sertorius before the arrival of the *proconsul* Quintus Caecilius Metellus Pius, so as to claim the victory alone; while his opponent was equally desirous to do battle before additional legions were able to join in.

In their haste, both generals arrayed their armies toward sunset, Pompey situated on the right wing and his *legatus* Lucius Afranius on the left. Opposing the Romans, Sertorius commanded from the right, with Perparna facing Pompey's cohorts. When Sertorius opened the battle, Afranius immediately found himself hard-pressed, but his legions managed to hold until a concerted attack by Pompey endangered Perperna's position and forced Sertorius to redeploy a portion of his troops to aid the flagging left. Perperna's men, though already in retreat, rallied and turned to charge the pursuing Romans. The unexpected counter-attack routed Pompey's legions. On the Roman left, the absence of Sertorius permitted Afranius to quickly defeat his opponents and drive the fugitives back to their camp. His cohorts briefly penetrated the enemy earthworks and pillaged the encampment before retiring. Once Sertorius completed the victory over Pompey, he returned to his previous location on the right, and in the darkness quickly overran many of Afranius' men straggling back in disarray, inflicting heavy casualties. The entire Roman line was put to flight after the defeat of Afranius.* The next morning, both armies again assembled for battle, but the timely arrival of Metellus' legions moved Sertorius to withdraw from the field.

Plutarch, *Sertorius*, 19.2.6, *Pompey*, 19.1–4; Lucius Annaeus Florus, *Epitomy*, 2.10.7; *both Appian and Livy suggest that Metellus was present, and note that one wing on each side defeated the enemy – Titus Livius (Livy), *Summaries*, 92; Appianus (Appian), *Civil Wars*, 1.8.110; see also Frontinus, *Stratagems*, 2.13.3.

Suessula, 343 BC – A Roman victory at Gaurus Mons did not deter the Samnites from gathering another army in preparation for a second battle against the legions of the *consul* Marcus Valerius Corvus. Alarmed by the situation, the citizens of Suessula appealed for assistance from the *consul*, who promptly assigned a strong garrison to guard his camp and baggage, and then moved the remainder of the army southward in light marching order toward the Campanian city. Arriving a short distance from the enemy's position, the *consul* encamped his soldiers within a very small perimeter since the maniples were unencumbered by draft stock, camp followers and supplies. The Samnites immediately assembled into battle formation on seeing the enemy in such close proximity, but they were soon compelled to advance to the very gates of the Roman camp when the legions failed to deploy with equal alacrity. Observing the Roman fortifications, the Samnite leadership concluded that the dimensions of the camp and the enemy's reluctance to engage implied the presence of a small force. Believing the Romans posed no real danger to their army, the commanders elected to disperse their troops in order to collect forage from the countryside. When Valerius observed what the Samnites were doing, he quickly gathered his forces and overran the unsuspecting enemy's camp. Then, deploying two legions to guard the location,

he next arrayed his remaining infantry on open ground outside the encampment before instructing the cavalry to make a wide sweep of the surrounding
fields in order to drive in the scattered foraging parties toward the awaiting
line of soldiers. Trapped between the stationary ranks of the maniples and the
advancing horsemen, the Samnites suffered heavy losses.

Titus Livius (Livy), *History of Rome*, 7.37.4–17.

Sulci, 258 BC (First Punic War) – Under a heavy fog, Roman and Punic
fleets clashed off the coast of southwestern Sardinia near the Gulf of Sulci. As
the Carthaginian vessels approached the anticipated location of their enemy,
the Roman commander Caius Sulpicius Paterculus ordered his ships to
attack. Undetected in the sea mist, the Romans caught the Punic fleet by
surprise. In the ensuing fight, the Romans destroyed the majority of the
Carthaginian ships. With the surviving remnants of his fleet, the Punic
admiral Hannibal fled to shore, where the survivors abandoned their ships
and took refuge in the town of Sulci (San Antioco). While there he was
murdered by his mutinous men.

John Zonaras, *Epitome of Histories*, 8.12; Paulus Orosius, *Seven Books of History against the Pagans*, 4.8.

Suthul, 109 BC, January (Jugurthine War) – The advent of the usurper
prince Jugurtha as ruler of Numidia eventually led to the outbreak of war
with Rome. In the course of the power struggle between members of the
Numidian royal family for control of the North African kingdom, a number
of Italian residents in the city of Cirta were inadvertently caught up in the
violence and killed. Public and political outrage in Rome over the atrocities
eventually forced the Senate to initiate military operations against the new
king in 111 BC. The first expedition, led by the *consul* Lucius Calpurnius
Bestia, fared poorly, as did a second campaign the following season directed
by Spurius Postumius Albinus, the junior *consul* for that year. When Spurius
left North Africa, he placed responsibility for the ongoing war in the hands of
his brother, the *propraetor* Aulus Postumius Albinus. In late 110 BC, Aulus
Postumius initiated another campaign against Jugurtha. Numbering 40,000,
the Roman army left its winter quarters and by forced marches in bad weather
reached the fortified town of Suthul, the repository for the king's treasures.
Because it was winter, seasonal rains had inundated the already marshy plain
around the community, making a siege impossible. Undeterred by the
circumstances, and driven by greed to employ his army as an instrument to
extort money from Jugurtha, Aulus pressed forward with his attack. After
assessing the situation, the king feigned intimidation, and by a ruse enticed
the Roman commander to abandon his intentions and pursue the Numidian
army into a more remote and inhospitable region of the country. During the

course of the march, Jugurtha covertly employed agents to bribe some of the Roman infantry and cavalry officers into deserting or otherwise betraying their military oaths. Once these arrangements were made, he took advantage of a dark, overcast night to surround Aulus' camp in the early morning hours. The sudden, unexpected appearance of the Numidian army caused confusion within the Roman camp, and their inability to discern the magnitude of the threat inspired further panic among the men. Some units of *auxilia* deserted in the midst of the chaos, including a cohort of Ligurian infantry and two troops of Thracian cavalry. At the same time, the *primus pilus* of the *Legio III* abandoned his post to allow the Numidians entrance through a camp gate. With the security of the *castrum* now compromised, the Roman army fled in disorder to a nearby hill. The next day, Jugurtha informed Aulus that he would not destroy the *propraetor*'s command if he agreed to withdraw his forces from Numidia within ten days, and if the army submitted to passing under the yoke. Left with no option, Aulus complied with the demands.

Caius Sallusticus Crispus (Sallust), *Jugurthine War*, 37–38; Paulus Orosius, *Seven Books of History against the Pagans*, 5.15.

Sutrium, 389 BC – Envoys from the community of Sutrium, an ally and neighbour of Rome located approximately 30 miles northwest of the Eternal City, presented themselves before the Senate to plead for military assistance against the Etruscans, who were presently besieging their town. In response, an army was dispatched under the command of the dictator Marcus Furius Camillus. As the legions entered the vicinity of the distressed community, they encountered a stream of refugees in flight. Camillus directed the Sutrines to stop and await the outcome of the Roman incursion. He then ordered the army to battle readiness and advanced in light marching order. On reaching the city walls, Camillus found the Etruscans fully involved in ransacking Sutrium and unaware of his army's presence. Exploiting the advantage of total surprise, the legions entered the open gates and quickly overwhelmed the enemy. The town was restored to the Sutrines by nightfall.

Titus Livius (Livy), *History of Rome*, 6.3; Diodorus Siculus, *Historical Library*, 14.117.4.

Sutrium, 311 BC (Second Samnite War, Samnite Wars) – In the fourteenth year of the Samnite conflict, the Etruscans, with the exception of the Arretini, entered into the war by besieging the city of Sutrium, an ally of Rome. In response, an army was dispatched under the *consul* Quintus Aemilius Barbula. As the city was not yet fully invested, the Sutrini were able to offer provisions to the Roman camp prior to the opening of hostilities. With the arrival of the legionary forces, the Etruscans resolved to initiate an assault to decide the matter and arrayed for battle at sunrise the following morning. After ensuring his army was well-fed and fully armed, Aemilius readily accepted the challenge, but caution compelled both armies to delay engaging in action until the afternoon, despite their being fully assembled in battle formation. The Etruscans finally elected to advance, shortly followed by the Romans, and the two armies rushed together, only to be drawn into a desperate, protracted struggle. Neither side conceded ground, and the engagement remained undecided for the better part of the day. The momentum of the fighting finally shifted in favour of Aemilius when his second line of infantry moved forward to relieve the exhausted front line of legionaries. Unable to provide fresh reserves, the Etruscans nevertheless continued to offer intense resistance, though the battle was inexorably shifting in favour of the Romans. Following hours of fighting, the engagement finally ended with nightfall, when both armies were recalled from the field by their commanders.

Titus Livius (Livy), *History of Rome*, 9.32.

Sutrium, 310 BC (Second Samnite War, Samnite Wars) – After learning that the Etruscans had once again besieged Sutrium, a legionary army under the command of the Roman *consul* Quintus Fabius Maximus Rullianus marched to relieve the community. On approaching the city, following the wooded foothills of Mount Ciminius, Fabius observed the enemy drawn up in battle formation on the adjacent plain. Able to ascertain the superior strength of the Etruscan army from his elevated location, the *consul* chose to withdraw into the surrounding hills, where the rugged terrain would serve to offset the numerical advantage possessed by the enemy. Observing the movements of the Romans, the Etruscans disregarded the dangers presented by the rough, stone-covered slopes, and rashly elected to attack Fabius' position. As the enemy rushed forward, Romans met the Etruscan charge with a barrage of javelins and stones. This action effectively checked the assault, and the open ground in the immediate vicinity offered the attackers no relief from the withering missle fire. The Etruscan line began to waver under such circumstances. Seeking to capitalize on this sudden unsteadiness in the enemy formation, the front two lines of Roman infantry, the *principes* and *hastati*, launched a charge that broke the ranks of the Etruscans, who then fled headlong toward their encampment on the plain below. As the enemy soldiers reached level ground, Roman cavalry swiftly cut the fugitives off from the safety of their camp, leaving them no alternative but to flee into the dense expanses of the nearby Ciminian Forest. Etruscan losses amounted to several thousand dead and the capture of thirty-eight standards.

Titus Livius (Livy), *History of Rome*, 9.35.

Sutrium, 310 BC (Second Samnite War, Samnite Wars) – Following his earlier victory over the Etruscans in the same vicinity, the Roman *consul* Quintus Fabius Maximus Rullianus again led an army near the city of Sutrium in central Etruria. There, the Etruscans once more mustered a large army in preparation for the coming conflict, and then gathered on a plain adjacent to the Ciminian forest in anticipation of a decisive encounter. After waiting futilely for Fabius to accept the challenge to battle, the Etruscans finally determined to march up to the very earthworks of the Roman camp. Still the legions refused to be enticed into an action, compelling the opposition to encamp for the night at the location. That evening, the *consul* instructed his soldiers to take their meal as usual and then be prepared for a call to immediate arms. After several hours had passed without incident, Fabius ordered his army to quietly assemble into battle formation. Just before dawn, the entire Roman army suddenly charged out of its camp and quickly overran the sleeping enemy. Startled, and thrown into confusion by the unexpected attack, the Etruscans abruptly lost 60,000 men killed or captured in the encounter.

Titus Livius (Livy), *History of Rome*, 9.37.1–10.

Syracuse, 212 BC (Second Punic War, Wars against Carthage) – Political turmoil between pro- and anti-Roman factions in the great Sicilian port city of Syracuse spilled over into the neighbouring community of Leontini (Lentini) to the northwest. The subsequent massacre of a local detachment of Roman guards by the pro-Carthaginian Leontinians earned the enmity of the Roman legate Marcus Claudius Marcellus, who quickly stormed the city with three legions. The resulting brutality directed against the community inspired an angry backlash from the Syracusians, who promptly renewed their city's alliance with Carthage and placed themselves under the leadership of the Punic agents Hippocrates and Epicydes. Marcellus immediately moved to end the growing hostility, first by negotiation. When these efforts failed, he prepared to use force. Drawing on the available military and naval resources under his command, Marcellus subjected the city to siege, beginning in 214 BC. Syracuse capably resisted all efforts to breach its defences, and Rome's refusal to lift the investment inevitably resulted in a protracted stalemate that lasted almost three years. After twenty months, the Romans finally gained access to the city in the spring of 212 BC during the Syracusian festival of Artemis. The legions proceeded to systematically reduce every section of the city by assault, a process that lasted well into the autumn. When the end was near, and all efforts by their Carthaginian allies to relieve the city had failed, the population appealed to Marcellus for mercy. The general declined the plea for clemency, and soon thereafter the legions sacked the city. Among the slain was the celebrated mathematician and engineer Archimedes, a native Syracusian instrumental in the city's defence during the previous months.

Titus Livius (Livy), *History of Rome*, 24.33.9–25.31; Plutarch, *Marcellus*, 15–19; Polybius, *Histories*, 8.37.

Syrian Gates, 39 BC (Parthian Wars) – After restoring Roman control over Cilicia, the *legatus* Publius Ventidius Bassus dispatched a cavalry detachment led by Poppaedius Silo to Amanus (Nur Daglari), a mountain range on the border of Cilicia and Syria. Once there, the Romans attempted to occupy the Syrian Gates – a narrow, strategically valuable pass – but were heavily defeated by a Parthian garrison already in possession of the location. Silo's command was only saved by the fortuitous arrival of additional Roman forces under Ventidius. While the battle raged, the legate suddenly attacked the unsuspecting Parthians with a numerically superior force. The assault drove off the enemy, who suffered numerous casualties, including loss of the garrison commander, Phranapates.

Dio Cassius, *Roman History*, 48.41.1–4; Plutarch, *Antony*, 33.4.

Tabor Mountain, 55 BC – see Mount Tabor, 55 BC.

Tagus River, 185 BC (Wars in Spain) – Following the Roman defeat near Toletum (Toledo) in central Spain, Caius Calpurnius Piso and Lucius Quinctius Crispinus – the praetors of *Hispania Ulterior* (Southern Spain) and *Hispania Citerior* (Eastern Spain) respectively – began to recruit additional auxiliary detachments from the various Spanish towns loyal to Rome in an effort to strengthen their existing armies, in anticipation of another battle with the Lusitani and their Celtiberian allies. When they were confident that their overall manpower was sufficient to again challenge the enemy, they moved their forces to a location approximately 12 miles from the Tagus (Tajo) River. At dawn the following day, the praetors assembled the legionary and auxiliary units in an *agmen quadratum*, or hollow square, and then advanced to the banks of the river in battle-readiness. Once the army reached a point directly across from the enemy encampment, the praetors divided their forces and forded the river at two separate locations, Calpurnius to the right and Quinctius on the left. The Lusitani and Celtiberi chose to attack during the crossing, but the Romans were able to successfully establish a beachhead on the opposite side. When the entire army was safely on the far shore, including the baggage train, the legions quickly drew up into battle formation. In the centre, Calpurnius posted the Fifth Legion, and Quinctius the *Legio VIII*. On the flanks were stationed the Latin allies and provincial auxiliaries. The Spaniards opened the battle with a fierce assault against the legionary line, but were unable to penetrate its ranks. Frustrated by their inability to disrupt the formation, the enemy formed into a *cuneus*, or wedge, and drove against the Roman centre. The intensity of the attack suddenly endangered the integrity of the legions' front line, forcing Calpurnius to order the legates Titus Quinctilius Varus and Lucius Juventius Talna to rally their troops against the onslaught. Then, leading the legions' cavalry to the right, while Quinctius advanced with the allied squadrons on the other wing,

Calpurnius and his fellow *praetor* simultaneously charged into the flanks of the Spanish wedge. The fighting rapidly intensified when the legions surged forward upon witnessing their generals in the midst of the melee. The pressure delivered by the combined attacks overwhelmed the enemy, who broke and fled in disarray. The opposing camp was then completely overrun, and 4,000 survivors of the battle driven into the surrounding countryside. Some 31,000 Lusitanian and Celtiberian troops died during the day's clash. Roman and Latin dead totalled more than 600, and the provincial auxiliaries lost about 150 men.

Titus Livius (Livy), *History of Rome*, 39.30.6–31.16.

Talium, 310 BC (Second Samnite War, Samnite Wars) – A Roman army led by the consuls Quintus Fabius Maximus Rullianus and Caius Marcius Rutilus Censorinus clashed with a Samnite force near a place called Talium. The fighting ended at nightfall but was resumed the next day. The Samnites were badly defeated in the second battle, suffering numerous fatalities during the course of the engagement. The Romans captured more than 2,200 of the enemy.

Diodorus Siculus, *Historical Library*, 20.26.3–4.

Tarentum, 282 BC – Not long after the Roman *consul* Caius Fabricius Luscinus stationed a garrison in Thurium, a city on the southern shore of the Tarentine Gulf, a small Roman fleet of *triremes* under Lucius Valerius anchored immediately off the port city of Tarentum (Taranto) to the north, on the Salentine Peninsula. The presence of the ships in the gulf violated an earlier treaty between the city and the Senate of Rome, and provoked the Tarentines to attack the stationary squadron. The surprise was total, and ended with numerous Roman vessels destroyed, including the admiral's flagship. Among the Roman dead was Valerius himself.

John Zonaras, *Epitome of Histories*, 8.2; Paulus Orosius, *Seven Books of History against the Pagans*, 4.1; Dio Cassius, *Roman History*, 9.5–6; Appianus (Appian), *Samnite History*, 7.1; Titus Livius (Livy), *Summaries*, 12.

Tarracina, 314 BC (Second Samnite War, Samnite Wars) – As a large Samnite army advanced into Campania, destroying those communities supportive of Rome, the consuls Marcus Poetelius Libo and Caius Sulpicius Longus led their armies southeastward from Latium, with the intentions of both aiding their allies and forcing the Samnites to a decisive contest. Approximately 55 miles from Rome, near the coastal town of Tarracina (Terracina), the two sides clashed in a bloody struggle that only ended when the legions drove their enemy from the field. Samnite dead totalled more than 10,000.

Diodorus Siculus, *Historical Library*, 19.76.1–2.

Tauris, 47 BC (Alexandrian War, Wars of the First Triumvirate) – While the Caesarian commander Publius Vatinius was at Brundisium, he received a series of appeals from the *propraetor* of Illyricum, Quintus Cornificius, to send aid to the province. The Pompeian admiral Marcus Octavius was presently employing both land and naval forces to attack a number of Caesarian garrisons in the region, including that at Epidauros. The two fleets joined in battle near the island of Tauris (Torcola). Octavius' ships were both larger in size and greater in number, compelling Vatinius to seize the momentum of the battle by taking the offensive. Turning his *quinquereme* to meet the approaching *quadrireme* of his counterpart, Vatinius' ship slammed into Octavius' vessel in a violent collision that crippled both craft. While the two flagships were locked together, galleys from both fleets concentrated around the two leaders, resulting in an intense contest for mastery of the narrow sea. As the battle matured, it became increasingly apparent that the ship-to-ship actions most imperiled Octavius' squadrons, for whenever two opposing ships were locked together, the aggressiveness of Vatinius' crews and combat troops almost invariably resulted in a victory for the Caesarians. A number of the Pompeian vessels were either captured or sunk by this means. When nightfall came, Vatinius retired from the fighting, having lost no ships. Among those seized by the victors were one *quinquereme*, two *triremes* and eight two-banked galleys.

Julius Caesar, *The Alexandrian War*, 44–47.

Tauromenium, 36 BC (Roman Civil Wars, Wars of the Second Triumvirate) – With three legions, 1,000 light-armed infantry and 2,000 colonial allies, Caius Octavius landed near the northeastern Sicilian city of Tauromenium with the intention of attacking the community if it refused to surrender. While preparing for the army's encampment, Octavian was suddenly surprised by the arrival of a large hostile fleet under the command of Sextus Pompeius. The *triumvir* was further alarmed by the deployment of Pompey's cavalry to one side of his encampment and the infantry to the other. As nightfall approached, the cavalry of Pompeius skirmished with Octavian's troops while the latter attempted to fortify their camp. By evening, Pompey's troops were positioned on the promontory of Coccynus and in the nearby town of Phoenix. Caius Octavius now feared the possibility of blockade by the enemy's fleet. In the early morning hours of the following day, Octavian placed his general, Cornificius, in command of the infantry, and he himself put to sea with his whole fleet, giving his lieutenant, Carisius, charge of the left wing and the right to Titinius. In the resulting naval battle, Octavian was soundly defeated and his ships scattered. Pompey's vessels captured and burned numerous craft, while others sailed for the coast of Italy. After a night spent in a small boat, Octavius finally reached the harbour of Abala with only a single attendant, and from there was conveyed to the camp of his general, Marcus Valerius Messala Corvinus.

Appianus (Appian), *Civil Wars*, 5.110–112.

Teanum, 90 BC (Social War/Marsic War) – While leading a force of 30,000 infantry and 5,000 cavalry through a rocky defile north of the Volturnus River, Lucius Julius Caesar was attacked by a Samnite army commanded by Marius Egnatius. The Romans fell back but were overtaken while trying to cross a stream where there was only a single bridge. Most of the army was destroyed. Lucius Julius, suffering from a dibilitating illness and confined to a litter, made his escape to the nearby town of Teanum together with the remainder of the army's survivors.

Appianus (Appian), *Civil Wars*, 1.45.

Teanus River, 89 BC (Social War/Marsic War) – A Roman army commanded by Mamercus Aemilius Lepidus Livianus* defeated an Italian force in a major engagement near the Teanus River. The Marsic leader Quintus Poppaedius Silo perished in the battle.

Appianus (Appian), *Civil Wars*, 1.53; Titus Livius (Livy), *Summaries*, 76; Paulus Orosius, *Seven Books of History against the Pagans*, 5.18; *Alternatively, Servius Sulpicius Galba or Quintus Caecilius Mettellus Pius.

Tegea, 47 BC (Roman Civil Wars, African War, Wars of the First Triumvirate) – In an effort to bring Senatorial forces to battle, Caius Julius Caesar advanced on the legions of Quintus Metellus Pius Scipio, encamped on a hill near the North African community of Tegea. Drawing close to the town, Caesar deployed his legionaries in three lines (*triplex acies*), with light troops and cavalry supporting each flank. Scipio responded by marching his infantry approximately a mile from camp to an elevated site above the village. He then ordered a garrison of 2,000 cavalry, maintained in Tegea, to take up station forward of the cohorts, and to the left and right of the town. Due to Scipio's obvious reluctance to relinquish the tactical advantage afforded by his hill position, Caesar opened the battle by dispatching some 400 horse, reinforced by light-armed elements, to harass the enemy cavalry and thereby draw the Senatorial forces into action. Pacideius, one of Scipio's junior commanders, responded to this ploy by manoeuvring detachments of cavalry to outflank the attacking Caesarian squadrons. Aware that his cavalry was now at risk of envelopment, Caesar countered by sending 300 legionaries from the closest cohorts in support of his horse. This escalation now compelled the senior commander of Senatorial cavalry, Titus Labienus, to commit a sizeable formation of mounted reinforcements to the battle. The weight of these additional troops threatened to overwhelm the Caesarian opposition before an

unexpected charge by a second wing of Caesar's cavalry rallied the beleaguered force, which then routed the Senatorial contingents with a counter-
assault and carried the day.

Julius Caesar (Aulus Hurtius), *The African War*, 78.

Telamon, 225 BC – Following their victory over a Roman army north of
Clusium in Eturia, an invading force of Gauls elected to return home, but
were immediately threatened by a second legionary army led by the *consul*
Lucius Aemilius Papus, which had marched southwest from the vicinity of the
Adriatic coast with the purpose of intercepting the intruders. Faced with this
danger, the Gauls withdrew southwest toward the Etrurian coast, intent on
remaining ahead of the pursuing Romans, unaware of the approach of yet
another consular army under Caius Atilius Regulus from Pisae (Pisa) to the
northwest. When the Gauls reached the Tyrrhenian Sea, they turned northward along the coastline, but were unexpectedly confronted by two Roman
armies near the seaside town of Telamon (Talamone). Initially observing
Roman cavalry atop a nearby hill to their front, the Gauls dispatched horsemen to contest the occupation, assuming they were merely an advanced
party deployed by their pursuers. To their consternation, the Gauls soon
learned from a prisoner that they were, in fact, trapped between the legions of
Atilius and Aemilius. Aware that they faced assault from two directions, the
Gauls assembled for battle, back-to-back; the Gaesatae and Insubres arrayed

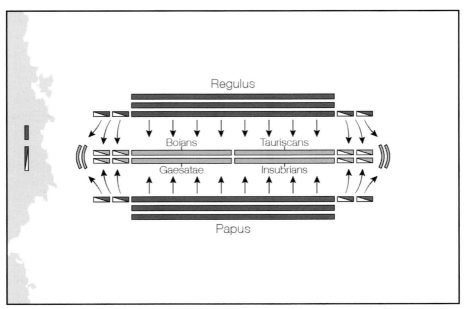

Battle of Telamon, 225 BC

against one consular formation, the Taurisci and Boii opposing the other. They positioned their chariots and wagons on either wing for protection, and placed their booty on a nearby hill with a strong guard. As the struggle continued for control of the hill, Aemilius sent his cavalry to aid those already engaged in the melee. After some time, the Romans succeeded in driving off the enemy and securing possession of the summit, but not before Atilius died in the fighting. Meanwhile, the two consular armies closed on the Gallic host. In the opening action, Roman *velites* inflicted considerable casualties among the Gaesatae, whose Gaulish shields failed to adequately protect them from javelins – but the remaining tribes offered formidable resistance. After intense infantry combat, a pronounced charge by Roman cavalry from the summit of the hill successfully broke the enemy formation. Directed against an exposed flank, the attack disrupted the ranks of the Gallic line and subjected the warriors to the full fury of the legionary assaults. Overwhelmed by the Romans, 40,000 Gauls died and an additional 10,000 were captured.

   Polybius, *Histories*, 2.27–31.2.

Tempyra, 188 BC – In the rugged defile of Tempyra, in southern Thracia, a local tribe called the Thrausi attempted to ambush a Roman army under the *consul* Cnaeus Manlius Vulso. Because the terrain was devoid of forests or other natural cover, the Romans quickly identified the enemy position and prepared for battle accordingly. The legions assembled into battle formation and advanced against the Thracians in close array. The Roman assault quickly broke the enemy's line in the ensuing engagement. Unable to recover, the Thrausi attempted to flee the field but were trapped by the narrow pass and slaughtered.

   Titus Livius (Livy), *History of Rome*, 38.41.1–8.

Tenedos, 85 BC (First Mithridatic War, Wars against Mithridates the Great) – While the renegade Roman general Caius Flavius Fimbria besieged the Pontic king Mithridates VI at the port of Pitane (Candarli) in the coastal region of Aiolia in Asia Minor; Lucius Licinius Lucullus continued his pursuit of the king's fleet. Lucullus discovered the enemy lying in wait off the island of Tenedos (Bozcaada), near the southern approach of the Hellespont. He immediately ordered an attack, and sailed out well ahead of the rest of the Roman fleet. In answer, the opposing commander Neoptolemus likewise outdistanced his own ships in a determined effort to ram Lucullus' smaller vessel. The two craft collided and were quickly joined by a general action between the warships of both fleets. Lucullus' squadrons finally put the enemy to flight following a lengthy struggle. After a close chase, the Romans broke off the action and rendezvoused with the army of Lucius Cornelius Sulla at the Chersonesus.

   Plutarch, *Lucullus*, 3.8–10.

Termantia, 141 BC (Numantine War, Wars in Spain) – Unable to capture the city of Numantia (Garray) on the upper Durius (Duero) River in northern Spain, the *proconsul* Quintus Pompeius Aulus shifted his operations against the community of Termantia (Montejo de Tiermes) south of the Sierra de Guadarrama. An initial engagement there ended with numerous Roman casualties, including 700 dead. On another occasion, a supply column led by one of the army's *tribuni militum* was attacked and driven off while delivering provisions to Pompeius' troops. In a third encounter that same day, the Termanti forced elements of the army into a rocky location where many of the soldiers, including both infantry and cavalry, were forced over a precipice. At dawn the following day, Pompeius was finally able to engage the enemy in a set piece battle, but after hours of fighting the encounter ended at nightfall with no clear victor. Unable to capture Termantia, the Romans were ultimately persuaded to abandon the assault and move against the smaller town of Malia.

Appianus (Appian), *Wars in Spain*, 13.77.

Thapsus, 46 BC, 6 April (Roman Civil Wars, African War) – Since the death of Cnaeus Pompeius Magnus in 48 BC, resistance against the growing power of Julius Caesar remained constant among supporters of the Senatorial class. On 4 April, as part of this ongoing civil war with the *optimates* of Rome, Julius Caesar invested the North African coastal town of Thapsus and its Pompeian garrison under the command of Caius Vergilius. This action compelled the leader of Senatorial forces in North Africa, Quintus Metellus Pius Scipio, to lead an army in relief of the besieged Vergilius. He was supported in this action by King Juba I of Numidia. Landward approaches to Thapsus were restricted to the west and south by a great inland salt marsh (Sebka di Moknine) situated approximately 2 miles southwest of the town. Scipio approached the port community from the south and established two camps near the southeastern edge of the marsh, 8 miles from Caesar's lines of circumvallation. However, a Ceasarian garrison of three cohorts blocked any northward movement by Scipio's legions because they occupied the neck of land south of Thapsus situated between the salt marsh and the coast. This circumstance ultimately forced the Roman commander to circumvent the marsh and advance from the west, whereupon he began construction of a third *castrum* within a mile-and-a-half of both the coast and the Caesarian camp. The close proximity of this new camp to his own lines of fortification now compelled Caesar to march against Scipio. Leaving the *proconsul* Lucius Asprenas Nonius and two legions to secure his own encampment, Caesar advanced to meet Scipio with the remainder of his force. Simultaneously, Caesar drew off a portion of the fleet besieging Thapsus and dispatched it along the coast in order to make a demonstration against the enemy's rear. Scipio marshalled his army for battle, posting legions in the centre, supported by strong formations of elephants and Numidian cavalry on both flanks. In response, Caesar deployed his army in three lines (*triplex acies*), with the *Legiones VIII* and *IX* arrayed on the left, and the Tenth and Seventh Legions on the right. Adjoining these forces were five cohorts of the *Legio V* posted on each wing, reinforced by archers and slingers. Cavalry were positioned on the extreme flanks, supported by light-armed elements. The battle was opened by a spontaneous charge of Caesar's right wing, followed by a general attack of the entire army. An intense assault by light troops against elephants positioned on Scipio's left flank quickly panicked the animals, throwing the entire left wing in disarray. With this disruption of the left wing, resistance by the Numidian cavalry rapidly eroded, thereby exposing the legions' left and triggering a rout. The infantry struggle remained undecided for some time until resistance on the Senatorial right and centre collapsed. The engagement was a total victory for Caesar. Scipio's command was decisively shattered, with certain sources relating manpower losses as high as 50,000. On 7 April, Caesar withdrew the bulk of his force from Thapsus, leaving the *proconsul* Caius Caninius Rebilus to complete the siege.

Dio Cassius, *Roman History*, 43.7–9.1; Plutarch, *Caesar*, 53; Appianus (Appian), *Civil Wars*, 2.96–97; Julius Caesar, *The African War*, 79–86.

Thaumaci, 191 BC (War against Antiochus III) – When the *consul* Manius Acilius Glabrio led a Roman army of 20,000 infantry, 2,000 cavalry and fifteen war elephants south from the city of Larisa toward the Malian Gulf, the column was attacked by troops from the small Thessalonian town of Thaumaci (Domokos), located on cliffs overlooking the pass of Coela at the entrance to the Thessalonian plain. The legions easily repelled the assault and Acilius thereafter attempted to negotiate with the enemy in an effort to avert further hostilities, but could not dissuade them from their suicidal purpose. Once it was apparent that the Thaumacians intended to persist in their course of action, the *consul* moved to put an end to the matter and deployed two maniples under a tribune to circumvent the enemy position and capture the town. The detachment quickly secured control of the undefended community and then occupied the road between Thaumaci and the defile below. When the Thaumacians heard what was happening above, they withdrew toward the town, but were caught in a Roman ambuscade and slaughtered. Afterward, the army continued its march southward.

Titus Livius (Livy), *History of Rome*, 36.14.12–15.

Thermae, 260 BC (First Punic War, Wars against Carthage) – After the defeat of a Punic war fleet off Mylae, Hamilcar, the general in command of Carthaginian forces in Sicily, learned that there was discord between the Romans and their allies, and that as a result the latter were encamped by themselves between the northern Sicilian coastal town of Thermae (Termini Imerese) and the Paropus River. Seeking to exploit the opportunity afforded by this dissension, Hamilcar secretly marched his army southeast from its base in the vicinity of Panormus (Palermo) to a location near the allied position and waited for a favourable moment to attack. While the enemy was preoccupied with striking camp, the Carthaginian commander launched a sudden assault with his entire force. At least 4,000 allied troops died in the struggle.

   Polybius, *Histories*, 1.24.3–4; Diodorus Siculus, *Historical Library*, 23.9.4.

Thermae Himeraeae, 260 BC – see Thermae, 260 BC.

Thermopylae, 191 BC (War against Antiochus III) – Angered by the Romans' unwillingness to grant their league more Thessalonian territory as part of the peace settlement ending the Second Macedonian War, the Aetolians invited the Seleucid king Antiochus III to intercede in Balkan affairs on behalf of the Greek peoples of the peninsula. The monarch willingly accepted the challenge, and in 192 BC landed at the port of Demetrias with 10,000 men. He initiated a campaign in Thessaly almost immediately, but soon learned that the Greeks, including the Achaean League, intended to provide him no support. Likewise, his former ally, Philip V of Macedon, refused to abandon the treaty. At the same time, the Romans mobilized an army of 20,000 infantry, 2,000 cavalry and fifteen war elephants under the *consul* Manius Acilius Glabrio to check the intrusion of Antiochus in eastern Greece. After landing on the Albanian coast near Apollonia, the Romans marched unopposed southeastward through the interior of Epirus and northern Greece before reaching Thessaly. The approach of Glabrio convinced Antiochus to retire south toward the pass at Thermopylae, where he elected to make a stand behind a line of defensive earthworks. On the day of the battle, the *consul* deployed his forces in the usual formation, but narrowed the front in order to conform to the topography of the defile. On the heights above the pass, 2,000 Aetolian troops occupied the peaks of Rhoduntia, Tichius and Callidromos. To neutralize this danger and secure access to the footpath over the mountain range, Glabrio dispatched a select force of 2,000 men under the *consulares legatos* Marcus Porcius Cato and Lucius Valerius Flaccus. Cato was charged with flushing out the enemy guarding Callidromos, and Flaccus those contingents holding the remaining pair of strongpoints. Below, Antiochus assembled his army on the open ground before the ramparts. Light troops and *peltast*s formed a front line ahead of the main heavy infantry phalanx. On the left flank, a detachment of archers, slingers, and javelineers secured the lower slopes of the adjacent mountains, and to the right the way was blocked near the sea by a line of elephants. Behind these latter, the king positioned his cavalry. Lastly, a second line of troops was held in reserve. Once battle was joined, the phalangites, in conjunction with the light infantry, easily repelled the Roman maniples. As Glabrio directed more pressure against the Syrian ranks, Antiochus was finally forced to withdraw behind the fortifications, where the Romans again found themselves frustrated by the enemy's reconstituted line. Meanwhile, Cato successfully outflanked the king's position after routing the 600 Aetolians guarding Callidromos. When Antiochus' troops realized that the foe was behind their defences, all resistance immediately collapsed. The sudden flight of his army forced the king to likewise abandon Thermopylae and withdraw southward toward Elatia. In the subsequent chase, the Romans were slowed by the narrowness of the pass, the earthen defences and the presence of elephants, which were retained at the rear of the retreating column in order to delay the enemy. Once the Roman infantry overcame the animals, either by capture or destruction, the cavalry pursued the Syrians as far as Scarphea. The next day, Glabrio again followed Antiochus as the king turned the remnants of his army southeast toward the Euboean port of Chalcis (Chalkida). Roman cavalry, ranging ahead of the legions, destroyed much of the exhausted army as it marched toward the coast, but the king, along with 500 other fugitives, survived to reach Asia. Roman dead amounted to 200.

Appianus (Appian), *Syrian Wars*, 17–20; Plutarch, *Cato Major*, 13–14.2; Titus Livius (Livy), *History of Rome*, 36.15–19; Lucius Annaeus Florus, *Epitomy*, 1.24.11.

Thuriae, 302 BC – While fighting continued between the Romans and Samnites, a Greek warfleet led by the Lakedaemonian mercenary general Kleonymus, a lesser son from the Spartan royal house of the Agidae, captured the Sallentinian city of Thuriae located on the Apulian Peninsula. The Roman Senate responded to this invasion by dispatching a consular army under Marcus Aemilius Paullus, which defeated the Greeks in a single battle and secured control of the city. The community was shortly thereafter restored to its inhabitants, as was peace to the whole of the Sallentine territory.

Titus Livius (Livy), *History of Rome*, 10.2.1–2.

Ticinus River, 218 BC, November (Second Punic War, Wars against Carthage) – This battle was fought in northern Italy on the eastern bank of the Ticinus River between a Carthaginian army of 6,000 cavalry under Hannibal Barca and a numerically inferior force commanded by the Roman *consul* Publius Cornelius Scipio. The Punic battle line consisted of Carthaginian and Spanish heavy cavalry deployed in the centre, flanked by squadrons of Numidian light horse. The Romans were arrayed in two lines: the first included a central formation of light infantry (*velites*) supported by detachments of Gallic horse on each flank; the second contained 2,000 Roman and

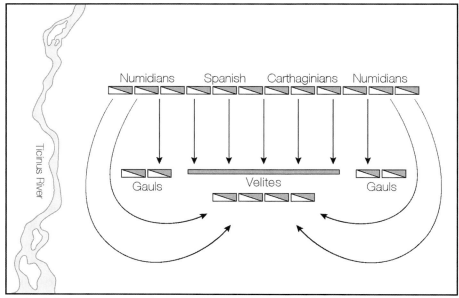

Battle of the Ticinus River, 218 BC

allied cavalry. The battle opened with a charge of Roman light infantry, which was quickly and efficiently turned by the Carthaginians – who then counter-charged the Roman line. Fighting was intense and protracted, until elements of Numidian horse succeeded in enveloping the exposed flanks of the Roman position and attacking from the rear. This assault, combined with continuous pressure from the Spanish and Punic cavalry, fragmented Scipio's entire battle formation, forcing the Romans to withdraw in disorder. Despite the victory, Polybius states that Carthaginian losses were heavier than those suffered by the Romans.

> Polybius, *Histories*, 3.65; Titus Livius (Livy), *History of Rome*, 21.45–46; Appianus (Appian), *Hannibalic War*, 2.5; Eutropius, *Abridgement of Roman History*, 3.9; John Zonaras, *Epitome of Histories*, 8.23.

Tifata, 83 BC – see Mount Tifatum, 83 BC.

Mount Tifatum, 83 BC (Roman Civil Wars) – After concluding a peace at Dardanus with the Pontic king Mithridates VI, Lucius Cornelius Sulla returned to Italy with 30,000 men to confront his political enemies, who were led by Caius Marius. The combined armies of Caius Marius the Younger and the *consul* Caius Norbanus Balbus challenged the legions of Lucius Cornelius Sulla near Mount Tifatum in Campania. Sulla routed his opponents in the resulting battle. Norbunus lost 7,000 men in the struggle, with an additional

6,000 captured, and was besieged in the city of Capua. Sulla's losses in the battle were minimal.

Plutarch, *Sulla* 27.5; Velleius Paterculus, *Roman History*, 2.25.2; Eutropius, *Abridgement of Roman History*, 5.7; Lucius Annaeus Florus, *Epitomy*, 2.9.19.

Tifernum, 305 BC (Second Samnite War, Samnite Wars) – Samnite raids into the Campanian district of Campus Stellatis provoked the Roman Senate to dispatch two armies, under the consuls Lucius Postumius Megellus and Tiberius Minucius Augurinus, to end the threat. While his colleague marched to confront the enemy near the Samnite capital of Bovianum (Boiano) in south-central Italy, Postumius moved against a second hostile army in the vicinity of the town of Tifernum. There, a protracted clash between the opposing sides ended in a draw. Feigning trepidation, Postumius abruptly withdrew his forces to the safety of the mountains, and once there constructed a *castrum*. The Samnites followed and established their camp approximately 2 miles from the Roman position. When, by his efforts to erect fortifications and provision the site, Postumius had convinced the enemy of his intention to remain at the location, he left a strong garrison in place, then secretly departed with his legions during the night to aid his colleague. Once at Bovianum, Postumius assisted Minucius in destroying the Samnite army protecting the town. Both consuls then led their victorious troops against the enemy force still encamped near Tifernum. The combined strength of the four consular legions completely routed the second Samnite army. Among those enemy soldiers captured near Tifernum was the Samnite commander Statius Gellius.

Titus Livius (Livy), *History of Rome*, 9.44.9–13.

Tifernum, 297 BC (Third Samnite War, Samnite Wars) – With the Etruscan threat largely extinguished by the Roman victory at Volaterrae the previous year, the consuls Quintus Fabius Maximus and Publius Decius Mus invaded Samnium. The two consular armies arrived on the borders of the enemy territory following separate routes; Fabius by way of Sora and Decius through the lands of the Sidicini. Scouts dispatched by Fabius soon located the Samnite army in a secluded valley, where they were prepared to ambush the unsuspecting Romans. In response, the *consul* ordered his forces to assemble into a hollow square formation before advancing directly against the enemy position. Once their cover was betrayed, the Samnites abruptly abandoned their place of concealment and descended to the level plain below, where they prepared to challenge the legions. The struggle proved difficult when the battle was joined. Neither army was able to gain advantage and it soon became a trial of strength, with each side suffering heavy casualties. With the infantry unable to achieve any lasting result, the *consul* was finally moved to order his cavalry to engage the enemy, but the effort to break the stalemate proved unsuccessful. Anticipating the possibility that his horsemen might fail to achieve their purpose, Fabius had also ordered his legate Lucius Cornelius Scipio to withdraw the *hastati* from the First Legion and, by a clandestine route, come upon the enemy rear. While the battle continued, the Samnites – still fighting with great vigour – were taken aback by the discovery of additional Roman forces approaching from behind. Fearing these new troops to be the leading elements of the second consular army under Decius, they quickly lost heart and fled the field. Some 3,400 Samnites were killed in the engagement, with an additional 830 captured.

Titus Livius (Livy), *History of Rome*, 10.14.

Tifernus Mons, 295 BC (Third Samnite War, Samnite Wars) – During the same campaign season when Roman legions under the consuls Quintus Fabius Maximus Rullianus and Publius Decius Mus achieved their great victory at Sentinum in Umbria; the *proconsul* Lucius Volumnius defeated a Samnite army on Mount Tifernus. Despite the difficult terrain, the cohorts of Volumnius pursued the enemy onto the base of Tifernus, routed and then completely dispersed the Samnite force across the slopes of the mountain.

Titus Livius (Livy), *History of Rome*, 10.30.7.

Tigranocerta, 69 BC, October (Third Mithridatic War, Wars against Mithridates the Great) – The crushing defeat of a Pontic army by Roman legions at Cabira drove Mithridates VI to Armenia, where the potentate sought the protection of his son-in-law, King Tigranes II the Great. After failing to attain the surrender of the Pontic ruler, Roman general Lucius Licinius Lucullus advanced with two legions, light infantry and several hundred horse southwestward by forced marches from Pontus to the Armenian city of Tigranocerta to confront the two monarchs. When Tigranes learned of the approaching army, he sent his lieutenant, Mithrobarzanes, with approximately 3,000 cavalry and a larger detachment of infantry to delay Lucullus' progress. The Armenian force arrived just as the Romans were preparing to encamp for the evening. Lucullus immediately dispatched the *legatus* Sextilius with 1,600 horsemen, and a roughly equal number of light and heavy infantry, to set up a screen and block the enemy from attacking while the legions were still in a state of disorder. The two sides clashed, resulting in the destruction of Mithrobarzanes and most of his command. Following this loss, Tigranes abandoned Tigranocerta to his subordinate Mancaeus and then began amassing a large army of mostly foreign levies, together with a force of several thousand *cataphracti*. Lucullus responded by sending both Sextilius and Murena to hinder the king's efforts, while he proceeded against the Armenian capital. Discarding Mithridates' advice to avoid a direct engagement with the Romans, Tigranes assembled an immense force to challenge his enemy in a decisive encounter. Meanwhile, leaving 6,000 men to continue the siege of Tigranocerta, Lucullus marched in person against Tigranes. As the Romans neared the Nicephorius (possibly mod. Batman-su) River to the southwest of the city, they observed the Armenian army gathered on the eastern bank. Lucullus quickly assembled his cohorts for battle, and then led the entire formation across the river. The king was initially taken aback to see the Romans assume the offensive and march against his much larger concentration of troops. Witnessing his opponent's approach, Tigranes drew up his own army into battle array, placing himself in the centre, and assigning the right wing to the king of the Medes and the left to the ruler of the Adiabeni. He positioned most of his *cataphracti* before the infantry on the right. Once the legions were across, Lucullus ordered his Thracian and Gallic cavalry to harass the king's heavy horse and then feign a retreat in order to induce the *cataphracti* to give chase. With the attention of Tigranes' army now focussed on the ongoing action, the Roman commander secretly led a select detachment of two cohorts in circumventing the enemy's position to arrive atop a hill behind the Armenian line. When Lucullus was satisfied that the *cataphracti* were sufficiently distracted by the Thracians and Gauls, he ordered his cohorts to charge the enemy baggage-train stationed to the rear of the king's army. The force of the unexpected assault drove the startled formation into the ranks of the infantry, and the infantry against the mounted squadrons, thereby shattering the cohesion of Tigranes' entire line. The chaos soon sparked a general rout, which was partially prevented by the density of the formation and the presence of the attending legions in front. At the same time, the Roman cavalry turned and charged the *cataphracti*. The pursuit of the defeated remnants of Tigranes' army continued for 14 miles, resulting in the slaughter of perhaps 100,000 men.

Plutarch, *Lucullus*, 25–28.6; Appianus (Appian), *Mithridatic Wars*, 12.84–85.

Timavus River, 178 BC – Following the resumption of hostilities between Rome and the Histri – a powerful Illyrian tribe occupying lands along the northeastern Adriatic coast – the *consul* Aulus Manlius Vulso led an army 12 miles east from the colony of Aquileia to a small freshwater lake called Timavus (mod. Lake Pietrarossa), approximately a mile from the Adriatic Sea. Within a short time, a Roman fleet, consisting of ten warships under the command of the *duumvir navalis* Caius Furius, arrived off the Illyrian coast near the mouth of the Timavus (Timavo) River. These vessels were soon joined by a number of transports, which then sailed to the nearest Histrian harbour. Volso followed the fleet's relocation, establishing his camp about 5 miles from the coast. Once contact was re-established, the ships' crews began offloading a substantial amount of supplies, which was then carried to the camp by troops of the Second Legion. In order to protect both the legionary

camp and the traffic moving inland from the harbour, the *consul* placed pickets
at various locations in the immediate vicinity. He stationed a recently levied
cohort from Placentia at a permanent outpost facing Histrian territory,
and deployed two maniples of the *Legio II* between the camp and harbour.
Some distance to the west, near the highway leading toward Aquileia, the
Third Legion was given the duty of protecting the army's foraging parties and
wood-cutters; in the same general area, approximately a mile from the legionary *castrum*, a secondary camp housed a contingent of some 3,000 Gallic
auxiliaries. Since their arrival at Lake Timavus, the Romans had failed to
detect the presence of a Histrian army shadowing their movements from
the surrounding hills. Under cover of an early morning fog, the Illyrians
seized the opportunity to attack the unsuspecting enemy. Silently, they
approached the outlying guard posts. When alert sentinels discovered their
presence, the unexpected sight of the amassed body of warriors panicked the
sentries. The heavy mist, partially dissipated by the sunlight, created the
illusion of a larger Histrian army than was actually present. The terrified
Placentine and legionary detachments fled to the Roman camp, where their
stories frightened the entire army. Once fear spread throughout the *castrum*,
the Second Legion abandoned the site in confusion and disorder. The chaotic
flight left the encampment virtually derelict, except for three maniples under
the tribune Marcus Licinius Strabo. Having entered the largely empty
palisade, the Histrians failed to encounter any resistance until they reached
the centre of the camp. There they discovered the troops of Strabo. The
resulting battle was stubbornly contested, but the Romans were eventually
overwhelmed by the Illyrians, who proceeded to plunder the army's supplies,
including its stocks of wine. In the meantime, Volso finally managed to
restore order among the remainder of the *Legio II* which were gathered near
the harbour, and simultaneously ordered the recall of the Third Legion and
Gallic auxiliaries. He then led the surviving maniples of the Second Legion
against the occupied camp and soundly defeated the inebriated enemy.
Approximately 8,000 Histrians died in the counter-assault. Roman losses
included Strabo and his command, plus an additional 237 killed in the
struggle to recover the camp.

Titus Livius (Livy), *History of Rome*, 41.2–4.

Tolenus River, 90 BC, 11 June (Social War/Marsic War) – During the
first year of war with the Italian *socii*, the Roman consul Publius Rutilius
Lupus and Caius Marius established two bridgeheads over the Tolenus River
in an effort to prosecute campaigns against the uprising. In response, rebel
general Vettius Scato encamped a Marsic army on the bank opposite that
occupied by the consular armies but nearer the bridge of Marius, and during
the night secretly deployed a sizeable force several miles upriver near the

bridge erected by Rutilius. The following morning, Rutilius crossed the river with a number of legionary cohorts, but once safely on dry ground was suddenly ambushed by the Marsic force lying in wait. In the engagement, 8,000 Romans were killed, many being driven into the river by the intensity of the assault. Rutilius was himself mortally wounded. Later that day, the appearance of Roman bodies floating downstream alerted Caius Marius to the fate of his co-*consul*'s legions. Quickly seizing the moment, he attacked the Italian contingents in his front, crossed over the Tolenus in force and overran the enemy camp, killing approximately 8,000 Marsi. Now denied supplies, the Italians were compelled to withdraw for lack of adequate provisions.

Appianus (Appian), *Civil Wars*, 1.43; Paulus Orosius, *Seven Books of History against the Pagans*, 5.18; Titus Livius (Livy), *Summaries*, 73; Publius Ovidius Naso (Ovid), *Calendar*, 6.563–566.

Toletum, 193 BC (Wars in Spain) – While prosecuting the war in Hispania, the Roman *praetor* Marcus Fulvius Nobilior defeated a combined army of Vettones, Vaccaei and Celtiberians near the town of Toletum (Toledo) located on the Tagus River in central Spain. The victory also resulted in the capture of Hilernus, king of the Celtic confederation.

Titus Livius (Livy), *History of Rome*, 35.7.8.

Toletum, 192 BC (Wars in Spain) – After seizing the Spanish towns of Vescelia, Helo, Noliba and Cusibis, the *propraetor* Marcus Fulvius Nobilior moved a Roman army against the central Iberian town of Toletum (Toledo). As the investment of the community proceeded, a large concentration of Celtic Vettones arrived in relief of the besieged Toletani. The subsequent engagement ended with the Vettones driven from the field. Following this victory, Fulvius completed the capture of Toletum.

Titus Livius (Livy), *History of Rome*, 35.22.6–8.

Toletum, 185 BC, spring (Wars in Spain) – During the early spring, Caius Calpurnius Piso, the *praetor* of *Hispania Ulterior* (Western Spain), and Lucius Quinctius Crispinus, his counterpart in *Hispania Citerior* (Eastern Spain), led their armies out of winter quarters. After uniting their forces in the region of Baeturia in southwestern Spain, the praetors marched northeastward into Carpetania to confront the Lusitani, then supported by the Celtiberi. Near the towns of Dipo and Toletum (Toledo), a skirmish erupted between foraging parties which soon developed into a set-piece battle between armies. Forced to fight on unfamiliar ground, and having committed their forces to the engagement in piecemeal fashion, Calpurnius and Quinctius were soon defeated and the legions driven back into their encampment in disorder. That night the praetors elected to abandon the camp rather than risk being trapped inside the fortifications the following day. Roman losses amounted to

5,000 men, including allied dead. At first light, the enemy pillaged the vacated *castrum* before withdrawing toward the Tagus River.

Titus Livius (Livy), *History of Rome*, 39.30.1–6.

Tongres, 54 BC – see Atuatuca, 54 BC.

Toros Hill, 262 BC (First Punic War, Wars against Carthage) – Shortly after arriving in Sicily, Roman legions under the command of the consuls Lucius Postumius Megellus and Quintus Mamilius Vitulus besieged the city of Agrigentum (Agrigento), a major Carthaginian supply depot located on the island's southwestern coast, presently occupied by an army led by Punic general Hannibal. The Romans established their camp less than a mile from the city preparatory to initiating siege operations. Approximately 20 miles away, in the Sicilian coastal town of Heraclea Minoa, Carthaginian commander Hanno learned of Agrigentum's plight and soon marched his forces southeast and encamped on Toros Hill, approximately a mile from the Roman position outside the beleaguered port community. Once there, Hanno failed to take any decisive action against the enemy for two months until the acute desperation of the starving army inside Agrigentum forced him to hazard an engagement against Postumius and Mamilius. Both armies assembled for battle on the small plain between the opposing camps. The legions deployed by maniples, while the Carthaginians arrayed their main divisions of troops behind a screen of war elephants. Hanno sent his mercenaries ahead of this formation. Once fighting began, the struggle remained undecided for some time before the Romans eventually overcame the forward line of Punic mercenary infantry. The defeat of the latter quickly produced a general rout as the retreating soldiers disrupted the line of elephants and remaining detachments of the army, throwing all into complete disorder. In the end, the remnants of Hanno's forces escaped to Heraclea Minoa, followed that night by those Carthaginian elements trapped in the city. The Romans entered Agrimentum unopposed the next day.

Polybius, *Histories*, 1.19.5–11; Diodorus Siculus, *Historical Library*, 23.8.1.

Trasimene, 217 BC – see Trasimeno Lake, 217 BC.

Trasimeno Lake, 217 BC (Second Punic War, Wars against Carthage) – With the advent of good weather in the spring, Carthaginian general Hannibal Barca led his army out of Cisalpine Gaul and southward into Etruria. Aware that a Roman army under the *consul* Caius Flaminius was presently located at Arretium (Arezzo), and that a second consular force led by Gnaeus Servilius Geminus would shortly arrive at Ariminum on the Adriatic coast, Hannibal elected to march his army through the Arnus River marshes following the course of the river to a point near Flaminius' position. In an attempt to provoke the *consul* to battle, the Carthaginians destroyed much of the country to the immediate southeast of the lower Val di Chiana between the hill town of Cortona and the northern shore of Trasimeno Lake. The devastation finally lured the rash and headstrong Flaminius from the security of Arretium in an effort to relieve the suffering of Rome's allies. While Hannibal continued to move southward toward the central plains of Italy, the *consul* took up the pursuit. Southeast of Cortona, the Carthaginians approached the lake through a defile called the Malpasso. Following the narrow road along the northern shore of the great inland body of water, Hannibal arrived at a small U-shaped plain contained on the south by the shoreline of Trasimeno, and surrounded to the north, west and east by thickly wooded hills. Once through the pass, Hannibal positioned his divisions of Spanish and African heavy infantry on a long ridge to the southeast which was clearly visible to anyone entering the area from the northwest. He then concealed his light infantry in the wooded hills to the north of the plain, and the Numidian cavalry, together with Gallic infantry and horsemen, on the western slopes near the defile. Several hours later, the Roman army reached the vicinity of the lake and encamped for the night to the northwest, outside Malpasso. The following morning, Flaminius blindly traversed the defile, recklessly electing to continue the legions' march without reconnaissance, despite the low visibility afforded by the presence of a light fog over the lake valley. On reaching the plain, the *consul* observed the Spanish and African divisions on the distant heights to the southeast, unaware that thousands of enemy troops were also deployed on the hills to his immediate left and rear. Delaying the signal to attack until the entire Roman column was through the defile, Hannibal allowed Flaminius' vanguard to progress the length of the plain and make contact with the African and Spanish ranks before ordering a general assault. Suddenly, the Carthaginian army erupted into a charge that swept through the mist and simultaneously struck the left side of the enemy column at all points. As the Roman troops reeled in confusion, unable to assemble into battle formation, the Numidians and Gauls thundered down the slopes near Malpasso, completing the ambuscade and denying the legions any means of escape through the defile. In the fog, the Romans were unable to fully comprehend the extent of the disaster before the situation passed beyond recovery. The force of the attack proved irresistible, overwhelming the centre and rearguard in such violence that thousands of legionaries died in their tracks or were driven into the lake. The chaos degenerated into slaughter. The Roman vanguard alone, after enduring tremendous punishment from Hannibal's heavy infantry, managed to carve its way through the Carthaginian phalanx. Upon reaching the crest of the ridgeline, these 6,000 survivors were able to see the full extent of the catastrophe through the dissipating mist, but were helpless to aid those remnants of the legions still trapped in the

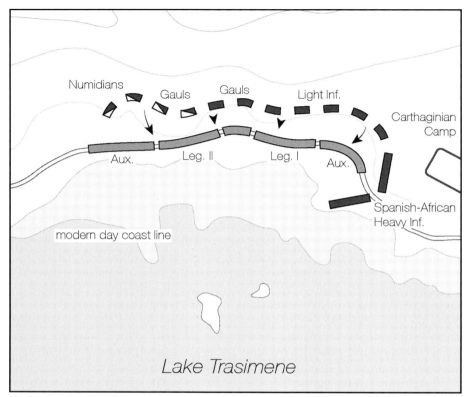

Numidians

Gauls   Gauls   Light Inf.

Carthaginian
Camp

Aux.   Leg. II   Leg. I   Aux.

Spanish-African
Heavy Inf.

modern day coast line

Lake Trasimene

Battle of Trasimeno Lake, 217 BC

carnage below. The fighting ended after some three hours. Some 15,000 Romans died in the fighting, including Flaminius, more than 15,000 were captured and 10,000 escaped the destruction. Carthaginian losses amounted to between 1,500 and 2,500 men.

Polybius, *Histories*, 3.83–84; Titus Livius (Livy), *History of Rome*, 22.4–7.3; Cornelius Nepos, *Great Generals of Foreign Nations*, 23.4.3; Appianus (Appian), *Hannibalic War*, 2.10; Eutropius, *Abridgement of Roman History*, 3.9; John Zonaras, *Epitome of Histories*, 8.25.

Trasimenus Lacum, 217 BC – see Trasimeno Lake, 217 BC.

Trebia River, 218 BC, December (Second Punic War, Wars against Carthage) – In an effort to check the advance of a Carthaginian army before it penetrated further into the Italian peninsula, the *consul* Tiberius Sempronius Longus prepared to challenge the invaders at the Trebia (Trebbia) River. Undeterred by the army's earlier defeat at the Ticinus River, Sempronius was eager to engage the Punic force before Rome's relationship with the neighbouring Gallic tribes was further eroded by the machinations of the enemy's commander, Hannibal Barca. Publius Cornelius Scipio, the second *consul*, was also present, but unable to command Roman forces in the current encounter because he was wounded at the Ticinus. The Roman camp was situated on the east bank of the river, while the Carthaginians remained on the farther shore some distance to the west. Before daybreak, Hannibal ordered his brother Mago to conceal a select force of 1,000 cavalry and an equal number of light infantry in heavy undergrowth along the banks of a nearby stream flowing away to the Padus (Po) River. At dawn, before the Romans had breakfasted, Hannibal then sent his Numidian cavalry to harass the enemy camp in an effort to lure Sempronius into prematurely deploying his army. As the African riders harried the opposing encampment, the *consul* dispatched his cavalry, together with 6,000 *velites*, against the attackers. After a brief skirmish, the Numidians feigned defeat and withdrew across the river, hotly pursued by the Roman horsemen. Their departure was quickly followed by the entire army. Determined to force a contest with the Carthaginians as soon as possible, Sempronius ordered the legions to ford the icy, chest-deep waters of the Trebia and assemble for battle on the opposite bank. Once the army was across the rain-swollen river, the maniples formed into ranks. The entire force consisted of 16,000 Roman and 20,000 allied foot, and 4,000 Roman and allied horse. In the bitter cold and light snow, the infantry drew up in three lines, with a screen of *velites* in front and the cavalry positioned on the flanks. All were cold, wet, hungry and fully exposed to the elements. Hannibal was by this time prepared for action. Well-fed and properly rested, the Carthaginians armed themselves around their campfires, and then advanced about a mile from their camp before gathering into battle formation. The Punic army arrayed in a single line, the Celts in the centre, accompanied by African infantry on both sides and the Iberians placed on the flanks. Deployed on the wings were 10,000 horsemen, including Celtic auxiliaries, and the army's contingent of war elephants. Thrown out ahead of this line were 8,000 light infantry skirmishers and 1,000 Balearic slingers. The engagement began with a contest between the light troops of both armies. The Roman *velites*, already largely spent as a result of their earlier encounter with the Numidians, were soon forced to retire. Shortly thereafter, the Carthaginian slingers and javelineers proved ineffective against the maniples and were sent to reinforce the cavalry. As the opposing lines of heavy infantry in the centre collided, the combination of Punic cavalry, light infantry and pachyderms put the squadrons of Roman horse on both wings to flight. This sudden loss exposed the flanks of the legionary formation to withering fire from Hannibal's slingers. Carthaginian phalangites and Numidian light horsemen soon joined in the melee. While the integrity of the Roman flanks was crumbling under these assaults, the elephants turned and bore down on Sempronius' centre, even as the 2,000 troops under Mago unexpectedly charged the legions' rear from

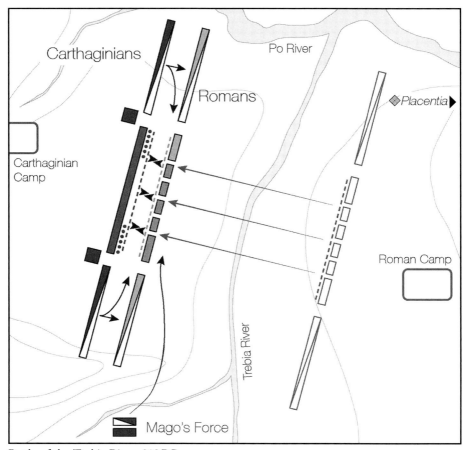

Battle of the Trebia River, 218 BC

their place of concealment. Despite such pressure, the legionaries managed to successfully drive off the war elephants and push back the Carthaginian centre. Hannibal then redirected the elephants against the Gallic auxiliaries on the Roman right flank, who fled before the beasts in great disorder. Now completely divested of their cavalry and allies, and fully contained by the enemy on all sides, only a portion of the Roman army was able to force a passage through the Carthaginian centre. Amidst this slaughter, 10,000 Romans managed to escape, but the remainder of the infantry died in the struggle. Following the defeat, many of the Roman survivors fled to nearby Placentia (Piacenza).

Polybius, *Histories*, 3.71–74; Titus Livius (Livy), *History of Rome*, 21.54–56.7; Cornelius Nepos, *Great Generals of Foreign Nations*, 23.4.2; Appianus (Appian), *Hannibalic War*, 2.7; Eutropius, *Abridgement of Roman History*, 3.9; John Zonaras, *Epitome of Histories*, 8.24.

Tribola, 147 BC (Viriathic War, Wars in Spain) – After a series of atrocities committed against their peoples by the Roman governors of *Hispania Ulterior* (Western Spain) and *Hispania Citerior* (Eastern Spain), a 10,000-man Lusitanian army invaded the region of Turditania, located in the Baetis (Guadalquivir) River Valley in southwestern Spain. The intruders successfully overran the territories, but were trapped the following year and compelled to parley by a Roman force of equal size commanded by the legate Caius Vetilius. Surrounded, and seemingly without any hope of flight, the capitulation of the Lusitani appeared a foregone conclusion when a minor chieftain named Viriathus inspired his fellow countrymen to implement a bold plan of escape. While the Romans watched, the Lusitanian infantry assembled into battle formation as though they intended to make a final stand, and then suddenly dispersed in all directions, leaving Viriathus and a select force of 1,000 horsemen on the field. Unable to effectively pursue the departing enemy with either infantry or cavalry while threatened with a possible mounted attack, Vetilius elected instead to launch a direct assault against Viriathus and his riders. The barbarian chieftain willingly accepted battle, and through a series of diversionary hit-and-run attacks that served as a rearguard action, adroitly covered the flight of the main Lusitanian army as it withdrew pell-mell toward the town of Tribola. The Romans immediately took up the chase when the skirmishing finally ended the following day. As Viriathus arrived in the vicinity of Tribola, he prepared an ambuscade in a dense thicket, concealing a portion of his warriors on both sides of the enemy's anticipated line of march, while he and the remainder of his men continued their trek toward the town. Once Vetilius' column unknowingly entered the ambush, Viriathus quickly wheeled about and attacked the Roman vanguard, as those men hidden in the underbrush burst from cover and charged the enemy's flanks. Approximately 4,000 Romans died in the struggle that followed, including Caius Vetilius, while the 6,000 survivors fled to the coastal city of Carpessus.

Appianus (Appian), *Wars in Spain*, 11.62–63.

Trifanum, 340 BC – Following the destruction of a combined Campanian and Latin army near the Veseris River by Roman legions under the *consul* Publius Decius Mus, the Latin general Numisius assembled a second army from among those Latin and Volsci peoples who were unaware of the earlier disaster. This force was met by an army led by the *consul* Titus Manlius Torquatus near Trifanum, a place located between the communities of Sinuessa and Minturnae on the Tyrrhenian coast. The belligerents elected to forgo construction of their encampments and immediately entered into battle. Numisius was defeated in the resulting fight, and Torquatus followed his victory by pillaging the enemy's fields. As punishment for their provocative actions, Latium and Capua were afterward compelled to surrender territory, which was partially redistributed among the Roman plebeian population.

Titus Livius (Livy), *History of Rome*, 8.11.5–13.

Tunes (i.e. Tunis), 255 BC – see Bagradas, 255 BC.

Tunis, 255 BC – see Hermaeum Promontorium, 255 BC.

Turda, 195 BC (Wars in Spain) – Roman efforts to secure control of the Iberian Peninsula after the Second Punic War resulted in the outbreak of an insurrection in 197 BC that required the diversion of resources already worn thin by the demands of the recently ended Punic and Macedonian wars. That year, word reached the Senate that a Roman army had been badly defeated in a battle in the province of Nearer Spain, and that the appointed *praetor*, Caius Sempronius Tudianus, was dead. The following year, legions were again deployed to the region under the *praetor* Quintus Minucius Thermus, but the struggle continued unabated and the Senate ultimately chose to dispatch a consular army led by Marcus Porcius Cato and his legate Publius Manlius. While these efforts were in preparation in Italy, Minucius achieved a signal victory over the Spanish generals Budares and Baesadines near the town of Turda. The Roman force thoroughly routed the enemy from the field. Some 12,000 Spanish tribesmen died in the battle, Budares was captured and the remainder of the army scattered beyond immediate tactical reconstitution.

Titus Livius (Livy), *History of Rome*, 33.25.8–9, 33.44.4–5.

Turis River, 75 BC (War against Sertorius) – Inland from the coastal city of Valentia (Valencia) in eastern Spain and near the banks of the Turis (Guadavial) River, a Roman army led by Cnaeus Pompeius Magnus engaged the Sertorian forces of Herennius and Perperna and defeated them. Pompey's troops killed more than 10,000 of the enemy.

Plutarch, *Pompey*, 18.3; Caius Sallusticus Crispus (Sallust), *Histories*, 2.86.6.

Turis River, 75 BC (War against Sertorius) – On the banks of the Turis (Guadavial) River in eastern Spain, the combined legions of Cnaeus Pompeius Magnus and Quintus Caecilius Metellus Pius defeated an army under the command of Quintus Sertorius.

Plutarch, *Pompey*, 18.1.

Cape Tyndaris, 257 BC (First Punic War, Wars against Carthage) – Near the cape of Tyndaris (Capo Tindaro on the Gollo di Patti), located on the northeastern Sicilian coast, a Roman fleet under the *consul* Caius Atilius Regulus engaged a Punic war fleet commanded by Hamilcar. In the waters off Tyndaris, the Roman fleet hastily gave chase in an effort to overtake a passing flotilla of enemy vessels. When the Carthaginians sighted the approaching ships, they immediately came about in order to offer battle. The two fleets quickly clashed, and the Carthaginians surrounded the leading Roman craft, capturing ten. Only Atilius' vessel avoided seizure. With the arrival of additional ships, the engagement turned in favour of the Romans, who captured ten Punic warships and sank another eight. The remainder of the Carthaginian fleet thereafter withdrew to the Liparaean Islands to the north. Zonaras' account of the Battle of Tyndaris differs dramatically from that given by Polybius.

Polybius, *Histories*, 1.25.1–4; John Zonaras, *Epitome of Histories*, 8.12.

Uscana, 170 BC (Third Macedonian War, Wars against Macedon) – Concerned with the growing danger presented by Gentius, king of the Illyrians, the Roman Senate decided to try and contain his influence in the Adriatic region, particularly in light of Rome's ongoing war with Macedon. To this end, the *consul* Aulus Hostilius Mancinus dispatched the legate Appius Claudius Centho and 4,000 infantry into southern Illyricum to provide protection for those peoples living immediately outside Illyrian territory. Uncertain that his existing troop numbers were sufficient to deal with the potential risks involved in the operation, Claudius raised an additional 4,000 auxiliaries from among the allies. The expeditionary force marched overland to the city of Lychnidos (Ohrid) on the eastern shore of Lake Lychnitis (Lake Ohrid). In this region, 2,000 Roman troops were already garrisoned at the request of the local Dassaretii and Illyrian peoples. Claudius then moved northwestward with the intention of recovering the community of Uscana, a city formerly held by a Roman garrison until its recent capture by the Macedonian king Perseus. The Romans established a camp 12 miles from the city before proceeding to their destination in the late afternoon. During the journey, the legate failed to maintain organization, with the result that the army arrived at the city's walls the next day in a state of disorder. The column of troops was badly attenuated after the long and confusing march in the darkness, and none of the maniples were prepared to repel a strong sally by the Illyrian inhabitants of Uscana. While the Romans slowly gathered outside the gates of the city, they were suddenly rushed by parties of attackers. The army's resistance completely crumbled when the first charge struck the unsuspecting Romans. With no hope of assembling his men into battle array, Claudius escaped along with his scattered command. Already exhausted after the night's travel, the legionary and allied soldiers were unable to offer sufficient resistance to ward off their pursuers, and fell in large numbers. By the time Claudius reached Lychnidos with the remnants of his army, approximately 5,000 men had died in the disaster.

Titus Livius (Livy), *History of Rome*, 43.10.

Utica, 204 BC (Second Punic War, Wars against Carthage) – When the Roman *proconsul* Publius Cornelius Scipio (Africanus) completed preparations in Sicily for the invasion of North Africa, he departed the island with an expeditionary force of 16,000 infantry and 1,600 cavalry aboard 400 transport ships. After arriving off Cape Apollinis (Ras Sidi Ali el Mekki), the army disembarked on the lee side of the promontory, where they established a camp approximately a mile from the city of Utica. Not far from Scipio's position was the Punic general Hasdrubal, son of Gisgo, with an army of 20,000 foot and 7,000 horse, supported by a sizeable contingent of 140 war elephants. While the two armies remained in their locations near the city, Scipio unexpectedly profited from an internal dispute between Syphax, king of western Numidia, and Masinissa, ruler of the Numidian Massylii in the east. The resulting intrigue shared by Syphax and Hasdrubal alienated Masinissa from the Carthaginians, and ultimately moved him to secretly ally with the Romans. Shortly thereafter, in a covert meeting between Scipio and Masinissa, the two commanders planned to ambush a 4,000-man force of Carthaginian cavalry presently bivouacked in the city of Selaeca, located about 15 miles from the Roman camp. When ready, the king's Numidian cavalry advanced to the very walls of the African city, and by means of a feigned withdrawal lured the enemy away from the security of Selaeca and onto open ground, where they were soon drawn into a running battle that carried the antagonists to within 4 miles of Utica. While the fighting raged near a tower built by the Syracusan tyrant Agathokles, a large formation of Roman cavalry suddenly attacked the Carthaginians from behind nearby hills. The charge quickly broke the ranks of the enemy. Exhausted by the long struggle, nearly 1,000 Carthaginians were trapped in the ambuscade and slain, along with their commander, Hanno. The Roman and Numidian horsemen thereafter pursued the fugitives in headlong flight for 30 miles. When the chase finally ended, an additional 2,000 Punic riders were dead or captured.

Appianus (Appian), *Punic Wars* 8.14; Titus Livius (Livy), *History of Rome*, 29.34; Dio Cassius, *Roman History*, 17.65–66; John Zonaras, *Epitome of Histories*, 9.12.

Utica, 203 BC (Second Punic War, Wars against Carthage) – After defeating a sizeable Carthaginian army in the Bagradas River valley, the Roman general Publius Cornelius Scipio (Africanus) seized control of a number of towns in the vicinity of the battlefield, and then marched his army 70 miles northeast toward the city of Carthage. As he neared the great port, Scipio diverted a portion of his troops and a large train of captives and booty north to the army's original camp near the besieged community of Utica. He led the remainder of his force to Tynes (Tunis), a town approximately 10 miles from Carthage which was earlier abandoned by an enemy garrison. From this vantage point the Romans had a view of the Punic capital and surrounding sea. As the army began construction of its camp, Scipio observed a number of ships sailing from Carthage to Utica, a distance of about 20 miles. Immediately recognizing the danger posed to Roman shipping in the harbour, Scipio ordered a cessation of all work and quickly moved to relocate his army to Utica. Within the confines of the African port were numerous vessels ill-conditioned for naval battle, including transport ships still heavily laden with artillery and siege engines and extremely vulnerable to attack. After reaching Utica, the Romans began to assemble a string of ships to block seaborne access to the harbour. Their efforts were inadvertently aided by the Carthaginians, whose irresolution delayed any assault until the following day. Scipio used this time to devise a proper defence of the ships and shoreline facilities. Near the entrance to the harbourage, he anchored the transports in four lines, stern to bow, and securely lashed the vessels together by an arrangement of yards, masts and rope. Planks were likewise extended from deck to deck to form a continuous gangway traversing the entire line of craft, and sufficient space was left below the bridges to permit smaller vessels the means to pass into open water and attack the enemy. Lastly, he placed 1,000 soldiers on board the transports along with a sufficient store of missiles. The next morning, after vainly waiting at sea for Roman warships to engage in battle, the Carthaginian fleet finally moved inshore to assault the front line of stationary vessels. The formation of ships proved difficult to attack in their unusual configuration, and missile fire from the opposing decks, the shoreline and the walls of the harbour continually battered the Punic *trireme*s. The Carthaginians again charged the Roman ships after failing in their initial attempt to breach the enemy line. In the chaotic struggle, the *trireme*s employed grappling hooks to successfully disrupt the front row of vessels and eventually force the Romans to cut away both the mooring cables and lashings between the leading ships. Set adrift in the fighting, about sixty transports were ultimately captured. The Punic flotilla suffered little damage in the encounter and returned to Carthage with its prizes.

Titus Livius (Livy), *History of Rome*, 30.9–10; Polybius, *Histories*, 14.10.2–12; Appianus (Appian), *Punic Wars*, 4.25.

Utica, 49 BC (Roman Civil Wars) – Near the North African port of Clupea (Kelibia), Caesarian general Caius Curio landed with two legions and 500 cavalry, and marched on the town of Utica. A Pompeian force under the leadership of Publius Attius Varus was encamped in a formidable location against the town's walls. When Curio reached the vicinity, he began the construction of his *castrum*. While the Caesarians were still in the process of excavating their earthworks, mounted sentries reported the approach of a large body of infantry and cavalry sent by King Juba I of Numidia to aid the Pompeian cause. A distant dust cloud marked the location of this army as it neared. Not anticipating the arrival of enemy reinforcements, Curio hastily dispatched his cavalry to intercept the new arrivals, and at the same time began to assemble his legions for battle. The arrangement of the Caesarian infantry ultimately proved unnecessary, as the king's forces – not expecting a hostile encounter – were caught completely unprepared to repel an attack by the Roman cavalry, and were routed. Several days later, both Curio and Varus gathered their legions in preparation for battle. Between the assembled battle lines lay a small valley. Each commander paused only briefly to judge his opponent's formation before a detachment of horsemen and light infantry on the Pompeian left wing descended into the valley. Curio countered by sending his cavalry and two cohorts of Marrucinian auxiliaries against them. Varus' horsemen fled at the first charge of the Caesarian squadrons, leaving Curio's forces to destroy the hapless infantrymen. The shock of this event demoralized the Pompeian army, inspiring a total rout once Curio's legions crossed the valley and challenged the awaiting line of troops. Varus incurred the loss of 600 killed and 1,000 wounded, while Curio suffered the death of only one soldier.

Julius Caesar, *Civil Wars*, 2.26–27, 34–35; Appianus (Appian), *Civil Wars*, 2.44.

Uxellodunum, 51 BC (Gallic War) – In the months following Caesar's decisive victory at Alesia, he and his lieutenants worked tirelessly to suppress isolated uprisings among the Gauls. During this unsettled time, two brigands – Lucterius of the Cadurci and a Senonian named Drappes – gathered a motley force of 2,000 ex-slaves, Gallic exiles, bandits and desperados of every kind, and proceeded to disrupt the shipment of Roman supplies and materials. The duo soon learned that they and their men were pursued by a Roman army, and fled to Uxellodunum (Puy d'Issolud), an *oppidum* located above the Duranius (Dordogne) River in southern Gaul. Within a short time, the Romans arrived below the town. The campaign commander, Caius Cabinius Rebilius, distributed his pair of legions into three camps situated on adjacent hills, and then prepared to invest the hilltop settlement. Fearful that a protracted siege would lead to starvation among the townspeople, Drappes and Lucterius sought to collect grain from the surrounding Cadurcan countryside. After gathering the requisite supplies, Lucterius attempted to smuggle an animal train laden with provisions into Uxellodunum, but Roman sentries were alerted to its presence, and scouts confirmed its identity. Just before dawn, a number of cohorts attacked the caravan and totally destroyed its escort. Only Lucterius and a few followers managed to escape. From prisoners captured in the clash, Cabinius learned that Drappes and the remainder of the foraging party were only about 12 miles away. The *legatus* ordered his cavalry and German infantry on ahead, and then followed with a single legion. The swifter *auxilia* surprised the enemy encampment on the banks of the river, and were already fully engaged with the Gauls when the legion arrived. Cabinius quickly drew up his cohorts for battle and then charged the enemy position from all sides. In the encounter, the entire Gallic force was killed or captured, and Drappes himself made prisoner.

Julius Caesar, *The Gallic War*, 32–36.

Vadimonian Lake, 310 BC (Second Samnite War, Samnite Wars) – After the defeat of the Samnites, a Roman army commanded by Quintus Fabius Maximus Rullianus met the Etruscans near Lake Vadimonis (*Vadimonis Lacum*). The resulting battle was savagely contested. Each army committed its total complement of troops. As the front ranks of infantry were exhausted or fell, each army advanced its second line of men, eventually to be followed by a third line of reserves. The engagement so depleted the Roman force that the cavalry was compelled to dismount in support of the infantry. This fresh infusion of men revitalized the Roman front line, which quickly mounted a new charge that broke the Etruscan formation. In the resulting flight, the Romans pursued the Etruscans and overran their encampment.

Titus Livius (Livy), *History of Rome*, 9.39.

Vadimonian Lake, 283 BC – Fearing a loss of their own lands following the Roman victory over the Gallic Senones at Arretium in the previous year, the Boii sought the support of the Etruscans. At Lake Vadimon in west-central Italy, approximately 80 miles north of Rome, the combined armies of the Boii and Etruscans fought a legion commanded by Publius Cornelius Dolabella. In the resulting struggle, the Romans virtually destroyed both opposing forces, with only a few of the Boii able to flee the battlefield. A subsequent battle the following year again ended in the total defeat of the Boii and Etruscans.

Polybius, *Histories*, 2.20.1–5.

Valentia, 75 BC – see Turis River 75 BC.

Valentia, 61 BC – In response to an uprising among the Allobriges, a Celtic tribe whose lands lay between the Rhodanus (Rhone) River and Lake Geneva, the Roman provincial governor of Gallia Narbonensis, Caius Pomptinus, dispatched legions into the field in an attempt to redress the situation. An army led by the legate Manlius Lentinus advanced against the city of Valentia, located on the eastern bank of the Rhone. This show of Roman force quickly intimidated the inhabitants of the community, but Lentinus' command was suddenly driven from the walls of the city when the neighbouring rural population attacked the unsuspecting cohorts. In retaliation, Lentinus devastated the surrounding countryside until the arrival of the Allobrigian chieftain

Catugnatus and a sizeable relief force temporarily ended Roman depredations. Unable to overwhelm the larger Celtic army in open battle, Lentinus elected to harass the enemy by means of frequent ambuscades. Finally, when Catugnatus determined to withdraw his warriors from the immediate area, Lentinus used the opportunity to launch a second assault against Valentia, destroying the town and overrunning the territory.

Dio Cassius, *Roman History*, 37.47–48.1.

Veascium, 390 BC (Gallic Invasion of Italy) – After withdrawing from Rome following their successful capture and occupation of the city, the Gauls purportedly besieged the city of Veascium, an ally of the Roman peoples. A Roman army led by the dictator Marcus Furius Camillus attacked the invaders without warning, inflicted heavy casualties on the unsuspecting enemy, and recovered the gold seized in Rome as well as much of the booty taken from the city.

Diodorus Siculus, *Historical Library*, 14.117.5.

Veii, 480 BC – During a period of intense political and social turmoil in Rome, the Senate was forced to grapple with a war against the nearby Etruscan community of Veii. The threat was exacerbated by an accord between the Veientes and other peoples in Etruria. At the same time, Latin ambassadors came seeking aid against the Aequi, who were presently besieging the city of Ortona. The current internal dissension between the plebeian and patrician classes in Rome threatened to hinder the successful prosecution of any campaigns, but the senators resolved to deploy two armies into the field under the consuls Gnaeus Manlius Cincinnatus and Marcus Fabius Vibulanus. Each consisted of two legions in addition to Latin and Hernician auxiliaries. The Roman armies encamped on adjacent hills near the city of Veii, while nearby the Veientine force was situated close to the city walls. Also present was a large concentration of Etruscan troops comparable in size to that of the Romans. Unsure of their armies' willingness to fight, the consuls hesitated to immediately enter into an engagement. The Etruscans greeted such reluctance with ridicule, and taunted the legions daily. Finally driven by shame, the legionaries demanded Manlius and Fabius lead them into battle. Concluding that the time was proper, the consuls assembled the Roman army on the nearby plain, Manlius in command of the right wing, Fabius the centre and the legate and *proconsul* Quintus Fabius the left. The opposing army was arrayed with a particularly strong formation of Etruscan troops on the right wing, which extended beyond the Roman left flank. The two armies fought desperately in the battle, and the Roman left was in danger of being overwhelmed before reinforcements led by Marcus Fabius drove back the enemy. The struggle remained savage for some time, with pockets of fighting also erupting around both legionary camps. Around sunset, the Etruscans finally abandoned the field and withdrew behind their fortifications. The following night, the enemy departed, leaving the Romans in possession of the plain. Of the 40,000 Roman and allied soldiers involved, many were killed and wounded, including the *consul* Gnaeus Manlius and pro*consul* Quintus Fabius. The Etruscan and Veientine armies also suffered heavy casualties.

Titus Livius (Livy), *History of Rome*, 2.43–47.9; Dionysius of Halicarnassus, *Roman Antiquities*, 9.5–9.13.3.

Veii, 475 BC – Following the outbreak of war, the Senate dispatched an army against the Etruscan city of Veii, 10 miles to the north of Rome. The *consul* Publius Valerius Publicola waged the campaign against both the Veientes and their allies, the Sabines. The legions, together with allied auxiliary detachments from the Latins and Hernici, launched a surprise attack against a Sabine camp immediately outside the walls of the community. The Veientes sent military support to the beleaguered Sabines during the fighting, and the unexpected arrival of these reinforcements briefly threw the Romans into disorder. The legions quickly recovered and the struggle continued unabated until a strong charge by Roman cavalry finally routed the Etruscans. The Romans soon overran the encampment, killing most of the occupants. When the day's action ended, the Romans had achieved a signal victory over two of their most implacable enemies.

Titus Livius (Livy), *History of Rome*, 2.53.1–3.

Veii, 396 BC – After nine years of siege war to subjugate the neighbouring community of Veii, the Senate appointed Marcus Furius Camillus as dictator. Camillus immediately set about prosecuting the war so as to bring the investment of the city to a successful conclusion. He began by restoring discipline and morale in the Roman army and enrolling new soldiers – including Latins and Hernicans – to resume the campaign. Once outside Veii, he refurbished and extended the siege works around the town, and began tunnelling a mine under the city walls and into the citadel. As construction of the mine neared completion, Furius launched an assault on all sides of the city in order to distract the Veientes from the sounds of the excavations near the town centre. While the battle raged on the ramparts of the city, Roman infantry suddenly exited from the opened mine into the temple of Juno on the Veientine citadel. The unexpected appearance of enemy soldiers within the sacred area resulted in bitter fighting throughout every precinct of Veii. Subjected to an intense and sustained assault from outside, and weakened by the presence of Roman troops in the heart of the city, Veientine resistance eventually collapsed. Having successfully overrun Veii, Furius ordered the

Romans to cease killing the noncombatant population. The victory decisively ended Rome's long struggle with her neighbouring rival.

Titus Livius (Livy), *History of Rome*, 5.19–21; Plutarch, *Camillus*, 5.1–5.

Velitrae, 382 BC – The colony of Velitrae revolted against Rome in 383 BC. In response, the Roman population declared war at the instigation of the Senate, but an outbreak of pestilence delayed the deployment of the legions against the Roman colony until the following year. When the rebellion continued unabated into the next campaign season, the Roman government sent an army under the tribunes Lucius Papirius Mugillanus and Spirius Papirius Crassus to end the uprising. Under the two commanders, the Romans decisively defeated the colonists and their reinforcements from the neighbouring town of Praeneste. The tribunes declined to attack the town after the battle out of recognition of its colonial status.

Titus Livius (Livy), *History of Rome*, 6.22.2–3.

Venafrum, 90 BC (Social War, Marsic War) – The Italian commander Marius Egnatius captured the town of Venafrum by treachery and destroyed two Roman cohorts.

Appianus (Appian), *Civil Wars*, 1.41.

Venusia, 207 BC – Still flushed from his victory over Hannibal Barca at Grumentum, the *consul* Caius Claudius Nero pursued the Punic army as it withdrew northward toward Apulia. Because of Hannibal's clandestine departure under cover of darkness, the two armies were separated by several hours as Claudius' legions delayed their march toward Apulia, electing to follow in the train of the Carthaginian column fully one day later. The Roman army finally overtook the Punic force near the southeastern Italian town of Venusia, located on the Aufidus River. A disorderly engagement similar to that fought at Grumentum followed, which also resulted in Hannibal's defeat. Carthaginian losses amounted to over 2,000 men. After Venusia, Hannibal turned his army southeast toward the coastal community of Metapontum and the support of the local Punic garrison. Claudius, likewise, resumed his pursuit of the enemy.

Titus Livius (Livy), *History of Rome*, 27.42.9–17.

Venus Mons, 146 BC (Viriathic War, Wars in Spain) – The Lusitanian army invaded the territory of Carpetania the year following the defeat of the legate Caius Vetilius at Tribola. The incursion prompted the Senate to dispatch a Roman army of 10,000 infantry and 1,300 cavalry under the command of the *praetor* Caius Plautius. An initial effort to defeat the Lusitani resulted in the total destruction of a 4,000-man army. When the enemy force, under the leadership of its chieftain Viriathus, crossed the Tagus (Tajo) River and encamped on the slopes of Venus Mons (Mt Veneris), Plautius overtook the marauders. The subsequent battle proved a complete disaster for the Roman army. Most of the troops were slaughtered in the encounter, and the few survivors who managed to escape fled in disorder to the surrounding towns. Viriathus thereafter overran the whole of the region unchecked.

Appianus (Appian), *Wars in Spain*, 11.64.

Venus Mons, 143 BC (Numantine War, Wars in Spain) – Following a couple of Roman victories over the Lusitani the year before, the Senate's war in Spain unexpectedly broadened when the Lusitanian leader Viriathus persuaded the Arevaci, Titthi and Belli tribes to abandon their allegiance with Rome and form a hostile coalition. After an initial defeat by a Roman army, Viriathus withdrew to the safety of Venus Mons (Mt Veneris) and prepared for further operations. When a Roman force under Quintus Pompeius Aulus later entered the region in search of the Lusitanians, Viriathus descended the slopes of the mountain and defeated his pursuers, killing approximately 1,000 of the governor's troops.

Appianus (Appian), *Wars in Spain*, 11.66.

Vercellae, 101 BC (German Invasions) – The destruction of the Teutoni and Ambroni the year before at Aquae Sextiae in southern Gaul removed the danger posed to Rome by those Germanic tribes, but Italy still faced the threat of invasion by a third barbarian people, the Cimbri. The Germans descended into the upper Padus (Po) Valley after crossing the Alps from central Europe. Moving southeastward, they encountered the Roman armies of Quintus Lutatius Catulus and Caius Marius outside the village of Vercellae (Vercelli) on a plain near the confluence of the Sesites (Sesia) and Padus rivers. With the arrival of the Cimbri, the two sides briefly engaged in a time of parleying before a day and place were mutually selected for battle. The armies assembled for action at the appointed time. In command of 20,300 men, Catulus formed the centre of the Roman line. His colleague, the *consul* Marius, distributed his 32,000 soldiers on both wings. German king Boeorix drew up his forces across the plain in a massive square, extending for 3¾ miles on each side. The amassed body of warriors totalled perhaps 180,000, including 15,000 cavalry. When the battle opened, the barbarian horsemen stationed on the right immediately swung to the right in an effort to position the Romans between themselves and the German infantry. The legions responded to this manoeuvre with a spontaneous charge. The cohorts were met by thousands of Cimbri foot-soldiers as they raced across the field. The resulting struggle was fiercely contested. Dust clouds quickly obscured much of the battlefield, temporarily delaying Marius' attack so that Catulus' troops alone bore the brunt of the fighting for much of the time. Combined with the summer heat, the intense combat quickly exhausted the Cimbri, permitting the Romans to gradually gain control of the battlefield before finally putting the enemy to general flight. Many of the fugitives, driven back on their encampment by the pressure of the Roman assault, were subsequently slain by their womenfolk, who then killed their offspring before committing suicide. The conflict ended with the capture of 60,000 Cimbri men, women and children. German dead may possibly have totalled 120,000.

Plutarch, *Marius*, 25.4–27.3; Paulus Orosius, *Seven Books of History against the Pagans*, 5.16; Velleius Paterculus, *Roman History*, 2.12.5; Eutropius, *Abridgement of Roman History*, 5.2; Titus Livius (Livy), *Summaries*, 68; Lucius Annaeus Florus, *Epitomy*, 1.38.11–18.

Veseris, 340 BC – Near a modest stream called the Veseris at the base of Mt Vesuvius, a Roman army of 21,000 men, led by the consuls Titus Manlius Imperiosus Torquatus and Publius Decius Mus, encountered a hostile Latin force of comparable size. The four consular legions deployed for battle. Manlius commanded the right wing and Decius the left. Having long served as allies of Rome in time of war, the Latins employed a Roman-style battle formation with heavy infantry arrayed in three lines; the *hastati* situated in the front, the *principes* arrayed in the centre and the veteran *triarii* stationed to the rear. Since the two sides were so evenly matched, the subsequent struggle continued unabated with neither able to gain an advantage over its opponent. After fighting at some length, the Latins eventually succeeded in driving back the Roman left, forcing the front line of *hastati* to recoil against the ranks of the *principes*. Unwilling to allow the remainder of the army to suffer the same fate as that experienced by the Roman infantry on the left, Decius and an attending priest named Marcus Valerius ritually invoked the aid of the gods. Upon completion of the solemnity, the *consul* then mounted his horse and charged directly into the midst of the enemy. The sacrificial act served to rally the left wing, which was soon joined by a contingent of fresh troops. The *rorarii*, *hastati* and *principes* drove back the Latin right in disorder. At about this same time on the Roman right, the maniples began to flag under the unrelenting pressure of the enemy assault, leading Manlius to send an additional detachment, the *accensi*, into action; but still withholding the *triarii*. In response, the Latin commanders committed their *triarii* to the struggle in the mistaken belief that the surviving *consul* had also committed his last reserve of fresh soldiers. Finally, after intense fighting, the Roman *triarii* suddenly charged into battle. This unexpected injection of fresh veteran troops completely shattered the exhausted body of Latin infantry. The rout was decisive. Three-quarters of the Latin army died on the field. The victory was further guaranteed by the presence of a sizeable Samnite army, assembled nearby in faithful recognition of their treaty with Rome the year before.

Titus Livius (Livy), *History of Rome*, 8.8.19–8.10.

Vesontio, 58 BC – see Vosges, 58 BC.

Mount Vesuvius, 340 BC – see Veseris, 340 BC.

Mount Vesuvius, 73 BC (War of Spartacus, Third Servile War) – A growing slave insurrection in Campania led by an escaped gladiator named Spartacus inevitably led the Senate to dispatch military forces to end the disturbance. A 3,000-man force, commanded by the *praetor* Caius Claudius Glaber, attempted to trap the fugitives on Mount Vesuvius, but was in turn surprised and defeated. While Glaber's cohorts were deployed around the base of the volcano, confident their quarry was contained, Spartacus and his band secretly descended from the heights by means of woven vine ropes. Once down, they routed Glaber's forces and seized the Roman camp by a sudden, unexpected attack. A subsequent effort by the *praetor* Publius Varinus to end the uprising was likewise beaten.

> Paulus Orosius, *Seven Books of History against the Pagans*, 5.24; Appianus (Appian), *Civil Wars*, 1.14.116; Plutarch, *Crassus*, 9.1–3; Titus Livius (Livy), *Summaries*, 95; Lucius Annaeus Florus, *Epitomy*, 2.8.4–5; Frontinus, *Stratagems*, 1.5.21.

Vindalium, 121 BC – A threat made against a local tribal people allied to Rome provoked retaliation from the *proconsul* Caius Sextius Calvinus, who initiated a campaign in 123 BC against the Celtoligurian Salluvii of the Druentia (Durance) River plain in southeastern Gaul. With his peoples soon subjugated by the Romans, the Salluvian king Toutomotulus sought assistance from the Allobroges, a powerful neighbouring tribe to the north. This support came readily, and the Allobroges further aggravated the situation by invading the lands of the Aedui, another Celtic tribe and ally of Rome. With the situation rapidly deteriorating in southeastern and central Gaul, the *consul* Gnaeus Domitius Ahenobarbus opened hostilities with the Allobroges. His efforts proved successful, and the following year the Senate granted him proconsular power in order to continue the struggle. His legions engaged the Allobroges and defeated them in an intense battle outside the city of Vindalium, near the confluence of the Sulgas (Sorgues) and Rhodanus (Rhone) rivers in southeastern France. The presence of Roman war elephants proved decisive, serving to frighten both the enemy warriors and their horses. Allobrogian losses totalled 20,000 dead and 3,000 captured.

> Paulus Orosius, *Seven Books of History against the Pagans*, 5.13; Titus Livius (Livy), *Summaries*, 61.

Volaterrae, 298 BC – A Roman consular army under the command of Lucius Cornelius Scipio engaged an Etruscan force arrayed in column (*instructo agmine*) near the community of Volaterrae in Etruria. Both armies incurred heavy casualties during the day-long struggle, though neither conceded the field. As a result, the action was broken off at nightfall with no apparent resolution to the contest. At dawn the next day, the Roman army again assembled into battle formation in preparation for a resumption of fighting, but the Etruscans had decamped and withdrawn during the night. Left in secure possession of the battlefield and the Etruscan outpost on the site, Scipio elected to retire his legions to Faliscan territory before initiating a sustained campaign into Etruria.

   Titus Livius (Livy), *History of Rome*, 10.12.1–6.

Volsinii, 294 BC (Third Samnite War, Samnite Wars) – A Roman army under the *consul* Lucius Postumius Megellus entered Etruria and laid waste to the lands around the city of Volsinii (Bolsena). The attack forced the Volsinienses to come out and defend their territory. Some 2,800 Etruscans died in the resulting battle before the rest fled to the safety of their walls. Afterward, Postumius led his legions northwest into the territories around Rusellae (Roselle).

   Titus Livius (Livy), *History of Rome*, 10.37.1–2.

Volturnus River, 296 BC (Third Samnite War, Samnite Wars) – While Roman forces concentrated on prosecuting a war in Etruria, the Samnites chose to take advantage of the situation and invade Campania and the Falernian district in southwestern Italy. At the same time, another Roman army under the leadership of the *consul* Lucius Volumnius Flamma Violens entered Samnium with the intention of initiating hostilities. Upon learning of the ongoing depredations in Campania, the Roman commander immediately marched his army into the region, only to hear from the native Caleni that the Samnites were presently withdrawing toward their homeland, heavily burdened by booty. Following the deployment of scouts, who confirmed these reports and located the enemy camp beside the Volturnus (Volturno) River, the Roman army moved northeastward in pursuit. Arriving in the vicinity of the Samnite position, the legions encamped sufficiently far away to avoid detection before approaching the enemy under cover of darkness. Shortly before dawn, spies reported to the *consul* that the Samnites were preparing to resume their march; the vanguard was in the process of departing, but the remainder of the column was not yet fully organized. Concluding that the moment was ideal for launching an attack, Volumnius assembled his army in preparation for battle and then advanced undetected against the opposing encampment. At daybreak, the Romans suddenly charged the enemy column. Hampered by their large quantity of plunder, and still mostly unarmed, the Samnites were thrown into complete disorder. The situation was made even more chaotic when numerous Roman prisoners detained within the column managed to escape and enter the struggle armed with their captors' weapons. The Romans quickly overran the entire enemy encampment in the confusion, which was followed by the unexpected capture of Samnite general Staius

Minatius. The fighting was briefly renewed with the return of the vanguard, but it too was inevitably overwhelmed by the legions. Samnite losses amounted to 6,000 dead and 2,500 captured.

Titus Livius (Livy), *History of Rome*, 10.20.

Volturnus River, 83 BC – see Tifatum, 83 BC.

Vosegus, 58 BC (Gallic War) – No sooner had Julius Caesar resolved the Helvetian issue at the Battle of Bibracte, than he faced the threat posed to Gallic territories by the German Suebi, led by their chieftain Ariovistus. Embassies from the Sequani, Aedui and Arverni appealed to the *consul* to aid their tribes against the encroachment of the Germans. The deteriorating situation increasingly concerned Caesar, who finally determined to take action to stop this unchecked movement of peoples across the Rhenus (Rhine) River. An initial proposal by the Roman commander to a parley with the Suebian leader was met with impudence. When Caesar learned that the Germans continued to cross the river unabated, he secured his grain-supply and promptly advanced against Ariovistus with six legions and accompanying *auxilia*. Three days later, he was informed that the German chieftain intended to seize the town of Vesontio (Besancon), the capital of the Sequani located on the Dubas (Doubs) River. Sitting atop a hill surrounded by a significant oxbow in the river, the community was a formidable site from which to conduct a war. It also possessed a large store of supplies. This news compelled Caesar to reach the town before the Germans, and by forced marches the legions managed to secure Vesontio ahead of Ariovistus' warriors. Roman occupation of the town served to stall the advance of the Suebi. Caesar encamped for several days near the town in order to collect additional supplies, and then resumed his march. Seven days later, the army drew to within 24 miles of the enemy. The two commanders briefly engaged in a final parley on a slight knoll in the midst of the plain of Alsace, before both retired to prepare for battle. Shortly thereafter, Ariovistus relocated his army nearer the Roman position, to a location at the foot of the Vosegus (Vosges) mountains. This action placed the armies about 6 miles from each other. The next day, the Suebi moved their camp 2 miles beyond Caesar's *castrum* in an effort to block the arrival of additional Roman grain supplies from the Sequani and Aedui. The manoeuvre prompted the Romans to offer battle on each of the next five days, but Ariovistus declined a major contest every time, preferring instead to deploy his cavalry in skirmishes against the Roman horse. Unable to entice his opponent to battle, Caesar eventually elected to relocate a portion of his army in order to restore access to the supply line. This second camp was constructed only about 500 yards from the Germans. The Roman threat was now too acute to ignore any longer, and when Caesar next arrayed for battle, Ariovistus accepted the challenge. Against the *consul*'s legions arrayed in three lines (*triplex acies*), the Germans assembled their formation by tribe: the Harudes, Marcomanni, Tribocci, Vangiones, Nemetes, Sedusii and Suebi. A train of wagons protected the rear and flanks of the amassed line of warriors, while likewise discouraging flight on the part of the tribesmen. Numbering perhaps only 40,000 men after their losses against the Helvetii, the Romans opened the battle with an assault against the German left, which Caesar observed to be the weakest point in Ariovistus' line. The attack was answered by a German countercharge which was so swift that it prevented the legionaries on the right from discharging their *pila*. After intense fighting, the Romans succeeded in routing the German left. At the same time, on the opposite end of the battlefield, the Roman left appeared to flag under the sustained pressure of Ariovistus' right, prompting Caesar's commander of cavalry, Publius Licinius Crassus, to redirect the maniples of the Roman third line against the German right. The arrival of these fresh reserves on the Roman left caused all German resistance in that part of the line to completely collapse. The disintegration of Ariovistus' right served as the catalyst for a general flight of the entire formation. As thousands of tribesmen and their women and children began to stream in disorder toward the Rhenus some 5 miles away, Caesar's Gallic cavalry initiated a vicious pursuit. Countless Germans died in the battle and subsequent chase. Ariovistus survived the disaster, but both of his wives

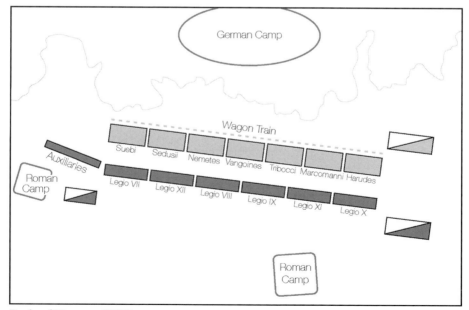

Battle of Vosegus, 58 BC

and a daughter died in the rout. A second daughter was among the fugitives captured. The remnants of the tribes evacuated Gallic lands and retreated across the river.

Julius Caesar, *The Gallic War*, 1.48–53.

Vosges, 58 BC – see Vosegus, 58 BC.

Zama, 202 BC (Second Punic War, Wars against Carthage) – This was the climactic battle of the second great war between Carthage and Rome for control of the western and central Mediterranean basin, fought near the ancient North African village of Zama. The Roman expeditionary army, commanded by the *proconsul* Publius Cornelius Scipio (Africanus), consisted of 25,000 legionaries and 2,500 Roman and Italian cavalry. The Romans were supported by 10,000 allied troops under Masinissa, son of King Gaia of the Massyles, an eastern Numidian people. Masinissa's force comprised 6,000 infantry and 4,000 cavalry. Opposing the Romans was a Carthaginian army under the leadership of Hannibal Barca. The Punic force of 40,000 infantry and 3,000 cavalry included 12,000 veteran Balearic, Ligurian and Celtic mercenaries formerly under the command of Hannibal's youngest brother, the now-deceased Mago Barca. These soldiers, like Hannibal's own 14,000 veterans, were only recently recalled from Italy by a Carthaginian Senate fearful of Scipio's invasion force. At Zama, Hannibal's command was strengthened by the addition of 14,000 recruits from Carthage, 1,000 Carthaginian cavalry, 2,000 Numidian horse under Tychaeus, and a corps of eighty war elephants. Hannibal positioned the elephants in a line-abreast formation before his army. The Punic infantry was then arrayed in three lines: the first included the 12,000 mercenaries of Mago's command, followed by the Carthaginian recruits and lastly Hannibal's veterans. The allied Numidian cavalry were stationed on the left, with the Carthaginian horse placed on the right wing. Like his counterpart, Scipio also deployed his legionaries in three lines; the maniples of *hastati*, *principes* and *triarii*. In customary fashion, the cavalry were deployed on the wings, with Roman horse under Laelius positioned to the left and the complete Numidian force of Masinissa on the right. The battle opened with an elephant charge. Anticipating such an assault, Scipio discarded the traditional checkerboard-pattern formation of the Roman infantry, and instead aligned the maniples of *principes* and *triarii* directly behind those of the *hastati* in an effort to channel the attacking animals through and away from the legions. The lightly armed *velites* served to harass and drive away the beasts. The tactical modification successfully minimized the impact of this initial assault on the Roman lines, though some Roman casualties resulted. In the confusion of this opening conflict, some of the pachyderms charged into their own Numidian cavalry on the left, disrupting

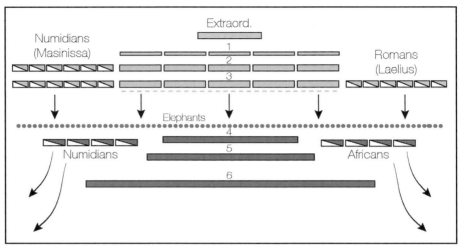

Battle of Zama, 202 BC (Phase 1) (1=Triarii; 2=Principes; 3=Hastati; 4=Ligurians/Gauls; 5=Africans/Carthaginians; 6=Italian Allies)

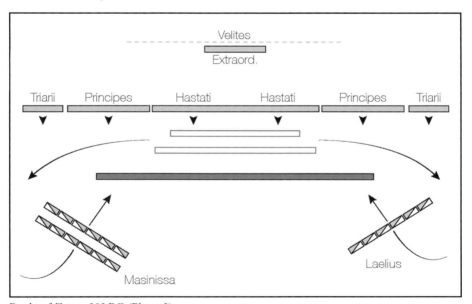

Battle of Zama, 202 BC (Phase 2)

that portion of the Carthaginian formation. Masinissa quickly used the opportunity to launch a sudden attack against the disorganized Numidians of Tychaeus and drive them off the battlefield. At the same time, Roman cavalry successfully shattered the Punic horse on the right. With the elephant threat neutralized and all enemy cavalry put to flight, Scripio now advanced his infantry against the Balearic, Ligurian and Celtic mercenary formations in the centre. After a protracted period of intense, bloody fighting, the maniples of Roman *hastati* were finally able to overcome Hannibal's allied mercenaries and then, with the aid of the *principes*, defeat the civic recruits of the second Carthaginian line. As Scipio prepared to commit his final maniples of *triarii* to battle, he ordered these reserve units to deploy with the *principes* on the flanks of the Roman line in an effort to encircle Hannibal's now depleted force. The sudden timely return of the Roman, Italian and allied Numidian cavalry completed the envelopment, and assured a Roman victory. In the rout which followed, 20,000 Carthaginians died, with a roughly equal number captured. Roman losses amounted to 1,500 killed and several thousand wounded. Hannibal was able to escape the field.

> Polybius, *Histories*, 15.9–14; Titus Livius (Livy), *History of Rome*, 30.32–35; Appianus (Appian), *Punic Wars*, 40–47; Eutropius, *Abridgement of Roman History*, 3.23.

Zela, 67 BC (Third Mithridatic War, Wars against Mithridates the Great) – Six years after the resumption of hostilities between Rome and Pontus, King Mithridates VI once again moved his armies against Roman forces, this time encamped near Gaziura. Following the arrival of the Pontic forces, Roman commander Caius Valerius Triarius refused all efforts by the enemy to draw him into a premature battle. The legate's rejection of these challenges finally compelled Mithridates to send a detachment of men to besiege the town of Dadasa, where the Romans' baggage was stored, in order to provoke Triarius to action. Word of this assault and news that Lucius Licinius Lucullus approached with a second Roman army, moved Caius Valerius to abandon his place of security and advance to the relief of the town. About 3 miles from the town of Zela (Zile), Mithridates' army suddenly attacked, surrounded and overwhelmed the Romans. The king's horsemen pursued and slaughtered the shattered remnants of Triarius' infantry and cavalry on the surrounding plain. Some Romans managed to survive the disaster, but 7,000 died, including 150 centurions and twenty-four tribunes.

> Dio Cassius, *Roman History*, 36.12–13.1; Plutarch, *Lucullus*, 35.1; Appianus (Appian), *Mithridatic Wars*, 8.89. The location of the battle is identified in Caesar's *The Alexandrine War*, 72.

Zela, 47 BC, 2 August (Roman Civil Wars, Wars of the First Triumvirate) - In the summer of 47 BC, Julius Caesar initiated a rapid campaign to suppress the expansionist aspirations of Pharnaces II, king of Bosphorus Cimmerius, who had seized much of northern Anatolia. Caesar moved his army northward from Tarsus on the Cilician coast to intercept the potentate, whose army was situated on a hill north of the town of Zela (Zile) in southern Pontus. Caesar's command consisted of two legions, the Thirty-sixth and the badly depleted veteran *Legio VI*. This force was accompanied by two additional Roman-trained legions provided by Deiotarus, king of Armenia and tetrarch of Galatia. Having located Pharnaces on 1 August, Caesar established the legions on an elevated site adjacent to the Bosphoran encampment. The enemy suddenly launched an attack as the Romans were completing their camp fortifications on 2 August. Caught off-guard by the assault, the legions reeled badly under the initial shock, but quickly organized into cohorts. Led by chariots, the unexpected charge penetrated the centre of Caesar's front line and threatened to split the entire Roman formation. On the right flank, the 1,000 legionaries of the Sixth Legion alone held their ground after absorbing the impact of this first attack. The stand of the *Legio VI* steadied the whole of the Roman defence, permitting Caesar the opportunity to redress the breach. After intense fighting, a counter-attack shattered all Bosphorian resistance. In the pursuit which followed, Pharnaces' army was annihilated, the king himself narrowly escaping the fate of his command.

Julius Caesar, *The Alexandrine War*, 72–76.

Notes

1. The feminine noun *legio* is derived from the Latin verb *legere*, meaning 'to bring together, gather, collect'.
2. Plutarch, *Romulus* 13.1. See Marcus Terentius Varro, *De lingua Latina*, 5.89; Titus Livius (Livy), 1.13.8; E. Rawson, 'The literary sources for the pre-Marian Army', *Papers of the British School at Rome* 39 (1971), pp. 13–31; and R.M. Ogilvie, *Early Rome and the Etruscans* (Glasgow 1976).
3. Diodorus Siculus, *Historical Library*, 23.2.1; and Athenaeus (*Deipnosophists*) 6.106, who states that 'from the Tyrrhenians they [the Romans] derived the practice of the entire army advancing to battle in close phalanx …' It is also equally reasonable to conclude that knowledge of the phalanx was acquired from the Greek coastal colonies in southern Italy. See also Livy and the *Ineditum Vaticanum*. See Hans von Arnim, 'Ineditum Vaticanum', *Hermes* 27 (1892), pp. 118–30, republished in Anders Björn Drachmann, *Diodors Römische Annalen bis 302 a. Chr. samt dem Ineditum Vaticanum* (Bonn, Marcus und Weber, 1912), and in Felix Jacoby, *Die Fragmente der griechischen Historiker* (*FGrHist*), 839.
4. There is no complete agreement among modern scholars as to which Etruscan communities formed the league of twelve cities. The following list includes those cities most often identified by modern historians: Arretium (Arezzo), Curtun (Cortona), Felathri (Volterra), Caere (Cerveteri), Vetluna (Vetulonia), Clevsin (Chiusi), Perusia (Perugia), Puplun (Populonia), Veii, Tarquinii (Tarquinia), Volsinii (Bolsena) and Vulci (Volci).
5. The Servius reforms introduced 'constitutional' changes that divided Roman territory into four urban and sixteen rural tribes and redistributed the population into classes, each determined by wealth. The four urban tribes were the Esquilina, Collina, Palatina and Sucusana. For voting purposes, the people were further organized into *centuriae* ('hundreds'), which also served as basic units for army recruiting. Following the Servian reforms, 193 centuries existed. The distribution of centuries into the classes was as follows: *Equites*, eighteen; First class, eighty; Second class, twenty; Third class, twenty; Fourth class, twenty; Fifth class, thirty; *Capitecensi*, five. See Livy, 1.42.5–1.43.8, and Dionysius of Halicarnassus, *Roman Antiquities*, 4.16.1–4.18.2 for an explanation of the Servian military reforms. Both historians provide comparable descriptions of the army, with only minor variations present.
6. In contrast to the accounts offered by Livy and Dionysius, other sources (Paulus ex Festo 100L, and Aulus Gellius, *Noctes Atticae*, 6.13) imply the grouping of the citizen population below the *equites* into a simplified bipartite division in which the wealthier segment of the community provided hoplites as part of the *classis* ('class'), while the remainder, designated *infra classem* ('below class'), supplied the needs for light-armed infantry. The consensus of evidence may very well suggest the presence of a rudimentary *classis/infra classem* system that was later modified by the application of a five-class structure and centuriate organization. Unfortunately, the information derived from the extant corpus is far from conclusive, making it difficult to definitively reconcile the disparate evidence pertaining to the extent and character of 'Servian' reform, a proper sequence and chronology regarding the introduction of reform, class and centuriate structure, and social and institutional influences on military organization. Nonetheless, a reasonably sober working model of military organization can be extrapolated from the available sources, despite the fragmentary and perceived anachronistic nature of some evidence.

7. Lawrence Keppie, *The Making of the Roman Army: From Republic to Empire* (B.T. Batsford, Ltd, 1984;, reprint, New York, Barnes and Noble Books, 1994), pp. 15–17; G.V. Sumner, 'The Legion and the Centuriate Organization', *The Journal of Roman Studies*, 60 (1970), pp. 61–78; and M.P. Nillson, 'The Introduction of Hoplite Tactics at Rome', *The Journal of Roman Studies* 19 (1929), pp. 1–11; the word *clipeus* was the Latin term used by Romans to identify the round hoplite shield of the ancient Greeks. See also R. Thomsen, *King Servius Tullius: A Historical Synthesis* (Copenhagen, 1980).

8. Livy, 1.42.5–1.43.8; Keppie, *Making of the Roman Army*, p. 17; from the eighteen centuries of *equites* were drawn not only the cavalry, but the legion's corps of officers.

9. Livy, *History of Rome*, 5.36.11–5.39.2; Diodorus Siculus, 14.113.3–115.2; Plutarch, *Camillus*, 18–19.

10. Livy, 1.42–43; Dionysius of Halicarnassus, 4.13–23.

11. Livy, 8.8–10; Polybius, *Histories*, trans. W.R. Paton et. al., Loeb Classical Library edition, six vols. (London, William Heinemann Limited, 1922–27), 3:6.21–23; Donathan Taylor, 'A Comparative Study of the Post-Alexandrian Macedonian Phalanx and the Roman Manipular Legion to the Battle of Pydna', *Ozark Historical Review*, vol. 22 (Spring 1993), pp. 18–31.

12. Livy 28.1.18 notes that in 211 BC, Roman authorities raised twenty-three legions.

13. Livy, 26.4.

14. Polybius, 6.21–23; F.E. Adcock, *The Roman Art of War under the Republic* (New York, Barnes and Noble Books, 1995); M. Bell, 'Tactical Reform in the Roman Republican Army', *Historia* 14 (1965), pp. 404–22; E. Gabba, *The Roman Republic, the Army and the Allies* (Oxford, 1976), trans. P.J. Cuff; and Hans Delbrück, *Warfare in Antiquity*, trans. Walter J. Renfroe, Jr., vol. 1 of *History of the Art of War* (Lincoln, University of Nebraska Press, 1975), pp. 272–82. See also Livy, 8.8.3–14 for a similar description of an early Roman manipular legion. Polybius notes that in times of extreme crisis, the number of *hastati* and *principes* might be increased, but the *triarii* remain unaltered (6.21.9–10). Among the heavy infantry in a manipular legion, the *hastati* consisted of younger men in their early 20s; the *principes* included more seasoned veterans, perhaps in their late 20s to mid-30s; and the *triarii* were drawn from the oldest and most experienced legionaries. The *velites* were those individuals identified by census as the poorest citizens eligible for military service.

15. Polybius, 6.21–23; Peter Connolly, *Greece and Rome at War* (Englewood Cliffs, NJ, Prentice-Hall Inc., 1981), p. 133; and Elmer C. May, Gerald P. Stradler and John F. Votaw, *Ancient and Medieval Warfare, The West Point Military History Series*, Thomas E. Griess (ed.) (Wayne, NJ, Avery Publishing Group Inc., 1984), p. 48.

16. Aulus Gellius, *Attic Nights*, 10.28.1: '[Aelius] Tubero, in the first book of his *History*, has written that King Servius Tullius, when he divided the Roman people into those five classes of older and younger men for the purpose of making the enrollment, regarded as *pueri*, or "boys", those who were less than seventeen years old; then, from their seventeenth year, when they were thought to be fit for service, he enrolled them as soldiers, calling them up to the age of forty-six *iuniores*, or "younger men", and beyond that age, *seniores*, or "elders".'

17. Gellius, 10.28.1; and Livy, 10.21, 22.11.9, 40.26.7, 42.31.4, 42.33.4, 43.7.11, 43.13.6. In an emergency, those citizens between 46 and 50, identified as *seniores*, were liable to military service.

18. Polybius, 6.21–23; and Connolly, *Greece and Rome at War*, p. 133.

19. For a thorough treatment of the cavalry of the Republic, see Jeremiah B. McCall, *The Cavalry of the Roman Republic* (New York, Routledge, 2002); Keppie, p. 35.

20. The term *ala* and accompanying description offered here should not be confused with the later auxiliary cavalry formation in the imperial army by the same name. In the Roman imperial army of the Principate, the term *ala* denoted a mounted unit commonly consisting of some 500 riders (*ala quingenaria*) recruited from non-citizens. A minority of such mounted units consisted of 1,000 horsemen each (*ala miliaria*).

21. Livy 25.21.5: 'The first legion and the left wing of the allied troops were drawn up in front.'; 27.2.6: 'On the Roman side the first legion and right *ala* ...'
22. Polybius, 6.26.7.
23. Polybius, 6.26.1–9.
24. Polybius, 6.40.1–8, and Livy, 10.34.
25. Polybius, vol. 4, *Histories* IX–XV (Loeb Classical Library, 1925), 11.33 and cf. 11.23.1; and Sallust, vol. 1. As a tactical unit, see M.J.V. Bell, 'Tactical Reform in the Roman Republican Army', *Historia* 14 (1965), pp. 404–22. See also Plinio Fraccaro, 'Della Guerra presso i Romani', *Opuscula* 4 (1975) Pavia, Presso la rivista Athenaeum.
26. Sallust, *War with Jugurtha*, 49.6, 46.7.
27. Polybius, 6.19.7.
28. Polybius, 6.19.8–9.
29. Polybius, 6.34.3.
30. Polybius, 15.9.7–9.
31. The *triplex acies* was the standard formation of a legion arrayed for battle. Numerous examples of a *triplex acies* exist from surviving texts. Caesar commonly employed the *triplex acies* during his campaigns in Gaul, and examples exist from Roman encounters with the Helvetii, the Suebi of Ariovistus, and the Usipetes and Tencteri. At the Battle of Ruspina (*African War*, 13) Caesar deployed his army in a *simplex acies*. An example of Caesar's use of a *duplex acies* is *Gallic War*, 3.24.
32. 'Acies erat Afraniana duplex legionum v; tertium in subsidiis locum alariae cohorts obtinebant; Caesaris triplex; sed primam aciem quaternae cohorts ex v legionibus tenebant, has subsidiariae ternae et rursus aliae totidem suae cuiusque legionis subsequebantur'; Caesar, *Civil Wars*, A.G. Peskett trans. (Loeb Classical Library, 1914) 1.83.
33. Vegetius, *Epitoma rei militaris*, 2.6. An instance where a *duplex acies* was perhaps used in battle during the imperial era is related by Arrian in *Acies contra Alanos*, 5–6, 15–18.
34. Dionysius of Halicarnassus, 14.10.18.
35. Polybius, 18.30.6.
36. Adrian Goldsworthy, *The Roman Army at War, 100 B.C.-A.D. 200* (New York, Clarendon Press, 1996), pp. 171–249; Philip Sabin, 'The Mechanics of Battle in the Second Punic War', in T. Cornell, B. Rankov and P. Sabin (eds), *The Second Punic War: A Reappraisal* (London, Institute of Classical Studies, 1996), pp. 59–79; Philip Sabin, 'The Face of Roman Battle', *Journal of Roman Studies* 90 (2000), pp. 1–17; and J.E. Lendon, *Soldiers and Ghosts: A History of Battle in Classical Antiquity* (New Haven, Yale University Press, 2005).
37. Polybius, 6.27–32.
38. Ibid.
39. See M.C. Bishop and J.N.C. Coulston, *Roman Military Equipment from the Punic Wars to the Fall of Rome* (Oxford, Oxbow Books, 2006), pp. 1–47, for an extremely valuable discussion of the three forms of evidence available for modern studies of Roman military equipment.
40. The sleeveless Mediterranean tunic remained the customary style of clothing until the late second or early third century AD, when a long-sleeved *tunica* was introduced into the army. For reference regarding the adoption of the long-sleeved tunic, see Dio Cassius, 78.3.3. Dio also notes the addition of the *sagum*, a heavy wool military cloak fastened on the right shoulder.
41. Herodian 2.13.10. *Balteus*, 'girdle, sword belt', said by Varro to be a word of Etruscan origin.
42. The colour of Roman legionary tunics remains a topic of scholarly debate. For a sound discussion of the issue, see Nick Fuentes' article, 'The Roman Military Tunic', *Roman Military Equipment: The Accoutrements of War*, edited by M. Dawson, Proceedings of the Third Roman Military Equipment Research Seminar, BAR 336 (Oxford, 1987), pp. 41–75.
43. Named after the village of Negau (Ž|enjak) in Slovenia where a large number of these helmet types were found in 1811.

44. H. Russell Robinson, *The Armour of Imperial Rome* (New York, Charles Scribner's Sons, 1975), pp. 13–14; Bishop and Coulston, pp. 65–66; and Polybius, 6.23.12. Polybius describes the crests as purple and black feathers: ἐπὶ δὲ πᾶσι τούτοις προσεπικοσμοῦνται πτερίνῳ στεφάνῳ καὶ πτεροῖς φοινικοῖς ἢ μέλασιν ὀρθοῖς τρισίν. (Polybius, 6.23.12).
45. Robinson, *The Armour of Imperial Rome*, pp. 26–39.
46. Polybius, 6.23.2–5.
47. Ibid.
48. Connolly, p. 131; and Bishop and Coulston, pp. 61–63.
49. In his account of the Roman infantry assault against the Punic line at the Battle of Zama (202 BC), Livy wrote that 'with the first attack the Romans at once dislodged the enemy's line. Then beating them back with their shoulders and the bosses of their shields', the legionaries pressed their attack, driving the Carthaginians from their original position (30.34.3).
50. Scale armour was used by soldiers throughout much of Roman history, though it was never as pervasive as mail armour, and no archaeological examples exist from the Republican era. Each coat of scale armour consisted of bronze or iron plates mounted to an undergarment of cloth or leather. The size and shape of the scales varied widely, but most were rectangular with rounded lower corners, and fastened together in rows. According to Robinson, individual scales measured from 2.8cm × 1.4cm (bronze example) to 8cm × 54cm (iron example), Robinson, pp. 153–57; and Bishop and Coulston, p. 64.
51. For visual representations, see the Aemilius Paullus victory frieze at Delphi, Greece, and the altar of Domitius Ahenobarbus, Musee du Louvre, Paris.
52. Varro, *De Lingua Latina*, 5.24.116.
53. In the *Histories*, 6.23, Polybius notes common soldiers wearing 'a breastplate of brass a span square, which they place in front of the heart and call the heart-protector, this completing their accoutrements; but those who are rated above 10,000 drachmas wear instead of this a coat of chain-mail'. (Loeb trans.)
54. Robinson, pp. 163–74.
55. The Etruscans used pieces of bronze armour to protect the thighs and arms (see the fragment from the central acroterium of the Sassi Caduti temple at Falerii Veteres).
56. Polybius, 6.23.8: πρὸς δέ τούτοις ὑσσοὶ δύο καὶ προκνημίς.
57. Polybius, 6.23.9.
58. Ibid, 6.23.10; and Connolly, *Greece and Rome at War*, pp. 131, 233. For modifications to the *pilum*, see Plutarch, *Marius*, 25.1; Arrian, *Order of Battle against the Alans* (*Ectaxis contra Alanos*), 17ff.; Appian, *Gallic Epitome*, 1.1; and Caesar, *The Gallic War*, 1.25. Each attests to the *pilum*'s iron shaft having been designed to bend upon striking a hard object. According to Caesar, 'The Gauls were greatly encumbered for the fight because several of their shields would be pierced and fastened together by a single javelin-cast; and as the iron became bent [*cum ferrum se inflexisset*], they could not pluck it forth, nor fight handily with the left arm encumbered.' (Loeb trans., *The Gallic War*, 1.25.)
59. Polybius, 6.23.10.
60. Polybius, 6.23.6–7.
61. Bishop and Coulston, pp. 54–56. Because of the accuracy afforded by the particular form of measurement, the centimetre is used throughout the text.
62. Bishop and Coulston, pp. 56–57.
63. Michael Pitassi, *The Navies of Rome* (Woodbridge, UK, The Boydell Press, 2009), pp. 18–39. For discussion of Roman naval development before the First Punic War, see Christa Steinby, *The Roman Republican Navy: From the Sixth Century to 167 BC, Commentationes humanarum litterarum, 123* (Helsinki, Societas Scientiarum Fennica, 2007); and Johannes Hendrik Thiel, *Studies on the History of Roman Sea Power in Republican Times* (Amsterdam, North Holland Publishing Company, 1946) and *A History of Roman Sea Power before the Second Punic War* (Amsterdam, North Holland Publishing Company, 1954).

64. Polybius 1.20.9–10.
65. Herman Tamo Wallinga, *The Boarding-Bridge of the Romans. Its Construction and its Function in the Naval Tactics of the First Punic War* (Groningue-D Jakarta, J.B. Wolters, 1956).
66. Michael Pitassi, *The Roman Navy: Ships, Men and Warfare, 350 BC–AD 475* (Barnsley, Seaforth Publishing, 2012), pp. 35–39. A less common ship was the *hexareme* (ἑξήρης). At the Battle of Ecnomus (256 BC), the consuls Manlius Vulso and Atilius Regulus each employed a *hexareme* as their flagship (Polybius, 1.26.11). Hexaremes, or 'Sixes', were infrequently used by the Romans for wartime, and most typically as a flagship, though a few were present in Octavian's fleet at Actium (31 BC).
67. Polybius 1.26.7–8.
68. John R. Hale, *Lords of the Sea* (New York, Viking Press, 2009), xxiv.
69. Stefan G. Chrissanthos, *Warfare in the Ancient World: From the Bronze Age to the Fall of Rome* (Westport, CT, Praeger Publishers, 2008), pp. 45–46.
70. Richard M. Berthold, *Rhodes in the Hellenistic Age* (Ithaca, Cornell University Press, 2009), pp. 199–212; and E.E. Rice, 'The Rhodian Navy in the Hellenistic Age', in W.R. Roberts and J. Sweetman (eds), *New Interpretations in Naval History: Selected Papers from the 9th Naval History Symposium* (Annapolis, MD, 1991), pp. 29–50.
71. Philip De Souza, *Piracy in the Graeco-Roman World* (Cambridge, Cambridge University Press, 2002), pp. 176–78.
72. Bruce W. Frier, *Libri Annales Pontificum Maximorum: the Origins of the Annalistic Tradition*. Papers and Monographs of the American Academy in Rome series, vol. 27 (Rome, American Academy in Rome, 1979).
73. John Dillery, 'Quintus Fabius Pictor and the Greco-Roman Historiography at Rome', in John F. Miller, Cynthia Damon and K. Sara Myers (eds), *Vertis in Usum: Studies in Honor of Edward Courtney* (Leipzig, K.G. Saur, 2002), pp. 1–23; and William Smith (ed.), *A Dictionary of Greek and Roma*. T.J. Cornell, E. Bispham, J.W. Rich and C.J. Smith (eds), *The Fragments of the Roman Historians*, three vols. (Oxford, Oxford University Press, 2013), pp. 160–78. Two other early annalists are the *consul* of 133 BC, Lucius Calpurnius Piso Frugi, and the late third century BC *praetor*, Lucius Cincius Alimentus. Cornell et. al., *The Fragments of the Roman Historians*, pp. 179–83, 230–39.
74. Other annalists include Aelius Tubero, Valerius Antias and Gaius Licinius Macer (d. 66 BC). Cornell et. al., *The Fragments of the Roman Historians*, pp. 293–304, 320–31, 361–67.

Bibliography

Modern Sources

Adcock, F.E., *The Roman Art of War Under the Republic*. New York, Barnes and Noble Books, 1995.

Bell, M.J.V., 'Tactical Reform in the Roman Republican Army', *Historia* 14 (1965), pp. 404–22.

Berthold, Richard M., *Rhodes in the Hellenistic Age*. Ithaca, Cornell University Press, 2009.

Bishop, M.C. and Coulston, J.N.C., *Roman Military Equipment from the Punic Wars to the Fall of Rome*. Oxford, Oxbow Books, 2006.

Burgess, R.W., 'Principes sum Tyrannis: Two Studies on the Kaisergeschichte and Its Tradition', *The Classical Quarterly*, New Series, vol. 43, no. 2 (1993), pp. 491–500.

Burgess, R.W., 'A common source for Jerome, Eutropius, Festus, Ammianus, and the *Epitome de Caesaribus* between 358 and 378, along with further thoughts on the date and nature of the *Kaisergeschichte*', *Classical Philology* 100 (2005), pp. 166–92.

Chrissanthos, Stefan G., *Warfare in the Ancient World: From the Bronze Age to the Fall of Rome*. Westport, CT, Praeger Publishers, 2008.

Connolly, Peter, *Greece and Rome at War*. Englewood Cliffs, NJ, Prentice-Hall Inc., 1981.

Cornell T.J. (ed.), *The Fragments of the Roman Historians*, 3 vols. Oxford, Oxford University Press, 2013.

Delbruck, Hans, *Warfare in Antiquity*, translated by Walter J. Renfroe, Jr, vol. 1, *History of the Art of War*. Lincoln, Nebraska, University of Nebraska Press, 1975.

De Souza, Philip, *Piracy in the Graeco-Roman World*. Cambridge, Cambridge University Press, 2002.

Dillery, John, 'Quintus Fabius Pictor and the Greco-Roman Historiography at Rome', in John F. Miller, Cynthia Damon, K. Sara Myers (eds.), *Vertis in Usum: Studies in Honor of Edward Courtney*, 1–23. Leipzig, K.G. Saur, 2002.

Fraccaro, Plinio, *Della Guerra presso i Romani*, volume 4, *Opuscula*. Pavia, Presso la Rivista 'Athenaeum', 1975.

Frier, Bruce W., *Libri Annales Pontificum Maximorum: the Origins of the Annalistic Tradition*. Papers and Monographs of the American Academy in Rome series, vol. 27. Rome, American Academy in Rome, 1979.

Fuentes, Nicholas, 'The Roman Military Tunic', in *Roman Military Equipment: The Accoutrements of War*, edited by M. Dawson. Proceedings of the Third Roman Military Equipment Research Seminar, BAR 336. Oxford, 1987, pp. 41–75.

Gabba, Emilio, *The Roman Republic, the Army and the Allies*. Translated by P.J. Cuff. Oxford, Blackwell, 1976.

Goldsworthy, Adrian, *The Roman Army at War, 100 BC–AD 200*. New York, Clarendon Press, 1996.

Hale, John R., *Lords of the Sea*. New York, Viking Press, 2009.

Keppie, Lawrence, *The Making of the Roman Army: From Republic to Empire*. New York, Barnes and Noble Books, 1994.

Lendon, J.E., *Soldiers and Ghosts: A History of Battle in Classical Antiquity*. New Haven, Yale University Press, 2005.

Loeb Classical Library.

May, Elmer C., Stradler, Gerald P. and Votaw, John F., *Ancient and Medieval Warfare, The West Point Military History Series*, Thomas E. Griess (ed.). Wayne, NJ, Avery Publishing Group Inc., 1984.

McCall, Jeremiah B., *The Cavalry of the Roman Republic*. New York, Routledge, 2002.

Nillson, M.P., 'The Introduction of Hoplite Tactics at Rome', *The Journal of Roman Studies* 19 (1929), pp. 1–11.

Pitassi, Michael, *The Navies of Rome*. Woodbridge, UK, The Boydell Press, 2009.

Pitassi, Michael, *The Roman Navy: Ships, Men and Warfare, 350 BC–AD 475*. Barnsley, Seaforth Publishing, 2012.

Rice, E.E., 'The Rhodian Navy in the Hellenistic Age', in W.R. Roberts and J. Sweetman (eds), *New Interpretations in Naval History: Selected Papers from the 9th Naval History Symposium*. Annapolis, MD, 1991.

Robinson, H. Russell, *The Armour of Imperial Rome*. New York, Charles Scribner's Sons, 1975.

Sabin, Philip, 'The Mechanics of Battle in the Second Punic War', in T. Cornell, B. Rankov and P. Sabin (eds), *The Second Punic War: A Reappraisal*. London, Institute of Classical Studies, 1996.

Sabin, Philip, 'The Face of Roman Battle', *Journal of Roman Studies* 90 (2000), pp. 1–17.

Smith, William (ed.), *A Dictionary of Greek and Roman Biography and Mythology: Oarses-Zygia*, 3 vols. London, John Murray, 1876.

Steinby, Christa, *The Roman Republican Navy: From the Sixth Century to 167 BC Commentationes humanarum litterarum, 123*. Helsinki, Societas Scientiarum Fennica, 2007.

Sumner, G.V., 'The Legion and the Centuriate Organization', *The Journal of Roman Studies*, 60 (1970), pp. 61–78.

Taylor, Donathan, 'A Comparative Study of the Post-Alexandrian Macedonian Phalanx and the Roman Manipular Legion to the Battle of Pydna', *Ozark Historical Review*, vol. 22 (Spring 1993), pp. 18–31.

Thiel, Johannes Hendrik, *Studies on the History of Roman Sea Power in Republican Times*. Amsterdam, North Holland Publishing Company, 1946.

Thiel, Johannes Hendrik, *A History of Roman Sea Power before the Second Punic War*. Amsterdam, North Holland Publishing Company, 1954.

Thomsen, Rudi, *King Servius Tullius: A Historical Synthesis* (Humanitas 5). Copenhagen, Gyldendal, 1980.

Wallinga, Herman Tamo, *The Boarding-Bridge of the Romans. Its Construction and its Function in the Naval Tactics of the First Punic War*. Groninge-D Jakarta, J.B. Wolters, 1956.

Additional sources consulted for the histories of the ancient authors

Burgess, R.W., 'Eutropius V.C. "Magister Memoriae?"', *Classical Philology* 96 (Jan., 2001), pp. 76–81.

Den Boer, Willem, *Some Minor Roman Historians*. Leiden, E.J. Brill, 1972.

Hill, H., 'Dionysius of Halicarnassus and the Origins of Rome', *The Journal of Roman Studies*, Vol. 51, Parts 1 and 2 (1961), pp. 88–93.

Kelly, Gavin, 'The Roman World of Festus' Breviarium', *Cambridge Classical Journal*, Supp. 34 (2010), pp. 72–91.

Meier, Christian, *Caesar, A Biography*. Translated by David McLintock. New York, Basic Books, 1982.

Rohrbacher, David, 'Eutropius' in *The Historians of Late Antiquity*. New York, Routledge, 2002.

Rohrbacher, David, 'Orosius' in *The Historians of Late Antiquity*. New York, Routledge, 2002.

Shutt, R.J.H., 'Dionysius of Halicarnassus', *Greece & Rome*, Vol. 4, No. 12 (1935), pp. 139–50.

Sihler, E.G., 'Polybius of Megalopolis', *The American Journal of Philology*, Vol. 48, No. 1 (1927), pp. 38–81.

Sumner, G.V., 'The Truth about Velleius Paterculus: Prolegomena', *Harvard Studies in Classical Philology*, Vol. 74 (1970), pp. 257–97.

Walbank, Frank William, *A Historical Commentary on Polybius: Commentary on Books 1–6*, Vol. 1. Oxford, Oxford University Press, 1957.

Yardley, J.C. and Barrett, Anthony A. (trans.), *The Roman History: From Romulus and the Foundation of Rome to the Reign of Tiberius*, by Velleius Paterculus. Indianapolis, Hackett Publishing Company, 2011.

Ancient Sources in Translation

The purpose of this list is to provide general readers with a reliable and user-friendly reference to English-language translations of ancient sources used in this work. I have cited almost exclusively from translations in the Loeb Classical Library for the compendium entries. When this was not possible, I necessarily consulted other translated works or scholarly publications. In such instances, only a single modern translation for each ancient writer was used in this study. If more than one work by any single ancient author was employed, then only one translation of each work was referenced. The following is a list of modern English translations of ancient works used by the author that are not part of the LCL.

Ancient Sources used in this work which are not part of the LCL Corpus

Athenaeus, *The Deipnosophists, or, Banquet of the Learned of Athenæus*, translated by C.D. Yonge, Volume I. London, Henry G. Bohn, 1854.

Aurelius Victor, Sextus, *De Caesaribus*, translated by H.W. Bird. Liverpool, Liverpool University Press, 1994.

Banchich, Thomas M. and Lane, Eugene N.(trans.), *The History of Zonaras from Alexander Severus to the death of Theodosius the Great.* New York, Routledge, 2009.

Index

Works consulted in this index include: John Hazel, *Who's Who in the Ancient World* (New York: Routledge, 2001); T. Robert S. Broughton, *The Magistrates of the Roman Republic: 509 B.C.–100 B.C.*, vol. I (Scholars Press, 1968); *The Magistrates of the Roman Republic: 99 B.C.–31 B.C.* with Supplement, vol. 2 (Scholars Press, 1968); *The Magistrates of the Roman Republic*: Supplement, vol. 3 (Scholars Press, 1968); Stillwell, Richard, William L. MacDonald, Marian Holland McAllister, *The Princeton Encyclopedia of Classical Sites* (Princeton, N.J.: Princeton University Press, 1976); William Smith (Ed), *Dictionary of Greek and Roman Geography*, 2 vols (London: John Murray, 1878); William Smith (Ed), *Dictionary of Greek and Roman Biography and Mythology*, 3 vols (Boston: Little, Brown, and Company, 1870); and the Loeb Classical Library.

Note regarding the consular designation used in the index: during certain periods of early Republican history (fifth and fourth centuries BC) military tribunes, commonly referred to in modern English usage as 'Consular Tribunes', exercised consular authority (*tribuni militum consulari potestate*) on behalf of the Roman state. To offer the reader clarity, the term 'Consul' is used exclusively throughout the text and index to denote individuals exercising such lateral authority, whether 'Consular Tribune', Consul, or Suffect Consul. For further discussion regarding consular tribunes see, F.E. Adcock 'Consular Tribunes and Their Successors', *The Journal of Roman Studies*, 47, 1/2 (1957): 9–14; and Robert E.A. Palmer, *The Archaic Community of the Romans* (Cambridge: Cambridge University Press, 1970), 224–43.

People

Places